Haunted Histories in America

Haunted Histories in America

True Stories behind the Nation's Most Feared Places

Nancy Hendricks

BLOOMSBURY ACADEMIC
NEW YORK • LONDON • OXFORD • NEW DELHI • SYDNEY

BLOOMSBURY ACADEMIC
Bloomsbury Publishing Inc
1385 Broadway, New York, NY 10018, USA
50 Bedford Square, London, WC1B 3DP, UK
29 Earlsfort Terrace, Dublin 2, Ireland

BLOOMSBURY, BLOOMSBURY ACADEMIC and the Diana logo
are trademarks of Bloomsbury Publishing Plc

First published in the United States of America by ABC-CLIO 2020
Paperback edition published by Bloomsbury Academic 2024

Copyright © Bloomsbury Publishing Inc, 2024

For legal purposes the Acknowledgments on p. xiii constitute
an extension of this copyright page.

Cover photo: (Thomas_Zsebok_Images/iStockphoto)

All rights reserved. No part of this publication may be reproduced or
transmitted in any form or by any means, electronic or mechanical,
including photocopying, recording, or any information storage or retrieval
system, without prior permission in writing from the publishers.

Bloomsbury Publishing Inc does not have any control over, or responsibility for,
any third-party websites referred to or in this book. All internet addresses given
in this book were correct at the time of going to press. The author and publisher
regret any inconvenience caused if addresses have changed or sites have
ceased to exist, but can accept no responsibility for any such changes.

Library of Congress Cataloging-in-Publication Data
Names: Hendricks, Nancy, author.
Title: Haunted histories in America : true stories behind the nation's most
feared places / Nancy Hendricks.
Description: Santa Barbara : ABC-CLIO, 2020. |
Includes bibliographical references and index.
Identifiers: LCCN 2020005478 (print) | LCCN 2020005479 (ebook) |
ISBN 9781440868702 (hardcover) | ISBN 9781440868719 (ebook)
Subjects: LCSH: Haunted places—United States. | Ghosts—United States.
Classification: LCC BF1472.U6 H457 2020 (print) |
LCC BF1472.U6 (ebook) | DDC 133.10973—dc23
LC record available at https://lccn.loc.gov/2020005478
LC ebook record available at https://lccn.loc.gov/2020005479

ISBN: HB: 978-1-4408-6870-2
PB: 979-8-7651-2966-1
ePDF: 978-1-4408-6871-9
eBook: 979-8-2160-9476-0

To find out more about our authors and books visit www.bloomsbury.com
and sign up for our newsletters.

Contents

Topical Guide to Haunted Sites   ix

Geographical Guide to Haunted Sites   xi

Acknowledgments   xiii

Introduction   xv

1 Alabama   1
2 Alaska   7
3 Arizona   13
4 Arkansas   19
5 California   25
6 Colorado   33
7 Connecticut   40
8 Delaware   47
9 District of Columbia   53
10 Florida   60
11 Georgia   66
12 Hawaii   72
13 Idaho   79
14 Illinois   85
15 Indiana   91
16 Iowa   97
17 Kansas   103

18 Kentucky   109
19 Louisiana 115
20 Maine 122
21 Maryland 128
22 Massachusetts 134
23 Michigan 140
24 Minnesota 146
25 Mississippi 152
26 Missouri 158
27 Montana 164
28 Nebraska 170
29 Nevada 176
30 New Hampshire 182
31 New Jersey 188
32 New Mexico 194
33 New York 200
34 North Carolina 208
35 North Dakota 214
36 Ohio 219
37 Oklahoma 225
38 Oregon 231
39 Pennsylvania 237
40 Rhode Island 243
41 South Carolina 249
42 South Dakota 255
43 Tennessee 261
44 Texas 267
45 Utah 273
46 Vermont 279
47 Virginia 285
48 Washington 291

49 West Virginia   297

50 Wisconsin   303

51 Wyoming   309

Appendix: Ghost Tour Road Trips by Region   315

    Eastern United States   315

    Central United States   316

    Western United States   317

Bibliography   319

Index   331

Topical Guide to Haunted Sites

Abandoned Mines—Arizona
Airships—New Jersey
Amusement Parks—West Virginia
Battlefields—Virginia
Breweries—Missouri
Bridges—Indiana
Brothels—Alaska
Canals—Maryland
Castles—New Hampshire
Caves—Idaho
Cemeteries—Georgia
Colleges—Vermont
Deadly Jobs—Alabama
Deadwood—South Dakota
Distilleries—Kentucky
Environmental Disasters—Pennsylvania
Factories—Connecticut
Forests and Woods—Illinois
Forts/Presidio System—Texas
Hangings—Minnesota
Health Spas—Arkansas
Hospitals—North Dakota
Hotels—Colorado
Immigration—New York
Inns—Delaware
Islands—Michigan
Jails—Iowa
Las Vegas—Nevada
Leper Colonies—Hawaii
Libraries—Kansas
Lighthouses—Florida
Little Bighorn—Montana
Mental Hospitals—Washington
Murders—Rhode Island
Museums—Nebraska
Piracy—North Carolina
Plantations—Tennessee
Potter's Fields—Ohio
Prisons—New Mexico
Rail Stations—Utah
Relocation Centers—Wyoming
Roads and Highways—Maine
Shanghaiing—Oregon
Summer Homes—Wisconsin
Taverns—Mississippi
Theaters—District of Columbia
Tuberculosis Sanitariums—South Carolina
Voodoo—Louisiana
Wagon Trains—California
Witch Hunts—Massachusetts
Women Soldiers—Oklahoma

Geographical Guide to Haunted Sites

Bonaventure Cemetery—Georgia
Buffalo Trace Distillery—Kentucky
Centralia—Pennsylvania
Chesapeake and Ohio Canal—Maryland
Cincinnati Music Hall—Ohio
Cold Harbor Battlefield—Virginia
Crescent Hotel—Arkansas
Deadwood—South Dakota
Deer Park Inn—Delaware
Donner Party—California
Edna Collings Bridge—Indiana
Ellis Island—New York
Ford's Theatre—District Columbia
Fort Gibson—Oklahoma
Greenville Tuberculosis Hospital—South Carolina
Heart Mountain Relocation Center—Wyoming
Hutchinson Library—Kansas
Kimball Castle—New Hampshire
King's Tavern—Mississippi
Lake Shawnee Amusement Park—West Virginia
Lakehurst—New Jersey

Las Vegas—Nevada
Lemp Brewery—Missouri
Little Bighorn—Montana
Mackinac Island—Michigan
Marie Laveau Gravesite—Louisiana
Minneapolis City Hall—Minnesota
Molokai—Hawaii
Museum of Shadows—Nebraska
Northern State Mental Hospital—Washington
Ocracoke Island—North Carolina
Presidio La Bahia Goliad—Texas
Red Onion Saloon—Alaska
Remington Arms—Connecticut
Rio Grande Depot—Utah
Robinson Woods—Illinois
Salem—Massachusetts
Santa Fe Prison—New Mexico
Shanghai Tunnels—Oregon
Shoshone Ice Caves—Idaho
Sloss Furnaces—Alabama
Sprague Mansion—Rhode Island
Squirrel Cage Jail—Iowa
St. Augustine Lighthouse—Florida

St. Joseph's Hospital—North Dakota
Stanley Park Hotel—Colorado
Summerwind—Wisconsin
University of Vermont—Vermont

U.S. Route 2A—Maine
Vulture Mine—Arizona
Wheatlands Plantation—Tennessee

Acknowledgments

The author wishes to thank editor Jane Glenn from ABC-CLIO; Dr. Guy Lancaster, editor of the *Encyclopedia of Arkansas History and Culture*; and Dr. Peg Lamphier of California State Polytechnic University, Pomona, as well as CEK who prefers anonymity but is an important part of this work.

Introduction

Who believes in ghosts? Many people do, claiming they have seen them, heard them, or experienced a feeling of being touched or watched by them.

Sometimes hauntings take place in an obvious spot like a cemetery at midnight. At other times, it might be a room at a historic inn or hotel where a previous guest may have met a sudden, violent death. Theaters are especially prone to alleged hauntings, with a high degree of emotion, superstition, drama, and ego that often takes place in the darkened surroundings of a playhouse. After all, the bare onstage light bulb that is always left burning when the theater is empty is universally called a "ghost light."

Sometimes hauntings are said to occur after lives are lost in accidents or other tragedies, or when someone sets out one day as usual only to vanish, never to be seen again.

Occasionally, an entire town is said to be haunted, especially if it is one that bears a history like Deadwood, South Dakota, or Salem, Massachusetts. Sometimes haunted sites are ghost towns from the past, or perhaps a modern-day ghost town like the abandoned community of Centralia, Pennsylvania, which is consumed by unending plumes of smoke pouring out of the ground, which some people say resembles the portals of Hell.

The living hell of bloody battlefields like the Little Bighorn or Cold Harbor often leads to stories of being haunted by the spirits of young soldiers who perished amid the terror they must have felt when taking their last agonized breath. A famous photo at the Library of Congress illustrates the tragedy of Civil War battles like Cold Harbor, showing not only skulls from unburied young men who fought and died there but also a foot with an intact shoe and pants-leg still attached. If the ghosts of these soldiers truly haunt the place where they died, it is hard not to feel their humanity.

SACRED GROUND

Hauntings are often said to happen in places where there was a tragedy or violence. This is nothing new. Throughout human history, there have not been many times when the world was free of strife, war, fear, famine, disease, natural disasters, or man-made catastrophes.

While the United States has been blessed with remarkable bounty since its inception, there have also been times when life in America was a struggle for many. When tormented lives ended in death, it was usually not the kind of happy ending that allowed them to "rest in peace."

The ghosts of enslaved people and those who were convicted of witchcraft are said to wander restlessly, seeking vengeance. Spirits of the dead are also believed to walk when housing developments are built atop sacred Native American burial grounds, or when strip malls are built on Civil War battlefields.

PAINLESS HISTORY

Perhaps if ghosts do exist all around us, they are there to remind the living that those events are part of our collective history. That is the perspective of this book. It is not intended to recount campfire tales of eternally lost Boy Scouts or urban myths that end with ". . . the calls were coming from *inside the house*!!!!"

The factual material presented in this book is meant to provide small doses of history for people who think they don't like history as well as those who do. The historical background is presented simply as part of our American tapestry. As humans, we tend to like stories and are intrigued by things that are unexplained. If they come to us in terms of the personal lives of real people—people like us—so much the better.

After all, the reason there are so many "haunted houses" is because that is where people lived their lives, comfortable in their day-to-day existence until something happened to change that. Since such life-changing moments usually happen in the blink of an eye, often their souls do not rest in peace in the afterlife, preferring to return to happier times in happier places.

SPIRITS OF THE PAST

Ghostly tales are hardly a modern phenomenon. In *Mosses from an Old Manse*, published in 1846, early American writer Nathaniel Hawthorne states that "houses of any antiquity in New England are so invariably possessed with spirits that the matter hardly seems worth alluding to." Other than Hawthorne's questionable grammar in ending the sentence with a preposition, his sentiment is shared by many. It is also worth noting that Hawthorne was in a position to know: his great-great-grandfather was a judge at Salem's witch trials in 1692.

By the time Hawthorne came along—and even before his witch-hunting ancestor's time—belief in the supernatural had been firmly established in human history for eons. Ghost stories with very similar themes can be found in such diverse ancient cultures as China, Egypt, Greece, Mesopotamia, India, and Rome, as well as the Celtic lands of Ireland and Scotland, and indigenous cultures in the Americas.

GHOSTLY PLOTS

When the western world's dramatic tradition emerged, some of the most important plot points in ancient theater involved ghosts. Classical Greek dramatist

Aeschylus utilized ghostly figures, most memorably in *The Eumenides*, featuring the ghost of Clytemnestra. Supernatural beings were found in Roman dramas like Seneca's *Agamemnon*, but the Romans also expanded roles for ghosts into comedies by casting them in farces like *Mostellaria* by Plautus, with the Latin title actually meaning "haunted house."

Shakespeare's plays were awash in ghosts, such as those in *Julius Caesar*, *Macbeth*, and *Richard III*, as well as the superstar of Elizabethan drama, the murdered king's ghost in *Hamlet*.

In literature, ghosts of the Victorian era stepped into starring roles in books like Charles Dickens's *A Christmas Carol*, which could hardly exist without its ghoulish figures. Writing around the same time, the gothic horror novels of Edgar Allan Poe set the gold standard.

THAT'S ENTERTAINMENT

In modern times, technology has really enabled haunting as entertainment. The first American on-screen depiction of the supernatural took place as far back as 1897 with George Albert Smith's *The X-Ray Fiend*, followed by his 1898 film *Photographing a Ghost*.

Movies focusing on the supernatural were enormously popular from the start. Cuddling in the dark, girls could squeal and snuggle closer to their boyfriends who assumed the role of the He-Man, calming her fears (although he probably harbored a few of his own).

A very small sample of movies through the years with the word "ghost" in the title include *Ghost*, *Ghostbusters*, and *The Ghost and Mrs. Muir*. Other Hollywood frights can be found in such films as *The Amityville Horror*, *Beetlejuice*, *The Blair Witch Project*, *The Haunting*, *The Nightmare Before Christmas*, *Poltergeist*, *The Shining*, and *Sleepy Hollow*, to name a mere fraction.

DARK TRAVELS

When it comes to ghosts, television rose to the ghoulish occasion early, from its humble beginnings to the current time.

In the year 2019 alone, a glance at the line-up for just one channel that used to broadcast sunny travelogues is revealing. It is now jam-packed with green screens in dark places, attesting to the popularity of such programs as *The Dead Files*, *Ghost Adventures*, *Ghost Bait*, *Ghost Stories*, *Haunted Case Files*, *Haunted Live*, *Haunted Things*, *Haunted USA*, *Kindred Spirits*, *Most Haunted*, *Most Haunted Towns*, *Most Terrifying Places in America*, *My Ghost Story*, *My Haunted House*, *Paranormal 911*, *Paranormal Caught on Camera*, *Paranormal Survivor*, *Portals to Hell*, and *These Woods Are Haunted*. That is just the line-up on one channel. Supernatural spirits are media darlings on other networks as well.

For those who enjoy the great outdoors, away from movie or TV screens, an entire niche of the travel industry has emerged: Dark Tourism. In many places, word of horrific habitués has been found to increase paying attendance at haunted sites and on ghost tours that explore them.

SEE THE UNITED STATES

This book itself can be seen as a ghostly guide to haunted hot spots across America. Readers can find restless souls haunting all fifty states from Alabama to Wyoming, including Alaska and Hawaii. The District of Columbia is also well represented.

This book illustrates everything from the turmoil of battlefields to the eerie (and deadly) peacefulness of the so-called health spas. There are pirates and prisoners, libraries and lighthouses. There are familiar names like Ford's Theatre as well as little-known spots like the Rio Grande Depot. The reader can visit Ellis Island where the ancestors of many Americans arrived, as well as discover the historical context of the Whiskey Rebellion, which almost derailed the new nation of America from the start.

Along the way are historical overviews of the kinds of things many Americans may take for granted today like mental health care and freedom from tuberculosis. We explore the history of airships and railroads, canals and cemeteries, amusement parks and breweries, deadly jobs and environmental disasters, with stops at Broadway and Hollywood.

Speaking of Hollywood, some of the haunts have become movie stars. These include Georgia's Bonaventure Cemetery (*Midnight in the Garden of Good and Evil*), Colorado's Stanley Park Hotel (*The Shining*), and the Grand Hotel (*Somewhere in Time*) at Mackinac Island, Michigan.

For those who may wish to visit these historic haunts in person, the book contains "Ghost Tour Road Trips" grouped by various regions of the United States.

WHY WE BELIEVE IN GHOSTS

Possibly because of the proliferation of "ghost reality" shows on TV, stories about the supernatural are currently in vogue. Many people truly have had experiences they just can't explain. Some have seen eerie sights, heard mysterious sounds, and felt strange sensations that they believe could only have been an encounter with the paranormal.

Humans have a need to know why things occur, and when an explanation is not readily at hand, many feel the reason may be the presence of the supernatural. In addition, many people are comforted by the thought of life after death. For those who believe in an afterlife, it is logical to assume that spirits are still among us.

As for the glut of movies and television shows about the supernatural, many people find the thought of spirits of the dead to be thrilling. Most believe ghosts are not evil, just lost souls searching for closure or justice from beyond the grave, or trapped between spheres and trying to cross over to the afterlife. Reasons might range from lack of proper burial, suicide, tragedy, unsolved murders, or other possibilities. Perhaps they are seeking redemption, or are pursuing revenge for past wrongs.

On the other hand, some believe certain ghosts return to spots that were special to them, places where they might have felt especially happy and comfortable. Some might be seeking a "do-over," a chance for things to work out differently than they did in life.

PRESIDENTS AND PRINCESSES

Sometimes animals are credited with a "sixth sense" about things beyond those that humans can interpret. In his book *But Enough About You*, author Christopher Buckley recounts an evening when he dined at the White House with President Ronald Reagan and two members of royalty, Princess Yasmin Aga Khan and Princess Caroline of Monaco. They were enjoying dinner in what is named the Prince of Wales Room (also called the President's Dining Room). During a pleasant chat about the surroundings, Mr. Reagan happened to remark that his dog would inexplicably start barking whenever it came into that particular room. There were no such displays by the canny canine anywhere else in the executive mansion. After further mentioning the historical fact that Abraham Lincoln had been embalmed there as he was prepared for burial, "suddenly the president of the United States and the two princesses were swapping personal ghost stories."

So to answer the question of who believes in ghosts, the response might be paraphrased from a quote attributed to the aforementioned Abraham Lincoln himself: all people some of the time and some people all the time. But regardless of the era we live in and to what degree ghosts are in vogue, it would appear that the belief in the supernatural has been with us since the earliest human history and is likely to stay that way for the foreseeable future.

1

Alabama

The U.S. Congress created the Alabama Territory in 1817, admitting Alabama as the nation's twenty-second state two years later. Before long, settlers and speculators arrived to take advantage of fertile land suitable for cotton cultivation.

Among the first were immigrant farmers such as the Scots Irish. Soon other immigrant groups arrived in Alabama, such as those from Germany, Greece, Italy, and Scandinavia, who sought work in new industries. In 1876, a process was developed for converting Alabama's local coal into fuel sources, and as Edwin Bridges states, "The enormous quantities of coal around Birmingham would be able to support iron production far into the future" (2016, 131).

The Industrial Revolution steadily transformed the nation from farms into factories. During the 1880s, Birmingham, Alabama, was booming as a center of the iron industry. New arrivals, the majority of whom from southern and eastern Europe, poured into Birmingham as they did in other large industrial cities. Those immigrants, who rarely spoke English and were often illiterate in their own language, were desperate for work and would often take the most dangerous jobs that no one else wanted.

With no workplace safety regulations, deaths from industrial accidents skyrocketed across the country. In less than one ten-year period alone, from 1901 to 1911, thousands died in mining accidents, factory fires, and tunnel construction. In New York's deadly Triangle Shirtwaist Factory catastrophe in 1911, almost one hundred fifty victims, mostly women and girls, perished in flames as exit doors were blocked.

That disaster caught the attention of the press and the public. As Mark Aldrich states, "Employers' interest in work safety was sharply influenced by public prodding" (1997, 50). In the late nineteenth and early twentieth centuries, employers found labor—and lives—to be cheap. Many industrial accidents went unreported. But after 1911, progressive era reformers sought changes. Journalists, often called "muckrakers," uncovered plentiful muck by writing about deadly jobs, while emerging labor unions pressed for workplace safety. Congress passed a few laws to protect American laborers, including laws concerning workers' compensation and fines for employers after worker fatalities.

A foreman at Alabama's Sloss Furnaces, built in 1881, pushed its immigrant workers to the limit. On the aptly named graveyard shift, the foreman mysteriously plummeted into molten iron. Soon, workers reported being harassed by an "unnatural presence" that looked like an angry, badly burned man. (Robbiebrewer/Dreamstime.com)

Unfortunately, progressive safety measures came too late for a third of the workers on the graveyard shift at **Sloss Furnaces** in Birmingham, Alabama. In 1881, Sloss was built to transform local coal and ore into the steel that was in demand nationwide for railroads, construction, and other industries. To meet the demand, a night shift was needed at Sloss Furnaces, supervised by a foreman named James "Slag" Wormwood. As Coleman states, "Slag made working on his shift literally a 'living hell'" (2008, 27).

Even during the nighttime, temperatures in the plant would hover around 100–120 degrees year-round. Visibility was low, workers were forbidden to take breaks, and Slag continually demanded that the exhausted workers take dangerous risks to speed up production. The laborers, usually newly arrived immigrants, were paid in tokens that could only be used in the company store, so they had no money with which to leave.

On the aptly named graveyard shift, the workers' fatality and accident rate was ten times that of other shifts, until one night in 1906 when Slag Wormwood mysteriously plummeted into a furnace of molten iron. Soon after, Sloss discontinued the graveyard shift, citing numerous reports of accidents and "strange incidents" that decreased steel production.

Workers complained of an "unnatural presence" throughout the work site. Reports of incidents increased, such as one in 1926 when a night watchman was injured after being "pushed from behind" while alone in the plant and ordered angrily by a deep voice "to get back to work." In 1947, three missing supervisors were found unconscious and locked in a small boiler room, with each of them stating that they were approached by a man who looked badly burned, shouting at them to "push some steel." In 1971, the evening before the plant closed, the night watchman said he suddenly faced the most frightening thing he had ever seen, something that beat him with fists. When examined, the watchman was found covered with intense burns and died before returning to Sloss.

Between the malevolent spirit of Slag Wormwood and the anonymous immigrant workers who perished, police in Birmingham have recorded hundreds of reports of paranormal activity at Sloss, according to the *Tuscaloosa News*.

During the era when those workers died or were injured, there were minimal government efforts to ensure workplace health and safety. Even if safety had been a concern to most employers, it was much less expensive to replace dead or injured workers than to develop safety measures. Injured employees no longer able to work or survivors of dead laborers usually found themselves destitute.

During the progressive era, after a series of highly publicized industrial accidents, Congress established the United States Bureau of Mines in 1910 to conduct research into mine safety, although it had no authority to regulate conditions. As the twentieth century progressed, workplace accident rates remained high as millions of workers died or were disabled. A few states, like California and New York, enacted workplace health and safety legislation, but by the end of World War II, the level of workplace protection in most states remained about the same as it was at the turn of the century.

However, in 1970, the Occupational Safety and Health Act (OSHA) was enacted by the federal government to set and enforce workplace safety standards for American workers. It aimed to ensure that employers provide employees with a workplace free from hazards like exposure to toxic chemicals, excessive noise levels, extreme heat or cold, mechanical dangers, or unsanitary conditions. OSHA was something that was not even dreamed of by the unfortunate men who worked at Sloss, and whose souls may haunt it still.

SOME OTHER REPORTEDLY HAUNTED PLACES IN ALABAMA

The **Boyington Oak** in Mobile is a Southern live oak tree that reportedly grew from the grave of Charles Boyington who was buried in the potter's field just outside the walls of Church Street Graveyard. In 1835, Boyington was executed for the murder of Nathaniel Frost, a friend from the rooming house where they had both lived. Before being hanged, Boyington said a tree would spring from his grave as proof of his innocence, a prediction that came true. Boyington worked as a printer, and legend has it that he fell in love with a young lady whose father was not in favor of a match with the near-penniless Boyington. In his despair, Boyington pined for his lost love, spending his time writing poetry. He was fired from his printing job for neglecting his work and was unable to find other employment. Boyington allegedly learned that Nathaniel Frost had a large sum of money in his room. The men were last seen walking together through the cemetery. When Frost did not return home, the landlady notified the sheriff, who discovered Frost's body covered in stab wounds. Boyington was found boarding a ship that was leaving town. After his arrest, Boyington repeatedly proclaimed his innocence, spending his time in jail writing love poems. Before his execution, Boyington vowed that a great oak tree would grow from his buried heart as proof of his innocence. A tree did so and can still be seen today, commanding a spot that is said to be haunted.

The **Dr. John R. Drish House** in Tuscaloosa is the site of ghostly lights that are said to have been seen emanating from the home. Its third-story tower was reported on numerous occasions to be on fire, while no evidence of fire could be found when authorities responded. Built in the late 1830s, the house belonged to John Drish and his wife Sarah. In 1867, after a night of drinking, Drish fell to his death from an upstairs balcony. The widowed Sarah was said to be devastated. Her late husband had left elaborate instructions for his funeral, which Sarah carried out precisely. Overcome with grief, Sarah insisted on having the exact funeral arrangements as her husband when *she* died. She carefully saved the candles that had been used at his wake so that they might also be burned at her funeral. Yet when Sarah herself died in 1884, she had safeguarded the candles so well that no one could find them in order to honor her dying wish. Some say her agitated spirit sparked the fire-related emanations in the tower of the Drish House, because the candles had not been burned at her funeral as she wanted. In addition to flames, some people have also reported to have seen strange ghostly lights being emitted from the top of the house, going up into the clouds. Ownership of the Drish House has changed many times, which some think is due to the unrest of spirits within.

The *Eliza Battle* is said to be a ghost ship, engulfed in flames, which can be seen on the river where she and her passengers had perished. The vessel was a steamboat that ran in the 1850s between Mobile, Alabama, and Columbus, Mississippi, on the Tombigbee River, one of the main commercial navigation routes in the southern United States. In her time, the *Eliza Battle* was one of the most luxurious riverboats plying Alabama waters. Former president Millard Fillmore was entertained during a reception on board the ship in Mobile in 1854. But on the freezing night of March 1, 1858, the fully loaded *Eliza Battle* became known not for her luxury but for the worst maritime disaster in the river's history. On a freezing windy night, the wooden-hulled paddle steamer caught fire around 2:00 a.m., sending passengers clad only in their nightclothes into the frigid waters of the river at flood stage. More than forty people were killed out of about a hundred souls on board. The human tragedy was captured in a poignant newspaper article that ran as far north as the *New York Times* of March 8, 1858: "Mrs. H. G. Turner and child, frozen; Dr. S. H. Jones, never seen; Nancy, chambermaid, belonging to S. G. Stone, master of the *Eliza Battle*, frozen; Mrs. B. Cromwell and child, died from cold in her husband's arms" (8). Today, a phantom burning ship has been reported where the *Eliza Battle* met her fate, especially on cold, windy nights, and said to warn rivermen of impending disaster.

Gaineswood is located in the town of Demopolis, which was first settled in 1817, becoming one of the oldest continuous settlements in Alabama. However, it is the ghost of an out-of-stater, a former housekeeper from Virginia, who reportedly haunts the stately Gaineswood plantation house. After the wife of Nathan

Bryan Whitfield, Gaineswood's owner, died, the widower hired a housekeeper. The young lady was musically talented, singing and playing the piano admirably. However, one winter she passed away, leaving a dying request that her body be taken to her family's burial ground in Virginia. Weather conditions and poor transportation made it impossible to do so upon her passing, so her body was sealed in a pine casket and stored beneath the manor house until spring, when it was shipped back to her home. In the meantime, her spirit may have become restless when it did not find itself at her family cemetery. According to the stories, a number of people over the years have reported hearing the sound of silk skirts rustling and footsteps on Gaineswood's long stairway. Furthermore, there have been reports of singing and playing the piano when no one was in the music room, which houses the original Gaineswood piano. It has missing keys and is badly out of tune, making it unsuitable to be played, except possibly by the spirit world. A painting called *The Burning of the* Eliza Battle was painted by Nathan Bryan Whitfield and is currently on display at Gaineswood.

Kenworthy Hall near Marion, Alabama, is a plantation home built just before the Civil War. The red-brick manor house is in an asymmetrical Italian villa style that was especially designed to suit the climate and plantation life of the South. It has none of the features often associated with plantation homes of the antebellum South, like stately white columns or spacious verandas. However, it has one special feature: what is said to be the ghost of a young woman who lived and died there. With brick walls twenty-eight inches thick, Kenworthy Hall's fourth-floor tower holds a room said to be haunted by Anne Carlisle, daughter of the home's original owners, Edward Kenworthy Carlisle and his wife. The legend goes that young Anne loved to climb the spiral staircase to the square tower room to be alone and dream, often about marriage to a neighbor boy whom she had loved since childhood. Although they talked of marriage, he was among the first from the county to volunteer for the Confederate Army at the start of the Civil War. He asked her to wait for him, which she did, sitting every day in the tower and awaiting news. One day a rider brought the word that her lover had been killed. She flung herself down the tower staircase to her death, calling his name. The haunted sightings reported by passers-by at Kenworthy Hall are of a young woman sitting at the window of the fourth-floor tower, long after the home had been abandoned.

Sweetwater Mansion in Florence was built in the early 1800s by General John Brahan, a veteran of America's War of 1812, but it was another conflict—the Civil War—that reportedly installed the mansion's resident ghosts. The eight-room home received both its name and the brick to build it from nearby Sweetwater Creek. Its first resident was Robert M. Patton, a post–Civil War governor of Alabama, who completed the mansion in 1835. The house served as headquarters for both Confederate and Union troops during the Civil War, which perhaps led to unsettled activity within. Having a handful of alleged ghosts on the premises, Sweetwater has been the subject of several paranormal investigations. One story is that a caretaker and others reported seeing the body of a soldier with a hole in his head lying in a coffin in the home's parlor. One of Patton's sons had been reportedly killed at the Battle of Shiloh when he was shot in the head. The ghostly coffin has always been reported as being in the exact spot in which the casket was laid during the boy's wake. Doors have allegedly slammed and locked themselves, even those with no actual deadbolts on them. One room has a tendency to lock unsuspecting women inside. During the taping of the television show *Paranormal State*, investigators saw a door move by itself and heard inexplicable footsteps. According to the Florence, Alabama, *Times Daily*, one investigator fell down the stairs after what he said felt like a nudge from behind and had a section of ceiling tile tossed past him. He immediately shot a photo in the direction of the flying tile, which later revealed an image of what appeared to be two children. Other reports include the sighting (as well as a photograph) of what appeared to be a Civil War soldier sitting on a log outside the mansion and holding a cannon ramrod. In a nod to equal opportunity, there have also been reports of a ghostly woman wearing nineteenth-century clothing and appearing at various spots on the property.

FURTHER READING

Aldrich, Mark. *Safety First: Technology, Labor and Business in the Building of Work Safety, 1870–1939.* Baltimore, MD: Johns Hopkins University Press, 1997.

Bridges, Edwin. *Alabama: The Making of an American State.* Tuscaloosa: University Alabama Press, 2016.

"Burning of Steamer Eliza Battle.; FORTY LIVES LOST!--TWELVE HUNDRED BALES COTTON LOST." *New York Times*, March 12, 1858, p. 8.

Coleman, Christopher. *Dixie Spirits: True Tales of the Strange and Supernatural in the South.* Nashville, TN: Cumberland House, 2008.

2

Alaska

Often called "America's Last Frontier," Alaska has a relatively sparse population rich in a rough-and-tumble history. Russians established settlements in Alaska to exploit wild animal furs but lost interest when overhunting depleted the supply of pelts. In 1867, they agreed to an offer by U.S. Secretary of State William Henry Seward of about $7 million—less than two cents an acre. Many Americans considered the sale "Seward's Folly," seeing only a frozen waste.

By 1896, even the naysayers saw something different: the glitter of gold. Thousands of prospectors flooded the region via the town of Skagway on their way to Yukon gold fields.

During the long Arctic nights, there was often nothing for the men to do but tell ghost stories. One story concerned the apparition of a beautiful Russian princess who haunted the abandoned Baranof Castle in Sitka. Newspaper articles picked up the story, reporting that the "Lady in Black" was the daughter of a Russian governor who forced her to marry a man she did not love, which ended in the princess killing herself on her wedding night. Her sprit was said to wander the deserted castle at midnight, although the story was later disproven by historians who found no such aristocratic family.

One ghostly apparition, however, has a basis in fact. Today's **Red Onion Saloon** in Skagway originally operated as a brothel, or a house of prostitution. The first floor of the Red Onion was a bar while the upper floor had ten small rooms where women entertained paying customers.

To avoid any altercations among the often-drunk saloon patrons, the downstairs bar area displayed ten dolls with different hair color and appearances, each representing one of the women upstairs. If the doll was sitting upright, it meant that the woman was available. After the customer made his choice, the doll was turned on her back. When he came back downstairs after visiting the woman's room, the doll was again turned upright into a sitting position, indicating she was once again available.

The Red Onion Saloon was not the only house of ill repute in Skagway during the gold rush. It was merely one of many establishments that catered to Skagway's

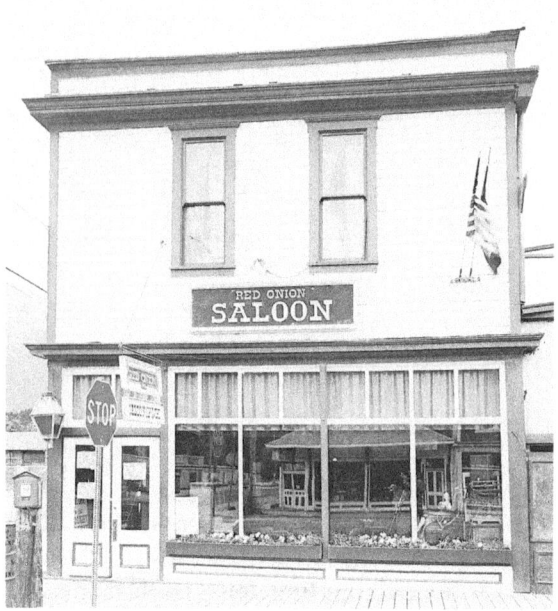

Alaska's Red Onion Saloon in Skagway was originally a house of prostitution. Most of the girls who worked there were desperately poor, had no other choices, and knew no other life. The spirit of one of the girls is said to haunt the Red Onion, perhaps because even in death, she has no place else to go. (Library of Congress)

transient population, which reached more than seven thousand men at the height of the gold rush. By one count, in 1898, there were almost ninety saloons in operation.

Author and historian Catherine Spude notes that in addition to would-be prospectors passing through town on their way to the gold fields, there was also a permanent population in Skagway. A number of prominent citizens were landlords of very profitable brothels, and some portion of the revenues and fines generated by prostitution often financed the town's schools and teachers (2015).

Today, the Red Onion Saloon is still in operation as a popular restaurant in Skagway. The establishment also houses the Red Onion Brothel Museum, which the owners say is filled with antiques from the gold rush days, as well as items that were found in the brothel. At the museum, costumed "madams," or brothel-keepers, take visitors on a tour and share stories.

One story concerns what the Red Onion calls its resident ghost, a female spirit known as Lydia. It is believed that Lydia was one of the prostitutes who once worked at the upstairs brothel. In addition to the sound of her footsteps on the second floor where the brothel used to operate, visitors also report unusual cold spots and a sudden strong scent of perfume. There have been reports of Lydia being seen as a full body apparition, walking around in the madam's room or running down the hall.

In one of the strangest manifestations, the soil around indoor potted plants is found to be damp when no one else acknowledges having watered them, an act of horticulture attributed to Lydia.

Paranormal investigators who have visited the Red Onion are said to have recorded voices, taken photos, and registered unexplained temperature drops in places around the building. Customers as well as long-time employees have not only felt Lydia's presence but have also witnessed items flying off the bar.

Some interpret Lydia's ghostly spirit as having remained in the building due to a broken heart over a man she loved but who abandoned her there. Some attribute it to her not wanting, or feeling able, to leave. It is possible that there may not have been a specific individual named Lydia but is rather a spiritual stand-in for all the young women who worked there and whose spirits did not rest in peace.

Like many present-day visitors to the Red Onion, who are shown around the Brothel Museum in the company of vivacious tour guides dressed as "madams," it is sometimes easy for people to believe the myths and misconceptions about the subject of prostitution. It was an activity born of desperation.

Often called the world's oldest profession, the act of women selling their bodies in a brothel was not unknown in colonial America. Tavern owners were occasionally prosecuted for operating "disorderly houses," but such cases were rare and the penalty was usually a small fine. When Boston minister Cotton Mather attempted to form a group to oppose brothels, most people, even the Puritans of Massachusetts, were indifferent since the activity was kept hidden. As an increased maritime trade brought sailors into port towns, and as American cities grew, so did the number of "red light districts" with their easily available brothels. While such houses did not advertise, their whereabouts were well-known, and brothel owners often paid local police for protection.

In America's Wild West frontier of the nineteenth century, men greatly outnumbered women. Saloons and brothels were common and were generally tolerated just as they were in Alaska, "America's Last Frontier." They were just another way for men to make money. In the days of the Yukon gold rush when businessmen paid no fees or licenses, "business-women paid huge rents to male landlords, and men controlled the politics of Skagway" (Spude 2015).

The women in the prostitution business often had few other chances for survival. Often they fell victim to "the four Ds" that afflicted scores of anonymous prostitutes: drink, drugs, disease, and death. "Respectable" options of job opportunities for women were extremely limited, to say the least.

According to Karen Abbott, most prostitutes came from lower classes, and many girls were desperately poor and frequently had to support parents, siblings, and/or children. The choice was often between earning $6 a week in a factory or several times that in a brothel. Abbott wrote, "Girls who turned to prostitution often suffered the death or desertion of one or both parents at an early age; witnessed their mother cohabitating with a series of strange men; fell victim to incest, alcoholism, tuberculosis, depression. For some the sporting life was simply the family business . . . [they] were reared in brothels and knew no other life" (2008, 20).

If Lydia's spirit still haunts the brothel rooms of Skagway's Red Onion, perhaps it is because in death, as in life, she has no place else to go.

SOME OTHER REPORTEDLY HAUNTED PLACES IN ALASKA

With its dark nights and forbidding forests edging against the side of many roadways, even some roads in Alaska are said to be haunted. One of the spookiest is a dirt stretch between Chitina and the abandoned copper mining camp of Kennicott. At this stretch, drivers have reported that in warmer weather, when their car windows are down, they can hear the sound of children laughing in the woods. In the late 1990s, construction on a housing project near the end of the road was terminated because workmen's tools were constantly disappearing right after being set down. Workers also reported hearing children laughing in the woods. However, no children can be heard laughing on **Badarka Road** in Chugiak, near Anchorage. The story is of a five-year-old girl who was watching her father chop firewood outside the cabin where her family lived near the isolated Badarka Road. Taking a break, her father embedded the razor-sharp ax in a tree to make sure the child did not fall on it. When he turned his back, the child tried pulling the heavy ax out of the tree which fell on her head, killing her instantly. The grief-stricken father refused to leave her, remaining in the woods clasping her bloody, lifeless body until he died of hypothermia. Today, it is said that drivers traveling down Badarka Road late on a winter's night may see the apparition of a man kneeling by the roadside at the edge of the woods, cradling the lifeless body of a child.

The general spookiness of **Begich Tower** in Whittier begins even before setting foot in what is often called the strangest, most haunted town in Alaska. Whittier lies on the western edge of Prince William Sound, about sixty miles southeast of Anchorage. Reaching Whittier requires driving through a two-and-a-half mile tunnel carved into a mountain. The eerie light at the end of the tunnel is said to be reminiscent of stories told about near-death experiences by those who have briefly visited the afterlife. Once out of the tunnel and reaching town, it becomes even stranger since there does not appear to be a "there" there. Whittier is home to about two hundred people, almost all of whom live in Begich Towers Condominium, earning Whittier another nickname: "The town under one roof." After the construction of the fourteen-story tower as part of a proposed U.S. Army complex in the early 1950s, it was only used by the military until the early 1960s. Today, it houses residential units, stores, churches, and public facilities. The building was named for Alaska Congressman Nick Begich, whose small plane vanished nearby in 1972 along with House Majority Leader Hale Boggs of Louisiana. Today, especially in winter months when occupants of the tower are snowed in, residents hear ghostly whistling in the halls, as well as heavy unseen footsteps stomping up and down hallways and stairs. The city manager has heard rustling noises in his kitchen, which made him reach for his gun before discovering that no one was there.

Fairbanks Memorial Hospital in Fairbanks is said to be one of the most haunted places in Alaska. The city's northerly location can sometimes produce eerie lighting effects. Named for Charles Fairbanks, who was U.S. vice president under Theodore Roosevelt, the town was essentially founded by mistake. In 1901, a trader was traveling by steamboat to his destination farther along the river where he hoped to open a trading post. However, the steamboat ran aground at the site of today's Fairbanks. When gold prospectors working in the hills saw the smoke from the boat's engines, they quickly came to the steamer seeking any supplies that might be on board. As more prospectors congregated, the trader set up shop, enticing other gold-seekers to the Fairbanks area. Today, Fairbanks is Alaska's largest interior city, with many fine public services, including Fairbanks Memorial Hospital, founded in 1972. Along with its staff of health-care providers, the hospital may be home to other residents. It has been reported that when an infant is close to death, mysterious apparitions appear in the nursery wing. Some have suggested that they are angels who comfort the dying infants as they cross over from this life. Other strange phenomena at the hospital include cold spots, sudden temperature drops, and the sound of crying babies coming from empty rooms. But it is the thought of angels comforting the dying infants that gives Fairbanks Memorial Hospital a reputation for being the home of kind, gentle spirits.

With almost three hundred thousand people, Anchorage is the most-populated city in Alaska, comprising more than 40 percent of the state's total population. Located in its downtown area, the **Historic Anchorage Hotel** prides itself on being featured on internet sites listings, such as "50 of the Most Historic Hotels in America" and "50 of the Most Haunted Wedding Venues in America." Historically, the hotel grew up with the city of Anchorage since its creation in 1914, and is cited on the National Register of Historic Places. But it is the hauntings that lead the hotel to also state on its website that it is a place "Where Ghosts Are More than Just Stories." Along with shower curtains swaying and pictures flying, the hotel can direct guests specifically to Rooms 215 and 217 with their hotspots, as well as reports of televisions turning on by themselves and bathroom faucets suddenly starting to run. The hallway of the second floor is where guests have seen the apparition of a young girl, while others have spotted a ghostly woman in a white dress. These figures remain anonymous, but the identity of another ghost is well-known: Jack Sturgus, the first Police Chief in Anchorage. In 1921, Sturgus was found outside the hotel, shot in the back with a bullet from his own gun. His ghost is said to keep returning to the hotel, haunting the scene of the crime to seek justice for a murder that is still unsolved.

Anchorage has no shortage of other haunted hotels even beyond its namesake Historic Anchorage Hotel. The **Hotel Captain Cook** in Anchorage is unique in having more than five hundred guest rooms spread among three buildings downtown. But there is one room in particular that seems to attract the most attention, at least from the spirit world. Both guests and staff members have reported seeing the apparition of a lady in a white dress who is said to be responsible for opening and closing doors, as well as turning the lights on and off in guest rooms. But her preferred accommodation is in the ladies' restroom. There, according to local legend, a woman committed suicide in the early 1970s. Since then, some guests have reported sightings of a female spirit dressed in white. It has been suggested that her suicide has bound her to the hotel rather than enjoying her afterlife elsewhere. The **Inlet Tower Hotel** in Anchorage is also said to be haunted by the spirit of a little girl who is often seen in the hallways. She is apparently in good humor, with reports indicating she has been heard laughing. Her pleasant nature differs from that of a male apparition who wordlessly makes an appearance in the hotel elevator, walks through the main entrance, and suddenly vanishes into thin air.

Palmer, Alaska, with its haunted **Motherlode Lodge**, had a unique transformation within about a year from its beginnings as a rail siding community. Named for George Palmer who built a nearby trading post, the town was the site of a New Deal relief experiment during the Great Depression of the 1930s as a planned agricultural colony. Today, many descendants of the original colonists still live in

Palmer. It is noted as the site of the annual Alaska State Fair where the town's agricultural spirit lives on. However, other spirits may also inhabit the area. At the fourteen-room Motherlode Lodge, built in 1942, guests have reported seeing a misty black apparition roaming the grounds on a number of occasions. People also looked into mirrors at the lodge and were surprised to spot an unknown figure in old-fashioned clothing standing behind them in the reflection when no one else was in the room. Other reports included unexplained loud banging noises, mysterious knocking sounds, and disembodied voices, as well as doors and curtains that opened and closed on their own late at night. In 2015, when the Motherlode was closed for repairs and renovation, the historic building burned to the ground under what were called suspicious circumstances. According to the owners, it was closed at the time; the lodge was not insured because it was not operating. Where did the Motherlode's spirits go?

Like many theaters, the **Wendy Williamson Auditorium** at the University of Alaska campus in Anchorage has its own resident ghosts. Along with reports of giggling children and a teenage boy haunting the theater, there is a cranky male spirit who has specific tastes in women's hair color. Apparently, he does not like brunettes since women with long brown hair have reported being pushed by an unseen presence in the auditorium. In addition, there have been reports of theatergoers getting more than their money's worth for their ticket price when a woman in white appeared during a performance. At first, the audience assumed she was a part of the show—until she vanished into thin air.

FURTHER READING

Abbott, Karen. *Sin in the Second City.* New York: Random House, 2008.

Devereaux, James P. *Spirits of Southeast Alaska: The History & Hauntings of Alaska's Panhandle.* Kenmore, WA: Epicenter Press, 2018.

Spude, Catherine Holder. *Saloons, Prostitutes and Temperance in Alaska Territory.* Norman: University of Oklahoma Press, 2015.

3

Arizona

Spanish settlers began to arrive in today's Arizona during the 1500s, which was home to Native Americans for thousands of years. In 1863, the Arizona Territory was created by the U.S. government, who had claimed it from Mexico in the Gadsden Purchase a decade earlier. President Abraham Lincoln approved the final name of "Arizona" for the territory, although Gadsonia, Montezuma, and Pimeria had all been considered. Ultimately, Arizona joined the Union in 1912, making it the forty-eighth and last of the contiguous states to be admitted.

Arizona has a rich mining history that goes back thousands of years when indigenous people gathered copper and turquoise from aboveground outcroppings for decoration or trade. William Ascarza states, "[I]t was the Spanish who were the first to extensively penetrate the earth in search of mineral wealth" in today's Arizona (2011, 7).

Mining in the United States has been practiced since colonial days, but with the advent of the Industrial Revolution in the nineteenth century and its demand for raw materials, mining became a major industry. The General Mining Act of 1872 provided for the free and open development of the vast expanses of western United States, which made prospecting available to anyone with a dream of becoming rich by discovering gold, silver, copper, or other minerals. Though towns sprang up, many died just as quickly. As James Crutchfield states, "Many of the ghost towns that haunt the American West owe their existence to the boom-bust nature of mining" (2017, 20).

The dream of instant wealth by discovering a vein of precious metal has led to some of the most celebrated mythology that surrounds Arizona's mining industry. Perhaps the most famous is the legend of the Lost Dutchman's mine, a rich gold deposit generally believed to be hidden in the Superstition Mountains of southeastern Arizona.

With "Dutchman" being a common American term for a person of German origin, the legendary mine was named after an immigrant from Germany ("Deutschland") who allegedly discovered the rich vein in the late 1800s and kept its location a secret. That German prospector was reportedly found dead in the

Arizona desert near Wickenburg alongside saddlebags filled with gold. Thousands of people have sought the Lost Dutchman's mine ever since.

In addition to legendary lost mines, Arizona is riddled with abandoned ones. Because much of the foundation of U.S. mining law was based on the "right to mine," states such as Arizona have been left with hundreds of abandoned mines after they played out or were found to be the mining equivalent of a "dry hole."

One such venture that has been abandoned by everyone except the spirit world is the **Vulture Mine**, a gold mine and settlement in southern Arizona. The mine's story started on a high note with its beginnings in 1863 when it became the most productive mine in Arizona history. From 1863 to 1942, the mine produced almost 350,000 ounces of gold and over 250,000 ounces of silver. It attracted thousands of people to the area, and is credited with the growth of the nearby town of Wickenburg, Arizona, as well as the eponymous town that served the mine, Vulture City.

According to the site's historical marker, "In 1863, Austrian Henry Wickenburg discovered gold, legend has it, while retrieving a vulture he had shot. The Vulture Mine went on to become one of Arizona's richest gold mines and sparked the development of Arizona and the city of Phoenix." Henry Wickenburg had inadvertently discovered a quartz deposit containing gold and began mining the outcrop. A mining town called Vulture City grew up nearby, becoming the home of about five thousand citizens, at least temporarily.

The Vulture Mine in southern Arizona is abandoned but may not be deserted. It is said to be haunted by the spirits of miners who were hanged outside the mine entrance for stealing gold. Some visitors claim that rocks were thrown at them, they felt cold spots, and they heard shouts of "Get out!" and "You're gonna die!" (Richard Charpentier/Dreamstime.com)

Just as the Vulture Mine's boom times began in the Civil War, ultimately producing tens of millions of dollars in gold, it was another war that led to its demise. In 1942, during World War II, the Vulture Mine was shut down by the federal government who directed all resources to be focused on the war effort. Ultimately, the mine reopened, but with less productivity than before. A few years later, the Vulture Mine closed permanently.

Currently, both the mine and ghost town are privately owned. Tours are offered of the remaining buildings of Vulture City to give visitors a glimpse of what was once a booming mining town. Other visitors are equally interested in the mine itself: paranormal investigators.

There are tales of angry evil spirits hiding among the abandoned buildings of the dusty town as well as down in the mine. Some visitors have reported apparitions, distant shuffling footsteps, faint disembodied voices, and dark shadowy forms on the walls when no one else is nearby.

One of the most persistent tales concerns the Vulture Mine's Hanging Tree. In much of the vast expanse of Arizona, as with most of the Old West, there were not always lawmen on duty to keep the peace, so vigilante justice prevailed. Also called "frontier justice," some civilians in the late 1800s adopted a self-appointed law enforcement role for themselves, without legal authority, to punish those whom they considered offenders. Gunfights and lynchings frequently ensued.

The rich bounty of the Vulture Mine in the late 1800s often induced its share of greed. The legend is that after being accused of stealing gold, eighteen miners swung from the Vulture Mine's Hanging Tree. Investigators point out that the hangings of that era were not "clean" executions with drop doors. The condemned man might be placed on a mule or a rock which was then kicked out from under him. According to some historians, the victim's death could take anywhere from two minutes to two hours.

Their spirits might still be haunting the last place they drew breath. Some visitors attest to having had rocks thrown at them, feeling cold spots, and hearing shouts of "You're gonna die" and "Get out!"

In another case, a young miner named Jimmy fell down a long shaft in the Vulture Mine, breaking most of the bones in his body. None of his fellow miners were able to reach him. Jimmy clung to life from about 10 p.m. to 3 a.m., with his final words being, "Someone help me, for God's sake!" Some present-day investigators said they have heard a man hollering in the distance. One who stayed alone overnight inside the mine reported hearing what sounded like a man begging for help. While Arizona's Vulture Mine has been abandoned, perhaps it is not deserted after all.

SOME OTHER REPORTEDLY HAUNTED PLACES IN ARIZONA

It should come as no surprise that the **Bird Cage Theatre** in the town of Tombstone, Arizona, is reportedly haunted. In fact, today it is called Tombstone's most haunted building. First settled in 1877, Tombstone itself, with its unnerving name, is no stranger to tales from the dark side. The Bird Cage opened as a legitimate theater in 1881, just two months after the legendary Gunfight at the OK Corral involving now-iconic figures like Wyatt Earp and Doc Holliday. Perhaps with such other forms of excitement to be found in Tombstone, the Bird Cage soon failed as a theater. It then reopened as a saloon, gambling hall, and brothel. Business picked up, and the Bird Cage operated twenty-four hours a day, 365 days a year. Today, the walls remain riddled with almost 150 bullet holes. In sixteen different deadly gunfights and knife fights, at least twenty-six people lost their lives at the Bird Cage. According to the *Arizona Capitol Times*, soon after the Bird Cage's opening, the *New York Times* called it the "the roughest, bawdiest, and most wicked night spot between Basin Street [in New Orleans] and the [San Francisco] Barbary Coast." Subsequent to a nearby silver strike, about fifteen thousand prospectors and settlers flocked to Tombstone hoping to strike it rich. With them came what has been reported as over three thousand prostitutes hoping to make money and/or find a husband in order to become "respectable." The Bird Cage was the site of what was called Tombstone's most grisly murder as a jealous prostitute brutally knifed another to death for allegedly stealing the affections of a male client. Other "fallen women" killed themselves out of despair, or succumbed to drink, drugs, or disease. Today, their ghosts are said to be joined at the Bird Cage by other uneasy spirits who left life too soon. Especially at night, investigators in the otherwise empty building have reported sounds of music playing, raucous laughter, glasses clinking, cards being shuffled, and dice being thrown. Visitors attest to seeing apparitions—sometimes an entire roomful—dressed in 1880s attire. Although the saloon closed in 1889 when the mines started to decline, a few spirits remain at the Bird Cage, perhaps dejected because like the silver, their lives did not pan out either.

The **Copper Queen Hotel**, a Victorian/Italian Villa style "grand dame" in Bisbee has been described as one of the last remaining historical gems of the Southwest, also claiming the title of Arizona's longest continuously operated hotel. It has remained in service as an upper-tier inn since it was built in 1902 as lodging for dignitaries and investors visiting nearby mines. The Copper Queen's rooms have been called atmospheric, an element that attracts some of its most enthusiastic guests: paranormal investigators. The town grew up around the same time as nearby Tombstone due to silver mining, as well as Bisbee's rich veins of copper, the hotel's namesake. Although arguably less obvious than in Tombstone, Bisbee had its share of vice, including prostitution. The spirit who haunts the Copper Queen Hotel was one of those women, and she even has a name: Julia Lowell. She is said to have used a room on the hotel's third floor to service her clients until she fell in love with one man, hoping to marry him and join respectable society. When she told him of her feelings, he rejected her. In despair, she killed herself. Julia's apparition is said to still spend time at the hotel, appearing seductively and whispering in the ear of male guests in Room 315. Other reports at the hotel include the apparition of a small boy named Billy, plus a disembodied caller to the lobby phone asking for "Howard," who was indeed a front desk clerk—but in the year 1910.

The seven-story **Hotel San Carlos** in Phoenix has operated continuously since 1928. It boasted an early form of air conditioning and the first elevators in the state, quickly becoming the center of social life in the burgeoning city of Phoenix. It also became a popular destination for Hollywood stars like Humphrey Bogart, Clark Gable, Cary Grant, Jean Harlow, Carole Lombard, and Marilyn Monroe. A "Star Walk" was created to denote the celebrities who frequented the hotel over the years, but one name is prized most of all by some hotel guests, a virtually unknown young woman named Leona Jensen. She had made her way across the country in May 1928 to marry her boyfriend, who was working in Phoenix. But when she arrived, he broke the news that he no longer loved her. She checked into Room 720 on the hotel's top floor, changed into a white evening gown, and made her way to the hotel's roof, jumping to her death. Since that time, visitors have claimed to see the ghostly vision of a woman in a long white dress roaming the hallways. Some reported a woman in evening attire on the roof, while others felt someone looking over their shoulder as they sipped drinks at the hotel's rooftop pool though no one else was ever there. Perhaps the forlorn spirit of Leona Jensen can take comfort in knowing she is perhaps more famous at the Hotel San Carlos than Marilyn Monroe.

The **Jerome Grand Hotel** is perched imperiously atop a steep ridge overlooking the eerie-feeling community of Jerome in northern Arizona. Several hundred people still remain in town as residents. Jerome was once a booming mining center but its primary economy today is based on tourism. Much of the town remains as a time capsule from the late 1800s through the early twentieth century. In 1927, the four-story United Verde Hospital was founded, a facility that helped serve miners injured on the job in the copper mines, as well as people with mental illness. The building was constructed on a ridge high above town where the land was felt to be more stable than ground level. Due to underground mining operations, a great deal of seismic shifting has taken place in Jerome, sometimes causing buildings to be damaged or simply collapse. This feeling of instability gives Jerome a sense of uncertainty that is unsettling to some visitors. Before the hospital closed in 1950, it is said that hundreds—perhaps thousands—of people died of injuries and illnesses in the hospital. In addition, the building contained the suffering of countless mental patients, as well as visiting family members who lost loved ones there. After its closure, the fully furnished hospital building lay empty for almost half a century, during which time a caretaker committed suicide. After a new owner bought the building in 1994, it was repurposed as a vintage hotel. Soon after, people reported disembodied screams, cries for help, ghostly figures, phantom phone calls to the front desk, the sound of a hospital gurney being pushed through the hallways, unexplained orbs of light, and even the apparition of a disgruntled head nurse. For guests to record paranormal experiences, the owners began keeping three hundred–page journals, which they say are filled every year.

The **Oliver House** bed-and-breakfast in Bisbee, a former boarding house dating back to the early twentieth century, attracts guests not just for its historic charm but also for the chance to encounter some of the spirits that are said to be in residence. There are claims of multiple murders in the building. Two particularly bloody ones involved the sensational element of adultery. In one, a police officer in 1920 found his wife at Oliver House with another man. He shot them both before wildly going on a killing spree throughout the building that resulted in a dozen fatalities. Over the years, guests at the Oliver House have reported hearing sounds of gunshots and ghostly footsteps in the hallways, as well as encountering doors and shutters that close by themselves. Another tale of an adulterous spouse, also in 1920, involves miner Nat Anderson. He was staying in the ominous-sounding Room 13 when a man to whom he owed money burst in. The moneylender found not only Nat but also his own wife, with whom Nat was having an affair. Nat was found dead outside his room, shot in the back. Despite the popular belief that the moneylender had killed Nat, a newspaper article in the legendary *Tombstone Epitaph* is titled "Find No Clues to Killing of Nat Anderson." With reports of footsteps, doors opening and closing, and the sound of running water, Nat is said to still haunt Room 13, perhaps because his case remains unsolved, thus adding insult to injury.

The **Thornton Road Domes** in Casa Grande became known as a spooky local attraction that rivaled nearby mysterious ruins from a thousand years ago. Near the Domes are the ancient ruins of Casa Grande, or "Great House," located about halfway between Phoenix and Tucson. According to the National Park Service, although the ancient adobe Casa Grande is one of the largest prehistoric structures ever built in North America, its purpose remains a mystery, as well as why the indigenous people of the Sonoran Desert abandoned it around the year 1450. Being listed on the National Register of Historic Places and cared for by the National Park Service, Casa Grande has fared better than the nearby Thornton Road Domes, which were built far more recently. The concrete UFO-like Domes were constructed in the 1980s on a five-acre plot south of Casa Grande. Built for an electronics manufacturer, the Domes were never completed and were abandoned. Varying in size and shape, they looked vaguely other-worldly, with one resembling a flying saucer while others in the shape of a giant caterpillar. Some investigators reported strange, unexplainable sounds, shadowy movements, and general spookiness, especially after dark. But with all the graffiti and smoke-blackened walls attributed to teenage vandals and partiers, ghostly apparitions would have trouble being seen. In any case, with the Domes deteriorating, the county ordered them to be demolished in 2017, although they stubbornly remained standing for a long time as an eerie shell of what they were intended to be.

FURTHER READING

Ascarza, William. *Southeastern Arizona Mining Towns*. Charleston, SC: Arcadia Publishing, 2011.

Crutchfield, James. *It Happened in Arizona: Remarkable Events That Shaped History*. Lanham, MD: Rowman & Littlefield, 2017.

Guinn, Jeff. *The Last Gunfight: The Real Story of the Shootout at the O.K. Corral and How It Changed the American West*. New York: Simon & Schuster, 2011.

4

Arkansas

Health spas and healing resorts have a long history. In ancient Greece, therapeutic baths were advocated by Hippocrates himself, the "Father of Western Medicine." The Roman baths were a common indulgence for citizens of ancient Rome. Many believe the word "spa" itself comes from a small Belgian village called Spa where hot mineral springs were used by Roman soldiers to treat battle wounds and aching muscles during the reign of Caesar Augustus, around the time of Christ. Classic European spas like Baden-Baden and Marienbad in Germany catered to the upper classes.

Local spas were popular in colonial America as well as after the American Revolution. Commercial enterprises sprang up where bathers could eat, drink, and find comfortable lodging. By 1815, Saratoga Springs in upstate New York was booming, soon offering more than five hundred rooms available to accommodate health-seekers year-round.

By the mid-twentieth century, Americans were traveling to such spa cities as Hot Springs, Arkansas; Mineral Wells, Texas; Warm Springs, Georgia; and White Sulphur Springs, West Virginia.

In some places where there was no warm therapeutic water bubbling from the ground, there were other ways to make money with the lure of good health. For example, in Arkansas, known for many years as "The Land of Opportunity," there were those who considered it a place with opportunities for a profit through any means possible. Arkansas was considered on the fringe of civilization even after becoming a state in 1836. According to Jeannie Whayne et al. (2013), "Those who hoped that statehood would improve Arkansas's image as a violent and lawless frontier found instead that subsequent events confirmed rather than refuted that image" (131).

Purported "health cures" mushroomed around Arkansas, with little regulation. One man opened a "clinic" in the state capital of Little Rock that promised to restore male potency by transplanting the organs of goats into the genitals of patients, many of whom died from the ordeal.

Located in the scenic, remote northwestern part of the state, Eureka Springs, Arkansas, boasted of having healing waters, but they were cold springs spread out all over town. In 1886, Eureka's five-story limestone **Crescent Hotel** opened with superior accommodations. However, to compensate for financial losses in the off seasons of fall, winter, and spring, in 1908, it opened the Crescent College and Conservatory for Young Women. One young lady fell or jumped from a window of the college. Some guests have seen her misty apparition at the window, wearing a white gown.

The Great Depression brought more financial struggles. In 1937, a man who called himself "Dr." Norman Baker turned the Crescent Hotel into a health resort where he painted virtually everything purple and claimed he could cure cancer.

Kay Danielson (2001) called Baker one of many: "Dozens of doctors came to the area, some of which were more reputable than others" (57). Baker's mailings boasted "World's Most Beautiful Health Spa [where] sick folks get well without operations, radium and X-ray," a slogan that would come to the attention of postal inspectors. As advertising, it was effective. Today's Crescent Hotel website states, "Many came, many were treated, many died."

For three years, desperate patients came for a cure only to find pain and suffering, loss of life savings, and often loss of life.

One patient, Lula Tunis, was brought to Baker's establishment by her husband John who was desperate to find some way to save her. After months of "treatments" that ranged from pathetically ineffective to horribly painful, Lula Tunis died. John Tunis testified in court against Baker at which point it was discovered Baker had absolutely no medical training and was simply a charlatan who preyed—very profitably—on desperate people. His "health resort" at the Crescent was found to be a hoax. The Assistant U.S. Attorney is said to have quoted Baker as saying he could "reap one million dollars out of the suckers in the state." Baker was convicted of mail fraud and imprisoned at the federal penitentiary at Leavenworth, Kansas, from 1941 to 1944.

Baker appeared enraged rather than remorseful. He wanted to be seen by the world as legitimate, blaming the American Medical Association, or "organized medicine," for his downfall. Today, some say his vengeful spirit haunts the hotel. He is said to wander around the old recreation room at the foot of the first floor stairs.

One guest reported hearing the sound of a squeaking gurney in the halls. Another, who saw a ghostly nurse pushing a gurney down a hallway and through a solid wall, was said to be unaware of the building's past history as a cancer treatment center.

Along with doomed patient Lula Tunis, the ghost of a fellow cancer victim named Theodora has been spotted in Room 419.

Much of the paranormal activity that haunts the Crescent can be traced back to Baker's activities in the building, especially in areas just over the old morgue and walk-in cooler where he kept cadavers. There have been reports of guests suddenly turning pale, falling against the wall, and sliding down in a faint. Loss of consciousness is brief but investigators say the phenomenon might substantiate the hotel's reputation for the paranormal, especially when it was discovered that

In Eureka Springs, Arkansas, the Crescent Hotel dates to 1886, serving for a time as a "health resort" where a charlatan profited on despair. Desperate patients found pain and suffering, loss of life savings, and often loss of life. The spirits of patients and staff are said to wander the halls, with reports of visitors suddenly turning pale before falling down in a dead faint. (Ashleydk52/Dreamstime.com)

the area in which people fainted was directly above the former morgue located in the hotel basement.

Investigators are often quick to point out that while many paranormal phenomena can be explained, some cannot. In the case of people fainting at the Crescent Hotel, it only seems to happen at one particular place, the location that sits directly above Baker's infamous morgue.

The Crescent is sometimes called "America's Most Haunted Hotel." Yet, Baker's dubious legacy is not the only source of hauntings. Just before the hotel opened in 1886, a construction worker named Michael was killed when he fell onto a beam located atop Room 218. Today, guests have reported seeing full-body apparitions in Room 218, feeling strange sensations, and hearing unexplained noises. Some say Michael's spirit remains—perhaps like a good workman, wanting to complete the job.

SOME OTHER REPORTEDLY HAUNTED PLACES IN ARKANSAS

The **Allen House** in the town of Monticello was built in 1906 for the family of businessman Joe Lee Allen. Not only has the Queen Anne/Gothic mansion been called one of the most beautiful houses in the state, it is also one of the most haunted. At least one member of Allen's family apparently refused to leave. Allen's daughter LaDell moved to Memphis, Tennessee, after marrying, but was later granted a divorce. In 1944, both her son and a beloved sister died. Amidst rumors that she was an alcoholic, LaDell returned to the Allen House where she occupied the master suite. There, on Christmas Day of 1948, she drank cyanide and died a few days later. After her funeral, which was held at the Allen House, her room was sealed by the family. That is how it remained until 1956 when the house was subdivided into rental apartments. Tenants began reporting paranormal experiences, like one resident who developed photographs he had taken of the house and found a clear image of LaDell in one of the mirrors. Another couple claimed to have seen LaDell's ghost in a closet; quickly shutting the closet door, they heard the sound of girlish giggling. When a retail shop was opened on the first floor, the storekeeper returned to open the locked shop on several mornings to find things missing or in disarray. Subsequent residents heard the sound of footsteps in the unoccupied upstairs floors, as well as crying from empty rooms. In 2009, new owners reported finding about ninety of LaDell's love letters from 1948, the year she killed herself, suggesting that the course of true love did not run smooth.

Dating to 1905, the **Basin Park Hotel** in Eureka Springs joins its neighbor, the Crescent, in providing accommodations for spirits in residence. Commonly sighted ghosts at the Basin Park Hotel include that of a young woman who is described as translucent, having steel blue eyes and blonde hair that some say resembles cotton candy. A little girl sporting pigtails and a yellow dress sometimes appears, as well as electromagnetic readings by investigators in Room 519 that seemed to be a man lying in the center of the bed. In addition, there are frequently what is said to be unexplained orbs of bright white light in the darkened, empty Ballroom, swooping and diving with no apparent source. The Ballroom seems to be an especially attractive place for spirits to gather, perhaps reliving merriment from the 1920s when the Basin Park Hotel was a popular prohibition-era speakeasy. Paranormal investigators have had the sense of a particularly strong presence in the hotel's basement where the underground cave was a storeroom for bootleg whiskey, perhaps a case of spirits attracting spirits.

The **Gurdon Light** in Gurdon, south of Little Rock, is a mysterious glow floating above isolated railroad tracks outside town. Its bright blue-white light tinted with a kind of orange refraction is said by some to look like lantern light. The Gurdon Light is seen to sway back and forth, usually on dark, overcast nights. First sighted during the 1930s, two legends that both involve railway workers have sprung up about the origin of the light. One is that a railroad worker accidentally fell on the tracks and was decapitated by an oncoming train. Now he is said to be swinging his railway lantern along the tracks looking for his missing head. The other legend involves an actual murder, given added weight by the Gurdon Light's first sighting occurring soon after the crime. In 1931, railroad foreman William McClain fired a worker, with one newspaper reporting that McClain accused the man of causing a train accident. After the accused man beat McClain to death, he was tried and executed in 1932. Soon the light appeared, with locals theorizing that the light is McClain's ghost haunting the tracks where he died prematurely, still on the job and swinging the lantern he would have carried for work. The movement of the Gurdon Light is indeed reminiscent of the characteristic swaying of a railwayman's lantern. With the lonely stretch of track outside Gurdon still used by the railroad, on a dark night the story is not difficult to believe.

The **Judge Parker's Courthouse** in Fort Smith was the hall of justice for Judge Isaac Parker, the "Hanging Judge," whose strict sentencing condemned about eighty people to hanging. Although he died in 1896 after over twenty years on the federal bench, Judge Parker may still dominate his old courthouse by haunting it. There have been reports of an unexplained mist in his courtroom, accompanied by the smack of a gavel, along with the sounds of men yelling and women crying. One observer described the apparition of a man in dusty clothes being dragged away by two men with badges. Notorious for his strict code of justice in some high-profile cases and sometimes clashing with the Supreme Court, the U.S. Congress reduced his jurisdiction in 1896. Parker, who died two months later, may have appealed that ruling by refusing to leave. A groundskeeper at the Fort Smith National Cemetery where Parker is buried reported leaving the graveyard on a cold December evening when he heard the sound of footsteps behind him crunching on the icy winter grass. Swinging around, his flashlight revealed an old man with white hair and a white beard, wearing an old-fashioned black suit. The old man stood staring and moving his mouth as if to speak, but made no sound. The groundskeeper realized he could see through the old man. Being familiar with the images he had seen at the Fort Smith Museum, the groundskeeper clearly recognized the old man as Judge Parker.

The **King Opera House** in Van Buren played a role in a doomed love story as tragic as anything on the theater's stage. Still in operation, the playhouse dates back to the late nineteenth century when it attracted traveling troupes of performers. A young actor who was part of a theater company presenting a play at the King Opera House around that time fell in love with the young daughter of the town doctor. She returned his affection, and the couple planned an elopement to avoid her disapproving father. The young actor went to Van Buren's train depot to buy tickets so they could leave town, but the doctor discovered their plan. Racing to the depot in his horse-drawn buggy, legend has it that the enraged doctor whipped the young actor to death. But even dead, the young man may have still portrayed the Romeo-and-Juliet storyline because his spirit is said to have returned to the King Opera House where employees state they can not only feel that there is someone in the room with them but have also experienced lights going on mysteriously. In addition, there have been reports of apparitions dressed in a top hat and Victorian-era coat with a long cape, perhaps the young actor hoping to spot his long-lost love in the audience.

Hot Springs, Arkansas, with its magnificent Victorian bathhouses along the Grand Promenade of Bathhouse Row is awash in history, including the haunted kind. With Bathhouse Row and its elaborate spa buildings designated a National Historic Landmark District, it is easy to feel in tune with the spirits of another time. Local businessmen quickly learned that bathers needed something to do when they dried off, and provided entertainment. The **Old Malco Theatre** was once the home of vaudeville shows and other productions, such as a nineteenth-century traveling magic show. As the story goes, the magician asked for a volunteer, selecting a young woman named Clara Southerland. After placing a silk sheet over her, he commanded her to "disappear," which she did. But when he commanded her to return, the stage remained empty. No matter how he tried, the now-panicked magician could not bring her back. No one ever saw or heard from her again. Today, the glowing image of a woman is often seen in the theater's basement, where disembodied voices and a woman crying can be heard. Some believe it is Clara trying to reappear. In 2017, the Old Malco building became home to famed illusionist Maxwell Blade who might be able to provide the right cue for Clara to return from her lengthy disappearing act.

The **Monte Ne Ruins** are found near the north Arkansas town of Rogers. Most of what is left of a once-thriving resort community lies underwater, submerged as a result of the creation of Beaver Lake by the Army Corps of Engineers in 1964. But from 1901 until 1936, Monte Ne was a popular 320-acre health resort that was owned and operated by William "Coin" Harvey. He said that the name Monte Ne meant "mountain water." On its spring-fed lake, he installed picturesque gondolas that met guests as they disembarked from their train. Today the long-abandoned resort has become a local legend, similar to the mythical Scottish town of Brigadoon that appears only when conditions are right. At Monte Ne, just a scarred concrete tower and some building foundations remain on dry land, which are eerie enough, but when lake waters are low due to drought, a submerged concrete amphitheater appears to rise like an apparition out of the depths. The general spookiness of the Monte Ne area has given rise to what some consider hauntings while others call them well-worn urban legends. Periodically, local newspapers report encounters with "Dear Darla," the spirit of a girl who was attacked after leaving a party at Monte Ne one night. She was reported to have run screaming through the woods toward the road, but even after a search of the area, she was never seen again—at least not in human form.

Bentonville, Arkansas, is not only the home office of megaretailer Walmart but also the **Peel Mansion**, which was built in 1875 by former U.S. Congressman Samuel Peel. The home is now said to be haunted by both Samuel and his daughter Minnie Belle. The apparition of Samuel Peel has been seen in various parts of the house, apparently keeping an eye on his property. Minnie Belle was an accomplished pianist in life, and apparently saw no reason to stop practicing after death. Reports indicate she can be seen wandering around Peel Mansion in a white gown as well as producing the sound of ghostly piano music in an otherwise empty room. Long-time Bentonville residents state that before the mansion's restoration, it looked like a stereotypically spooky spot, with some calling it "The House on Haunted Hill."

FURTHER READING

Danielson, Kay. *Eureka Springs, Arkansas.* Chicago, IL: Arcadia Publishing, 2001.

Lowe, Alan, and Jason Hall. *Supernatural Arkansas: Ghosts, Monsters, and the Unexplained.* Atglen, PA: Schiffer Publishing, 2012.

Whayne, Jeannie M., Thomas A. DeBlack, George Sabo, and Morris S. Arnold. *Arkansas: A Narrative History.* Fayetteville: University of Arkansas Press, 2013.

5

California

California has been called America's own "Shangri-La," the term for a fictional utopia. Coincidentally, the state that became the Shangri-La for countless seekers of the American Dream actually began life being named *for* a fictitious utopia. The state's name is taken from a popular 1510 Spanish novel titled *The Adventures of Esplandián*, which concerns what the book calls the "Island called California, very close to an Earthly Paradise."

In the later 1500s, Spanish explorers coming upon today's Baja California thought it was an island and are said to have named it after the mythical land in the book. Later becoming a part of Mexico, California was reluctantly ceded to the United States by a treaty ending the Mexican War in 1848.

What the Mexican diplomats did not know when they signed the treaty was that gold had just been discovered in northern California. Prospectors and settlers flooded into California. Bypassing the usual lengthy process for statehood, California, often called "The Golden State," became America's thirty-first state in 1850.

Blessed with a pleasant climate, fertile fields, mineral wealth, and spectacular natural beauty, California attracted its share of get-rich-quick schemers. It also brought American Dreamers, who believed in the idea that with hard work, anyone in the United States can become successful regardless of their background.

Before the rise of the transcontinental railroad after the Civil War, many schemers and dreamers headed for California overland. Caravans of wagons traveled about two miles an hour across the vast American West. From a typical starting point like Independence, Missouri, the two thousand–mile overland journey took about five months—provided travelers had good weather, capable leadership, skillful guides, no breakdowns, no loss of animals hauling the wagons, and no attacks by marauders or hostile Native Americans. The most critical requirement was an abundance of good luck.

The image of wagon trains has been captured in books, movies, and television shows. Groups of about twenty to forty wagons banded together for mutual protection, often led by a professional wagon master and/or experienced guide. Author Andrew Rolle (2015) describes one of the earliest wagon trains: after

Hollywood

In Los Angeles, a number of spirits are said to call the City of Angels their home, especially in the part of town known worldwide as Hollywood. One is Falcon's Lair, a Hollywood haunt that was the home of cinema's famed heartthrob Rudolph Valentino who died tragically in 1926 at the age of thirty-one but whose ghost apparently still appears in his old bedroom at Falcon's Lair. Valentino is also said to haunt his final resting place, the Hollywood Forever cemetery, where the phantom of mogul William Randolph Hearst, on whom the movie *Citizen Kane* was based, has also been known to make an appearance. The ghost of Culver Studios founder Thomas Ince has been spotted in his private screening room after dying in 1924 under mysterious circumstances aboard Hearst's yacht. On Stage 28 at Universal Studios, which housed the set for the 1925 production of *Phantom of the Opera*, the film's star Lon Chaney died in 1930 but still shows up for work dressed in a black cape. Paramount Studios welcomes the busy phantom of Rudolph Valentino who occasionally reports to the costume department. Rudy has also been seen accompanying the late Marilyn Monroe at the Hollywood Knickerbocker Hotel. At the Hollywood Roosevelt Hotel, Monroe's face has been said to appear in mirrors. Among the cement footprints outside Graumann's Chinese Theater, the ghost of elderly character actor Victor Kilian, who was murdered nearby during a 1982 robbery, is said to stalk the front of the theater looking for his killer who was never caught. The iconic Hollywood sign itself, where struggling actress Peg Entwistle jumped to her death in 1932, is the location of reports of a ghostly young woman throwing herself off the forty-five-foot tall white block letters.

---

leaving Missouri in 1841, green pastures were replaced by deserts and alkali flats where "the weary travelers had no choice but to jettison heavy furniture, wash-pans, butter churns, baggage, and lastly their wagons in order to keep going" (91). The animals pulling those wagons didn't fare too well either.

Still, California dreamers kept coming. In the spring of 1846, a group of eighty-seven men, women, and children headed west. The group was spearheaded by Illinois farmer George Donner, who had been reading a new book, *The Emigrants' Guide to Oregon and California*, written by Lansford Hastings. It was said that Hastings had visions of building an empire for himself in California and needed to attract settlers. Hastings described a new "shortcut" on easy terrain that he claimed would save travelers 350–400 miles. What the **Donner Party** did not know was that Hastings had never traveled the "Hastings Route." It was misinformation—the route had not actually been attempted.

Using the Hastings' book as a guide, by the time the Donner group reached the "shortcut" at northern California's steep, rugged Truckee Pass, they had already had their share of troubles. Without water in the desert, many of their horses and oxen died. Wagons were abandoned; entire families had to ride with others.

Near the Wasatch Mountains, the owner of a trading post decided his business would increase if travelers heading west used the still-untried Hastings Route, promoting its sight-unseen to the Donner Party as a smooth trip.

When the Donner Party reached the Hastings Route, they found it was so steep that their wagons kept rolling backward. The trail was not marked, so travelers were forced to clear brush, cut down trees, and heave rocks to make room for the wagons. After many accidents and delays, the Donner family's wagon broke a wheel. Stopping to make repairs, the next morning they found a thick coating of

California's Donner Pass was the site of a tragedy where people on a wagon train seeking a better life found only a horrible death. Trapped in the winter of 1846–1847 in snow reaching twenty-two feet high, members of the Donner Party froze to death, died of starvation, or were killed by disease. Disputed reports of "cannibalism" focused on sensationalism rather than the travelers' heroism. (Tommy Song/Dreamstime.com)

snow although it was only October. They had been told that the pass would not be snowed in until mid-November.

From what they could determine, the path ahead was worse than what they had already encountered. They decided to stop and rest, not knowing that it spelled their doom.

What came next for the ill-fated group was one of the worst snowstorms of the century, with snow reaching twenty-two feet high in spots. A few tried going for help. While some in the help parties survived, others were never seen again. Men, women, and children who stayed behind steadily froze to death or died of starvation or disease. To stay alive, some of the desperate people ate their animals, family dogs, as well as what were said to be the remains of dead people, although the latter has been disputed.

Trapped from October 1846 to April 1847, only around forty starving and frostbitten men, women, and children out of the eighty-seven original members of the Donner Party managed to avoid death. The number of survivors includes those who had remained alive by leaving with the help parties instead of staying behind.

After the news got out, what might have been an otherwise anonymous wagon train captured the country's imagination. Some sensationalized reports of "cannibalism" focused on the macabre rather than the travelers' ordeals and miraculous survival. Many newspapers, along with members of the U.S. Congress who supported Manifest Destiny, portrayed the Donner Party as unprepared, with the trail west leading to a paradise worthy of their sacrifices. Author John Unruh (1993) cites one California newspaper editor who promoted the overland journey, "provided the emigrants took normal precautions and did not delay inordinately—as he intimated the Donner Party had done."

In June 1847, after survivors were rescued, a U.S. Army detachment arrived at the former Donner encampment. Soldiers were ordered to burn any remaining shelters, clothing, and personal items so nothing would be left behind in connection with the site. A museum exists at the site today, housing some artifacts that were somehow spared from destruction.

As early as 1854, the site of the Donner encampment became a tourist attraction. In 1927, California created the **Donner Memorial State Park**, attracting hundreds of thousands of visitors each year.

Some who visit the site have reported paranormal experiences, like someone tugging at their clothes, or that they later found ghostly, unexplained images in photos. Some report overwhelming feelings of gloom and sadness, of being watched, of spirits that were trying to speak to them, or seeing ghosts of the entire starving, desperate Donner Party in the woods staring back at them.

Some people may have been more haunted than others. The orphaned Elitha Donner, who was fourteen when she was rescued, died in Sacramento, California, in 1923 at age ninety. She never talked about her dead family's ordeal but it is reported that every year when a nearby school studied a historical unit on the Donner Party, Elitha Donner sat in the classroom, listening silently from the back row.

SOME OTHER REPORTEDLY HAUNTED PLACES IN CALIFORNIA

Since its closing in 1963, **Alcatraz**, a former maximum-security men's prison on an island in San Francisco Bay might still remain the home of some captive spirits who refuse to leave. Local Native Americans had usually steered clear of the island, considering it a gathering place for evil spirits. Alcatraz opened in 1934 to house the worst of the worst, including mobster Al Capone. After Alcatraz was designated a National Historic Landmark in 1986 and tourists arrived, there have been stories of supernatural occurrences. Some psychics have said that the facility is soaked in anger, fear, pain, regret, and death, which some consider a breeding ground for the paranormal. Along with strange noises, cold spots, and the feeling of being touched, there are sounds of disembodied voices, sobbing, screams, and banging of cell doors. There has been the unexplained sound of a banjo, the instrument Al Capone played during his last years as a prisoner. It is said that an entity known simply as "The Thing" with red glowing eyes has been seen not only by visitors today but by prisoners and staff when Alcatraz was in operation. In Cell 14D, a prisoner locked in solitary screamed throughout the night that a creature with glowing eyes was killing him; the next day guards found the prisoner strangled to death. Even the wardens were not immune, as one discovered while showing guests around the prison. The group heard sobbing from inside the prison walls before encountering a noticeably cold wind whisking past that could never quite be explained.

Bodie, California, south of Lake Tahoe, was once home to thousands of residents but became a ghost town like many of the boom-and-bust communities during the days of the gold rush. In 1859, gold was discovered by prospectors including W. S. Bodey. Attempting to go for supplies, Bodey perished in a blizzard. When a richer vein of gold was uncovered in 1876, Bodey's small mining camp exploded into a boomtown. W. S. Bodey never got to see it, and although the town was named for him, it was misspelled "Bodie." Within three years, Bodie housed up to seven thousand people, with its mines producing millions of dollars in gold. But the town dwindled along with the gold. By 1943, there were only three people remaining, including a caretaker to prevent vandalism. In 1962, the town was designated as Bodie State Historic Park and named by California legislature as the official state gold rush ghost town. Its eerie nature is said to be due to the town's state of "arrested decay" where many interiors remain exactly as they were left, stocked with goods. The Bodie Curse maintains that if any items are taken, the crook will be plagued with bad luck. Some would-be thieves have returned what they took, along with apology notes, hoping to remove the curse. Perhaps the town was cursed by Mr. Bodey, offended at misspelling his name for the town he founded.

The **Cecil Hotel** in downtown Los Angeles has been said to contain so many menacing spirits that tragedies descended not only on those staying at the hotel but even people innocently walking outside the building. The Cecil opened in the 1920s, falling into disrepair with the economic downturn of the Great Depression in the 1930s. The first in a series of suicides occurred in 1931 when a traveler from Chicago took poison in his room. In 1947, would-be starlet Elizabeth Short was said to have been drinking at the bar of the Cecil just prior to her gruesome unsolved murder, after which she posthumously became famous as the Black Dahlia. Another unsolved murder involving the Cecil was that of a well-liked elderly resident at the hotel who was raped, beaten, and murdered in her room. Several serial killers stayed at the hotel during their homicidal sprees. Suicides occurred amidst what were said to be the dark spirits in residence. One woman was last seen behaving bizarrely in a hotel elevator, as if possessed. Her decomposing body was found several weeks after her mysterious death in a rooftop water tank that was covered by a heavy lid, during which time hotel guests had been drinking and bathing in the tainted water. The "curse" of the Cecil extended to a sixty-five-year-old pedestrian walking outside the hotel when a suicidal woman leaped from a ninth-floor window, landing on top of him and killing them both.

The **Greystone Mansion** in Beverly Hills is said to be the residence of dark spirits allegedly haunting the fifty-five-room limestone building with walls that are three feet thick. It was built in 1928 for the wealthy Doheny family. But just four months after Ned Doheny Jr. moved in with his wife and children, Doheny's close friend and secretary, Hugh Plunkett, allegedly shot Doheny before turning the gun on himself. Some said Plunkett was angry over being denied a raise. But others said Plunkett was despondent over investigations of his involvement in the infamous Teapot Dome scandal on behalf of the oil-rich Doheny family, learning that they planned to have him committed to a mental asylum before he could testify. It was also hinted that Ned Doheny or his wife fired both shots, fearing disclosure that Doheny and Plunkett were romantically involved. The case was ruled a murder-suicide, and historians say what really happened in the Greystone Mansion will probably never be known. Since that time, there have been allegations that the spirits of Plunkett and Doheny have been sighted, still roaming the mansion. In addition, a pool of blood is said to appear and disappear on the floor of the guest bedroom where the deaths allegedly took place. The exterior of the Greystone Mansion has been seen on television programs like *Columbo*, *Murder She Wrote*, and *Dark Shadows*, all of which seem appropriate.

San Diego's popular **Hotel del Coronado**, lovingly called The Del, boasts a unique Victorian design that sets it apart from other hotels in the country and is well deserving of its National Historic Landmark status. Built in 1888, it is also popular with the undead, such as the famed ghost of a woman named Kate Morgan who arrived in 1892 and apparently never checked out. Depending on the storyteller, her dead body was found in her former guestroom (number 3327) or on a stairway leading to the beach. She was shot once in the head, which the coroner determined to be self-inflicted. Some say the jilted Kate committed suicide over a man who abandoned her, while others believe he murdered her. Either way, her spirit is said to roam the scenic grounds before retiring to her former room where guests have reported unexplained breezes, faucets, and television turning on and off by themselves, sightings of a woman in a black Victorian dress, and the covers tossed off the bed while they slept. In another room, number 3519, a maid was said to have hanged herself, making it one of the most haunted rooms with several guests reporting disembodied voices, mysterious temperature changes, the sound of footsteps, and the feeling of unseen hands touching them. Guestrooms do not have a monopoly on hauntings at the Del. There have also been reports of glassware, pictures, and other items flying off the shelves at the hotel's gift shop.

Los Coches Adobe is located in the northern California town of Soledad, not far from the magnificent vistas of Monterey, Big Sur, and Carmel. But Soledad ("solitude" in Spanish) is considered by some to be less than idyllic, housing two prisons, serving as the setting of John Steinbeck's tragic novel, *Of Mice and Men*, and becoming known as one of the most haunted places in California. Originally a mining community, there have been claims of seeing the ghost of a man hanging from a tree on the property, which was often the punishment for individuals accused of stealing precious metals from mines in the Old West. There is also the tale of visitations by a spectral woman in black who allegedly robbed and murdered miners who were looking for a good time before she dumped their bodies in a well on the property, a spot that seems to be the center of other paranormal activity. A mining accident trapped thirty miners underground where they were unable to be rescued. Area residents as well as visitors to Los Coches Adobe have reported hearing the screams of the doomed miners' spirits emanating from the old well. Many reports come from those brave enough to approach the well after nightfall, surrounded by the same kind of terrifying darkness in which the miners perished.

The former ocean liner **R.M.S. *Queen Mary*** is now permanently docked at Long Beach where it serves as a floating hotel. Many of its guests today are paranormal researchers checking in at what is called one of the most haunted places in California. The luxurious vessel sailed the Atlantic from 1936 to 1967, carrying celebrities as well as serving as a World War II troopship when the ship was popularly known as the "Grey Ghost." After the war, she was restored to her former glory but was docked perpetually at Long Beach in 1967. During her time at sea, the *Queen Mary* saw numerous deaths. The First Class swimming pool area is said to be haunted by the spirits of two women in old-fashioned swimsuits and several children who reportedly drowned there. Wet footprints have been spied leading from the empty, now-dry pool to the changing rooms. Other First Class haunts include a male specter in 1930s attire, a lady in white in the Queen's Salon, and the unexplained sounds of children playing in the First Class suites. The areas below decks have their own apparitions, especially the engine room which is said to be a hotbed of paranormal activity. Its infamous "Door 13" crushed several men to death; the apparition of one of them, a young crew member dressed in blue coveralls, has often been spied walking through the engine room before disappearing at Door 13.

The historic **Whaley House** in San Diego, built in 1857, has been cited as one of the most haunted houses in the nation by no less than *Life* magazine, the television program *America's Most Haunted*, and even TV host Regis Philbin. The earliest documentation concerns the ghost of convicted thief James "Yankee Jim" Robinson who was hanged in 1852 on the grounds where the Whaley House would later be built. One of the spectators was Thomas Whaley who bought the property a few years later to build his family home. Soon after the family moved in, they reported hearing heavy footsteps moving about the house, like a large man in the kind of thick boots Robinson had worn. Members of Whaley's family, who lived in the residence until 1953, were convinced that the ghost of "Yankee Jim" haunted the house. In addition, the family apparently determined that they had as much right as Yankee Jim to remain in the house after their deaths. It is said that both guests and museum staffers occasionally glimpse the ghost of family members who died inside the house, including Violet Whaley, who in 1885 fatally shot herself in the heart at age twenty-two when her new husband abandoned her. On television's *The Haunting of Regis Philbin*, the entertainer claimed while some people "pooh-pooh it because they can't see it . . . there was something going on in that house."

Even with other world-class hauntings in California, the **Winchester Mystery House** in San Jose stands apart. Sarah Winchester commissioned construction on the house in 1886, after the death in infancy of her only child as well as the passing of her husband, weapons manufacturer William Winchester, who died of tuberculosis in 1884 at age forty-three. It is said that Sarah believed she would be haunted by the ghosts of those killed by Winchester rifles unless she started building nonstop, which some said was to confuse dark, evil spirits pursuing her. Using her inheritance, she employed builders to work nonstop until her death in 1922. With almost two hundred rooms, secret passageways, mismatched levels, doors opening into thin air, and staircases that dead-end at ceilings, today the Winchester Mystery House is said to also be occupied by the ghost of eccentric Sarah herself. Staff and visitors have reported encounters with various spirits. Quoted in

People magazine, Winchester House historian Janan Boehme states that over the course of her forty-year association with the residence, she has sensed a good energy that is sometimes sad and lonely but mostly kind, adding that while she never feels unsafe in the house, she never feels alone there either.

FURTHER READING

Dennett, Preston. *California Ghosts: True Accounts of Hauntings in the Golden State.* Atglen, PA: Schiffer Publishing, 2004.

Rolle, Andrew, and Arthur Verge. *California: A History.* 8th ed. Malden, MA: Wiley-Blackwell, 2015.

Unruh, John D. *The Plains Across: The Overland Emigrants and the Trans-Mississippi West, 1840–60.* Urbana: University of Illinois Press, 1993.

Warner, Kara. "America's Most Haunted House?" *People*, February 12, 2018, pp. 56–59.

6

Colorado

Straddling the Rocky Mountains, Colorado was named by Spanish explorers for the Río Colorado ("red-colored river") that cuts through it with its reddish-brown silt carried by water running down from the mountains. The Territory of Colorado was organized in 1861, just before the nation became embroiled in the Civil War. Colorado was admitted to the Union as the thirty-eighth state in 1876, the year America celebrated its hundredth birthday; therefore, Colorado became nicknamed the "Centennial State."

Colorado is split by the Continental Divide, in which water on the west side of the Rockies flows westward and water on the east side flows to the east. Some say this rift gives Colorado an added dimension in addition to its majestic beauty. But another part of Colorado's allure came from the glitter of gold and silver beneath the land. Even before statehood, prospectors arrived, developing mines and mining towns.

A significant silver strike in 1864 was followed by the coming of the transcontinental railroad in 1869, linking the riches of Colorado to the rest of the world. Another major silver strike took place in 1872. In 1878, the discovery of a rich lode of silver near the town of Leadville triggered what was called the Colorado Silver Boom.

The U.S. Congress boosted Colorado's mining industry by passing the Sherman Silver Purchase Act in 1890, mandating the federal government to purchase nearly twice as much silver as before to increase the amount of money in circulation. A few months after its passage, Colorado's last and greatest gold strike took place at Cripple Creek, enticing more prospectors hungry for instant wealth, which many found, including J. J. Brown who made a fortune through the unexpected discovery of copper.

However, what Congress gives, Congress can also take away. In 1893, the Silver Purchase Act was repealed, leading to a collapse of Colorado's mining industry and putting a severe dent in the state's economy. But due to what Carl Abbott (2013) calls scenery, health, and tourism, Colorado found a new source of economic wealth: tourist dollars.

Molly Brown House

Located in Denver, the Molly Brown House is renowned throughout the state. It was once the home of the millionaire philanthropist Margaret Tobin Brown. Visitors enjoy the rags-to-riches tale of a woman who married for love and found herself a millionaire. She became popularly known as the "Unsinkable Molly Brown" as a courageous survivor of the *Titanic* disaster, in which she helped others to lifeboats, ordered crewmen to go back for survivors in the water, and even grabbed an oar to help row. She and her husband James Joseph "J. J." Brown purchased the house in 1898, apparently liking it so much that they never left. Currently serving as a museum, empty rooms are said to suddenly smell strongly of tobacco smoke in today's nonsmoking building where J. J. was an avid smoker. There have also been reports of sudden unexplained cold spots in Molly's former bedroom, dark shadows moving in rooms where there is no light to produce them, furniture being rearranged, light bulbs inexplicably undone, curtains and blinds opening or closing on their own, piano keys moving but making no sound, and apparitions of Victorian-era women said to be Molly or her mother, with ghostly figures sometimes being seen sitting in chairs. As a world traveler, when she boarded the *Titanic* in 1912, Mrs. Brown had just had her fortune told in Egypt, being warned to stay away from water. She lived until 1932 and apparently then returned to her beloved Denver home. Someone who was "unsinkable" enough to survive the doomed *Titanic* in grand style can probably go anywhere she wants, even after death.

In the late 1800s, crowded conditions and industrial pollution in Northern cities often drove the spread of deadly tuberculosis, a highly infectious disease. Doctors frequently recommended that patients go to dry, sunny climates for their health. By the 1880s, Colorado, with its cool, clean mountain air, was nicknamed "The World's Sanitarium."

Not all visitors needed to be placed in sanitariums. Friends and families of patients as well as tourists seeking Colorado's natural splendors sought other accommodations. Hotels began springing up like Rocky Mountain wildflowers.

The history of hotels goes back at least as far as the ancient Greeks and Romans as places where travelers could find food and lodging. The templates for modern hotels were the inns of medieval Europe, often run by religious orders at monasteries. In the early nineteenth century, American hotels began catering to well-heeled guests who demanded luxury. Tremont House in Boston, Massachusetts, opened in 1829 as the first hotel to offer such novelties as indoor toilets and baths, bellboys to carry luggage, and complimentary soap.

Hotels across the United States have traditionally welcomed guests of all tastes. Among the wide variety are caboose hotels (in old rail cars), capsule hotels (with tiny "cabins"), container hotels (even smaller accommodations), cave hotels and cliff hotels, both self-explanatory. Some people find the most popular variety to be haunted hotels.

At a hotel, there is often a sense of anonymity and loneliness. According to Levander (2017), hotels are not passive sites but bring a power of their own due to transience and dislocation. They are frequently the site of suicides as well as the death of those who pass away of natural causes far from home. With such restless

The eerie sensations at the Stanley Hotel in Estes Park, Colorado, were even able to frighten master of the macabre, author Stephen King. King especially noted the disorienting feeling of the hotel's looping, empty corridors. After a disturbing dream one night while staying there, King sketched out the plot for what became his best seller, The Shining. (Coljh09/Dreamstime.com)

spirits, paranormal investigators frequently cite hotels as some of the nation's most haunted places.

One spooky spot that immediately comes to mind is the **Stanley Hotel** in Estes Park, Colorado. It was built by wealthy Freelan Oscar Stanley in 1909 to provide luxurious accommodations amid Colorado's scenic splendor for his upper-class friends. But what put the hotel on the map was frightening the monarch of the macabre, author Stephen King. The night before Halloween in 1974, he and his wife stumbled upon the hotel, looking for lodging just as the Stanley was about to close for the winter. According to Pittman (2015), King described the eerie sensation of being the only guests. He especially noted what he called the looping, empty corridors in the 142-room hotel. After a disturbing dream that night about his young son, King got up and sketched out the plot for what ultimately became the 1977 best seller, *The Shining*.

In King's novel, the fictional hotel inspired by the Stanley is an evil entity haunted by malevolent spirits and their victims. A couple and their young son act as caretakers during the off-season. When a winter storm leaves them snowbound and stranded, supernatural forces inhabiting the hotel disrupt the sanity of one of the characters, putting the others in grave danger.

During his stay at the Stanley, King stayed in Room 217, which was changed to Room 237 for the film. Today, Room 237 is the hotel's most requested accommodation. Although the 1980 movie adaption of *The Shining* was not shot at the Stanley, the 1996 TV miniseries was.

In addition to show business types, the Stanley may be attractive to original owners F. O. and Flora Stanley who reportedly never left. According to staff, Mrs. Stanley can be heard playing her piano in the music room at night, and the image of Mr. Stanley occasionally shows up in photographs. There have also been reports of bags being mysteriously unpacked, echoes of children's laughter in the hallways, and lights inexplicably turning on and off. Paranormal experts call the Stanley Hotel one of the nation's most active ghost sites, which is understandable in a place that has guest rooms with a television channel that plays *The Shining* continuously twenty-four hours a day.

SOME OTHER REPORTEDLY HAUNTED PLACES IN COLORADO

Many consider cemeteries to be among the most haunted places, and if restless souls are a cause of the haunting, Denver's **Cheesman Park** has to be among the most haunted. When the old Prospect Hill Cemetery, dating back to 1859, was commandeered by the city for a downtown park in 1893, a contractor was hired to remove the five thousand unclaimed bodies that remained with the requirement that he put them into fresh coffins. Realizing he could make more money by purchasing inexpensive child-sized coffins, he hacked up adult bodies before stuffing as many as he could into the miniature caskets. Newspaper accounts state that bystanders were sickened at the sight of bones and body parts strewn around the grounds. The city cancelled its contract but did not hire a replacement to deal with the open graves and desecrated bodies. In 1907, Cheesman Park was named for a local pioneer who created the park space without removing the rest of the bodies and simply bulldozing over the open graves. Today, joggers and others using the park at night report an uneasy feeling that some ascribe to it being haunted by those whose bodies were desecrated without being allowed to rest in peace. Writer Russell Hunter has stated that he based many elements of his Seattle-based 1980 horror movie *The Changeling* on his experiences living in Denver on the edge of Cheesman Park, even naming the center of the paranormal action as the "Cheesman House."

The **Hotel Colorado** in Glenwood Springs is known for its hauntings. It opened in 1893, and during World War II, it served as a naval hospital, giving rise to the enduring legend of a chambermaid of that era who was murdered by a jealous lover, with her screams being heard in the room where she died. Staff and guests have also reported activities like an elevator that moves between floors with no passengers, knocking sounds at doors with no one there, lights turning on and off by themselves, locked doors mysteriously opening, and televisions changing channels. A young girl in a Victorian dress playing with a ball has reportedly been seen playing throughout the hotel, as well as a female apparition who peers over male guests in their beds. Room 551 is especially active, with a ghost who may have dreamed of becoming an interior decorator. In a hotel renovation, wallpaper that was applied to the room was found the next day rolled neatly on the floor. The wallpaper was replaced, but again found on the floor in the morning. After several attempts, various wallpaper samples were placed on the bed in Room 551. The next morning, all but one of the samples was on the floor. The wallpaper from the sample that was left on the bed was applied to the walls, where it remains today.

A popular bar in downtown Denver was once a popular brothel, **Mattie's House of Mirrors**. At one time, all of its wall space was covered in mirrors. In 1910, Mattie Silks took over the building, which dated back to 1889. She established a restaurant on the lower floor with a brothel above. Paranormal researchers report that the spirit of a woman named Ella Wellington might still reside upstairs. According to the story, Ella was a former owner of the business who had left her husband and children in Omaha. One evening, amid a gala party downstairs, some businessmen from Omaha arrived, including a former friend of Ella and her husband. He recounted how happy her husband and children were. "I too am happy," she is reported to have said, "Oh, so very happy." Whereupon she went upstairs to her room and fatally shot herself in the head. Since then, there have been reports of unusual activities in the room where Wellington died, as well as other areas of the building, such as staffers hearing parties when no one else was in the building, a piano playing upstairs, the elevator moving between floors when nobody called it, footsteps being heard throughout the building when staff members were downstairs alone, and reports of faces reflected in the mirrors at the bar. Some staff members refuse to go to the second floor alone. As for Mattie Silks, nothing seems to have bothered her—she married for the last time at age seventy-seven.

With a history going back to 1916, the popular **Melting Pot** restaurant in Littleton originally served as a library before becoming the police headquarters complete with jail. That transition took place after a child drowned in the library's outdoor fountain, leading to rumors of a poltergeist returning after the tragedy to haunt the facility. After being taken over by the jail, a story circulated that an inmate and jailer died during a failed escaped attempt. Today, the restaurant sits on what was once a flood plain where dozens of people died when the Platte River flooded. There have been numerous stories attributed to the staff, such as bartenders having their feet grabbed, women being pushed in the restroom, mysterious sounds, eerie voices, and a newly installed cappuccino machine flying across the bar. One staffer who was working alone in an upstairs room is said to have been putting glasses on a table. After hearing noises, the worker went to a nearby room, but upon returning, found that the glasses had been moved from the table to a bench. Some say that the Melting Pot feels like it could indeed be haunted with its low ceilings and a cavernous, maze-like layout. A dark basement section of the building is said to feel like a catacomb, although even there, no cappuccino-based incidents have been reported.

Riverdale Road in Thornton, north of Denver, is reportedly one of the most haunted roads in the nation due to the many terrifying tales attributed to it. Reportedly, the road was built on Native American burial grounds, accounting for vengeful spirits. It is also said to have been the site of tragic accidents and bloody doings. There have been reports of apparitions of people hanging from trees, figures suddenly appearing and disappearing, strange voices chanting, a phantom jogger who was killed by a car accosting drivers along the roadway, and bloody handprints splattered on signs which is said to be the work of a child who was hit by a car while walking along the road. Large metal gates near the road, familiarly known as the Gates of Hell, were left behind from a mansion where a man reportedly burned down the house with his family inside.

Between the towns of Silver Cliff and Westcliffe in southern Colorado lies the **Silver Cliff Cemetery**, which dates back to the 1880s and is home not only to the dead but also to what have been called the Ghost Lights of Silver Cliff. Soon after dark, there have been reports of small lights that ranged from blue to green to white to yellow, and with various combinations of these colors. As nighttime hours passed, the lights were said to become larger, more numerous, and more active. Some appeared to dart between the weathered headstones without stopping. Some appeared to follow individuals and dance around them. Other orbs seemed to float lazily, landing in the grass as well as on headstones. Within an hour, some were reported as large as three to four inches in diameter, glowing brightly. Some observers have reported that they spotted an orange glow that became larger and appeared to luminesce, like the glow of a campfire. It was said that the orbs seemed attracted to the orange glow, but as investigators approached, the lights became dimmer. At one point, the side of a headstone appeared to be the site of tiny illuminations that resembled Christmas lights shooting toward the sky. While some have tried debunking the lights as reflections from electric lights in the town rather than supernatural phenomena, others ask why the dancing orb lights were first reported by nineteenth-century miners using the cemetery as a shortcut—before there was electricity in the area.

The **St. Elmo Ghost Town** in Chaffee County, southwest of Denver, is a popular destination for getting a glimpse into Colorado's mining past. But those who explore the remaining buildings might also glimpse St. Elmo's most well-known former (and possibly current) resident, Annabelle Stark. Annabelle and her parents arrived in 1881. Her mother kept her isolated from the rough-and-tumble characters in the mining town until she was sent to work in a nearby town. There she married, but apparently the union was unsuccessful because Annabelle returned to St. Elmo. In her later days, she was said to prowl around the ghost town with her rifle to protect St. Elmo from vandals. Some reported seeing her apparition in the window of her now-deserted home, still keeping an eye out to discourage trespassers.

Located near Aurora, the **Third Bridge** has a history steeped not only in ghostlore but also in brutal real-life history. In a bloody incident near Third Bridge, a white settler killed a Native American in cold blood for attempting to take a horse, leading Native warriors to kill and mutilate the settler along with his family. The family's bodies were brought to Denver, where their deaths spurred government-sanctioned violence against Native Americans in the run-up to 1864's Sand Creek Massacre, which occurred elsewhere and became notorious for the slaughter of Indian women, children, and the elderly. In 1997, two car loads of teenagers at the bridge met with an accident that left some killed and others paralyzed. In 2010, drivers on Third Bridge discovered the body of a teacher who was found with a bag over his head, a belt around his neck, and hands bound behind his back. His murder remains unsolved. There have been reports of hearing loud cries for help, seeing the apparition of a crying young girl that suddenly disappears, and hearing the sounds of drums. In one case, a group checking out reports of the haunted bridge found a photographic image of a jagged green line near one of them amid the darkness. Another member of the group began to experience unexplained jagged scratches on her arm, neck, torso, and face although the group was not near any bushes, branches, or other potential causes. Some said the scratches were in the shape of a "W," which was the letter that began the last name of the murdered man.

FURTHER READING

Abbott, Carl, and Stephen J. Leonard. *Colorado: A History of the Centennial State*. 5th ed. Boulder: University Press of Colorado, 2013.

Levander, Caroline Field, and Matthew Pratt Guterl. *Hotel Life: The Story of a Place Where Anything Can Happen*. Chapel Hill: University of North Carolina Press, 2017.

Pittman, Rebecca. *The History and Haunting of the Stanley Hotel*. Loveland, CO: Wonderland Productions, 2015.

7

Connecticut

Connecticut is named for the Connecticut River that bisects the state, with the word itself derived from an anglicized version of the Algonquian term for "long tidal river." The state has traditionally enjoyed a high standard of living and a reputation for upscale tastefulness.

However, tastefulness does not mean Connecticut does not attract its share of the supernatural. According to Farnsworth (2006), Connecticut is also known for its haunted islands; phantom ships, planes, and trains; sightings of UFOs and aliens; and encounters with Bigfoot, as well as an evil ghostly black dog. There are even rumors of hauntings at the former American Shakespeare Festival Theatre in Stratford, Connecticut, which is quite tasteful.

English colonists established major settlements in Connecticut during the 1630s. After ratifying the U.S. Constitution in 1788, Connecticut became the fifth state admitted to the Union. The state went on to prosper in the era following American independence, with flourishing seaports and thriving fisheries. With the arrival of the Industrial Revolution, textile mills and factories sprang up.

A factory (previously called a "manufactory") is a large industrial facility where goods are manufactured. In the past, harnessing energy through waterwheels and windmills had helped facilitate the production of items like food products. Most sources regard the first modern factories to stem from eighteenth-century Britain, and then transported to the English colonies. By that time, most factories resembled large warehouses that contained heavy equipment operated by a large number of people performing the same task over and over.

It was efficient for administration and for distributing raw materials to individual workers. By the late 1700s, steam power was harnessed, leading to the development of industrial textile factories, where precision machines and interchangeable parts allowed greater efficiency and standardization, enabling the production of huge quantities of identical goods.

In the twentieth century, Henry Ford further revolutionized the factory concept through mass production, in which workers stationed alongside rolling ramps built automobiles a piece at a time. This concept usually decreased production costs, increased profits for factory owners, and brought about the age of consumerism, which in turn led to greater demand for products.

However, for many workers, what the factories of the Industrial Age brought about was a life of hardship. Many people were moving away from the kind of subsistence farming that had previously been the mainstay of America's economy. In addition, immigrants were increasingly coming to America. Many were illiterate, unskilled farm laborers, and often found themselves in city slums and "factory towns," where one industry dominated the economy.

Freeman (2018) notes the factory of that era as "a new kind of prison with the clock a new kind of jailer" (20). He cites textile mills whose "owners preferred women and children who they could pay less" (23). Freeman also describes harsh conditions for mill workers that were often terrifying with the noise and motion of the machinery, foul air full of cotton dust, and temperatures that were kept oppressively hot to reduce breakage. Freeman (2018) says there was ". . . the sweat of hundreds of laboring people; the pale countenances and sickly bodies of the workers; the fierce demeanor of the overseers, some of whom carried belts or whips to enforce their discipline" (23).

Generally, with Sunday the only day off, workweeks of over seventy hours were common. To economize, some factory owners turned to poorhouses for a steady supply of widows and orphans, with some children as young as five years old. In some places it was a criminal offense for children to run away from mill work.

Fortunately, not all factories were so austere. When World War I broke out in 1914, Connecticut became a major supplier of weapons for the U.S. military. Along with Winchester in New Haven and Colt in Hartford, **Remington Arms** in Bridgeport produced half the weaponry used by the U.S. Army.

Remington was founded in 1816 by Eliphalet Remington, and is reputed to be not only the country's oldest gun maker but also the oldest factory in America that still makes its original product. Remington remains the largest U.S. producer of shotguns and rifles. According to Marcot (2005), before the concept of a factory was fully developed, Remington organized groups of workers into specific tasks in a way that would be recognizable today as a rudimentary factory assembly line.

In 1867, the Union Metallic Cartridge Company opened a factory in Bridgeport, later merging with Remington. The Bridgeport plant went on to produce tons of ammunition and weapons each year for domestic and military use.

To meet the demand of World War I, Remington's Bridgeport factory expanded to thirty-eight buildings on almost seventy-five acres, employing about seventeen thousand people and churning out around ten thousand rifles per day.

In a factory of that size, workplace accidents were not uncommon. Many workers lost fingers in the presses or suffered injuries from accidents with chemicals and gunpowder. Some accidents were fatal, such as a 1905 explosion that killed three men and filled the building with lead dust that slowly poisoned workers with prolonged contact. When about a hundred workers went on strike at Remington in 1914, Bridgeport police attacked the strikers, killing one and injuring scores of others. On three separate occasions, workers were reported as falling into a

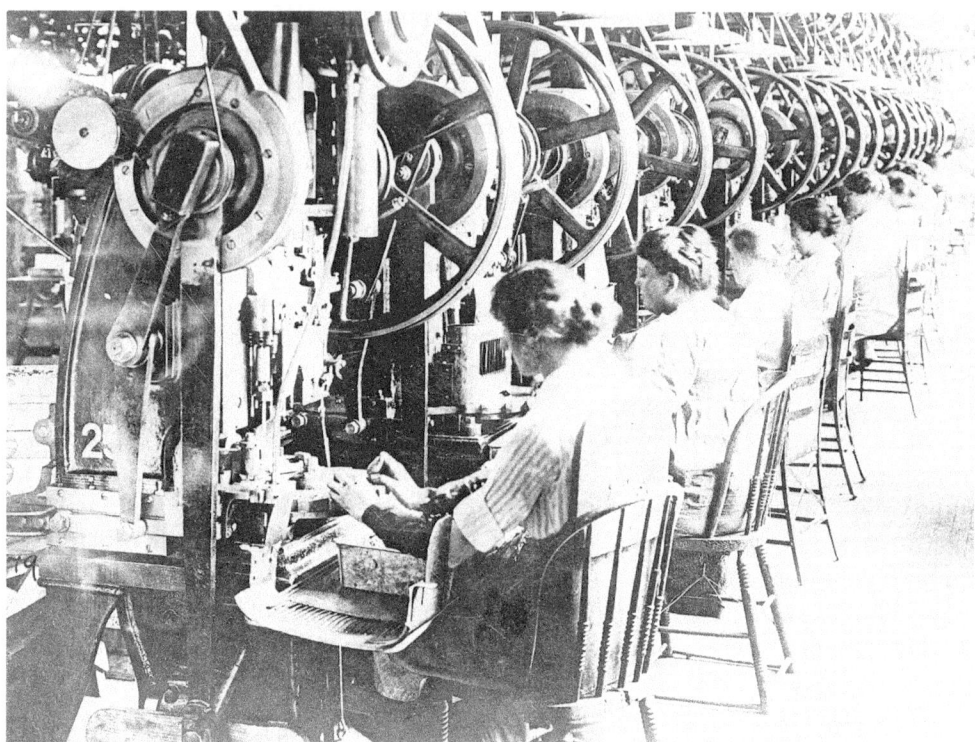

In munitions factories like Remington Arms in Bridgeport, Connecticut, workplace accidents were not uncommon. Workers like the women seen here suffered injuries from accidents with chemicals and gunpowder, while others lost their lives in explosions. At the abandoned Bridgeport plant, there have been reports of ghostly shadows, eerie lights, and disembodied screams. (Library of Congress)

cauldron of molten metal. In 1942, an explosion in one of the munitions buildings took the lives of almost twenty people and injured about a hundred. In addition, the fire from the explosion set off countless bullets that ripped through nearby buildings and neighborhoods.

Over time, Remington Arms has closed older factories as it moved to more modern facilities elsewhere. The Bridgeport factory closed in 1986. Since then, police patrolling the grounds of the abandoned buildings have reported seeing ghostly moving shadows and eerie lights, hearing disembodied voices and screams, and generally feeling a sense of dread. Some ascribe it to the uneasy souls of factory workers killed there. With the multitudes of now-broken windows staring like accusing eyes, it is not hard to see why.

SOME OTHER REPORTEDLY HAUNTED PLACES IN CONNECTICUT

The **American Shakespeare Festival Theatre** at Stratford, Connecticut, is reputed to stand on the site of the town's first settlement. The theater began with great promise in 1955. No less than Winston Churchill remarked that it completed the third side of a triangle composed of towns named Stratford in England, Canada, and the United States. He expressed hope that Shakespeare's works would help bring English-speaking people of the world closer together. In its heyday, the American Shakespeare Festival hosted such actors as Katharine Hepburn, Ruby Dee, Helen Hayes, Hal Holbrook, Lynne Redgrave, and Christopher Walken. But by 1983, amid dwindling ticket sales, the property was sold to the state of Connecticut. There were attempts at reviving the theater, but by 1990, newspapers were citing strange problems at the playhouse that included everything from broken air conditioning to repeated hospitalizations of a lead actor causing the show to be cancelled. Electronic equipment malfunctioned, the lighting system failed, and at one point, the theater was filled with smoke due to faulty installation. Then there came reports of incidents on the grounds, including assault, a bloody murder, and an old man freezing to death. Even the elm trees lining the street outside the theater died. In the years before it burned in January 2019, the public was not admitted and it was said that only raccoons could be found onstage. But paranormal investigators described communal energy clusters at the theater and a general feeling of uneasiness, as well as the ghostly apparition of a woman's face in a window. Some wonder if there are uneasy spirits from Stratford's early settlement under the property along with the shades of actors haunting the theater, reluctant to make their exit.

Bara-Hack near Pomfret, Connecticut, is an oddly named ghost settlement that is reportedly haunted. Although it was abandoned more than 125 years ago, this "village of ghostly voices" still welcomes curious visitors who hope to encounter some old residents who may never have left. In the late 1700s, Obadiah Higginbotham and Johnathan Randall were settlers in the remote forest outpost. It is generally accepted that the men, being of Welsh heritage, named the settlement Bara-Hack, which is said to mean "breaking of bread" in Welsh, although some declare that the name was a later invention. Making their living supplying flax to surrounding areas, the residents of Bara-Hack established a waterwheel and mill along with a communal graveyard. But the small village met economic hardships after the passing of the founding families. Most remaining residents moved away, leaving Bara-Hack abandoned by the late 1800s. Today, there are overgrown ruins where the settlement used to be, scarcely more than a wide spot in the road with a few stone foundations and clearings for cellars. Yet, it attracts not only tourists but also paranormal investigators intrigued by tales of a bearded face appearing in the cemetery, a ghost baby spotted in a tree, and streaking lights and orbs. Strange sounds have also been reported amid the silent ruins, such as the braying of farm animals, children laughing, disembodied voices, horse-drawn wagons on a road that is no longer there, and the general atmosphere of a small rural community in a place that no longer exists. These are not recent occurrences; it is reported that the original observers of the ghost baby were servants of the Randall family in the 1790s, leading to speculation that the ground itself was—and is—inhabited by the spirit world.

Like Bara-Hack, the **Dudleytown** community exists as an abandoned place with its only remains being some stone foundations and cellar holes. Several related families named Dudley moved to this section of Cornwall, Connecticut, beginning in the mid-1700s where they cleared a spot in the gloomy, shadowy woods later dubbed "Dark Entry Forest." At its peak in the mid-1850s, records show the town had no more than about twenty-five people. But what the community *did* have was its own curse. According to some, the Dudley family was cursed after trying to usurp the English throne at the time of Henry VIII, an offense against the belief that rulers were anointed by God. Dudley descendants who settled in Connecticut did seem to have more than their share of ill fortune. Their village was in the middle of three large hills that kept the town dark even at noon. At a fifteen hundred–foot elevation, winters were so harsh that trees were stunted from the cold. The rocky land was ill-suited to grow their food, although the curse may have eased somewhat when iron ore was discovered nearby, providing a steady income. Whether a curse or constantly dark days that some psychologists say can affect the mind, Dudleytown seems to have suffered more than its share of insanity among its residents. Some simply vanished forever into the woods where unexplained "creatures" had been spotted. Paranormal investigators report strange apparitions in photographs, mysterious lights, overwhelming feelings of terror, and sometimes of being touched, pushed, and scratched by unseen hands. Today, the land is owned by the Dark Forest Entry Association, where trespassers might encounter not only wrathful spirits but also local police.

Hannah Cranna's Grave is located in Gregory's Four Corners Burial Ground on the edge of Monroe, Connecticut, where an old woman called "The Wicked Witch of Monroe" lived in the mid-1800s. Hannah apparently lived an uneventful life until her husband went walking one evening and met an untimely death by toppling off a cliff. Hannah was suspected of "bewitching" him. There were no contemporary reports suggesting the possible involvement of alcohol or a simple misstep in the dark. Accused of witchcraft, Hannah was at least fortunate that it was no longer a capital crime in Connecticut. In fact, black-clad Hannah used her witchy-woman reputation to her advantage, scaring trespassers away from her property where she lived alone, discouraging fishing on her land, and even manipulating her neighbors into giving her food. It was said she punished those who refused by casting a spell on them but rewarded kind neighbors with good fortune. Her legend grew impressively when she predicted her own death, stating that she wanted her casket carried to the cemetery on foot, not by wagon. When she died in winter with deep snow on the ground, the pallbearers went against her wishes and used a wagon. But the casket rolled off the wagon again and again, even with men sitting on top of it. Finally forced to carry the coffin on foot, they returned to the village where Hannah's home was burning to the ground. Today, visitors claim to see a ghostly woman wandering the cemetery, with an accompanying legend stating that motorists regularly swerve off the road to avoid a woman in the street, crashing into Hannah's tombstone, which is somehow still intact.

The sixteen-acre **New Haven Green** was established in 1638 as a pasture, marketplace, and the colony's first burial ground. In 1821, after several serious yellow fever epidemics, the Green, which held thousands of gravesites, was felt to be too crowded with the dead. Headstones were moved to a newer cemetery. But something noteworthy remained at the Green—the dead bodies which were not disinterred but left to deteriorate namelessly where they lay. There was not much in the way of an orderly pattern. In the mid-1800s, while trying to erect a monument to a prominent citizen, workers unearthed the remains of sixteen people in a twelve-foot space just two feet below the surface. Over the years, people have reported shadowy or misty figures that disappear when approached. Sometimes whispering voices are heard when there is no one else there. Visitors also complain of what they call a spirit-draining energy. Some say that ghosts walk the Green in search of their headstones, none too pleased that their bodies are still under the ground where people stroll above. According to one recent newspaper report, an uprooted tree exposed a human skeleton in the tree roots. In springtime, the New Haven Green is a popular spot for romantic college students to cuddle, not realizing that intimations of mortality lie just beneath their feet. One disgruntled subterranean resident may be an early governor of the colony who warned that the Green was not a healthy place for a burying ground. A year after making that statement, he died—and was buried beneath the Green.

Over the years, there have been tales of a large, hairy creature spotted in remote regions. The Native Americans called it Sasquatch, arctic regions have the Abominable Snowman, and the residents of Tibet claim the Yeti. America has its legend of Bigfoot, most often reported in the Pacific Northwest. One creature may have chosen another northwestern region to call home, in this case, the town of Winsted in northwestern Connecticut, becoming known as the **Winsted Wildman**. For such a small state, Connecticut has spawned a large number of reported Bigfoot encounters. One Bigfoot-type creature allegedly chased a horse and a rider in 1997, one was spotted near the town of Barkhamsted in 2002, and another allegedly crossed the highway in Woodstock during 2004. Connecticut was also home to sightings near East Hampton, another in Norwich, and even what was called a "young" Bigfoot in Bristol in 2005. Perhaps coincidentally, those years happened to span the rise of the internet. But the legend of the Winsted Wildman predates the internet age. In 1895, the local newspaper stated that a town councilman was walking along the road with his bulldog. Suddenly, the dog became frightened, whining and cowering at his master's feet. Soon a creature covered with thick black hair allegedly jumped out of the bushes, yelling incoherently at the terrified man and dog before running back into the woods. The six-foot-tall Wildman creature was reportedly spotted again at various times that year. Those sightings stopped until the mid-1970s when there were again reports of a hairy humanoid. Terrorizing the locals over the next few weeks, the Wildman was purportedly seen by several witnesses. Descriptions generally matched, with all agreeing it was definitely *not* a bear. The local newspaper speculated that the Wildman may have been an escaped mental patient from a nearby sanitarium. Others theorized that the elusive creature may be some sort of multi-dimensional being able to teleport between universes, visiting various spots, and vanishing before getting caught or leaving tracks. Therefore, while perhaps not technically haunted, the woods around Winsted might be a good place to avoid on a dark night.

FURTHER READING

Farnsworth, Cheri. *Haunted Connecticut: Ghosts and Strange Phenomena of the Constitution State.* Mechanicsburg, PA: Stackpole Books, 2006.

Freeman, Joshua. *Behemoth: A History of the Factory and the Making of the Modern World.* New York: W. W. Norton, 2018.

Marcot, Roy. *The History of Remington Firearms: The History of One of the World's Most Famous Gun Makers.* Guilford, CT: Lyons Press, 2005.

8

Delaware

Delaware, one of the Mid-Atlantic states, took its name from colonial governor Baron De La Warr. It is the nation's second smallest state (after Rhode Island), and was first colonized in 1631. As one of the original thirteen colonies, in 1787, Delaware became the very first to ratify the Constitution of the United States, prompting Delaware's official nickname, "The First State."

Delaware also ranks first in another significant area. According to Russell Words (2014), "Thanks to the Delaware General Corporation Law, more than half of all the publicly traded corporations in the United States are incorporated in Delaware" (26). With its business-friendly laws, the state is home to more corporations than people.

In the 1760s, Delaware's boundaries were established by legendary surveyors Charles Mason and Jeremiah Dixon. Although Delaware was situated below the Mason-Dixon Line, and thus designated as a Southern territory or "slave state," it remained in the Union during the Civil War.

Located near large early American cities like New York, Philadelphia, and the newly established capital, Washington, D.C., Delaware was crisscrossed with turnpike roads and stagecoach lines. Even though the state was small, it often took a long time to travel through Delaware due to bad roads. Travelers usually had to stop overnight for food and lodging at one of the many inns that dotted the state.

In early America, small inns were the norm, patterned on those in medieval Europe. An inn could also stable and feed the travelers' horses, as well as serving as a kind of community center where people could gather in its tavern and hear the latest news from far-flung locations. In America, many inns were simply farmhouses that had extra rooms available for rent. The owner would answer the door for visitors and judge the people to see if they would be allowed to come in.

Inns attracted a cross-section of humanity, primarily male, traveling on journeys that were made out of necessity, not leisure. In a large room the guests could find food and wash it down with beverages like beer, ale, or cider. They might encounter farmers making their way to market, merchants going to the city, soldiers on their way to camp, or adventurers of all sorts, which sometimes made for a volatile mix.

The standard of hospitality varied widely from inn to inn. There were no rules or regulations and no frills. Several travelers usually had to share a room, or even share the same bed. Inns of the past bore little resemblance to modern hotels.

The standard risks along early American roadways included accidents, bandits, conflicts with Native Americans, disease, injury, and natural threats like blizzards or flash floods. Generally, friendly looking lights in the distance were a welcome sight.

On the other hand, spending the night in an isolated inn might pose yet another peril. A lone guest might be assaulted and robbed by fellow travelers, or even by the innkeepers themselves. There were tales of trap doors and bloody basements concealing murderous deeds. Some travelers simply disappeared. With travel itself being dangerous, plus limited communications that prevented knowing what happened or where, families of unlucky travelers might never welcome their loved ones back home.

One of the most famous—and mysterious—incidents involving an early American inn revolves around the death of explorer Meriwether Lewis of the Lewis and Clark expedition. When they returned in 1806, they were publicly acclaimed, but three years later, Lewis was dead at the age of thirty-five. Traveling along the hazardous Natchez Trace in 1809, Lewis was on his way to meet Thomas Jefferson when he stopped at a small log cabin/inn along the isolated route in today's Tennessee. The next morning, Lewis was found dead with gunshot wounds to his head and stomach. Some called it suicide. Others speculated that bandits roaming the notoriously dangerous Trace killed Lewis after robbing him of the large amount of money he was said to be carrying but which was not among his possessions when he was found. Some researchers have pointed the finger at the innkeepers, reconstructing cycles of the moon to prove that the innkeeper's wife could not have seen what she claimed on that moonless night. Ambrose (1997) states that a friend finally retraced the journey Lewis would have taken and informed Thomas Jefferson that he buried Lewis "as decently as I could" (476). Near today's Nashville, close to a replica of the log cabin inn where he stayed, a simple broken monument marks the end of the trail for Meriwether Lewis.

In Delaware, another inn has a story to tell. The land where the **Deer Park Inn** stands at Newark, Delaware, dates back to 1747, where a previous inn stood before burning down. In 1848, the property was purchased and the Deer Park Inn was established. With Delaware a slave state, the inn's front porch became a gathering place in the 1800s where slave traders trafficked in their human wares before adjourning to the tavern inside the inn to celebrate their salesmanship.

As if the unhappy spirits of trafficked humans were not enough, the Deer Park Inn comes with its own celebrity curse. According to the Newark Historical Society, writer Edgar Allan Poe, master of the macabre, arrived at the inn one rainy night, tripped, and fell into mud outside the building. Being none too cheerful at the best of times, the angry Poe reportedly exclaimed, "A curse on this place!" It is not known how effective he was at casting hexes, but Martinelli (2006) states that reportedly Poe wrote his gloomy masterpiece, "The Raven," at Deer Park Inn.

Since then, patrons of Delaware's Deer Park Inn have reported hearing footsteps on landings near blocked-off stairwells, and the front door swinging open and shut on its own as if to admit unseen guests. Martinelli says, "Perhaps it is Poe's ghost . . . seeking sanctuary in one of the taverns in which he felt most at home" (53). Or perhaps it may be the spirits of enslaved people, finally coming in from the front porch.

SOME OTHER REPORTEDLY HAUNTED PLACES IN DELAWARE

The **Addy Sea** in Bethany is today a Victorian-style bed and breakfast with stunning sea views. While most guests appreciate its homey atmosphere, others are more in tune with an atmosphere that smacks of the otherworldly. Dating back to 1901, John Addy, one of Bethany's original settlers who moved to Pittsburgh, Pennsylvania, built the home as a summer retreat for his family. The Addy Sea was the first in the area to have such amenities as gaslight and indoor plumbing, thanks to the forward-thinking Mr. Addy,

The Deer Park Inn in Newark, Delaware, comes with its own celebrity curse. Horror writer Edgar Allan Poe, seen here, reportedly became angry outside the inn, exclaiming, "A curse on this place!" Some sources claim Poe wrote his gloomy masterpiece, "The Raven," at Deer Park Inn where visitors have reported hearing disembodied footsteps. (Library of Congress)

who also had helpful plumbing skills. However, with the Great Depression in the 1930s, the next generation opened the house for paying guests. Apparently, today there are also some nonpaying ones, who occupy three of the thirteen rooms. Room 1 is the location of the Addy Sea's famous haunted bathroom with the original copper tub that John Addy brought with him from Pittsburgh. Bathers seeking a comforting, hot bath have been startled when the tub starts inexplicably shaking violently—with them in it. Room 6 graciously provides what has been called has hauntingly beautiful organ music which is heard by passers-by, even though there is no organ in the room. Room 11 is said to be haunted by the ghost of a handyman at the Addy Sea. He apparently liked the place so much that after being killed elsewhere in a construction accident, his spirit came back to his old room at the Addy Sea where his apparition has been seen sitting on the bed or standing by it. Not to be slighted, the hallways attract a ghost who reportedly runs through the halls in the evening. It may be the spirit of one of the Addy sons who died after falling from the roof of the home, where his restless rooftop footsteps can be heard by dark of night, making his presence known.

The **Christiana Fire Company Station 12** in Christiana is said to be home to not just one but two ghosts, eternally at odds with each other. One is a menacing, evil spirit that is said to appear in the doorway of the engineer's room as a dark, shadowy figure. This spirit does not get much further than that point because the other resident spirit is a kind, benevolent one who is rarely seen but is felt when the evil spirit appears, stopping the evil from going any further into the hallway, acting as a kind of protector for the station. Witnesses say it is an ongoing battle between good and evil, and that when it happens, anyone present can definitely feel it.

With the state aligning itself alongside the Union during the Civil War, **Fort Delaware** at Delaware City was used as a prison for Confederate soldiers. Today, it is inactive as a defensive facility, for which it was originally built, but is said to be one of the most actively haunted locations in Delaware. Much like Alcatraz in California, Fort Delaware is situated on an island, with a ferry being the only way to get there and a drawbridge over a moat the only way to get in or out. Its construction began in 1848, although it was not declared complete until 1868. Unfortunately, it was put to use before that time. Instead of being a fortress to keep enemies out, it was used to keep people in. By the end of the Civil War, about thirty-three thousand prisoners were jammed into the facility, which was built for a small garrison of about five hundred troops. Conditions were brutal. Prisoners had very little food or water and no beds, sleeping on the floor of rat-infested dungeons. Thousands died as disease and death ran rampant. Many of these tormented, restless spirits are said to inhabit the fort to this day. In fact, it is said that today it is unusual if visitors do *not* hear disembodied voices, see shadowy figures, experience cold spots, or hear the sound of chains rattling. Cameras have captured both orbs and full body apparitions. An investigator who tried spending the night at Fort Delaware was alone in a bedroom when an oil lamp inexplicably slid across the window sill, crashing to the floor next to him and spraying him with broken glass. One of the spirits who remains at Fort Delaware may be a young drummer boy who planned an escape by hiding in a coffin. The plan did not work, with the boy ending up being buried alive. Today, it is said that the drummer boy haunts the grounds, still dutifully playing his drum.

Delaware can boast its own spooky tale of a **Headless Horseman**, one that can be found in the town of Newark, site of the previously mentioned and allegedly haunted Deer Park Inn. The story began with a historic "first" for Delaware, soon to be known as "The First State" for being quick to ratify the U.S. Constitution. On September 3, 1777, the Battle of Cooch's Bridge at Newark was the only battle of the American Revolution to be fought on Delaware soil. However, it carried an important distinction: it marked the first time that the new American flag, today known as the Stars and Stripes, was flown in battle. Delaware militiamen were holding the line against British forces in order to give General Washington and his troops time to escape. One legend states that during the skirmish between the Americans and the Redcoats, a British soldier got his head shot off. On foggy moonless nights, some people claim to see the Headless British Soldier stalking along the roads in the area. However, giving equal time to the Americans, there is also the legend of young Charlie Miller, a colonial volunteer during the Battle of Cooch's Bridge, who was decapitated by a British cannonball. It is not unlikely that with cannonballs flying, two soldiers would have lost their heads in the heat of battle and who continue to search for a place to hang their hats. Newark, Delaware, can also claim an additional haunted tale, one that has a Poe-like quality. In fact, it was on the site of the current Deer Park Inn, the hostelry cursed by Edgar Allan Poe, where Charles Mason and Jeremiah Dixon, of the Mason-Dixon Line fame, established a headquarters. Mason was also an inventor and a mathematician who sought a prize for the first person to develop a chronometer that would accurately measure longitude at sea. Legend has it that a small boy wandered into Mason's tent, and as small boys have been known to do, put Mason's miniscule invention in his mouth and swallowed it. But the small metal device continued to tick inside the youngster's body. Mason, incensed, cursed the boy, stating: "May my creation function until the end of time, proof that I would have won the celebrated prize." The boy, named Fithian Minuet, grew up to a ripe old age and ultimately was buried beneath a flat stone marker. There it is said that the sound of a ticking clock emanating from the grave can be heard.

Wilmington's **Rockwood Mansion** is a magnificent 165-year-old home that boasts both history and hauntings. Joseph Shipley, born in 1795, made his fortune as a merchant banker in England. Returning to his American homeland, he hired a British architect to build a stately home in the best English manner. Rockwood Mansion was completed in 1854 in the Rural Gothic Revival style with grounds on which Shipley spared no expense. He ordered more than one thousand two hundred trees and shrubs, some of which remain on the property to this day. Apparently, so do the spirits of some of the people who lived there. Joseph Shipley died in 1867, passing the estate to his sisters. As time passed, the property found its way into the hands of family descendants, including a grandniece, Mary. Residing at Rockwood until she died at age hundred, Mary's own niece donated the property to the county, who created a museum and estate tour. Despite that altruism, it may be that the previous owners loved the residence so much they did not want to leave. Over the years, people have claimed to have experienced apparitions, unexplained balls of light, cold spots, and footsteps in empty rooms along with the sounds of children playing throughout the night. One museum official reported seeing visions of the former owner sitting in the Tea Room wearing a red smoking jacket, in the style of a proper English country gentleman. When the official glanced away and looked back, the specter was gone. The room that belonged to Mary, who lived to be hundred, is considered the most haunted in the mansion. In her later years, Mary became blind and crippled; today, she likes her privacy and does not appreciate people in her room. Visitors have felt ill or passed out there, and investigators have said that the energy in Mary's room is so strong that they are reluctant to enter. Photographs have allegedly captured a strange mist appearing to be a human shape in a hunched, crippled position. The scent of lilac has also been reported with no reason for being there, very tasteful in an Old English kind of way.

FURTHER READING

Ambrose, Stephen. *Undaunted Courage: Meriwether Lewis, Thomas Jefferson, and the Opening of the American West.* New York: Simon & Schuster, 1997.

Martinelli, Patricia. *Haunted Delaware: Ghosts and Strange Phenomena of the First State.* Mechanicsburg, PA: Stackpole Books, 2006.

Words, Russell C. *So, You're Moving to Delaware!: A Handbook to Being a Delawarean.* Flat Rock, NC: Cruden Bay Books, 2014.

9

District of Columbia

According to Tom Lewis (2015), in 1791, the commissioners tasked with creating a capital city for the brand-new United States of America opted to call it "City of Washington, in the Federal District of Columbia" (16). Lewis hints that settling on the bulky name might have been the easy part: "Creating a city, even a small one, was almost unheard of in the eighteenth century" (33).

Today, the nation's capital is generally called Washington, D.C., or the District of Columbia. In an effort to avoid the appearance of favoritism, the founding fathers decided to locate the new seat of federal government about halfway between the Northern states and the South, replacing the country's previous capital cities like New York and Philadelphia. It was named for America's first president, George Washington, as well as referencing Christopher Columbus. The states of Maryland and Virginia each donated land to form the new federal district located along the Potomac River.

Pierre L'Enfant was an officer during the American Revolution who served with George Washington at Valley Forge. L'Enfant was appointed the planner and architect for the new capital city, although his plans were never fully adopted. L'Enfant spent much of the rest of his life trying to get paid by Congress for his work, ultimately dying in poverty in 1825.

The city of Washington began life as a muddy backwater, which many foreign diplomats considered deserving of hardship pay for staffing the embassies. Today, the city hosts almost two hundred foreign embassies as well as the headquarters for many national and international organizations. Proximity to Congress makes it attractive to those working as lobbyists, individuals seeking to influence legislation affecting their particular organization or cause.

Along with the federal government, the District of Columbia is also home to many majestic national monuments and captivating museums. The city attracts an estimated twenty million tourists each year, making it one of the most visited cities in the world. Part of the allure is the city's cultural life. Its theaters include such institutions as the John F. Kennedy Center for the Performing Arts, Arena Stage,

First Ladies

The role of America's First Lady has never been clearly defined. While some have not been active, some very much *were* and a few have even continued being active well into the afterlife. As the first to live in the White House, Abigail Adams hung the family laundry up to dry in the drafty, unfinished East Room. Soon after her death in 1818, the ghost of the formidable Abigail has been seen in the East Room, arms extended as if she were still carrying laundry, accompanied by an unexplained scent of soap. The ghost of Frances Cleveland, who was married to President Grover Cleveland in the Blue Room of the White House in 1886, is said to have appeared there after her death in 1947. No First Lady may have enjoyed her time in the White House as much as Dolley Madison. After ex-President James Madison died in 1836, Dolley moved to the Cutts-Madison House on Lafayette Square across the street where she lived until her death in 1849. She apparently still couldn't bear to move too far from the White House. Soon after her death and into the present day, witnesses have claimed to see Dolley's smiling ghost in a rocking chair on the front porch of the Cutts-Madison House. In the 1960s, the house was almost destroyed to erect office buildings. Then-First Lady Jacqueline Kennedy lobbied to stop the demolition, saving her predecessor's home—something more for Dolley's ghost to smile about.

and Shakespeare Theatre Company. There are also niche-oriented theater groups like the GALA Hispanic Theatre, National Center for the Latino Performing Arts, and the U Street Corridor, known as "Washington's Black Broadway," home to institutions like the Howard Theatre and the Lincoln Theatre.

However, any mention of the words "Lincoln" and "theater" usually brings one particular playhouse to mind. The historic **Ford's Theatre**, site of the assassination of President Abraham Lincoln, continues to operate as a functioning performance space as well as a museum. But there may be visitors at Ford's who did not pay for an admission ticket.

According to Ogden (2009), "[f]or some reason, it seems that more spirits have taken up residence in playhouses than just about any other type of venue" (x). Some say it may be due to the level of drama and superstition associated with stagecraft, but it might also pertain to a song in the modern play *A Chorus Line*: "What I Did for Love." Theater people simply love the theater and love being *in* theaters. Some are reluctant to leave even after their earthly curtain is rung down. And theaters can be welcoming places to spend life after death. After all, the bare onstage light bulb that is always left on when the darkened theater is unoccupied is universally called a "ghost light."

Although the genre of theater goes back to the ancient Greeks and Romans, it arrived in America relatively recently. A theater was built in colonial Williamsburg, Virginia, in 1716, and the original Dock Street Theatre opened in Charleston, South Carolina, in 1736. Many cite the birth of professional theater in America to 1752 when one Lewis Hallam arrived in Williamsburg with his professional theatrical troupe. They brought classics by Shakespeare but encountered religious opposition so they soon decamped to New York.

District of Columbia

Ford's Theatre in Washington, D.C., was the site of the 1865 assassination of President Abraham Lincoln as seen in this artist's rendering. Today, the ghost of Lincoln's assassin, John Wilkes Booth, is said to stalk the playhouse. There are claims that Booth's footsteps have been heard running up the staircase toward the presidential box, as well as the sound of a gunshot and a disembodied voice screaming, "Murder!" (Ridpath, John Clark, *Ridpath's History of the World,* 1901)

Around the time of the American Revolution, onstage political satire could be found in works by Mercy Otis Warren and Robert Munford. After independence and through the Civil War era, a unique theatrical character gained widespread popularity, the comically rough-edged "Yankee" whose quick wit usually got the best of his "betters."

In fact, in 1865, it was a comedic Yankee character whose antics were guaranteed to get a huge laugh that ironically set the stage for tragedy. The farce, *Our American Cousin*, was being performed at Ford's Theatre in Washington at the close of the Civil War, when everyone was ready for some much-needed humor. The person who needed light comedy most of all was President Abraham Lincoln who many said carried the weight of the war on his shoulders.

On April 14, 1865, Lincoln was having a thoroughly good time watching the play from a private box at the theater. Meanwhile, a popular actor who was not in the show but who had often performed at Ford's in the past was making his way toward the box. That actor, a Confederate sympathizer named John Wilkes Booth, was familiar with *Our American Cousin*. He knew that a big laugh would come when the Yankee character uttered the line, "Well, I guess I know enough to turn you inside out, old gal—you sockdologizing old man-trap!" With the audience's raucous laughter masking the sound of his gunshot, Booth chose that moment to

Smithsonian Castle

Fondly nicknamed "The Nation's Attic" housing all manner of relics and administered from a building called The Castle that looks like something out of a brooding Victorian novel, the Smithsonian Institution is a prime suspect to be solidly haunted. Although most officials deny tales from the dark side, a few ghost stories prevail. Along with allegations of hauntings by the institution's benefactor, Englishman James Smithson, there are reports of visits by the ghosts of an administrator and his son, both of whom died in the family quarters of The Castle in the late 1800s. Another ethereal presence is rumored to be a paleontologist with the unlikely name of Fielding B. Meek, who lived with his cat in the Smithsonian's Castle where he died of tuberculosis in 1876. Some staffers have claimed to encounter former administrators, still on the job although long dead. During dark nights at the museum, staffers have reported books moving off the shelves in the library, doors opening and closing by themselves, and lights going on and off when the building was closed and presumed to be unoccupied. This is nothing new. Stories in Washington newspapers were appearing as early as 1900, reporting on museum guards claiming to hear strange footsteps in empty corridors along with unseen voices and ghostly screams in the night. However, it may be that with the Smithsonian one of the most popular destinations in the world, the only souls haunting The Castle are lost, hungry tourists.

---

fatally shoot Lincoln in the back of the head. Lincoln, thus, became the first American president to be assassinated.

It might seem that the spirit of someone like Lincoln who was taken from life so abruptly would not rest in peace. Ogden (2016) states that "Abraham Lincoln's spectre has appeared with some frequency at the White House" (137), but curiously, not at Ford's Theater.

However, someone else's does. Ogden (2009) says, "Lincoln may not return to the scene of his assassination—would you?—but the ghost of John Wilkes Booth does stalk the stage at Ford's Theatre in Washington, D.C. His presence has been felt and heard throughout the playhouse, and his aura may have even turned up in an old Matthew Brady photograph" (157).

Booth's footsteps are said to have been heard running up the back staircase toward the presidential box, as well as the sound of a gunshot followed by someone screaming, "Murder!" A specter of Mrs. Lincoln is said to lean out of the box with a hysterical cry, pointing in the direction of Booth's escape route out of the theater, shouting "He has killed the president!" Lights at Ford's have been reported to turn on and off, apparitions appear at center stage, icy sensations have been felt in various spots, and there have been numerous reports of disembodied laughter and strange voices on various occasions.

Another notable District of Columbia ghost is said to appear not at Ford's Theatre but at another frequent site of theatricality, the U.S. Capitol. Witnesses have claimed to see the spirit of architect Pierre L'Enfant walking through the Capitol with his head down, murmuring to himself. L'Enfant's specter allegedly carries his plans for the capital city tucked under his arm, presumably accompanied by yet another unpaid bill to Congress for the services he rendered.

SOME OTHER REPORTEDLY HAUNTED PLACES IN THE DISTRICT OF COLUMBIA

The **Capitol Building** is reputedly haunted by a number of spirits, from governmental officials to workers who died during its construction to a "demon black cat" that is said to appear just before national tragedies and/or changes in Presidential administrations. The spectral feline was first seen soon after the White House was built and has allegedly been seen by night watchmen and members of the Capitol Police. It is said to have appeared before the assassination of President Abraham Lincoln, the 1929 stock market crash, and the assassination of President John F. Kennedy. Meanwhile, a worker who fell to his death during the construction of the rotunda can occasionally be seen as a ghostly spirit floating beneath the dome carrying a tray of woodworking tools. A stonemason who died after being crushed beneath a wall that collapsed is sometimes seen in the Old Senate chambers or passing through a wall in the basement beneath the Senate. A number of former congressmen have been spied even after their lives were term-limited. One, former U.S. president and then-representative John Quincy Adams suffered a stroke in 1848 at his desk in the House chamber where some have heard his ghostly whisper. Today, it may be that fewer recent ex-congressmen haunt the Capitol because they can find a home as lobbyists.

In a less majestic part of its history, the District of Columbia is said to have been home to the largest slave market in North America. Along with large slave markets, there were numerous smaller "slave pens" in nearly every neighborhood. One, the **Yellow House** slave pen, is said by some to be the approximate location of today's Federal Aviation Administration headquarters. The modest two-story Yellow House concealed a windowless basement in which slaves were chained to walls, while an outside yard within a high brick wall provided space for training and selling enslaved people. At the Yellow House, as well as other places where Washington's slave pens used to operate, witnesses say that on dark nights, they have heard screams and the clinking of chains. Unexplained sounds have also been heard in the basement at the **Halcyon House,** where a tunnel was allegedly dug as a secret stop on the Underground Railroad. Along with footsteps being heard creaking in the unoccupied attic, moans and sobs can be heard in the basement, allegedly the spirits of numerous runaway slaves who died there before their escape to freedom. Also unexplained is a bedroom where guests have reported being levitated in the middle of the night.

The **Hay-Adams Hotel** may host a nonpaying guest, the spirit of socialite and pioneering photographer Marian Hooper Adams who has been cited as the inspiration for the nineteenth-century novels *Daisy Miller* and *The Portrait of a Lady*. Nicknamed "Clover," Marian was exceptionally close to her beloved father. After he died in 1885, she sank into a deep depression. Her husband, writer Henry Adams, was having a luxurious new home constructed next to their friend, statesman John Hay. Just before they were to move in, a few months after her father's death, the distraught Marian committed suicide. When the Hay and Adams homes were later demolished, the Hay-Adams Hotel was built on the site. Some say Marian's spirit has moved into the hotel, with staff reporting being hugged by an invisible presence, as well as hearing the disembodied sound of a woman sobbing. Locked doors have been said to open and close, radios turn themselves on and off, and a woman's voice has been heard to whisper, "What do you want?" The incidents usually occur during early December; Marian died on December 6. After her suicide, Henry Adams destroyed most of her much-admired photographs as well as her letters. Rather than being erased from history, perhaps at the Hay-Adams, "Clover" lives on.

The **Octagon House** was built in 1801 for the prominent Tayloe family. There is evidence that its walled backyard may have served as a slave market, as well as housing the Tayloe family's slaves. After the White House was burned in the War of 1812, President James and Dolley Madison lived at Octagon House for over a year. It was also where Madison signed the Treaty of Ghent, ending that war. Today, as a museum, staffers and members of the public have reported other residents, those from the spirit world. Two daughters of the original Tayloe family are said to haunt Octagon House. One quarreled with her father on the second floor landing about her relationship with a British officer. The daughter turned in anger, falling from the landing to her death. Her specter has been reported, crumpled at the bottom of the stairs. A few years later, another daughter eloped with a young man, infuriating her father. When she returned home to reconcile with Tayloe, they argued on the third floor landing. This daughter, too, fell to her death. Her shade is alleged to haunt the landing and the nearby staircase. In addition, one of the household's enslaved girls was allegedly killed by a British soldier during the War of 1812 by being thrown from the third floor landing, where witnesses today report hearing her scream. Visitors to the Octagon House might consider avoiding the spiritually crowded staircase.

While small in size, the **Old Stone House** is home to a large number of spirits. Built in 1765, over the centuries it has seen a number of residents who have apparently returned. The sightings are remarkably detailed, including a woman in a brown dress standing near the fireplace, women cooking in the kitchen, a woman in a rocking chair on the third floor, and a heavy-set woman standing on the staircase. Male spirits include a man wearing colonial-style knee breeches and long stockings standing in the master bedroom, another man dressed in colonial-era clothing on the second floor, and a man with long blond hair who is wearing a blue jacket. The laughter of invisible children is also in evidence, along with the translucent images of a young girl with curly hair running up and down the staircase, as well as a small boy scampering down the third floor hallway. The Old Stone House may also contain one of Washington's only malevolent spirits, not counting Capitol Hill. Nicknamed "George," he has allegedly choked and pushed visitors, with his presence indicated by an extremely cold spot, leaving witnesses with an understandably intense feeling of dread.

The **Walsh Mansion** today houses the Indonesian Embassy as well as several distinctly non-Indonesian nationals. In 1869, the penniless Thomas J. Walsh emigrated from Ireland and ultimately struck gold, literally and figuratively, becoming a multimillionaire in the course of his new life in America. Moving to Washington, D.C., the sixty-room Walsh Mansion was constructed in 1903 as the most expensive residence in the city at the time. In 1908, his daughter Evalyn

Walsh married Edward "Ned" McLean, whose family owned the *Washington Post*. Ned and Evalyn moved into the Walsh Mansion after her father's death in 1910. That same year, Ned McLean bought the allegedly cursed Hope Diamond for his wife. To cover significant debts after they died, the Walsh Mansion was sold in 1952 to the Government of Indonesia, but embassy staffers have reported Evalyn Walsh McLean may never have vacated the home, with her spirit seen gliding down the mansion's grand central staircase. In addition, there have also been reports of a naked lady's spectral form in the mansion, but since she carries no identification, no one knows exactly who she is.

Although unfinished at the time, the **White House** welcomed its first occupants, President John and Abigail Adams, in 1800. Since that time, it has also provided a welcoming space for some former residents, notably the one who lived there from 1861 to 1865, Abraham Lincoln. The first person who is said to report seeing Lincoln's spirit was First Lady Grace Coolidge, who lived in the White House with her husband "Silent Cal" in the 1920s. She said she saw the ghost of Lincoln standing at a window in the Yellow Oval Room, staring out at the Potomac. Luminaries like Winston Churchill and Theodore Roosevelt claimed to see the specter of Lincoln in the White House, but probably the most famous incident was in 1942 when visiting Queen Wilhelmina of the Netherlands heard footsteps outside her White House bedroom. Going to the door, she encountered Lincoln in a frock coat and top hat standing right in front of her. Her Majesty promptly fainted. Although today's Lincoln Bedroom was actually used as a meeting room during his administration, some witnesses have claimed to see the shade of Abraham Lincoln lying down on the bed or sitting at the edge, putting his boots on. His son Willie, who was especially close to his father, may have returned after dying in 1862. Willie's ghost was first reportedly seen in the White House during the 1870s by staff members of the Grant administration. In the 1960s, President Lyndon Johnson's daughter Lynda claimed she saw Willie's ghost and talked to him, First Family to First Family. Others have claimed to encounter spirits of dead presidents like William Henry Harrison, Andrew Jackson, Thomas Jefferson, and John Tyler. As if the Secret Service didn't have enough to worry about.

FURTHER READING

Lewis, Tom. *Washington: A History of Our National City.* New York: Basic Books, 2015.

Ogden, Tom. *Haunted Theaters: Playhouse Phantoms, Opera House Horrors, and Backstage Banshees.* Guilford, CT: Globe Pequot Press, 2009.

Ogden, Tom. *Haunted Washington, DC: Federal Phantoms, Government Ghosts, and Beltway Banshees.* Guilford, CT: Globe Pequot Press, 2016.

10

Florida

Florida, the Spanish term for a place of flowers, was named by conquistador Juan Ponce de León who spotted the peninsula in 1513. According to legend, the Spaniard was seeking the rumored fountain of youth, but according to Gannon (2018), "Probably more important to Juan Ponce were the gold and the glory of conquest" (19).

Florida became the first region of the continental United States to be explored and settled by Europeans, a century before the English pilgrims aboard the *Mayflower* landed at Massachusetts's Plymouth Rock in 1620.

The Florida city of St. Augustine was founded in 1565, becoming what is generally known as the oldest continuously occupied European settlement in the United States. As England's presence in mainland America grew throughout the 1600s, 1700s, and 1800s, the Spanish foothold in its southernmost region became what the English considered something of a nuisance.

Florida was a haven for escaped slaves and a base for Native American attacks against the United States. As Anglo-Americans began moving into northern Florida, such immigration was discouraged by Spanish authorities, but they were unable to control the border between Florida and the United States. Finally, after lengthy negotiations, U.S. Secretary of State John Quincy Adams achieved a diplomatic victory for America in 1819 with the purchase of Florida from Spain at a cost of about $5 million.

After that, Anglo settlements in Florida increased, and removing Native Americans from the territory became a priority for the United States. By the mid-1800s, tribes like the Seminoles had either been forcibly moved west of the Mississippi River or eradicated.

In 1845, Florida was admitted as the twenty-seventh state of the Union. Being declared a slave state, it was no longer a sanctuary for enslaved runaways.

Until the advent of air conditioning in the twentieth century, permanent settlement of Florida grew relatively slowly. However, Florida did attract wealthy vacationers from the North who were escaping cold winters, especially after the development of railroads. Nicknamed "The Sunshine State," tourism remains a foundation of Florida's economy.

Since Florida is a peninsula, there is plenty of room for visitors on all those sunny beaches. The state rests between the Atlantic Ocean on the east and the Gulf of Mexico on the west. To its south, the Florida Straits flow between the Gulf and the Atlantic.

Florida is the only state that borders both the Atlantic Ocean and the Gulf of Mexico. With all that water, the state is in the middle of some of the world's busiest shipping lanes. Before the invention of navigational aids like radar and GPS, Florida was a critical factor in helping to save sailors and cargo by providing the same kind of nautical lifesaver that guided ancient Egyptian ships into the harbor at Alexandria: lighthouses.

At its most basic, a lighthouse is a structure designed to produce light that serves as a navigational aid for sea-going vessels or those on inland waterways. In addition to denoting safe entry into ports and harbors, lighthouses mark dangerous coastlines, hazardous shoals, reefs, rocks, and other hazards that could result in tragedy.

In ancient times, fires were built on hilltops to guide mariners. Raising fire on a platform made it even more visible at sea. Finally, constructing a high tower to emit light became a commonly seen structure around the busy Mediterranean from Egypt to Spain.

According to Dolin (2016), in 1716, "[The] Boston Lighthouse was lit, becoming America's first lighthouse" (9). Lighthouses of the colonial era utilized an open flame, and were built all along the Atlantic Coast where navigation could be treacherous. Since trees were readily available in the American colonies, many early lighthouses with their open flame were made of wood—until the design flaw became obvious.

To diminish the ever-present threat of fire, masonry towers were built. Many stood the test of time, including today's oldest standing masonry tower, the Sandy Hook Lighthouse in New Jersey, built in 1764.

As a source of illumination, coal started to be used after wood pyres were found to be undesirable. But with some lighthouses consuming up to four hundred tons of coal a year, it was an expensive proposition. Banks of candles or oil lamps backed by concave mirrors were used until the 1782 invention of the Argand lamp that burned whale oil. Then came gas, and finally, electricity.

By definition, lighthouses emit powerful light, often rotating in several directions. They must be built near the coastline, often on islands or in lonely, desolate places away from more populated areas. Their locations are isolated and storm-prone, requiring constant vigilance to keep the light visible. Often lighthouse-keepers found themselves in rough waters, especially in a storm, trying to save hapless sailors who miscalculated the shoreline. The weight of responsibility for seafaring lives often fell heavily on the shoulders of lighthouse-keepers. Sometimes men could ease the loneliness by having families living with them, but the wives and children often suffered from the same isolation that gives lighthouses an eerie atmosphere.

Florida's **St. Augustine Lighthouse** was originally built in 1824 and still stands at the north end of St. Augustine's Anastasia Island. In the mid-1800s, lighthouses came under government control; St. Augustine Lighthouse was privately owned

Sometimes lighthouse-keepers and their families suffered from the eerie isolation. Florida's St. Augustine Lighthouse, dating to 1824, is said to be inhabited by the ghost of a former lighthouse-keeper who never left. There have been reports of a spirit in old-fashioned clothing, along with the smell of cigar smoke, and the sound of ghostly footsteps on otherwise-empty stairs. (Library of Congress)

until the government came calling. The owner was offered what he considered to be far less than its value, followed by the government's threat of taking it from him by force. He was outraged and vowed never to leave. That is exactly what happened according to some visitors who claim the specter of the disgruntled lighthouse-keeper in old-fashioned clothing has been sighted around the property.

Apparently, later lighthouse-keepers followed his example. There have been reports of at least two separate keepers whose spirits have appeared. One is usually accompanied by the smell of cigar smoke, which he was known to favor, and the ghostly footsteps of another can be heard on the otherwise-empty stairs. Other spirits are said to be a lighthouse-keeper's two young daughters who drowned when they were swept into the ocean while playing. According to Randall (2013), "Ever since those girls passed away, people have seen them . . . in the lighthouse and running around the grounds. They've heard them whispering and singing" (100). Apparently, all that Florida sunshine cannot completely banish dark, unexplained forces.

SOME OTHER REPORTEDLY HAUNTED PLACES IN FLORIDA

At one time, the **Apollo 1 Launch Complex 34** at Cape Canaveral was the crown jewel of America's space program. In a flash, it turned into a burned-out husk, with the official order "Abandon in Place" imprinted on it. Today, it is allegedly haunted by the souls of the men who died there. On January 27, 1967, astronauts Gus Grissom, Roger Chaffee, and Ed White were three weeks away from their historic journey to the Moon and back. In a routine prelaunch test, they were enclosed in the oxygen-filled space capsule. Suddenly, a flash fire broke out, trapping the doomed men inside. An investigation of their deaths led to design changes for greater safety, and the complex was permanently closed in 1968 by the National Aeronautics and Space Administration (NASA). What was one of the largest and most prominent of NASA's launch pads is today only an abandoned concrete platform and rusted steel hulk on a barren, windswept landscape. Visitors have occasionally been allowed special access to the deserted site where many report an overwhelming sense of dread, sadness, or fear when approaching it. Some have claimed to hear disembodied screams or see floating apparitions, leading to speculation that the gruesome landmark is haunted. With its bleak, foreboding form looking like something supernatural, it is a reminder that even boasting the height of technology for its time, our modern world can produce phenomena as spine-chilling as an ancient cemetery.

In St. Augustine, which lays claim to being the oldest city in the United States, there is a structure which, according to the National Park Service, is the oldest seventeenth-century masonry fortress in the country. The **Castillo de San Marcos** on Matanzas Bay was constructed by the Spanish beginning in 1672. Through the five centuries of its existence, Florida, and by extension the Castillo or "castle," has been under Spanish, British, and American control. Along with being utilized as a defensive outpost by the Spanish and British, the Castillo was used by the Americans to imprison Native Americans, including the Seminole war chief Osceola. With so much pain, despair, violence, and death within its thick walls, it is no surprise that the Castillo is said to harbor some ghostly spirits who did not rest in peace. Visitors have reported seeing apparitions of soldiers patrolling the battlements of the Castillo and the spirits of Native Americans jumping from the walls of the fortress. There have also been strange orbs of light reported inside the darkened Castillo. But one ghost story is a tale of love, at least until its finale. Apparently, in the late 1800s, the colonel who was the fort's commanding officer suspected his wife of being romantically involved with an army captain. Suddenly, the pair of lovers inexplicably vanished, never to be seen again until witnesses described seeing the apparition of a forlorn-looking woman dressed in white who was thought to be the colonel's dead wife. Whether she is seeking her husband or her unfortunate lover within its walls is unknown.

Built in 1926, Miami's **Coral Gables Biltmore Hotel** is a striking Mediterranean-style luxury hotel featuring fountains, terraces, and Moorish-looking columns in its lobby. Because of its gracious ambience, the hotel has long been a favorite of celebrities and dignitaries along with the general public. It might also be a favorite haunt of long-dead guests who checked back in to spend eternity in such posh accommodations. One of those spirits is said to be Thomas "Fatty" Walsh, a New York mobster who was killed at the hotel during a gambling dispute in 1929. Walsh was an associate of Dutch Schultz (born Arthur Flegenheimer) and Charles "Lucky" Luciano (born Salvatore Lucania), as well as being a bodyguard for gangster Arnold Rothstein (apparently born Arnold Rothstein). Walsh was involved in the narcotics racket and was questioned regarding Rothstein's 1928 gangland slaying, although Walsh was later released. It is not known if Walsh appreciated his "Fatty" nickname, but it was enshrined after his death in breathless headlines like "Rothstein bodyguard killed at Coral Gables—Fatty Walsh shot dead in Hotel Room—Card party interrupted by bullets at Miami Biltmore." Most card players hate to have their game interrupted, especially by bullets, so apparently Walsh returned to the scene. Despite his girth and chosen career, Walsh was said to be a gentleman, a tradition that continued after death. He is said to open doors for the waitresses as they carry trays in and out of the restaurant. It has been claimed that his ghost has also been known to write messages on mirrors, as well as haunting the hotel elevator, opening and closing its doors and depositing guests on the wrong floor, usually the thirteenth—the floor on which he was killed.

The **Cuban Club** in Ybor City was built in 1917 as a gathering spot for the growing number of Cubans who migrated to the Sunshine State. The board of directors wanted something elegant for the club's members. The building, with a neoclassical design, featured a ballroom, bowling alley, cantina, gymnasium, library, swimming pool, and theater. Although the club steadily lost members through the late twentieth century resulting in the building's decline, the Cuban Club Foundation was formed in 1992 to save and restore the structure. Some of its former habitués apparently liked what they saw because they came back even after death. Among the reported deaths in the building are an actor who committed suicide onstage, as well as a member of the board who was found in the boardroom after an argument with another member, dead from a gunshot to the face. Both of those spirits are said to haunt the building, but the apparitions are not limited to males. There have also been reports of a woman dressed in white wearing red high heels who climbs up and down the stairs and can sometimes be heard wailing. A piano plays by itself and orbs of light are also common in the club. One of the most energetic of the ghosts is a young boy believed to have drowned in the Cuban Club's pool when he was about eight years old. His psychic energy has apparently remained, as guests report hearing the voice of a small boy, seeing balls move that have been set on the floor, doors being pushed open, and strange shapes appearing before their eyes, which they attribute to the mischievous boy.

The Mediterranean/Moorish-style **Don CeSar Hotel** in St. Pete Beach dates back to 1928 during Florida's heyday when it attracted the top celebrities of the Roaring Twenties. According to the hotel, it is said to be haunted by its original owner, Thomas Rowe, who was forbidden to marry his great love, a Spanish opera star named Lucinda who sang the leading role in the opera *Maritana*. Before her family's intervention, the pair met secretly by a secluded fountain, affectionately calling each other Maritana and Don Cesar, the opera's romantic leads. In what was said to be in remembrance of her, he chose the name Don CeSar for his hotel. Years later, Rowe received notice of her death accompanied by a note addressed to "My beloved Don Cesar." From her deathbed she left him her pledge of eternal love, writing, "Time is infinite. I wait for you by our fountain." After Rowe's death, it was reported that apparitions of the couple were seen by the hotel's courtyard fountain, said to be an exact replica of the one where the young Thomas and Lucinda had rendezvoused. The female spirit was reportedly wearing a Spanish peasant dress, Maritana's costume in the opera. In addition, the apparition of a man wearing a white summer suit and a Panama hat has been spotted strolling the grounds, possibly Rowe still keeping an eye on his beloved hotel. There have also been tales of doors opening, disembodied knocks, and showers turning on by themselves. In perhaps the strangest manifestation, a kitchen staffer once reported that he left a sink full of dirty dishes when he went for a break, but returned to find them clean and stacked in the middle of the floor. While it might have been Rowe's spirit keeping his hotel tidy, it is unknown why the dishes ended up on the floor, which seems an unlikely spot to deposit them, even in the spirit world.

Located at the tip of the Florida Keys, the **Key West Cemetery** is almost two hundred years old and is the final resting place for more than one hundred thousand people who are buried there. More precisely, it may not be the final resting place for *everyone* buried there, with sightings of various spirits haunting the graveyard. Some gravesites date back to 1829, having been moved there after a hurricane dislodged them at an older cemetery on another part of the island. Perhaps their occupants did not appreciate being disturbed during what was supposed to have been their eternal rest. One of the more commonly reported stories at Key West Cemetery involves a woman who is said to appear both day and night. She becomes angry if visitors sit on headstones, walk across graves, or in any other way fail to show respect for the departed. Her manifestation reportedly expresses her anger by making threatening gestures against the offenders, only to vanish before their eyes. Along with the sound of disembodied voices, other apparitions have been spotted at the cemetery. It has also been reported that some photographers at the historic graveyard later discover odd, unexplained shadows in their otherwise sunny snapshots.

The **Vinoy Renaissance Hotel** in St. Petersburg was built during the Roaring Twenties when Florida was, literally and figuratively, the nation's hotspot for celebrity sightings. With baseball teams holding their practice seasons during Florida's warm winter months, many visitors to popular hotels like the Vinoy could spy players like baseball legend Babe Ruth. Built in 1925, the Vinoy is also said to attract its share of ghosts who apparently enjoyed their stay, spicing up the afterlife by playing tricks. Guests and staffers have reported lights flickering on and off, toilets flushing on their own, phantom footsteps in empty corridors, and the semitransparent image of a man. One of the stranger manifestations reported by some guests is a feeling that they are being held down on the bed as they sleep.

FURTHER READING

Dolin, Eric Jay. *Brilliant Beacons: A History of the American Lighthouse.* New York: Liveright, 2016.
Gannon, Michael. *The History of Florida.* Gainesville: University Press of Florida, 2018.
Randall, Elizabeth. *Haunted St. Augustine and St. Johns County.* Charleston, SC: The History Press, 2013.

11

Georgia

Named for Britain's King George II, today's state of Georgia became the last and southernmost of the original thirteen English colonies when it was founded in 1733. Georgia was chartered when James Oglethorpe noted the wretched conditions in the debtor's prisons of England, and according to Sullivan (2010), "recommended the release of thousands of debtors to form the basis of a new colony" (16). Oglethorpe's charter originally banned slavery, an ideal that faded in the face of huge profits to be made in the cotton industry through unpaid labor.

In addition to offering a fresh start for debtors who could not repay their debts if they were languishing in English prisons, the Georgia colony would also serve as a buffer zone. Running from the South Carolina colony to its north to Spanish Florida in the south to the French territory of Louisiana in the west, Georgia quickly affirmed its allegiance to the new United States in 1788 as the fourth state to ratify the U.S. Constitution.

In 1829, gold was discovered in northern Georgia, leading to an influx of white settlers and a push to seize Cherokee land. In 1838, federal troops forcibly marched Georgia's Cherokee population west of the Mississippi River. Known as the Trail of Tears, thousands of Native American people died.

Georgia seceded from the Union in 1861 as one of the original Confederate states, becoming the site of major Civil War battles like Chickamauga and Kennesaw Mountain. A huge "scorched earth" swath of the state from Atlanta to Savannah was destroyed during Union General William Tecumseh Sherman's "March to the Sea." Thousands of soldiers and civilians died. In 1870, Georgia became the last state to be restored to the Union.

Often called the Peach State for its bounteous harvest of the fuzzy fruit, many people know Georgia as the setting for the iconic book and movie *Gone with the Wind* with its striking portrayal of the burning of Atlanta.

With so much Civil War–era death and destruction, it is no wonder that Georgia has a lot of cemeteries in which to bury the departed. Remarkably, before 1831, America did not have any cemeteries, at least not as we know them today. Rural families (which most early Americans were) buried their dead in small family plots. City dwellers generally utilized churchyards, town commons, or municipal burial grounds, but those were small land-locked spaces dating from colonial times that were often seen as hotbeds for diseases like cholera or yellow fever that killed the people buried there. When graveyards filled up, it was not unusual for burials five or six coffins deep.

In Cambridge, Massachusetts, Mount Auburn Cemetery was created in 1831 as the final resting place for the growing population in Boston. As it also grew, New York City established large burial grounds in nearby Brooklyn.

Not only was there more room in outlying areas but those cities of the dead initiated the modern system of separating the living from the departed. Ornate entrance gates marked the end of one world and the beginning of the other.

With more room came the tradition of making cemeteries park-like spaces with trees, flowering plants, and grave markers that were often exquisite works of art. Especially, during the nineteenth century, graves were often adorned with elaborate pieces of sculpture. This was especially the case with the graves of children, which were often marked with weeping angels, cherubs, a sleeping child atop the tombstone, and as Keister (2004) says, "lambs that marked the graves of children, particularly infants" (46).

One of the most well-known cemeteries in America is also home to some of the most iconic cemetery art, as well as the haunted legends they inspire. **Bonaventure Cemetery** in Savannah, Georgia, attained worldwide fame thanks to the novel and movie *Midnight in the Garden of Good and Evil*.

It is located on the site of the former Bonaventure Plantation, which according to Johnson (1998) means "Good Fortune" (9). The city of Savannah purchased the

One of the best-known cemeteries in America is also home to some haunted legends. Bonaventure Cemetery in Savannah, Georgia, attained world-wide fame through the novel and movie *Midnight in the Garden of Good and Evil*. People have claimed to hear giggling children and a crying baby near an infant's grave, see the apparition of a Voodoo priestess, and have a statue smile at them. (Library of Congress)

site in 1907, establishing it as Bonaventure Cemetery. The graveyard became the final resting place for a number of notable citizens of Savannah, including musician Johnny Mercer and novelist Conrad Aiken, along with many state officials, leading minsters, and Civil War generals. But none are as famous as a little girl named Gracie Watson.

"Little Gracie," born in 1883, was an adored only child. At age six, Gracie died of pneumonia. Her grieving family commissioned the life-sized, delicately detailed marble statue of Gracie that sits at her grave. The statue was said by contemporaries to bear a striking resemblance to the dead child, with her hair in bangs framing a sweet face. Legend has it that in the cold of winter, when the moon is full, the face of the marble statue is warm. Some say they have seen Gracie's ghost making the cemetery her playground. Many visitors leave coins at her grave or toys for her ghost to play with. There are claims that she cries (sometimes, tears of blood) if anyone removes the trinkets.

The ethereal spirit of another young girl has become synonymous with Bonaventure Cemetery. The book cover for 1994's *Midnight in the Garden of Good and Evil* features the statue of a young girl holding a bowl in each outstretched hand. For over fifty years, it had stood in the cemetery, essentially unnoticed. The statue was created by artist Sylvia Shaw Judson who called it Little Wendy. Also known as the "Bird Girl," the statue stood sentinel over a family plot, but once the book became a best seller, droves of fans came from around the world to commune with what they said was Wendy's spirit. They disturbed the peace of the family's gravesite, trampling adjacent plots to get a closer look, and even attempted to chip off pieces of the statue as souvenirs. The owners finally donated Little Wendy to a museum to avoid her destruction. Still, people come to Bonaventure looking for her.

People have also claimed to hear giggling children, a crying baby near an infant's grave, seeing the apparition of Minerva the Voodoo Priestess, and having a statue called "Corinne" smile at them. But it is the ethereal presence of Gracie and the now-departed Little Wendy who are the stars of Bonaventure's spirit world.

SOME OTHER REPORTEDLY HAUNTED PLACES IN GEORGIA

Even in a state with a rich history of distinguished homes, the **Hay House** in Macon, Georgia, stands apart. Built in 1859 with touches like plaster work containing twenty-four-carat gold leafing, apparently no expense was spared. Luckily, the Hay House survived the Civil War, and was loved by those who called it home. The original family, William Butler Johnston and Ann Tracy Johnston, modeled the house on mansions they had seen in Florence and Rome during their honeymoon. As a jeweler and treasurer for the Confederacy, William Johnston understood appearances, constructing the eighteen thousand–square-foot Italian Renaissance Revival mansion on seven levels. After it was declared a national historic landmark, the last private owner, financier Parks Lee Hay, conveyed the property in 1977 to the Georgia Trust for Historic Preservation. While the Trust tends to downplay the home's tales from the dark side, a number of stories have been circulated and printed in newspaper articles. Along with reports of unexplained cold spots, doors slamming for no reason, footsteps in empty parts of the building, and lights dimming on their own, strange apparitions have been reported. One in particular, the transparent figure of a lady in a long white gown and with hair styled in an old-fashioned bun at the back of her head, has been spied at the top of a stairwell and strolling on the lawn, and has been seen by neighbors in the top floor windows during early morning hours. The ghost is believed to be Ann Tracy Johnston, no doubt still keeping an eye on the home she loved.

Established in 1853, **Laurel Grove Cemetery** in Savannah was unique for its time by reserving four of its sixty-seven acres for the city's African American community, including both free blacks and enslaved people. Along with more than one thousand five hundred Southern soldiers and what seems like almost as many Confederate generals and politicians, Laurel Grove is also the final resting place of Juliette Gordon Low, founder of the Girl Scouts. Amid its lush floral displays and intricately carved gravesite statuary, Laurel Grove also attracts guests like the apparition of a woman dressed in a wedding gown wandering the grounds who has not been positively identified but no doubt has quite a story to tell. Visitors have also heard the sounds of heavy footsteps when no one was nearby. But one of the strangest tales dates back to 1894 when people on a trolley line traveling past the cemetery reported that every time a certain car (#28) passed the cemetery, the sound of a child crying could clearly be heard. No one could ever see a child either inside or outside the car. The crying sound continued every day for years until finally workers aboard car #28 reported that although the sounds were eerie and pitiful, after a while they simply got used to it.

Madison Square is a small park in a pleasant Savannah neighborhood where there have been reports of shadow people and ghostly figures strolling amid its manicured grounds. Although the square is named for U.S. president James Madison, it is a bronze statue of Sergeant William Jasper, dating from 1837, that is the park's central figure. Jasper's monument, as well as what may be other restless spirits haunting the Square, serves as a reminder that while Savannah is usually associated with the Civil War, it was also a battleground during American Revolution. In 1778 and 1779, hard-fought battles between American colonists and British soldiers resulted in the siege and capture of Savannah. Although the American defenders fought bravely, the city remained in British hands until the end of the war. Sergeant Jasper was one of many American militiamen killed during the battle of Savannah, whose bodies were thrown into a mass grave around the location of today's Madison Square. Even worse are the stories that men who were wounded in battle but not dead were also tossed in, doomed to be buried alive. In addition, during the construction of homes around the Square, bodies of buried British soldiers were found, men who lost their lives far from home. While Madison Square itself is an enchanting spot during the day, it is said to be one of the most haunted outdoor places in Savannah after the sun goes down. Some people who walked through the Square at night report a tall, dark, shadowy figure coming directly toward them and then suddenly disappearing. Others report strange sounds, unexplained shadows, and feeling a distinct chill in the air even on the warmest Georgia night.

In the mid-1800s, the city of Savannah doubled in population, spurred by the railroad boom. Built in 1851, the **Marshall House** hotel was unusual for its time for being developed by a woman, Mary Marshall, whose family was among the first group of settlers to colonize Georgia. In 1854, just a few years after it opened, the Marshall House was turned into a hospital for victims of Savannah's deadly yellow fever epidemic of 1854. Then, during the Civil War, the Marshall House was taken over by Union General William Tecumseh Sherman's troops in the winter of 1864 to be used as a hospital for his soldiers. When the troops occupied the hotel, the ground was frozen, so doctors were forced to bury the amputated arms and legs of patients under the floorboards of the room used for surgery during the war. Perhaps with the souls of all those who died at the Marshall House hotel when it served as a hospital, or uneasy spirits looking for their severed arms and legs, there seem to have been a few guests who did not check out. There have been reports of faucets turning on by themselves, ghost sightings, and even the sound of children running down the empty hall at night. The Marshall House has made the "Top Ten" list of haunts by several newspaper and television shows, which has led to speculation that the knocking current hotel patrons hear at their door may not actually be housekeeping. Incidentally, one of the most prized possessions of the Marshall House is a portrait of Mary Marshall that the hotel acquired from the estate of the dead Jim Williams whose story was told in *Midnight in the Garden of Good and Evil* and who was portrayed in the movie by Kevin Spacey.

Another Savannah haunt, today called the **Pirates' House**, has the distinction of being named the oldest building still standing in Georgia, dating back to 1753. Today it is a popular tavern and restaurant, but during one era of its long history, the Pirates' House served up something far more sinister than ale. Being on the coast, the Pirates' House was a familiar gathering place for sailors. Sea captains would often visit the establishment. Some of the less reputable ones might occasionally find themselves short on crew members, and would use the Pirates' House as a kind of recruiting office. Sometimes unwary men might find themselves getting drunk and passing out one minute, then waking up the next day far out to sea against their will, forced to work or be thrown overboard. Although often disputed, rumors continue that there are numerous underground tunnels throughout the city of Savannah. One allegedly was beneath the Pirates' House and is said to have been the way unconscious sailors were smuggled onto pirate ships. There have been reports of voices and moaning from beneath the floor where the tunnels are said to be, ghostly shadows, the sound of footsteps when no one is around, and unexplained reflections through the windows.

Mention the town of **Roswell** and most people think of UFO landings in Roswell, New Mexico. But there is another Roswell, the one in Georgia, which also has its share of UFOs—unexplained freaky occurrences. Bulloch Hall is said to be haunted by a teenage girl who was enslaved on the plantation, and either fell or was thrown into a well in the backyard. Her apparition is occasionally seen, usually accompanied by electrical disturbances. A private house in Roswell is said to be home to the ghost of a Confederate soldier who makes his allegiance clear: when pictures of a Union soldier and a Confederate soldier were hung on the wall, the owners would later find the Union soldier's picture lying in the middle of the floor with the glass shattered. In another manifestation, a group of junior high students were said to be touring the home when they saw a little girl playing in the house, even though there was no one in the building. When the ghostly girl ran right at the students, it is said that they ran screaming down the street.

Back in Savannah, which seems to have general spookiness in its DNA, for a place to become known as the most haunted building in town is quite a distinction. But that is the case of Savannah's **Sorrel-Weed House** which is noted not only for its elegant Greek revival architecture but also rumored paranormal activity. Dating back to 1840, the Sorrel-Weed House belonged to wealthy shipping merchant Francis Sorrel. Though Francis was married, legend has it that his fancy turned to a beautiful slave named Molly who was installed to live in private quarters above the carriage house. Sorrel's wife Matilda discovered the affair, and feeling betrayed, Matilda is reported to have jumped to her death from a balcony. Soon after, Molly was found hanging from a noose in the carriage house. Now, both women reportedly haunt the Sorrel-Weed mansion, making their presence known with unexplained sounds, disembodied voices, shadowy forms, and the sound of screaming. Many visitors also report feeling violently ill with headache, nausea, and dizziness. Although documentation on Matilda and Molly's connection to the Sorell-Weed House is sparse, many believe the property itself is haunted, having served as a battleground during the American Revolution. In what many people consider the ultimate in the power of the spirit world, it has been reported that camera and phone batteries seem to completely drain during tours of the property. This, they feel, might suggest that the Sorrel-Weed House is a top vortex for hauntings in the city. If the city in question is Savannah, that's saying a lot.

FURTHER READING

Johnson, Mandi Dale, and Amie Marie Wilson. *Historic Bonaventure Cemetery*. Charleston, SC: The History Press, 1998.

Keister, Douglas. *Stories in Stone: A Field Guide to Cemetery Symbolism and Iconography*. Layton, UT: Gibbs Smith Publishing, 2004.

Sullivan, Buddy. *Georgia: A State History*. Charleston, SC: Arcadia Publishing, 2010.

12

Hawaii

Hawaii is the most recent territory to join the Union, becoming the fiftieth state in 1959. Lying in the Pacific Ocean, it is the only U.S. state located outside North America. Composed entirely of islands, they include Kauai, Lanai, Maui, Molokai, Oahu, and the Island of Hawaii, which is often called the "Big Island" to avoid confusion.

With a warm tropical climate, Hawaii's beaches and majestic natural beauty make it a popular destination for everyone from tourists and surfers to biologists and volcanologists. The state is said to derive its name from Hawai'iloa, a figure from native mythology.

Although some may have arrived earlier, historians say that by the eleventh century, Polynesian explorers probably came to Hawaii from places like Bora Bora and Tahiti.

In the first documented contact by Europeans, British explorer James Cook arrived in 1778. Cook chose the name "Sandwich Islands" in honor of his sponsor, the Earl of Sandwich. When Cook returned the following year, he was killed by native people. Moore (2015) states that the British crew did not seek vengeance. After they sailed away, "as far as is known, no other foreign ship visited Hawai'i for the next seven years" (73).

But inevitably, Cook's reports about the tropical paradise attracted many Europeans to the Hawaiian Islands, including explorers, traders, and whalers. Sadly, just as had happened in North America, South America, and the Caribbean, the Europeans introduced diseases like influenza and smallpox that were new to the island people after centuries of isolation. By 1820, more than half of the Native Hawaiian population had died from disease and other causes. During the 1850s, measles alone killed one-fifth of the Native Hawaiians who remained.

In the late eighteenth century, the islands came under the control of King Kamehameha I. The Kamehameha dynasty ruled the Kingdom of Hawaii until 1872. After that time, the Islands experienced various governmental takeovers until Hawaii became a territory of the United States in 1898 before ultimately becoming a state in 1959.

Iolani Palace

The nation's capital, Washington, D.C., may have a building called the Smithsonian Castle, but Honolulu, Hawaii, is the home of America's only true palace. Built in 1882, Iolani Palace was once the official home of the Kingdom of Hawaii's ruling royalty. The dynasty ended with Queen Liliuokalani who ruled from 1891 until the overthrow of the Hawaiian monarchy in 1893. Following that coup, which according to *Smithsonian.com* was led by American sugar and pineapple growers, Queen Liliuokalani was imprisoned in her palace bedroom for eight months following the overthrow. Although she passed away in 1917, it is believed that her spirit may still call the Iolani Palace home. Both staff and visitors have reported hearing the sound of unexplained footsteps, as well as a piano mysteriously playing in the unoccupied Blue Room of the palace. Others claim to hear chanting or Hawaiian music playing when they enter the upstairs bedroom where Queen Liliuokalani was imprisoned. Some witnesses report seeing the silhouette of a woman standing in the window of what once was the Queen's bedroom. Witnesses say that ghostly figure can sometimes be observed looking out her bedroom window around 5:30 a.m. In addition, there are banyan trees that were planted on the grounds of Iolani in the 1880s. It is rumored that these trees are home to the spirits of the dead, and not just royalty. Some say that the banyan trees welcome the souls of departed Hawaiians who didn't have families to care for them.

The U.S. influence grew especially strong in the early 1800s when a number of American Protestant missionaries arrived to convert Hawaiians to Christianity, which they considered civilizing the natives as well as saving them from paganism. Haley (2015) states, "As with other aspects of native culture, control of the narrative today goes a long way toward controlling who knows what" (83).

Americans of all sorts assumed active roles in the Islands' commercial and political affairs. Some established large plantations, importing Chinese laborers to work the fields. It is generally believed that leprosy was introduced by Chinese workers around 1830, with disastrous results. In Hawaii, the disease had been unknown; Hawaiians had no resistance to it.

Throughout history, leprosy (today called Hansen's disease) was terrifying because it was incurable, causing disability and very visible disfigurement. It was commonly believed to be highly contagious, leading to the establishment of "leper colonies" where its victims were quarantined for life. Many were located in remote locations like mountaintops, or in the case of Hawaii, on an island.

Kalaupapa, sometimes simply called **Molokai** (for the island where it was located) was founded in 1866 to prevent transmission of leprosy by isolating individuals, including children, who had been struck by the disease. By 1890, more than a thousand people were living there. Over the course of a century, about eight thousand people were sent into exile at Kalaupapa. In some cases, spouses and other family members came with them, including healthy children who accompanied family members to Kalaupapa to live out their lives in isolation.

However, many lepers had to leave family behind, leading to the pain of homesickness and loneliness along with the sense of isolation and social stigma. There was not an actual medical staff at Kalaupapa, but missionary priests from Belgium were among those who came to Molokai to care for persons with leprosy.

Hawaii's Molokai was founded in 1866 to prevent transmission of leprosy, isolating individuals with the disease. Thousands lived there in exile, sometimes including healthy children who accompanied parents only to live out their lives in isolation. Currently abandoned, including Father Damien's Saint Philomena Church, seen here, there are said to be phantom spirits on Molokai of those who endured the pain of separation from mainstream society. (Library of Congress)

The most well-known of the Belgian priests was Father Damien, who arrived at the facility in 1873. Father Damien died of leprosy in 1889; for his work, he was canonized as a saint by the Roman Catholic Church in 2009. Among other missionaries and caregivers, Mother Marianne Cope of the Sisters of St. Francis from Syracuse, New York, came to the Molokai colony in 1883. Despite direct contact with the patients over many years, she did not contract the disease, remaining in Hawaii until 1918 when she died at the age of eighty. In 2012, Mother Cope was declared a saint by Pope Benedict XVI.

Unfortunately, those missionaries did not live long enough to see leprosy become curable in the 1940s through the use of modern antibiotics. In 1969, the quarantine restrictions were lifted from the Molokai colony and it was officially closed.

Today, it is said that Kalaupapa on Molokai is basically a ghost town, with its phantom inhabitants reportedly including the spirits of those who were taken from their families, lived in isolation, and felt the pain of being unable to join mainstream society. Relatively few visitors come to Molokai today, despite its natural beauty. Some who have come reported strange, powerful feelings of dread and despair.

Native Hawaiians traditionally shunned mysterious Molokai for generations because of legends and rumors about angry gods, evil spirits, and ghostly warriors. In fact, one of the reasons Molokai was chosen for the leper colony was because the Hawaiian Board of Health felt that such a facility would not damage the island's reputation since it was already considered fearsome and taboo.

Even in modern times, tourists tend to shun Molokai. As Tayman (2006) says, "Though modern medicine has stripped the illness of its horrors, on a social level, leprosy remains among the most feared of all diseases" (3).

SOME OTHER REPORTEDLY HAUNTED PLACES IN HAWAII

While some haunted spaces evoke past eras like the 1700s or 1800s, Hawaii contains two that were pivotal to events in the twentieth century. Along with Pearl Harbor, there is **Hickam Air Force Base** on Oahu. Hickam Field, as it was known then, was built to be a state-of-the-art military facility. Personnel began moving into the barracks in early 1940. By the end of that same year, it was fully occupied and the largest facility of its kind on an American military installation. Designed to accommodate the B-17 Flying Fortress bomber, the base was named for an early advocate of airpower, Lieutenant Colonel Horace Meek Hickam, who was an officer in what was then the U.S. Army Air Corps. A year after its opening, on December 7, 1941, in a surprise attack, Japanese planes struck American military installations on Oahu. They bombed and strafed Hickam Field to eliminate air opposition and to prevent U.S. planes from pursuing them back to their aircraft carriers. Hickam Field suffered extensive damage and loss of aircraft, with almost two hundred people killed and over three hundred wounded. But the base regrouped to serve as a major center for training pilots and assembling aircraft during World War II, as well as serving as the hub of the Pacific air network, a role it repeated during the Korean and Vietnam wars. Since that "day that will live in infamy" in 1941, it is said that a number of unusual incidents have occurred at Hickam. While at the base, people have claimed to hear the sounds of soldiers moaning in their death throes. Others have reported hearing the sounds of bombs exploding. Still others claim to have seen soldiers in World War II–era fatigues drifting around various areas of the base. One prankster of a ghost, nicknamed Charley, apparently likes to switch radio stations and throw objects at the unwary. Some witnesses claim that a guard shack on the base is haunted, reporting that they saw the ghost of a soldier in his uniform. The soldier is believed by many to have been killed while on duty in the guard shack on that fateful morning in 1941, and still remains at his post.

Highway 1 on Oahu is a roadway passing through the Ko'olau Mountains. However, it is not actually a mountain range as most people would know it due to its having been formed as a single mountain called Ko'olau Volcano. What remains is the western half of the volcano that suffered a cataclysm when in prehistoric times the eastern half slid into the Pacific Ocean. After being dormant for millennia, Ko'olau Volcano erupted several times over the past five hundred thousand years, creating such landmarks as Oahu's iconic Diamond Head. As dramatic as that may be, to some people, the Ko'olau Mountains are especially noteworthy for allegedly being haunted. Legend has it that ancient warriors perished in those mountains. That saga would seem to be supported by the bones of ancient warriors being excavated during the construction of Highway 1. Moving those bones is said to have disturbed the warriors' final resting place, resulting in their other-worldly revenge. Building the highway took years longer than expected. One reason for the delay was that terrified workers claimed to see ghosts, left work, and never returned. Today, unsuspecting motorists on Highway 1 have claimed to see ghosts or hear war cries and the warriors' voices speaking to them, especially inside the roadway's tunnels. Highway 1 has been described by many as one of the scariest places in Hawaii. With the angry spirits of ancient warriors making themselves known, it adds a new interpretation to road rage.

The **Hilton Hawaiian Village** is located on Oahu's beachfront. In addition to luxurious hotel amenities, guests at the Hawaiian Village might also experience some onsite paranormal activity. There have been reports of a young woman appearing and vanishing right before the eyes of witnesses, with the young woman in question apparently being murdered years before in her room at the hotel. Some say the ghostly presence of another woman, this time wearing a red dress, has been seen in the hotel's hallways as well as on the beach. Some speculate that the woman in red is actually a manifestation of Pele, the volcano goddess (also known as the fire goddess) who was exiled to Hawaii from her native Tahiti due to her terrible temper. But amid the natural splendor and mellow vibes of the Hawaiian Islands, apparently Pele is happy now and enjoys beachfront hotels like everyone else. Perhaps sometimes her bad temper returns, resulting in the eruption of one of Hawaii's volcanoes like Mauna Loa. But even those tantrums may be more benign—the oozing Kilauea Volcano has been continuously erupting since 1983, and there is still Hawaiian beachfront for Pele and others to enjoy.

The **Honolulu Airport** on Oahu opened in 1927, attracting thousands of arrivals and departures each day ever since. One story related by locals might indicate that amid the comings and goings at the bustling airport, at least one person decided never to leave. The apparition of a blonde woman in a white dress has been spotted in different parts of the airport, being dubbed the Lady in Waiting. Her tale was apparently another love story gone wrong. According to the legend, she had fallen in love with a man who said he wanted to marry her. Instead, her lover left on a flight out of Honolulu Airport and never returned. Some say the lady was so devastated that she took her own life, and today, her ghostly spirit roams around the airport, waiting for her erstwhile lover to return to her.

The **Iao Theater** in Wailuku, Maui, opened its doors in 1928 as both a movie and vaudeville house. Vaudeville died, films moved to multiscreen cineplexes, and the Iao Theater fell into disrepair in the 1980s, facing possible demolition. Thanks to local efforts including the Maui Community Theatre, there was a reprieve for the Spanish Mission-style playhouse. Cited as the oldest theater building in Hawaii, the Iao was listed on Hawaii's Register of Historic Places in 1994, and on the National Register of Historic Places the following year. While such organizations have strict guidelines for historic buildings, apparently paranormal activities are acceptable. Over the years, actors, staffers, and audience members have experienced cold spots, disembodied voices, items flying off dressing room shelves, and lights flickering. Shadowy figures of ancient Hawaiian warriors are said to have manifested themselves in the theater's basement, which may have been built over a site in the Iao Valley where they died in battle centuries ago. The valley itself is said to be a burial ground for ancient Hawaiian royalty. But if there is one drama queen at the Iao Theater, it is a misty, luminescent ghost who answers to "Emma." She has been seen both onstage and sitting in the audience. Some speculate she was an actress from the 1920s since she is most active during productions based in that era like *Chicago*. At those times, light boards malfunction for no apparent reason until Emma's presence is acknowledged by calling her by name. The story goes that cast and crew tried saying different names out loud. After calling "Emma," there was a cool, breezy feeling in the air and her spirit has been friendly ever since. It is unknown if a woman named Emma was actually associated with the theater, how she died, or what her backstory might be. But when a ninety-year-old time capsule encased in concrete outside the Iao Theater was unearthed, it contained a strip of film. When played on a projector, the film shows a woman's face, perhaps an actress named Emma whose benign spirit provides a bit of drama for the theater to this day.

The **Nu'uanu Pali Highway** on the island of Oahu is a main thoroughfare that connects the windward side of the island with downtown Honolulu. Construction on the original road started in 1845 and has seen a lot of history. The valley itself goes back even further. At the highway's Pali Lookout, people who are unfamiliar with Hawaiian history claim to have seen what looked like ancient Hawaiian soldiers being tossed off the cliff. In fact, one of the bloodiest battles in Hawaii's history occurred at the Pali Lookout. It was there that King Kamehameha I united the Hawaiian Islands, but part of the process involved Kamehameha's warriors pushing hundreds of enemy soldiers to their deaths off the cliff. Their ghosts are said to haunt the Pali, especially at night. But probably the strangest manifestation of the paranormal involves a meat product that can often be found in people's home: pork. According to legend, a Hawaiian fertility demigod named Kamapua'a is half man and half hog. He and fire goddess Pele became romantically involved, but almost inevitably it was followed by a bad breakup. Kamapua'a is said to live on the windward side of the island while Pele's turf is on the leeward side. They agreed to adopt a status of peaceful coexistence. But, taking pork from one side to the other would symbolically break that agreement. Some drivers who were carrying hot dogs for lunch or even SPAM® have claimed their cars mysteriously stalled on the highway. After they threw the pork product out the window, their vehicles started up again. Pedestrians carrying pork-related foods while walking alongside the highway have reported that their flashlights died when they stepped over the boundary to the leeward side, but after tossing the pork back to windward, the lights came alive again. It is unknown how the animosity between the hog deity and the fire goddess affects the well-known Hawaiian luau, which involves roasting a pig in a pit of fire, but no diners seem to have reported any problems.

Like neighboring Hickam Field, **Pearl Harbor Naval Station** on Oahu suffered devastating losses when Japan attacked on December 7, 1941. Thousands of people lost their lives or were wounded during the attack, which also crippled America's Pacific Fleet. Since that tragic morning, countless visitors to Pearl

Harbor have stated they experienced a feeling of extreme pain and overwhelming sadness. Some say they suddenly felt incredibly frightened for no apparent reason. This is especially true at the memorial site of the USS *Arizona* where sailors were trapped below decks when the ship was bombarded and sank into the waters of Pearl Harbor within minutes. More than one thousand officers and crewmen are still entombed inside, nearly half of all those killed in the devastating aerial bombing of Pearl Harbor by Japanese forces. Visitors to the site have stated they have seen apparitions of servicemen around the sunken vessel, as well as the ghost of a lone sailor wandering the deck of the doomed *Arizona*.

FURTHER READING

Haley, James L. *Captive Paradise: A History of Hawaii.* New York: St. Martin's Griffin, 2015.

Moore, Susanna. *Paradise of the Pacific: Approaching Hawaii.* New York: Farrar, Straus and Giroux, 2015.

Tayman, John. *The Colony: The Harrowing True Story of the Exiles of Molokai.* New York: Scribner, 2006.

13

Idaho

Before the arrival of European settlers, Idaho was inhabited by Native American people. Today, some of their descendants still remain there. Sharing a border with Canada, Idaho was the center of a dispute between the United States and Great Britain until Idaho officially became a U.S. territory as part of the Oregon Treaty in 1846. A separate Idaho Territory was not organized until 1863, but by 1890, Idaho was ready to be admitted to the Union as the forty-third state.

Idaho holds a special place in the hearts of people who love chips and french fries. The state produces about one-third of the nation's entire crop of potatoes. Some early settlers planted the first confirmed potato crop as early as 1838. But except to hardcore tater fans, Idaho's history did not actually begin with the succulent spud. Excavations have revealed evidence that humans may have been present there as long as 14,500 years ago, with arrowheads ranking among the oldest dated artifacts in America.

Native tribes included the Nez Percé and Shoshone. The arrival of Europeans was led by the early presence of French-Canadian fur trappers. Their influence on the Idaho countryside is reflected in place names taken from the French language like Boisé (meaning "wooded") and Cœur d'Alène ("heart of an awl," indicating a tough trader).

The Lewis and Clark expedition passed through Idaho going westward in 1805 and again on their eastbound return journey in 1806. After some short-lived settlements sprang up, the first permanent community of note was Lewiston in 1861, just two years before Idaho was officially dubbed a U.S. territory.

The state's name is something of a mystery. A local booster named George Willing, whose business practices were sometimes described as questionable, lobbied federal officials in favor of the name "Idaho," which he claimed at the time to be derived from the Shoshone language term "ee-da-how," meaning "the sun comes from the mountains" or "gem of the mountains." Later, he claimed to have simply made up the name after being inspired by a girl named Ida. Despite his later disclaimer, many references still repeat Willing's account that the name was derived from the Shoshone.

Sometimes Idaho is said to be somewhat disjointed, having two time zones (Mountain Time and Pacific Time). In addition, its elevation runs from Borah Peak at almost thirteen thousand feet high to the lowest point in Lewiston, just over seven hundred feet. According to Kratz and Maughan (2014), "Idaho has a more diverse natural topography within its borders than most places" (7). With all that variety, the landscape of Idaho includes rushing rivers, steep canyons, snow-capped mountains, and sparkling lakes. Hells Canyon (no apostrophe, by the way), cut by the fast-moving Snake River, is the deepest gorge on the continent. Shoshone Falls plunges down a stony rim one thousand feet across from a height taller than Niagara Falls. The rugged landscape of Idaho includes stretches of the Rocky Mountains and encompasses some of the largest unspoiled natural areas in the United States.

With so much geological diversity, it is not surprising that Idaho's majestic mountains would be riddled with caves. A cave is simply a natural hollow place in the ground that is large enough for a human to enter. Silvestru (2008) puts it poetically: "There is a landscape beneath the landscape. We know it as caves. . . . A long, long time ago our ancestors entered this 'underland' with eyes full of fear . . . and hearts pounding with excitement" (6).

Most caves are formed by the weathering of rock, usually by water, and often extend deep underground. According to the National Speleological Society, two of the world's longest documented caves are in the United States: Mammoth Cave in Kentucky and Jewel Cave in South Dakota.

Throughout history, people have used caves. The earliest human fossils are found in caves, which some early humanoid species made into their home, ergo the term "cave man." Some caves were used for shelter; others were used for burials or as religious sites. In a dramatic use of caves as primitive galleries, prehistoric cave art has been found at various locations around the world.

In the United States, Idaho boasts an underground feature that is one of the most unique natural cave formations on the planet, the **Shoshone Ice Caves**. The thousand-foot-long lava tube is the largest such cave in the world that is open to the public. It contains ice up to thirty feet thick in a massive sea of jagged lava rock that is between eight and thirty feet high, remaining permanently frozen at a constant temperature between twenty-four and thirty-two degrees year-round. The ice was caused by cold air flowing through the lava tubes, causing subterranean water to freeze.

The Shoshone Ice Caves have an additional feature that makes them even more chilling than their freezing temperatures: they are said to be haunted. Located near the town of Shoshone, about two hours from Boise, they seem to exemplify what Natalie Lunis (2012) writes, "Why do caves attract so many ghosts? Some say that the underground spaces serve as passageways between the world of the living and the spirit world. . . . Others believe that those who lost their lives in the underground spaces are unable to ever leave the caves again" (5).

The legend is that a Native American princess was buried in the ice mass within the cave decades ago during one of its rare thaws, and is patiently waiting to re-emerge. It is said that after the caves are closed to the public for the night, staffers can hear phantom footsteps and hushed, disembodied voices. The legend further alleges that if the cave ice were somehow to melt, the princess would rise again, but in keeping with the legend of the dead being trapped underground forever, she would be destined to walk the Shoshone Ice Caves for eternity.

SOME OTHER REPORTEDLY HAUNTED PLACES IN IDAHO

If the **Bates Motel** in Coeur d'Alene had remained with its original use, it would probably never have become immortalized as a universal shorthand for horror. It began life as officers' barracks for the nearby Farragut Naval Training Station. When Farragut was established in 1942, in the early days of World War II, the base had a population of fifty-five thousand, making it the largest community in the state and the second-largest training center in the world (behind Great Lakes Naval Station near Chicago). Before the war ended, about three hundred thousand recruits would pass through Farragut for their basic training. The base was also used as an Army prisoner of war camp in 1945 for about nine hundred Germans. But in 1946, after the war, Farragut was decommissioned. The barracks facility in Coeur d'Alene, no longer needed, was sold and converted into a motel known as The Roadway Inn. Finally, when it came time to sell the building yet again, a local accountant named Randy Bates came along and renamed it The Bates Motel. Legend has it that Robert Bloch, the author of a 1959 thriller novel titled *Psycho*, had stayed at the motel during the 1950s and made note of the name. In 1960, the classic thriller movie *Psycho* was released, directed by master of suspense Alfred Hitchcock. With its bloody murder scene taking place in the shower of a room at the fictional Bates Motel, the name is imprinted on the psyches of anyone who saw the film. Today, at the real-life Bates Motel in Idaho, employees and guests claim that there is a steady flow of paranormal activity, with the majority of the unexplained occurrences taking place in Rooms One and Three. Guests in those rooms often report having the feeling of being watched along with experiencing cold spots, lights turning on and off, strange noises, and ashtrays being knocked off tabletops or moved to another spot. At this writing, however, there have been no confirmed reports of bloody stabbings in the shower.

The abovementioned Farragut Naval Training Station also figures in another allegedly haunted spot in Idaho, today's **Brig at Farragut State Park** in the Coeur d'Alene Mountains at the southern tip of Lake Pend Oreille. During its time as a naval basic training facility in World War II, the Brig served as a military jail. During that time, the Brig was said to have been the site of at least one murder as well as at least one suicide. After the war, the base was decommissioned and several thousand acres were ultimately transferred to the Idaho Department of Parks and Recreation. Farragut State Park was created in 1966. The Brig is one of the few structures remaining of the 776 buildings that were once on the base. The building houses a museum dedicated to the boot camp as well as naval and war memorabilia. It may also house something else. No one can definitively say who it is that actually haunts the Brig, but most witnesses agree that there is an apparition which appears to be in some kind of uniform. There is some debate among witnesses as to whether it is a military uniform or prison garb, both of which would be plausible for a building used as a military jail. It is also said that there could be two or more different apparitions. Over the years, visitors and staffers have described the apparition in detail saying that it appears to be a living person—apart from being transparent and having the ability to suddenly vanish into thin air. In addition, there are also reports of objects flying across the old cells and large, heavy objects being moved to different spots when the building is unoccupied.

Many people can come up with excuses not to exercise, but perhaps the occurrences at the **Canyon Hill Cemetery** in Caldwell, Idaho, might motivate them. At the cemetery, there have been reports of a jogger who not only runs at midnight but is also legless. The story is that visitors who drive up to the gates of the cemetery around midnight and park the car there see an apparition of a jogger with no legs that floats up to the driver's side window and taps on the glass. The Midnight Jogger has definitely been reported as a female, and is said to just hover. Other than tapping on the glass, no further contact is made, certainly not an invitation for the visitor to join her in a quick sprint around the graveyard. Another apparition that has been reported at Canyon Hill Cemetery is that of an elderly lady who has been seen sitting on a bench in the middle of the night when it is quiet and everyone else has left. Witnesses say that when they looked away for a moment and looked back, she had vanished. Visitors report a sudden drop in temperature as they walk the grounds and an uneasy feeling that they are being watched. Dating to the 1800s, Canyon Hill Cemetery is the final resting place for murder victims, suicides, and other tragic departures.

The **Old Idaho State Penitentiary** in Boise has long been considered one of the most haunted places in Idaho. In its original incarnation, it was a single-cell jailhouse for the territory, opening in 1870. But as crime grew in Idaho, so did the jail. It closed at the end of 1973, with over a century of housing what the Idaho State Historical Society calls some of the West's most desperate criminals. Two hundred and fifteen of its thirteen thousand inmates were women. One of them was Lyda Trueblood Dooley McHaffle Lewis Meyer Southard, one of America's first known female serial killers. She was accused of using arsenic from flypaper to kill four husbands, a brother-in-law, and her three-year-old daughter between 1915 and 1920 to collect their life insurance money. After being convicted, she escaped from the Old Idaho State Penitentiary but was returned to prison. Conditions there were said to be horrible, including a lack of indoor plumbing. The cells were unbearably hot in summer and freezing cold in winter. In 1952, there were severe riots over conditions at the prison. Some say that along with the pain, despair, hopelessness, and executions inside the prison walls, some deaths due to brutal conditions may have gone unreported, resulting in troubled spirits. Today, those on prison tours report hearing disembodied voices and phantom footsteps echoing, along with a feeling of being watched, touched, and even pushed by unseen hands. Shadow figures have been spotted, especially in what is said to be the most haunted spot at the old penitentiary, 5 House. There, a serial killer known as Idaho's answer to Jack the Ripper was executed. Raymond Allen Snowden confessed to the murder of one woman but bragged to fellow inmates he killed others. In 1957, his execution was the last to occur at the Old Idaho Penitentiary.

The Old Idaho State Penitentiary in Boise, opening in 1870, has long been considered one of the most haunted places in the state. Some say that along with the pain, despair, hopelessness, and executions inside the prison, deaths due to brutal conditions may have gone unreported, resulting in troubled spirits. Today, those on prison tours report hearing disembodied voices and even a feeling of being pushed by unseen hands. (Glenn Nagel/Dreamstime.com)

However, his hanging did not snap his neck as planned, and he hung at the gallows for around fifteen minutes, struggling for breath. Some visitors have reported stepping into the gallows room and hearing the sounds of someone fighting to breathe. Currently, Snowden lies in an unmarked grave in the prison cemetery, which may further offend his spirit. It is said that his malevolent soul still haunts the prison, with visitors and staff sensing a sudden feeling of dread, pain, and cruelty.

In a state that contains the Bates Motel, it is something of a distinction to be known as a lodging that is equally scary. The **Owyhee Plaza Hotel** in Boise has been a landmark in that city since the lodging opened in 1910. With its dignified classical architecture, the Owyhee was a popular nightspot containing a fashionable rooftop garden, restaurant, and dance floor with live music. Although its popularity waned, it apparently retained its allure for the spirit world. Staffers and hotel guests have reported strange sounds, feeling of being watched, and seeing a full body apparition, especially the one in Room 136. There, a guest awoke during the night to see a female spirit standing in the room. However, the unflappable guest said she was not frightened, but actually felt a sense of calm come over her. The guest asked the spirit who she was, what she wanted, and why the spirit was in the room, but rather than chat, the ghostly roommate faded away. Other guests reported similar apparitions wandering in different parts of the hotel, including the basement and meeting rooms. Staffers report cleaning supplies being replaced as well as materials disappearing and reappearing the next day. One woman who was cleaning the offices late at night reported hearing the voices of a group of people talking when she was the only person in the area. She also said she saw a man walking out the door, which is when she realized the door never opened or shut after him. Even with all that, one of the biggest mysteries is what the word "Owyhee" means. It shows up in numerous place names around Idaho as well as Nevada and Oregon, and is said to come from an 1819 fur trapping expedition in which three of its members were natives of Hawaii. After one was found murdered and the others mysteriously gone without a trace, places were named with the word to honor them, with "Owyhee" said to be an early spelling of "Hawaii."

FURTHER READING

Kratz, Luke, and Jackie Maughan. *Hiking Idaho: A Guide to the State's Greatest Hiking Adventures*. Guilford, CT: Globe Pequot, 2014.

Lunis, Natalie. *Haunted Caves*. New York: Bearport Publishing, 2012.

Silvestru, Emil. *The Cave Book*. Green Forest, AR: Master Books, 2008.

14

Illinois

The state of Illinois received its name from early French explorers and missionaries who adapted it from the language of the Native American tribes who inhabited the region and spoke a common language. Although current residents of the state often prefer the interpretation of the word that means "tribe of superior men," according to the Illinois State Museum, the state's name may have originated from the word "irenweewa" or "ilinwe," meaning "he speaks in the ordinary way."

With due respect to certain athletic teams, the Illinois State Museum also says the term "Illini" has been used to refer to local Indians but does not appear to be valid, historically or linguistically.

The current spelling of Illinois began appearing in the 1670s with the arrival of French explorers like Jacques Marquette and Louis Jolliet. Illinois was a territory that was claimed by France until 1763 when it passed to the British after they defeated the French in the Seven Years' War.

At first, the British made it part of a region reserved for Native Americans, but that soon ended. After the Revolutionary War, American settlers began arriving in what was then called the Territory of East Mississippi. By 1818, there was enough of a white population there for Illinois to become America's twenty-first state. When the opening of the Erie Canal increased trade through the Great Lakes, and from there to the world, Chicago was founded in the 1830s on the banks of the Chicago River and Lake Michigan. Chicago went on to become the largest metropolis in America's Midwest and a nationally renowned city.

Illinois became an industrial center in the twentieth century, with the lure of jobs attracting African Americans from the Jim Crow South as part of the Great Migration to the North. Chicago became central to the emerging African American-based jazz and blues culture.

But it was in the 1920s that Chicago took its place among cities that were known around the world, and it was *not* for its culture. According to Danzer (2011), prohibition, or the federal ban on alcoholic beverages nationwide, created new opportunities for gangsters already operating in the nation's cities. "Al Capone soon emerged as the most powerful mobster in Chicago, and perhaps the most famous, or infamous, citizen of the state" (156).

On the other hand, three U.S. presidents have been elected while living in Illinois: Abraham Lincoln, Ulysses Grant, and Barack Obama.

Chicago can boast a number of superlatives. In 1942, the University of Chicago conducted the first sustained nuclear chain reaction, ushering in the Atomic Age. Although geographically it is in the middle of the United States, Chicago became an ocean-going seaport when the Saint Lawrence Seaway opened in 1959. It was renowned as a cultural center for its art and architecture, comedy (notably the Second City improvisational troupe), film, food, literature, music, and theater. But to some, the most significant achievement in the state's history occurred in 1960 when businessman Ray Kroc opened the world's first McDonald's franchise in Des Plains, Illinois.

Even with the staggering rise of Chicago as an urban center, many Illinois residents lived in rural areas for much of the state's history. When settlers arrived in Illinois, as with most of the rest of America, one of the first things they did was to start cutting down the trees that covered the landscape. They used wood to build houses, barns, furniture, fences, and tools. It was used for fuel and eventually for timber that could be sold.

It is said that before Europeans arrived in what is now the United States, a squirrel could scamper treetop-to-treetop all the way from New York City to Chicago without ever setting foot on the ground. Forests in the United States covered nearly a billion acres. But as the population grew, deforestation decimated wooded areas and wildlife, not to mention the Native American people who depended on forests to hunt for their food.

To Europeans, forests were a nuisance that needed to be cleared away in order to build farms and construct European-style towns. Cutting down trees and taming them ultimately proved useful. Rutkow (2012) says, ". . . trees changed from enemy, to friend, to potential savior . . . trees imbued the great cities with life" (7). The last point was ironically discovered during the Great Chicago Fire of 1871 that killed hundreds of people and destroyed the city—a city that was built mostly of wood.

But forests also held a sense of memory for European settlers. In fairy tales like those of the Brothers Grimm, the forest is a dark, dangerous, foreboding place. Forests were considered breeding grounds for dragons, goblins, sorcerers, trolls, warlocks, witches, and Big Bad Wolves. Snow White, Sleeping Beauty, and Hansel and Gretel all had tribulations in the woods. Even in more modern times, in works from *Lord of the Rings* to *Lord of the Flies*, going into the woods could be a risky business.

It is not unusual, then, for woods and forests to find themselves as the center of hauntings. However, it is somewhat unusual for those woods to be in a major urban metroplex like Chicago. But hauntings are often believed to emanate from bloodshed, passion, and violence. And as Taylor (2008) says, "From the first days of statehood, passion and tragedy ruled Illinois" (2).

Robinson Woods in Chicago is said to be one of the most haunted places in Illinois. Some say the land is cursed by disrespecting its prior use as a Native American burial ground. Contemporary reports include hearing phantom sounds of tribal drums being played. In 1814, a Chicago resident named Andrew

Robinson acquired the land, one way or another, from Native Americans. Soon, his life was plagued by misfortune. His home was destroyed by fire that ended his family's claim to the property since there was no longer a homestead on it. Then, three bodies were found lying naked and strangled in a ditch at the edge of Robinson Woods. Visitors, including police who were called to investigate, began to report various strange occurrences, such as disembodied voices and unexplained lights, sounds, and smells. A stone marks the burial site of Andrew Robinson himself, and it is in this area where many of the strange occurrences have been reported. Apparently, the spirits that lie buried beneath Robinson Woods do not rest in peace.

SOME OTHER REPORTEDLY HAUNTED PLACES IN ILLINOIS

Bachelor's Grove Cemetery in Bremen Township, Cook County, near Chicago, is a small, abandoned burial ground, which has a reputation for being one of the most haunted spots in Illinois. Sometimes called Bachelor Grove, Batchelor Grove, Batchelder's Grove, Everden, or Everdon, it was not consecrated as a burial ground until the 1840s, although there are headstones predating that. Some say the cemetery has been desecrated because of reported satanic rituals being conducted there. Perhaps it is the suspected devil worship that disturbs the peace of deceased people buried there. Possibly as a spiritual antidote, witnesses have reported seeing a number of ghostly figures dressed in the robes of religious monks wandering throughout the cemetery. The most commonly reported phenomenon involves orbs or red flickers of light floating over tombstones. There have also been reports of a lady in white, dubbed by locals as "The Madonna of Bachelor's Grove," walking the grounds during the full moon carrying an infant. She sometimes appears on top of one of the tombstones and looks out toward the thick woods close to the cemetery. Some say her image was captured in a newspaper photograph, purportedly showing a transparent woman sitting on a tombstone. The apparition, however, was not visible when the photograph was taken. In addition, a ghostly farmhouse is said to shimmer and float, shrinking as witnesses approach it until it vanishes altogether. Other tales involve the restless spirits of a farmer and his plow-horse who were dragged down to their watery deaths after getting submerged in a watery marsh. Some claim to have seen the manifestation of a black dog at the cemetery entrance that would disappear when they approached it. In one of the strangest incidents, a young boy was heard crying about a lost silver coin. An investigation was allegedly conducted in which the investigator is said to have gone into a trance-like state, wandering into the knee-deep water of a muddy pond on the property. He is said to have bent down and retrieved a silver half dollar from the bottom of the pond. Since then, the little boy's spirit has not been reported making any more sounds.

The **Congress Plaza Hotel** on Chicago's famed Michigan Avenue was built in 1893, and during that time, has played host to celebrities, dignitaries, performers, and presidents. Apparently, it has also hosted a few unregistered guests. There

The Congress Plaza Hotel in Chicago has played host to celebrities and dignitaries as well as apparently a few unregistered guests. Appliances throughout the hotel are said to turn on and off by themselves, strange noises come from empty hotel ballrooms, and apparitions in the hotel's hallways are said to include 1920s gangster Al Capone. (Maxironwas/Dreamstime.com)

have been reports of appliances throughout the hotel that are said to turn on and off by themselves, strange noises coming from the hotel ballrooms when they are empty, and sudden apparitions in the hotel's many hallways, which are said to include one of the building's alleged Jazz-Age owners in the 1920s, gangster Al Capone. Some guests state they have seen Capone walking the halls amid the rat-ta-tat sounds of his highly polished two-tone wingtip shoes. But the most frequently reported manifestation is not the famous (or infamous) Capone but an anonymous construction worker who was somehow trapped behind some drywall when the property was being built and ended up being walled in. What has been dubbed the "Hand of Mystery" allegedly sticks out of a wall in the area behind the balcony of the hotel's ballroom called the Gold Room. Witnesses report seeing a ghostly gloved hand sticking out of the wall; that hand is said to be all that the dead worker has been able to free. He remains trapped in his tomb and is apparently doomed to wave for all eternity in an attempt to get help. Also in the Gold Room, which is often used for formal weddings, there have been rumors that some of the bridesmaids who gather around the piano for photographs of the bridal party are later inexplicably found not to have shown up in the pictures. Apart from the Gold Room, there are several other ballrooms and event spaces in the hotel. There, disembodied voices are heard in those cavernous areas even when they are empty. Moving upstairs, there are tales that the manifestation of a man roams the eighth floor, a level where the elevator is said to stop frequently even though no one pushed an elevator button for that floor. In Room 441, guests have reported seeing the identical apparition: the shadowy outline of a woman who shakes the bed while the guest is still in it. She appears there so often that Room 441 is the place where hotel security is called more than any other room. On the twelfth floor, there is a room alleged to be so frightening that hotel staff sealed it and removed the door handle. The tale is that ghostly children haunt the twelfth floor because their mother lost her mind in the early 1900s, throwing them from there to their death.

The **Hotel Baker** in St. Charles, dating back to 1928, was built as a luxurious boutique hotel that was advanced for its time. It boasted its own hydroelectric facility and a radio station in addition to a parking garage for the then-increasing number of Model T cars plus a serene formal English rose garden for those who felt the world of the Jazz Age was moving too fast. The hotel was known in the greater Chicago area as "The Honeymoon Hotel." Today, some happy couples celebrate their nuptials by renting the sixth floor Penthouse Suite, which includes a separate sitting area, a spectacular view of the Fox River, and a winding staircase that leads to a deck with its hot tub built for two. But in this cozy lodging, some people have reported an uninvited guest. Along with the sounds of disembodied voices and mournful cries within the privacy of the suite, guests have reported feeling as if an unseen force was tugging on the bedding and that their bedsheets were disturbed while they were in another part of the suite, even though no one else had access to their room. Someone who *might* have access is the spirit of a former chambermaid who committed suicide by drowning herself in the Fox River after being jilted at the altar. As it happens, before it was converted, the sixth floor Penthouse Suite was formerly used as employees' quarters where the lovelorn chambermaid is said to have spent her final day, one that did not include a happy honeymoon.

Showmen's Rest in Forest Park is a cemetery within a cemetery, with its boundaries marked by five elephant statues at Woodlawn Cemetery. In the early 1900s, one of the most popular forms of entertainment, especially in the heartland of Mid-America, was the circus. One of the traveling troupes was the Hagenbeck-Wallace Circus. In the middle of the night on June 22, 1918, a circus train was heading from Illinois toward its next stop at Hammond, Indiana. Several hundred performers, roustabouts, and temporary workers were slumbering in the sleeper cars at the rear. Due to an overheated axle box, the train was halted and warning flares were lit. Most of the circus train was on a side track, but the last five cars, including four wooden sleeper cars, remained on the main track. Suddenly, another train appeared behind them on the same track, driven by an engineer who was said to be dozing and stated he did not see the flares or several warning signals. His fast-moving steel frame locomotive crashed through the three cars at the back of the circus train before coming to a stop on top of the fourth. About eighty-six of the sleeping circus personnel perished in the first seconds of the crash with about a hundred injured, as well as some circus animals. The circus train then caught on fire, burning survivors of the initial impact beyond recognition. A few days after the crash, survivors gathered at Woodlawn Cemetery, where the victims were buried in a mass grave that had been purchased by the Showmen's League, a fraternal order created in 1913 to support men and women in show business. With so many unidentifiable remains and some birth names unknown, only five of the victims had names on their markers. Most are inscribed with such tombstone epitaphs as "Baldy," "4 Horse Driver," "Smiley," "Unknown Male No. 44," or "Unknown Female No. 43." The dates of death are all marked June 22, 1918. Their graveyard came to be called Showmen's Rest and is still used as a burial ground for circus folk and show people. The cemetery is said to be haunted by their tragic spirits. Some locals say the phantom sounds of ghostly elephants can be heard at night. In a postscript, following the tradition of "the show must go on," the Hagenbeck-Wallace Circus only cancelled two performances. Competitors like the Ringling Brothers and Barnum & Bailey Circus lent equipment and performers to the decimated troupe. The engineer of the train who had plowed into them blamed the circus for using rail cars that were made out of wood, not steel; he lived for three more decades.

FURTHER READING

Danzer, Gerald A. *Illinois: A History in Pictures*. Urbana: University of Illinois Press, 2011.

"The Illinois: Identity," *Illinois State Museum*, 2000. http://www.museum.state.il.us/muslink/nat_amer/post/htmls/il_id.html.

Rutkow, Eric. *American Canopy: Trees, Forests, and the Making of a Nation*. New York: Scribner, 2012.

Taylor, Troy. *Haunted Illinois: Ghosts and Strange Phenomena of the Prairie State*. Mechanicsburg, PA: Stackpole, 2008.

15

Indiana

Indiana, which became the nineteenth state of the Union in 1816, was officially named for its original Native American inhabitants, with the meaning essentially being "land of the Indians." According to Willis (2012), Indiana can boast distinctions like "more interstate highway per square mile than any other state, wonderful covered bridges, and of course the Indianapolis 500" (5), in addition to what some consider its crowning achievement, the Indianapolis Colts football team.

An overriding question that many people have about Indiana relates to the Colts whose home turf was formerly called the Hoosier Dome, begging the question, "What is a 'Hoosier'?"

Its derivation is disputed. The Indiana Historical Society cites "Hoosier" as being a term possibly traceable to England. Its American usage began in states like Tennessee and Virginia, where many new arrivals to Indiana originated. In those states, the term "Hoosier" is said to have meant a backwoodsman or a country bumpkin. Hoosier lore spread after being popularized in an 1833 poem by Indiana resident John Finley, who was originally from Virginia. Finley's poem, "The Hoosier's Nest," included such lines as "Blest Indiana! in thy soil . . . a stranger found a *Hoosier's Nest* / In other words, a buckeye cabin. . . ."

The term helped define Indiana's identity toward rugged individualism. Anyone born in Indiana or a current resident can be considered a Hoosier. After lobbying by Indiana congressmen, in 2017 the U.S. Government Publishing Office changed the official designation for Indiana residents from "Indianans" to "Hoosiers," making Indiana the only state whose people do not have part of the state's name in their title, such as "Texans."

As for the Indians for whom the state was named, a British proclamation in 1763 authorized the land west of the Appalachian Mountains for Native Americans, barring white colonists. But during the American Revolution (1775–1783), George Rogers Clark of Virginia raised an army to fight the English in the west. Clark won battles such as those at Vincennes, Indiana, that have been credited with helping win the war. As part of the peace treaty, the newly formed United States took control of Indiana's Native American land.

In 1825, the state capital was moved from Corydon to Indianapolis. Thomas (2012) says, "Leave Indy behind and head in any direction, and in minutes you will find yourself in the heart of rural Indiana" (2).

What early settlers found in Indiana was *extremely* rural. Pioneers came from eastern states as well as Europe, neither of which were generally used to the kind of ultrarustic frontier conditions they encountered across Indiana. Thick forests were interspersed with wide rivers such as the Ohio River, Wabash, and soon-to-be politically useful Tippecanoe. With forests all around them, the pioneers did the obvious: they cut down trees to build bridges.

In its simplest sense, a bridge is a structure built to span obstacles like a river to allow people and goods to cross. The earliest bridges in prehistoric times were probably fallen trees, but by the era of the ancient Greeks and Romans, bridge-building became an art. Some arched stone bridges built by those civilizations before the birth of Christ are still standing today.

According to Newman (2016), especially during the Civil War era, bridges were utilized as the site of hangings (5). Such a practice was immortalized in the 1890 story by Civil War veteran Ambrose Bierce titled "An Occurrence at Owl Creek Bridge." That evocative tale is generally burned into the memories of students who read it in school.

Although probably not as famous as the fictionalized Owl Creek Bridge, Indiana has its own noteworthy setting in the **Edna Collings Bridge**. Located in

Indiana's Edna Collings Bridge, located in Putnam County, comes with its own legend. A little girl named Edna Collings enjoyed swimming in Walnut Creek, which it spans. One day, Edna's dead body was found downstream. Some suggest she was murdered. It is said that if drivers stop on the bridge, Edna's ghost will appear, accompanied by the sound of a little girl giggling. (Kenneth Keifer/Dreamstime.com)

Putnam County, Indiana, the covered bridge was built over Little Walnut Creek in 1922 and is also known as the Edna Collins Bridge even though the sign on the bridge entrance clearly spells it as "Collings."

According to legend, a little girl named Edna Collings (or Collins) enjoyed swimming in Walnut Creek along with her dog. Her indulgent parents would drop the child off to swim when they went to market at a nearby town. Upon their return, they would drive onto the bridge and honk three times to let Edna know it was time to get into the car and go home. However, tragedy ensued when one day, Edna didn't come when they honked. Her body was later found downstream. Most stories say she was trying to rescue her dog, although others suggest she was murdered. Today, it is said that if drivers stop on the bridge, turn off the car engine, and honk three times, the ghost of little Edna will appear on the bridge and try to get into the car. Some people claim to have found a child's handprints on their car after they drive away, accompanied by the sound of a little girl giggling.

The town of Avon, Indiana, has its own haunted bridge, this one located across White Lick Creek. It is said to house the spirit of a construction worker who was building the railroad bridge when he fell into a vat of wet concrete that was used to harden into the bridge pylons. As he sank into the vat, his fellow workers had no way to save him. They could hear him knocking and screaming from inside the pylon until it dried, a sound that is said to still be heard at the bridge by dark of night.

SOME OTHER REPORTEDLY HAUNTED PLACES IN INDIANA

No look at Indiana's haunted places can fail to include the **Carolina Street Demon House** in Gary, Indiana. It has also been called the "House of 200 Demons" for the population density of alleged spirits who called it home. Making nationwide news during 2011, witnesses reported a boy walking backward up a wall, a girl levitating from bed, mysterious footprints, the shadowy apparition of a man pacing the living room, and hordes of black flies that swarmed the porch in the frigid month of December and kept returning even after efforts at extermination. There were reports of the devil possessing the three children who lived there with their mother and grandmother, who claimed to have been choked by an unseen entity. Caseworkers from Indiana's Department of Child Services, police, a doctor, and a priest were called to the scene, with the latter performing three exorcisms and calling the house a "portal to demons." But the landlord stated the family was behind on rent and were claiming paranormal activities to avoid payments. The family moved to Indianapolis in 2012 after which events at the Demon House were said to have stopped. The tenant who moved in after them reportedly did not experience any paranormal incidents. However, the story took on another dimension in 2014 when Zak Bagans of TV's *Ghost Adventures* purchased the house. After making a film titled *Demon House*, Bagans had the home demolished in 2016.

Completed in 1869, the **Culbertson Mansion** in New Albany, Indiana, was originally the home of wealthy William Culbertson. In the 1930s, it was purchased by a new owner who transformed the Culbertson Mansion into a rental property. In 1933, the family of Dr. Harold Webb moved in, with Webb using the mansion as both his home and office. Soon, the Webb children said a man was entering their bedrooms through the walls at night. They heard noises underneath the house, including the sound of screams and rattling chains, and a terrible odor came up through the floor. Although Dr. Webb said he investigated thoroughly, he claimed to have found nothing, assuring the family everything was fine. At the same time, many of Dr. Webb's patients did not come back for return visits, which he attributed to untrue dark rumors about the mansion. After several of Dr. Webb's patients went missing in 1934, local police arrived to find the house abandoned—except for Webb's entire family, who had been slaughtered. In the basement they found the tortured remains of Webb's patients. Riddled throughout the house were secret passages and doors hidden in walls. Today used as an event facility and—not surprisingly—a spook house, staff and visitors report strange sounds after hours and mysterious figures moving from room to room.

The **Elkhart Civic Theatre**, also known as the Bristol Opera House in Bristol, Indiana, is housed in a historic building that dates back to 1897. Amid the theatricals that are still presented are special effects, including books and papers flying off shelves, sewing machines running by themselves, unexplained shadows and shafts of light, small objects being levitated, tools being rearranged, and people being grabbed by an unseen presence. The effects are not part of the show; they are said to be the ghost of a former handyman named Percival "Percy" Hilbert who lived in the basement of the theater with his wife and two daughters after they lost their home during the Great Depression. The family was not only grateful for a place to live but apparently they took a proprietary interest in the place. The ghosts of two little girls have been spotted peeking out from behind the curtain and peering out into the audience as well as in the aisles. Perhaps something of a theatrical "ham," Percy's apparition is said to have turned up in a photo during a ghost hunt. His supernatural dramatic tastes do not seem to include musical comedies because annoying incidents like lost props seem to happen most often when musicals are being staged. Actors have felt like they were being jerked backward as they are making their entrance onstage. Regarding actresses, Percy's ghost also seems to enjoy hanging around the women's dressing rooms.

Dating back to 1845, the historic resort lodging called the **French Lick Springs Hotel** in French Lick is said to be haunted by former owner Thomas Taggart. His spirit can be recognized by a noticeable mist and the smell of tobacco smoke, which he apparently favored. It is said that when hotel staff are busy, Taggart's spirit helps by opening and closing the elevator door, which usually requires pushing a button. The same elevator is said to run between floors by itself in the middle of the night. Taggart was not always so diligent; he apparently enjoyed riding his horse down hotel hallways or in the ballroom. Today, there are reports of the sound of a horse trotting down the halls or seeing the ghostly figure of a horse and rider in the ballroom. Hotel staffers say they have heard the sound of a party going on, complete with clinking china, party music, and festive voices in the ballroom when there is no one in the room. Less festive is a guestroom where a man committed suicide and his distraught bride killed herself in the bathtub. There are reports that the tub in that room has a recurring red stain that reappears whenever it is replaced. In addition, phone calls are made to the front desk from a room on the sixth floor, but when answered, there is no one on the line. It was even more remarkable when the phantom phone call came to the front desk and there was not even a phone installed in the room at the time.

The **James Allison Mansion** in Indianapolis was completed in 1913 as the dream home of businessman James Allison who became rich in the early aircraft and automobile industries. With Allison's wealth, his mansion lacked for nothing. It boasted a basement swimming pool, billiard room, elevator, sleeping porches (a pleasant amenity in the days before air conditioning), and a magnificent kitchen in which ice water could be pumped, also a rare luxury item in those days. Today, the mansion has an added feature: it appears to be haunted. With all his money, James Allison's life did not end happily. He divorced his long-time wife in order to marry his much younger secretary. Soon after his second marriage, he is said to have contracted a fatal case of pneumonia, dying at the age of fifty-six. The mansion was put up for sale, and is used as a small college. Since then, witnesses have reported the sound of cries coming from the basement, keys disappearing, tables and chairs being rearranged, voices in the attic, and objects that move by themselves or disappear. The apparition of a little girl who drowned in the basement pool can sometimes be seen. But in one of the strangest occurrences, the furniture and books in the college library have been completely rearranged. Perhaps it is the manifestation of James Allison himself, continuing to oversee his mansion from the afterlife since he did not get to enjoy it for long while he was alive.

The **Roads Hotel** in Atlanta, Indiana, was a historic spot even when it was being patronized by the likes of gangsters from the 1920s, such as Al Capone and John Dillinger. Built in 1893, it was a layover stop for the railroad that passed through the town's business district. Being on the line between Chicago and Indianapolis, the hotel had an unusually large number of comings and goings for a small town. The property was purchased by a man named Newton Roads who ran the hotel with his wife and family. First, his son was diagnosed with tuberculosis at age nineteen and confined to isolation in the hotel until he died. Then, Newton Roads's wife, stepmother, and Roads himself all died in the hotel. During the prohibition era of the 1920s, the hotel became a local brothel and a speakeasy. Today, some of the guests who visited the Roads Hotel have apparently never left. Witnesses have reported apparitions of men, women, and children, disembodied voices, doors that open and slam shut by themselves, and lights that turn on and off on their own. There are unexplained footsteps and shadows, what sounds like conversations from past guests, and a playful entity that chuckles when teasing the living for otherworldly entertainment.

The small, abandoned **Stepp Cemetery** near Bloomington, Indiana, is said to be one of the most haunted cemeteries in the state. Located in the Morgan-Monroe State Forest, it appears desolate and lonely, isolated at the end of a narrow dirt trail that leads into the wilderness. With only about two dozen old grave markers, the cemetery might have been forgotten if it had not found a kind of celebrity status by allegedly being haunted. The stories concern a ghostly woman in black who watches over a gravesite at the cemetery, seated on an old tree stump. She is said to be a young wife and mother whose husband was killed at work in a quarry accident. Her daughter was later killed in a car accident. Both were buried at Stepp Cemetery. Soon, the distraught woman began making nightly visits to their graves, sobbing and talking to her now-departed loved ones. After the woman died (some say by suicide), she too was buried at Stepp Cemetery and apparently saw no reason to discontinue her nightly visits to the old tree stump where she could sit and watch over the graves of her family. Visitors have reported the sounds of sobbing, but when police investigate, they find no one there, at least no one who is among the living.

The **Whispers Estate** in Mitchell, Indiana, received its name from the many reports by people who claim to have heard whispering coming from all directions in the building when it was operating as a bed-and-breakfast. Visitors to the estate have also reported apparitions, disembodied voices, doorknobs that jiggle, furniture that shakes, and unexplained odors. Built in 1899, the estate was home to a doctor and his wife who adopted three children. However, one little girl started a fire in the front parlor and died after being burned, after which the strange events at Whispers Estate began as her apparition was seen around the grounds of the estate. Soon after her death, the ten-month-old infant who was adopted by the couple was reported to have died in the master bedroom. Today, people who go to that room report the unexplained scent of baby powder and hearing the disembodied sound of a baby crying. Losing two of their children deeply affected the parents, with the mother developing a severe case of pneumonia shortly after the children's deaths. She died in the same room as her departed infant. Visitors today report hearing the sound of coughing and experiencing difficulty breathing as if there is a strong pressure on their chest.

FURTHER READING

Newman, Rich. *Haunted Bridges: Over 300 of America's Creepiest Crossings*. Woodbury, MN: Llewellyn Publications, 2016.

Thomas, Phyllis. *Indiana off the Beaten Path: A Guide to Unique Places*. Guilford, CT: Globe Pequot Press, 2012.

Willis, James A. *Haunted Indiana: Ghosts and Strange Phenomena of the Hoosier State*. Mechanicsburg, PA: Stackpole Books, 2012.

16

Iowa

The state of Iowa derives its name from the Ioway people, a Native American tribe who occupied the region at the time of European exploration. In the 1830s, Iowa's Native Americans were removed from the state that bears their name to reservations in Kansas and Nebraska; some later moved to Oklahoma to become the Iowa Tribe of Oklahoma.

The first known European explorers to document today's Iowa were Jacques Marquette and Louis Jolliet in 1673. According to Schwieder (1996), "At the time of the 1673 expedition, the future state of Iowa was unclaimed by any European power. English, French and Spanish settlements lay far to the north, east and south" (22).

France stepped into the breach, claiming Iowa until 1763 when, embroiled in the French and Indian War, ownership was transferred to France's ally, Spain. At that time, Iowa was part of a territory known as La Louisiane or Louisiana.

Spain's influence in Iowa was minor. French and British traders were licensed to establish trading posts where they dealt in furs. In 1800, Napoleon Bonaparte regained France's claim on La Louisiane through a treaty with Spain, which ended after America's Louisiana Purchase in 1803.

After settlers began arriving, Iowa was granted U.S. territorial status in 1838, with residents immediately aiming for statehood. In 1846, Iowa became the twenty-ninth state in the Union.

Today, Iowa is often named as one of the safest states to live. But that was not always the case. During the late 1800s, sparse law enforcement over long distances sometimes led to a free-for-all among criminals. The population of agricultural Iowa was isolated and spread out. Iowa's small towns with tiny banks proved irresistible to criminals. Banks were easily robbed and offered convenient escape.

In 1871, the notorious gang led by Jesse James was suspected in a bank robbery at Corydon, Iowa. The bank contacted Chicago's Pinkerton Detective Agency, marking the first involvement of the relentless detectives in pursuing the James gang.

In the 1930s, criminals continued to believe sleepy Iowa was ripe for the picking. John Dillinger, "Pretty Boy" Floyd, and the Clyde Barrow-Bonnie Parker gang all showed up to rob banks in Iowa. They had shootouts with local police, and hid out in small Iowa towns. In fact, it was at Dexter, Iowa, where the Barrow gang barely survived the shootout with Iowa law enforcement in 1933 that severely wounded Bonnie and Clyde, was fatal to Buck Barrow, and blinded Buck's wife Blanche, who was captured.

Long before Bonnie and Clyde, however, it became apparent that even peaceful Iowa was in need of jails.

The use of some sort of penal institutions as punishment for a crime dates back to well before the birth of Christ. Some ancient Greek philosophers like Plato considered the concept of trying to reform prisoners since imprisonment was generally used for those who could not afford to pay their fines.

Ancient Rome, as usual, spun what the Greeks had begun. Prisoners were housed in places, such as the basements of public buildings, metal cages, rock quarries, and the bottom of ships where they were chained to oars as galley slaves. One Roman prison was a dungeon located in a sewer beneath the city where prisoners were trapped in squalid conditions, awash in human waste.

Fast-forwarding to early America, there was increased popular resistance to public execution, torture, and the kind of "cruel and unusual punishment" that was prohibited by the Eighth Amendment to the U.S. Constitution. Still, some form of incarceration was needed for those convicted of committing a crime.

As peaceful Iowa was not immune to criminal activity, in 1885, residents of the town of Council Bluffs decided to experiment with a type of jail that they felt was not only safer for both jailers and prisoners but also cheaper for the frugal citizens of Council Bluffs to build. Jones and Coffey (2009) describe what came to be known as the **Squirrel Cage Jail** as a three-story rotating cell drum inside a cage with only one opening per floor, "[which] was hailed as an improvement over other jails of the period. And that thought will make you even more terrified if you choose to visit" (142).

The Squirrel Cage Jail, which was in continuous use until 1969, had a rotary or "Lazy Susan" design in which prisoners were housed in pie-shaped cells that were rotated with a crank inside a cage and centered around one opening. Only one jailer was necessary to oversee each of the three stories, with the levels housing over ninety prisoners apiece. This design narrowed it down to a single entrance and exit for the jail, providing what the designers called "maximum security with minimum jailer attention."

Officially known as the Pottawattamie County Jail, Iowa's Squirrel Cage was one of the eighteen revolving jails in the nation but was the only three-story unit ever built. With ten cells on each floor, a hand crank was needed to move about ninety thousand pounds of iron. When the ground settled due to its location atop a water table, the building would shift, the gears would go out of balance, and it was both difficult and dangerous to rotate. Arms and legs were lost when the "Lazy Susan" did not function well.

Today, the jail is a museum where the spirits of both prisoners and jailers are said to be confined. Reportedly, the shadowy ghost of a guard still wanders the halls. Disembodied footsteps are heard on unoccupied levels. Visitors report feelings of being watched or followed. Spirits are said to primarily be prisoners who died in the Squirrel Cage, although two of the stranger manifestations are the voice of a little girl and the presence of two ghost cats.

SOME OTHER REPORTEDLY HAUNTED PLACES IN IOWA

Local lore maintains that anyone who reaches out to touch the hand of the **Black Angel of Fairview Cemetery** in Council Bluffs will soon meet their doom. The bronze statue, officially called the Ruth Anne Dodge Memorial, was completed in 1918 to honor a local woman who, her daughters said, was visited in her dreams by an angel for three days prior to her death from cancer. The family hired a sculptor to cast a statue commemorating the angel. After the statue's dedication, local residents began reporting strange occurrences, including one claim in which the statue left its pedestal and floated above the cemetery grounds. The statue's kindly faced angel is also said to visit fresh graves at night, perhaps to welcome the new occupants. But other reports are darker, with one stating that children were observed walking behind the base of the statue before vanishing, never to be seen again. Others say anyone who looks into the angel's eyes at midnight will soon be dead. Incidentally, the statue's creator was American sculptor Daniel Chester French who said he considered Black Angel of Council Bluffs to be his greatest work. This was high praise considering that he was also the creator of the iconic marble statue of Abraham Lincoln at the Lincoln Memorial in Washington, D.C.

Iowa can boast not one but two Black Angel statues. The winged **Black Angel of Oakland Cemetery** in Iowa City looks somewhat less benign than its counterpart in Council Bluffs. The eerie statue by Mario Korbel was erected as a memorial to a local family. Since then, the statue has been associated with superstition and tales of the paranormal, being dubbed the "Angel of Death." Local lore maintains that staring directly at the statue at midnight will result in being fatally cursed. It is said that when the statue was officially installed in 1912, it was shimmering gold. But soon, the bright golden statue suddenly began to turn black, starting with the eyes. By the time the blackness had overtaken the angel's body, it seemed to stare menacingly at the cemetery. One local tale involved a young woman who defied the curse and kissed the feet of the statue during a full moon; within six months, the young woman was dead. Another tells of a skeptical man who visited the Black Angel with friends, touched the statue, and died on the spot of a massive heart attack. Paranormal investigators say they recorded ghostly voices at the statue as well as strange floating lights. One claimed to have captured temperature fluctuations with thermal cameras, indicating that the statue's temperature had risen dramatically during their investigation, which took place on a cold winter night.

Edinburgh Manor in Scotch Grove has a history of pain and despair dating from the 1800s to the time it closed in 2010. Those are a lot of years for a site to breed the kind of anguished spirits who do not tend to rest in peace. According to 1910's *History of Jones County*, as cited on the *Jones County IA GenWeb* website, the land was donated in 1840 to house the county "Poor Farm." In one memorable phrase, the description states that despite the county's policy not to provide a comfortable retreat for "the lazy, able-bodied, willingly dependent applicants of its charities" and cognizant that "the county is burdened with several who are incurably insane," an attempt would be made to treat those unfortunates humanely. People with disabilities were also housed at the Poor Farm, with an adjacent cemetery offering a final resting place for the eighty documented deaths that occurred at the facility. In 1910, the Poor Farm was torn down and Edinburgh Manor was built in its place for those with disabilities and extreme mental illness, as well as the elderly. A hundred years later it closed, and today there are reports of supernatural activity. Disembodied voices and whistling can be heard, with reports of plates flying across the room. There are claims of an evil spirit called the "Joker," who has been known to choke visitors. The atmosphere is made even more eerie by the fact that Edinburgh Manor was abandoned with its furnishings and personal belongings—even documents and patient records—still in place, as if its residents were expecting to return to find their beds still neatly made.

Dating back to the 1800s, **Malvern Manor** in Malvern, Iowa, started life as a comfortable, pleasant hotel catering to traveling salesmen disembarking from the nearby railway line. It ended in a far less benign manner. Today, it is available as a rental for an event or a private paranormal investigation. Even its asymmetrical appearance seems to put an observer off balance. Visitors have reported phenomena such as moans, orbs of light, sounds of footsteps and voices, unexplained shadows, flashlights that turn on and off by themselves, and the feeling of being watched or being touched when no one was nearby. It is even rumored that the Villisca ax murderer (see entry) may have stayed at Malvern Manor the night before the ghastly massacre. Some investigators have said that when a building has gone through many incarnations, it retains a type of energy, as if the spirits residing inside are fighting to have the building remembered as it was when they were alive. In the case of Malvern Manor, the rise of the automobile in the early twentieth century and the decline of railroads as the preferred transportation for traveling salesmen led to Malvern Manor being converted from a hotel into what was called a convalescent home where care was minimal at best. Residents suffered from various disabilities, with conditions ranging from alcoholism to schizophrenia, multiple personalities to self-mutilation. Abuse and neglect were said to run rampant, which is the main reason paranormal investigators believe the building is haunted by disturbed, tormented spirits. A particularly malevolent energy is often felt in the rooms below the attic where two patients resided before it was discovered that one spent years physically and sexually abusing the other.

The historic **Mason House Inn** at Keosauqua can boast several distinctions. Not only does it date back to 1846, it served as a station on the Underground Railroad to help escaping slaves and was also used as a hospital during the Civil War. It is known as being rich in paranormal activity, allegedly housing five separate spirits. But in a welcome departure from the dark side, the manifestations at the Mason House appear to be friendly. Three of the inn's previous owners died in the hotel, and may still be keeping an eye on the property. In Room 8, a floating head has been seen. There is also the ghost of a lady in a white nightgown and an old man who likes to stare at people before suddenly vanishing into thin air. Guests have reported seeing the apparition of a young boy in Room 5 who apparently likes to play tricks on people. One guest, a minister who was staying in Room 5, said that he felt his pajama shirt being tugged while he lay sleeping. He thought it was his wife, wanting him to switch over to the other side of the bed. But then he remembered that his wife did not come with him on that trip.

At the **Roseman Covered Bridge** in Winterset, which was originally built in 1883, area residents have reported strange, high-pitched noises, muffled laughter, unexplained yelling, and the sounds of wagon wheels crossing over the bridge's floorboards. Apparitions and a cold spot in the middle of the structure have also been reported. People walking their dogs across the bridge state that the hackles rise on the animal's back, as if sensing something it cannot see. In 1892, according to local legend, a Madison County jail escapee was cornered inside the covered bridge by law enforcement, with policemen at either end. Suddenly, they heard a bloodcurdling scream from the convict. Rushing inside the bridge to investigate, they discovered he was gone, having vanished into thin air. The escapee, who was never found, might have been comforted to know that it was determined that anyone capable of such a vanishing act must be innocent of all charges. Haunted or not, the fact that the bridge is located in Madison County, Iowa, might be of interest to alert readers. The Roseman Covered Bridge is the place that the hero of the romantic novel, *The Bridges of Madison County*, is seeking when he stops at a local woman's home for directions. It is also the spot where the heroine leaves him a note inviting him to dinner, a rendezvous which proves fateful. As the center point for the novel's story, if bridges could receive royalty checks, Roseman would no doubt qualify.

It may seem obvious that a place called the **Villisca Ax Murder House** would be home to supernatural activities. Often called "The Scariest Place in Iowa," visitors report banging sounds, a bedroom door opening and closing on its own, falling lamps, inexplicable cold spots, objects moving, the sound of voices and laughter from children when none are present, and unexplained sensations of being pinched or shoved. The house was "Exhibit A" in the horrific murder of an entire family that took place in the peaceful small town of Villisca during the summer of 1912, a bloodbath that remains unsolved to this day. Many people believe that the spirits of the murdered family may still remain in the house where they once lived and then tragically died, perhaps seeking justice for their slaughter a century ago. Reports state that one morning, eight bloody corpses were discovered in the house. The skulls of the victims were crushed with an ax. It was the J. B. Moore family, who were well-liked members of the community. They were found murdered in their beds, along with two overnight guests, children who had come home with them after a church program the night before and were houseguests of the Moore children. Along with parents Josiah and Sarah Moore, the victims' ages ranged from eleven to five. After the news of the massacre spread throughout the small town, friends and curiosity seekers descended on the Moore house, even taking souvenirs from the crime scene before Villisca's National Guard unit arrived to secure the home for state police investigators. Along with earning a spot in American crime history, the Moore house in Villisca also joined

Often called the scariest place in Iowa, the Villisca Ax Murder House sounds like it would be a natural home for the supernatural. It was the site of the horrific murder of an entire family in 1912, a bloodbath that remains unsolved. Many people believe the ghostly spirits of the murdered family still remain in the house where they tragically died, perhaps seeking justice for their slaughter a century ago. (Cjh Photography LLC/Dreamstime.com)

the roll of ghostly places. The house has been restored and the mystery remains inside its walls, from the identity of the murderer to how he was able to carry out his dark deeds without awakening the occupants of the house, and more to the point: why? Perhaps the ghosts of the Villisca Ax Murder House will someday share their secrets.

FURTHER READING

"County Poor Farm." *Jones County IA GenWeb.* 2015. http://iagenweb.org/jones/directories/PoorFarm.html

Jones, Eric, and Dan Coffey. *Iowa Curiosities: Quirky Characters, Roadside Oddities & Other Offbeat Stuff.* Guilford, CT: Globe Pequot Press, 2009.

Schwieder, Dorothy. *Iowa: The Middle Land.* Iowa City: University of Iowa Press, 1996.

17

Kansas

Kansas is often considered the quintessential middle-American state, with the line from *The Wizard of Oz*, "We're not in Kansas anymore," shorthand for leaving someplace familiar to find oneself in strange new surroundings. Like many states, Kansas is named after the Native Americans who had lived there, in this case the Kansa tribe.

Spanish conquistador Coronado explored the area in 1541, but the first documented European settlement was not until 1812, after most of Kansas was acquired by the United States in the Louisiana Purchase of 1803. The Santa Fe Trail crossed Kansas from 1821 to 1880, transporting goods and people whose wagon ruts are still visible in the prairie today.

After the Kansas-Nebraska Act was passed by the U.S. Congress in 1854, opening the area to increased settlement, Kansas became embroiled in the conflict over slavery. Both pro and antislavery settlers arrived, hoping to determine whether Kansas would be a free state or a slave state. As those forces violently collided, it became known as Bleeding Kansas.

In 1861, Kansas became the thirty-fourth state to join the Union, entering as a free state. After the Civil War, waves of immigrants turned the Kansas prairie into farmland. The state adopted the sunflower as its symbol. Miner (2002) states that while it may not be glamorous, the sunflower is cheerful and tenacious, adding that it "bespoke regional history that was not flashy but deep, enduring, and when familiar, inspiring" (15).

Many African Americans looked to Kansas as a home after the Civil War. Led by freedmen like Benjamin "Pap" Singleton, they began establishing black settlements in the state. Around the same time, the Chisholm Trail was opened, placing Kansas in the heart of the Wild West. In such Kansas towns as Abilene and Dodge City, legendary figures like Wyatt Earp, Wild Bill Hickok, and Bat Masterson served as lawmen.

In 1881, Kansas was the first U.S. state to adopt a constitutional amendment prohibiting alcoholic beverages. State prohibition lasted well into the twentieth century, not being repealed until 1948.

In other high-minded endeavors, Kansans placed an emphasis on education. In rural areas, where the population was sparse, local libraries allowed young people to be exposed to the wider world through books.

Whether privately owned or public, a library is a collection of materials that can be read for enjoyment and/or sources of information, either studied for reference onsite or available on loan. Libraries can range in size from a few bookshelves to several million items.

Centuries before the birth of Christ, libraries were known in classical Greece. But the greatest library of the ancient world was the one at Alexandria, Egypt, where tens of thousands of scrolls were said to be accidentally burned by Julius Caesar during the days of the Roman Empire.

According to author Susan Orlean (2018), "In the library, time is dammed up—not just stopped but saved" (11). The loss of the library at Alexandria, as well as library or museum fires in the present day, can result in irreplaceable losses.

Whether in ancient or modern times, public libraries usually also provide the services of librarians. Traditionally, these people can easily find and organize necessary materials, as well as interpret the informational needs of patrons. Librarians could be called the human forerunners of Google.

Libraries were highly valued by one somewhat unlikely source, a man who was often called a nineteenth-century "robber baron," industrialist Andrew Carnegie. As a young Scottish immigrant working in the factories of Pittsburgh, Pennsylvania, Carnegie borrowed books from the personal library of his employer, who shared his collection with workers. Carnegie later wrote of the great esteem he felt for the employer who had provided that opportunity despite critics who said laborers should *not* be entitled to books or the chance to improve themselves.

After Carnegie indeed improved himself by becoming a multimillionaire, he set about funding libraries across America. His formula would today be called a matching grant. By requiring some local funds, he felt it showed a community commitment to their library.

Starting in 1883 near his adopted hometown of Pittsburgh, Carnegie funded about thirty-five hundred libraries in American cities and towns before the last grant was made in 1919, the year of his death.

In Kansas, fifty-nine Carnegie libraries were built in towns ranging alphabetically from Abilene to Yates Center. One of these was the **Hutchinson Public Library** in Hutchinson, Kansas. The project was initiated in 1901 by the local women's club, which had collected about five hundred books to donate. They set up a temporary library facility before contacting Andrew Carnegie in 1902. He responded with a gift of $15,000 (almost $450,000 in 2017 dollars). In 1916, Carnegie donated $15,000 more for an addition to the building.

Today, the Hutchinson Public Library reveres two names as a special part of its history: the first is of course Andrew Carnegie. The second is a woman who was an essential part of the library's operation not only for most of her life but also apparently in the afterlife.

Ida Day Holzapfel served as head librarian from 1915 to 1925 (when she left to attend college and get married) and again from 1947 to 1954. She ran the library with rigorousness worthy of an army drill sergeant. She developed programs not only within the library, such as modernizing its cataloging system, but also mobilized books for soldiers during World War I and initiated an outreach program for shut-ins.

It was said that her employees were afraid of her, especially when committing infractions like disrupting the silence of the library.

Ida died within a year of resigning, but apparently felt her work was not finished. Heitz (1997) declares that not long after Ida's death, former coworkers "began reporting strange incidents, sounds, and even ghostly apparitions around the library" (27). One young librarian was humming while shelving documents in the basement when she came face to face with the apparition of a stern-looking old woman who emerged from the shadows to challenge her by demanding, "What are you doing?" Perhaps it was the humming that irritated Ida's ghost.

SOME OTHER REPORTEDLY HAUNTED PLACES IN KANSAS

Some might say there are bound to be interesting stories involving a place that was built by a colorfully named character like the (self-titled) Colonel Napoleon Bonaparte Brown of Concordia, Kansas. In the early 1900s, Brown, a wealthy local banker, announced that he would build a grand opera house for the community. He followed through, and after the formal opening of Concordia's **Brown Grand Theatre** in 1907, it was said to be the most elegant theater between Kansas City and Denver. His son Earl Van Dorn Brown became the theater manager. With Earl's skillful management and Concordia's location on the railroad line, renowned acting troupes and orchestras from around the nation were booked at the theater. The theater thrived until Napoleon Brown died in 1910, and the following year, Earl died after surgery for gall stones in a Kansas City hospital. The local newspaper reported the tragedy, stating that Earl, at age forty, was in the prime of his life. Earl apparently thought so too, and may have returned to oversee the theater that bears his family's name into the present time. Today, there are reports of Earl's apparition being spotted in the theater's balcony, dressed in his finest. There have also been claims of the shadow of a person walking on the stage toward a nearby utility room, as well as a disembodied voice with no apparent source. Although the theater went into decline after the deaths of the Browns and the rise of motion pictures, the community rallied to restore the playhouse and held its grand reopening in 1980. There was a restaging of *The Vanderbilt Cup*, the first play that was presented in 1907. According to the theater, there were three ladies present in the front row who had attended the theater's opening seventy-three years before. With those ties to the past, the familiar figure of Earl Brown's ghost may have been in the audience as well.

The **Brown Mansion** is located in Coffeyville, Kansas. Its owners were presumably not related to the Brown family of Concordia, although they were contemporaries and shared a degree of tragedy. The ornate, three-story Brown Mansion was completed in 1906 to serve as the family home of wealthy William Pitzer Brown, who had gotten rich in lumber, mining, and having the good fortune

The elegant Brown Grand Theatre in Concordia, Kansas, was apparently too pleasant for its owner to leave. Dying unexpectedly after routine surgery in 1910, Earl Van Dorn Brown, age 40, was said to be in the prime of life. His apparition has been spotted in the balcony dressed in formal clothing, apparently overseeing the playhouse that still bears his family's name. (Photograph taken by Paul McDonald)

to discover one of the largest natural gas wells in the country. As is often the case, the mansion came with all the amenities money could buy, including some that were ahead of their time such as an alarm system, elevator, and a walk-in "ice box." Many of the features, like steps, were designed to accommodate Brown's petite wife, Nancy, who stood under five feet tall. Of their five children, two died at birth. One of the surviving children later died from pneumonia at age four and yet another died from complications of diabetes when he was eleven. The last survivor, Violet Elizabeth Brown, married at age nineteen, but divorced shortly after their only child died. She married a second time and divorced again. In the 1930s, Violet moved back to the family home to take care of her parents, who left the mansion to Violet when they died. In 1970, Violet sold the mansion to the Coffeyville Historical Society to use as a museum. She took only what she would need at the nursing home where she lived until her death in 1973. All other family possessions were left in the house. There were soon reports that the mansion was haunted, with observers seeing strange glowing green lights around the mansion grounds, even after electric power had been turned off. Ghostly presences in the mansion have been reported, thought to be Mr. and Mrs. Brown, the manifestations of their children, and a servant named Charlie. Witnesses have claimed to hear the sound of crying, as well as to smell pipe smoke as favored by Mr. Brown.

The legendary **Fort Leavenworth** in Leavenworth, Kansas, is said to be one of the most haunted military bases in the United States. Established in 1827, it is the oldest active U.S. Army post west of the Mississippi River and has had a lot of years to accrue its share of ghostly manifestations. There are said to be at least nine spirits haunting the base. One of the most poignant is Catherine Sutler whose family was on their way west around 1880 when they made camp at Fort Leavenworth in early winter. Catherine sent her children, Ethan and Mary, to collect firewood, but they never returned. Catherine refused to join her husband when he left, staying at Fort Leavenworth in hopes of finding her children. All winter, she walked through the snow calling for Ethan and Mary until she contracted pneumonia and died. Since then, residents have reported seeing the apparition of a woman in 1800s clothing walking among the Leavenworth National Cemetery's tombstones on the coldest nights carrying a lantern, still calling "Ethan" and "Mary." There is also a house on the base with one of the stranger manifestations. She has been described by residents as a middle-aged woman in a black dress who lives in the house's attic, where unexplained footsteps can be heard. One night, the family was surprised to see this matronly apparition washing their dinner dishes at the kitchen sink. One of their children said that a "nice lady" would read stories to him at bedtime, after which the parents found a book in the child's room that didn't belong to them and which they had never seen before. They would sometimes feel her presence while walking up or down the stairs, brushing against their arms and leaving a cold spot where she touched them. While the manifestation apparently loved the family, she had little use for the children's grandmothers and babysitters, who would sometimes feel themselves being pushed out of the upstairs nursery by unseen hands, or find the children's beds neatly remade after they had turned down the covers for bedtime. There are also reports of other hauntings in base housing at Fort Leavenworth, such as ghostly men in Army uniforms appearing in the mirror, a dark-haired man in the bathroom shaving with an old-fashioned razor, the unexplained sound of a harmonica playing, and a ghost who likes to ride horses through the old infantry barracks. They all appear to be friendly spirits, but the one most residents really want to encounter is the ghostly Mrs. Doubtfire who does the dishes and helps with the kids.

There are those who say that if the **Stull Cemetery** in Stull, Kansas, is haunted, it is not so much the work of the devil as efforts of students from the University of Kansas. Nonetheless, any spot that has become known in American popular culture as one of the "Seven Gateways to Hell" deserves special mention. Stull is a tiny unincorporated community that lies near Lawrence, home of the University of Kansas. The tiny settlement, named after its only postmaster, Sylvester Stull, was founded in 1857. At its height, the population of Stull barely reached fifty people. For such a small settlement, Stull has become infamous. Stull suffered a misfortune in the late 1800s when hopes for a railroad coming through town were dashed, extinguishing any dreams of growth for the community. Even the post office for which the town was named shut down in 1903. However, neither explained what happened to Stull starting in November 1974 with a post-Halloween issue of *The University Daily Kansan*, the student newspaper of the University of Kansas. With a headline stating "Legend of Devil Haunts Tiny Town," the student-written story began with a reference to a movie, *The Exorcist*, which had been popular that year. The article cited alleged legends of Stull's diabolical supernatural happenings, claiming that the devil appeared at Stull Cemetery on Halloween and the spring equinox. No confirmation is available as to whether the story was completely fabricated as a Halloween ruse, if the writer was reporting on what was already local lore, or indeed why Stull was singled out. But even before the days of the Internet, the rumor took hold that the Stull Cemetery was one of the "Seven Gateways to Hell," and that the nearby ruin of the abandoned (and now demolished) Evangelical Emmanuel Church was possessed by the devil. Since then, trespassers have descended on the cemetery, vandalizing it, and even stealing tombstones. The tale of Stull Cemetery has been spread in rock music, on television shows, and in horror movies. There are those who say that if Stull Cemetery is indeed haunted by anything at all, it is by a student prank that went viral before the word was invented.

Across America, scores of small local grocery stores have been supercentered out of existence, which is haunting to some. The now-empty **Wilbur's Grocery** in Towanda, Kansas, was a recent victim of that fate, but not before it achieved a level of fame for having ghosts among the groceries. Towanda is a rural community of fewer than fifteen hundred people located west of El Dorado, Kansas. Locals say that Wilbur's Grocery was housed in a structure that was one of the oldest buildings in town. Before becoming a grocery store, they say the building originally served as an orphanage for the county and a shelter for unwed mothers, which may have engendered its share of sad, restless spirits. Perhaps, like their human counterparts, the spirits did not leave because they had nowhere else to go. After becoming a grocery store, employees reported that they smelled the aroma of fresh coffee brewing when there was none, objects moving on their own, unexplained cold spots, and even being touched and having their hair mussed by an unseen presence. Grocery carts were reported to have moved around on their own, and potato chips (literally) flew off the shelves. Mops and brooms were found lying in a pile on the floor, and employees' aprons were constantly being mysteriously untied. After doors to the freezer were found open after being closed for the night, employees placed heavy objects in front of the freezer doors to keep them solidly shut. The next morning, they would find that the freezer doors were open and the heavy objects had been moved out of the way. However, even the intervention of spirits from the supernatural realm were not enough to save Wilbur's Grocery from closing in the face of modern-day progress.

FURTHER READING

Heitz, Lisa Hefner. *Haunted Kansas*. Lawrence: University Press of Kansas, 1997.

Miner, Craig. *Kansas: The History of the Sunflower State*. Lawrence: University Press of Kansas, 2002.

Orlean, Susan. *The Library Book*. New York: Simon & Schuster, 2018.

18

Kentucky

Kentucky is said by some historians to have been named for the Kentucky River whose name itself probably came from an Iroquois term referring to a meadow. If that meadow was covered with grass in a distinctive shade of blue, it would account for Kentucky's nickname, "The Bluegrass State." While bluegrass is actually green, in the spring its buds appear blue when allowed to grow to its natural height of two to three feet, which it rarely did after white settlers arrived.

In the late 1600s, the French explorer La Salle claimed all of the Mississippi River Valley for France, including today's Kentucky. By the late 1700s, white settlers heading west into Kentucky clashed with Native Americans who were already there. In 1786, George Rogers Clark led more than one thousand two hundred armed Americans to fight the Shawnee. Harrison and Klotter (1997) state that although the Shawnee probably numbered no more than four thousand when white settlement began, the Native Americans were a formidable threat to Kentucky settlers until 1795, adding a childcare note: "Many a pioneer housewife cautioned a crying child, 'Hush or the Shawnee will get you'" (9).

In 1776, the area of Virginia beyond the Appalachian Mountains was known as Kentucky County. In 1792, Kentucky became the fifteenth state to join the Union. However, like bluegrass not actually being blue, Kentucky is not technically a state. It joins Massachusetts, Pennsylvania, and Virginia in being constituted as a "commonwealth." While equal to an American state, the traditional use of the term "commonwealth," derived from English common law, symbolically identifies it as a government based on the common consent of the people.

Whatever its status, Kentucky has become familiar around the world for its Kentucky Derby thoroughbred horse race and the state's association with Kentucky Fried Chicken franchises that can be found in countries from Azerbaijan to Zimbabwe.

Of greater interest to some is the fact that Kentucky produces 95 percent of the world's supply of bourbon. It is said that there are more barrels of bourbon being aged in Kentucky than the state's entire population.

Kentucky is the birthplace of bourbon, which is made primarily from corn and is the only native spirit of the United States, as declared by the U.S. Congress. Bourbon must contain a minimum of 51 percent corn and must be aged in charred oak barrels, giving bourbon its warm reddish-copper color.

Bourbon has been distilled in the United States since the 1700s. Distilling was most likely brought to present-day Kentucky by settlers from the British Isles. The exact inspiration for the whiskey's name is unclear, although it ultimately evolves from a reference to the Bourbon dynasty of France. Some historians link it to the large western Virginia county that was founded by settlers moving west and named after the French royal family in 1785. This region included a number of modern-day Kentucky counties, including the current Bourbon County. It became part of the Bluegrass State when Kentucky separated from Virginia in 1792.

The standard usage of the term "bourbon" for the alcoholic beverage has been traced to the 1820s, and to this day, it is strongly associated with Kentucky. However, by that time, distilling "liquid gold" almost derailed the new nation of the United States due to the Whiskey Rebellion.

The Whiskey Rebellion was a tax protest from 1791 to 1794 during George Washington's presidency. As the first tariff levied on a domestic product, in 1791, a whiskey tax was imposed by the federal government, then in its infancy. It was intended to generate revenue to pay for the country's Revolutionary War debts.

Farmers of the western frontier, far away from the East Coast establishment, were accustomed to distilling their surplus crops into whiskey. In some cases, whiskey often served as a mode of trade for the cash-poor farmers. They resisted the tax, feeling that as war veterans, they had fought for the principles of the American Revolution, in particular, against taxation without representation.

Protesters refused to pay the tax, sometimes using violence to attack federal revenue collectors. In response, President George Washington himself led an army to suppress the rebellion.

Kentucky was found to be especially resistant to paying the tax. Scores of Kentucky distillers were convicted of violating the tax law. Although the power (and army) of the federal government proved stronger than the scattered militias of rural farmers, bad feeling was instilled in America's western settlers against the central government after the Whiskey Rebellion was essentially defeated in 1794.

The whiskey tax was repealed in the early 1800s during the Jefferson administration. However, the conflict contributed to the formation of divisive political parties and a mindset of Westerners versus Easterners, which led to the rise of populists like Andrew Jackson.

According to Hogeland (2010), "What people in the western backcountry recognized, and most Congressmen lacked the expertise to understand, were mechanisms embedded in the tax for keeping wealth in the hands of the few while denying western laborers and small farmers their last, slim chances for economic opportunity" (28).

Another blow to distillers by the federal government came in the twentieth century with the enactment of Prohibition. One of those affected was today's **Buffalo Trace Distillery** in Frankfort, Kentucky. According to the company, there was a working distillery of some type on its current property since 1787. It managed to

In 1791, the Whiskey Rebellion almost derailed the new nation of the United States, requiring President George Washington himself to suppress the uprising. With a working distillery on its property since 1787, Buffalo Trace Distillery in Frankfort, Kentucky, has a long history that may attract spirits not found in barrels. Shadowy figures are said to generate cold spots, phantom footsteps, and unexplained noises. (Volgariver/Dreamstime.com)

stay afloat during Prohibition by being granted one of the rare permits to make a small amount of whiskey for "medicinal purposes."

With its long history, the distillery has attracted spirits that may not be found in barrels. An apparition of the long-dead company president Albert Blanton has been seen around the property, generating cold spots, phantom footsteps in the warehouse, shadowy figures, and strange, unexplained noises. Two male paranormal investigators reported having their bottoms pinched by an unseen hand.

Brown (2009) says that while other states have their mysteries as well, "the dark side of the Bluegrass State seems particularly dark" (2). When people are outnumbered by barrels of bourbon, anything is possible.

SOME OTHER REPORTEDLY HAUNTED PLACES IN KENTUCKY

The website for **Bobby Mackey's Music World** in Wilder, Kentucky, includes the cordial invitation, "Come for the Ghosts and Stay for the Music!" Often called the most haunted nightclub in America, its life as a roadhouse was preceded by serving as a slaughterhouse. A well in the basement was used to dispose of animal blood and remains. Even after the slaughterhouse closed down in the 1890s, it is said that the well continued its use as a ghastly repository. Supposedly, the basement was used for satanic rites, with the well hiding the remains of small animals used as a "sacrifice." Those rituals became public knowledge in a sensational trial during 1896 in which two men were accused of murdering a young woman whose body was cut up. Her head was never found and was said to have ended up in the well. However, the victim's long, luxurious blond hair was found in the suitcase of one of the accused. The abandoned slaughterhouse was eventually torn down and a roadhouse was constructed on the site, becoming a popular prohibition-era speakeasy and casino. It is said that the owner's pregnant daughter, distraught over her father having her lover killed, took her own life in the basement. In 1978, Bobby Mackey, a popular local musician, purchased the building to turn it into a country bar. Soon, patrons and employees began reporting phenomena, such as lights turning on and off by themselves, securely locked doors becoming unlocked, an unplugged jukebox that started playing by itself, objects that moved around on their own, a feeling of being grabbed, the sound of disembodied voices and laughter, and the apparition of a headless female in turn-of-the-century clothing that was often accompanied by the unexplained scent of roses, said to have been a favorite scent of the long-dead decapitated blond woman. The current website says, "Country Music Lives On" at Bobby Mackey's. So, apparently, do other things.

Cave Hill Cemetery in Louisville is the final resting place for such colorful personalities as boxer Muhammad Ali and Kentucky Fried Chicken's Colonel Harland Sanders, neither of whom necessarily account for the strange occurrences at the cemetery's abandoned eastern portion. Dating to the 1840s, it is one of the oldest graveyards in Louisville. It was noteworthy for allowing cremations before they were generally accepted, as well as being one of the first in the nation to allow the burial of people of different races on the same property. However, it was discovered that bodies, including infants, were being buried in graves that were already occupied by corpses, with family plots having been resold and reused multiple times. There have also been newspaper reports of headstones and bodies being moved without informing the families of the deceased, resulting in mismatched bodies and headstones that make it impossible to know where a loved one actually rests. In some cases, bodies were buried within a foot of the surface. Today, there are reports of phantom footsteps and unexplained sounds in the cemetery, as well as ghostly orbs of light that are said to have both appeared at night and been captured on film. Even though ornate tombstones and statues stand guard, the spirits of the dead, so close to the surface, are said to wander.

The small community of **Camp Taylor** southeast of Louisville was once a massive military post named after Army General and twelfth U.S. president Zachary Taylor (not to be confused with Fort Zachary Taylor at Key West, Florida, which was opened in 1971). Kentucky's Camp Taylor opened in 1917 as a World War I training base, the largest of more than a dozen such camps across the United States. The camp held more than two thousand buildings, and housed over forty thousand troops at any given time. Young soldiers, many just off the farm, wrote home about Camp Taylor's good accommodations and hot meals. But within a year of its opening, the boys stationed at Camp Taylor ran out of luck even before being shipped overseas. The deadly 1918 influenza outbreak killed almost one thousand soldiers at Camp Taylor in just three weeks, putting over ten thousand in the hospital. Many previously healthy young men died within hours of going on sick calls. Reports said that in some of the buildings, bodies were stacked from floor to ceiling. Within three years, military operations were moved to what became the nearby Fort Knox. Camp Taylor was closed and the buildings torn down, with the wood from the structures being repurposed into constructing nearby houses, which some say is the source of paranormal activity. Perhaps some of the departed spirits within the buildings came with the neighborhood. There are claims that phantom soldiers can be seen in the community today, earnestly marching in formation down the residential streets. Camp Taylor may also live not only in the spirit realm but also in the literary world. Author F. Scott Fitzgerald was stationed at the camp in 1918, drawing inspiration for his classic novel *The Great Gatsby* in which heroine Daisy Buchanan resided in Louisville.

Built in 1886, the **Kentucky State Penitentiary** (KSP) overlooking the town of Eddyville is the oldest prison in the state and is considered an architectural work of art that belies its purpose. Also known as the "Castle on the Cumberland," it was constructed as an Italianate medieval fortress that was not only meant to house the prisoners inside but to be a warning to those outside: choose a life of crime and here you'll do the time. By 1889, just three years after opening, the penitentiary was overcrowded. Until modern initiatives toward more humane conditions, there were no attempts toward rehabilitation at KSP, only appallingly unsanitary conditions, disease, poor food, and a high death toll, of which only a part was from legal executions. Inmates died after suffering extreme isolation, hard labor, and being brutalized by vicious fellow inmates. Children who stole as much as a loaf of bread were housed within the general population, as did hungry locals who tried their hand at bootlegging during Prohibition in the 1920s and the Great Depression of the 1930s. The ball and chain was still used on offenders until the 1940s, the same decade when the prison began to transfer inmates under age eighteen to a reformatory. With the penitentiary housing Kentucky's male death row inmates, executions were not unusual; the gallows in the prison yard served as a continual reminder. Some say hauntings can occur where there is despair, fear, pain, and death in tragic circumstances. Some of the troubled souls at KSP may have been transformed into dark spirits whose manifestations have been reported by modern guards and inmates alike. Reports include a dark spectral "energy" without cohesive shape but visible nonetheless, alternating with a pale streak of light. There are also claims of seeing bluish-white orbs and unexplained smoke or vapor. Some have heard the clank of leg irons, disembodied voices in unoccupied cells, footsteps in empty corridors, screams, and the sound of children crying. Perhaps some spirits remained at KSP after their human sentence ended, one way or the other.

Liberty Hall in Frankfort was carved out of the Kentucky wilderness in 1796. However, the four-acre estate with magnificent gardens was never a humble log cabin. Its owner, John Brown, was one of Kentucky's first senators. The plans for the stately Georgian mansion were designed by Thomas Jefferson, with whom Brown had studied law. The Brown family hosted the social and political elite of the new American nation, such as President James Monroe and future presidents Andrew Jackson and Zachary Taylor. With all that history, the mansion is today called a "living museum of Kentucky history" and is not without visits from the *un*-living. Several spirits, in particular, continue to reside at Liberty Hall. One, the elderly Margaret Varick, is also known as the Gray Lady. After traveling eight hundred miles over rough roads from New York to a family funeral at Liberty Hall in 1817, she died of a heart attack in an upstairs bedroom soon after arriving. She was first buried in the garden, but it is said that her body was later moved to a location that has been lost to time after the family plot was transferred to a larger cemetery in Frankfort. Although she was lost, Mrs. Varick's restless spirit is said to be kindly and calm, wandering the house and grounds, opening and closing doors, playing music on an unwound music box, sometimes gently stroking the faces of sleeping guests, and wandering in apparitions wearing gray. Other manifestations who roam the grounds at Liberty Hall include the apparition of a War of 1812 soldier dressed in a British uniform who has been reported gazing into ground floor windows with a forlorn expression on his face. In addition, there is a beautiful young opera star who visited the mansion in 1805. During a party in her honor, she stepped outside to view the gardens in the moonlight but abruptly vanished, never to be seen again.

Built in 1779, the **Old Talbott Tavern** in Bardstown is said to be the oldest tavern in Kentucky, as well as the oldest western stagecoach stop in early America. It was the western end of the coach road between Pennsylvania and Virginia, and attracted a good number of guests, including some who may have never completely checked out. According to legend, while in exile from France, King Louis Phillippe wished to see the New World. He and a small entourage stayed at the tavern in 1797. During that time, an apparently artistically minded member of the group was reported to have painted murals on the plaster walls. In the late 1800s, outlaw Jesse James is said to have stayed at the inn while in Kentucky during one of the times when he was in hiding from the law. The legend is that after being "over-served" in the tavern, a drunken Jesse went upstairs to sleep it off. Thinking he saw something moving, either an intruder in his room or the birds in the murals, he started shooting, leaving behind about a dozen bullet holes in the wall that can be seen today. Perhaps he enjoyed his experience at the tavern so much that his spirit returned, appearing around the building. Another reported visitor from the spirit world is called the "Lady in White" who, like James, also shows up in apparitions, although she is apparently unarmed.

FURTHER READING

Brown, Alan. *Haunted Kentucky: Ghosts and Strange Phenomena of the Bluegrass State.* Mechanicsburg, PA: Stackpole Books, 2009.

Harrison, Lowell, and James Klotter. *A New History of Kentucky.* Lexington: University Press of Kentucky, 1997.

Hogeland, William. *The Whiskey Rebellion: George Washington, Alexander Hamilton, and the Frontier Rebels Who Challenged America's Newfound Sovereignty.* New York: Simon & Schuster, 2010.

19

Louisiana

Louisiana is said to be the most "foreign" of all American states. Part of that exoticism comes from its colorful past when ownership of the region alternated between France and Spain before becoming the centerpiece of the greatest land deal in U.S. history, the Louisiana Purchase.

Louisiana is also notable for its rich mix of cultures, including African, Cajun, Creole, French, Haitian, Native American, and Spanish. According to Wall et al. (2014), this blend gives Louisiana "a multicultural diversity and variety perhaps unequaled in telling the story of any other state" (11).

Native Americans were the state's first inhabitants, having lived there for thousands of years and producing the earliest mound complex in North America. The first documented European incursion into the region of Louisiana came in 1543 when Spaniard Hernando de Soto followed the Mississippi River to the Gulf of Mexico. After that, Spanish interest in Louisiana faded.

In the late 1600s, France would lay claim to a vast region of North America stretching from the Gulf of Mexico to Canada. In 1682, the French explorer La Salle claimed the territory drained by the Mississippi River for France, naming it La Louisiane after the then-current French King Louis XIV. The name would ultimately be Anglicized into "Louisiana."

The first permanent settlement, Fort Maurepas, was founded in 1699 by Pierre d'Iberville. The town of Natchitoches, established in 1714, became the oldest permanent European settlement in today's state of Louisiana. When it was determined that mass cultivation of sugar cane and cotton could become cash crops, African slaves were imported to do the grueling work in the fields.

Europe's Seven Years' War was called the French and Indian War in North America where it was fought between 1754 and 1763. With the French defeated by England, France's territorial claim to La Louisiane was transferred to Spain. In 1765, during Spanish rule, thousands of French-speaking refugees from the eastern Canadian region called Acadia were expelled to Louisiana. Later, when the word "Acadians" was Americanized, they became known as "Cajuns."

In 1800, the imperial pendulum would swing again. Napoleon Bonaparte of France secretly reacquired the Louisiana Territory from Spain. When Napoleon needed money to fight another war, Louisiana was offered for sale to the newly created United States of America. U.S. president Thomas Jefferson was an advocate of western expansion, and the sale was enacted by statute on October 31, 1803. For less than three cents an acre, eventually all or parts of fifteen American states were formed out of the region in what became known as the Louisiana Purchase, including Louisiana itself.

In 1812, Louisiana joined the Union as the eighteenth state. Stemming from its French and Spanish past, Louisiana is the only U.S. state whose political subdivisions are derived from the Catholic Church, the predominant religion of both France and Spain. In answer to the trivia question, "How many counties are there in Louisiana?" the answer is: *None*. In Louisiana, they are called "parishes."

Filan (2011) says that starting in colonial days, "A shortage of labor in Louisiana encouraged the importation of slaves, and the shortage of eligible French women led to mixed marriages and a growing mulatto population ... and encouraged the cultural exchanges that later became New Orleans voodoo" (11). Since many enslaved people came from the same region of West Africa, as well as those arriving from Haiti, they had a shared culture of spiritual folkways rooted in a belief system called "Vodun."

In French Louisiana, voodoo mingled with Catholicism and was often kept underground as a faith practice until the coming of twentieth century technology when voodoo exploded into mainstream consciousness. A popular 1932 feature film called *White Zombie* portrayed voodoo as an exotic (and erotic) tradition that included such habits as hexing enemies by sticking pins into dolls.

While there were leading male practitioners like "Doctor John," who were called voodoo kings, it was their female counterparts, termed voodoo queens, who caught the popular imagination. Among those powerful women was the most eminent voodoo queen, Marie Laveau, who lived between 1801 and 1881. It was said that along with attracting slaves and people in lower economic classes to her practice, wealthy businessmen and powerful politicians consulted with her before making important decisions.

Marie Catherine Laveau was a free woman of color who was of African, French, and Native American descent. Also being Roman Catholic, she encouraged her followers to attend Mass and incorporated some Catholic elements into her practice of voodoo. Clients came to her for voodoo dolls, potions, and amulets, which are believed to bring good luck to the wearer and/or protect them from misfortune. According to Ward (2004), Marie "did what she had to do, what she knew how to do, to fulfill Voodoo's obligation, to earn Voodoo's greatest gift" (92).

Even after her death in the late 1800s, Marie Laveau remains an influential figure in New Orleans. Gamblers are said to shout her name when throwing dice. The **Marie Laveau Gravesite** attracts tourists as well as people who believe in voodoo, praying to her spirit to ask for favors and to offer gifts. Madame Laveau may also continue to carry out her busy schedule, with multiple sightings of her apparition being reported.

Even after her death in the 1800s, voodoo practitioner Marie Laveau is an influential figure. Generally believed to be buried in a crypt at Saint Louis Cemetery No. 1 in New Orleans, visitors pray to her spirit and offer gifts. The apparition of Madame Laveau has also been said to appear around the cemetery, the oldest in New Orleans. (Karen Foley/Dreamstime.com)

Marie Laveau is generally believed to have been buried in a crypt at Saint Louis Cemetery No. 1 in New Orleans. Created in 1789, it is the oldest cemetery in New Orleans and is located near the city's old section, the French Quarter. Today, visitors must be accompanied by a licensed tour guide to what has been called one of the most haunted burial sites in America. Saint Louis Cemetery No. 1 occupies a small area but is said to be the final resting place for tens of thousands of the city's dead. Perhaps because of crowded conditions below, many of the deceased are thought to roam aboveground.

The most distinctive apparition is of voodoo queen Marie Laveau. But another ghostly wanderer is said to be the entity of Henry Vignes who appears to unsuspecting visitors as a full-body apparition, sometimes tapping them politely on the shoulder, looking for his family's lost tomb. Only once was he said to be cranky, insisting, "I need to rest!"

Another is the entity of a young man named Alphonse who will take a person's hand into his ice cold one and ask for help in going to his home. He is said to appear lonely, although sometimes Alphonse has been seen carrying flowers and vases taken from other vaults, which is not a way to win friends.

At Saint Louis Cemetery No. 1, visitors have also claimed to see the phantoms of Civil War soldiers and what may have been victims of the frequent yellow fever epidemics that killed thousands in New Orleans.

With the Louisiana Purchase enacted on October 31, 1803—Halloween—hauntings may be business as usual in the state that bears its name.

SOME OTHER REPORTEDLY HAUNTED PLACES IN LOUISIANA

The ghosts who frequent the upscale **Arnaud's Restaurant** in New Orleans are as classy as the establishment itself, which is to say *very much so*. The restaurant's Richelieu Bar area dates back to the 1700s while the restaurant's famed dining room was created in 1918 by a Frenchman, Arnaud Cazenave, who is said to appear in the main dining room dressed in his tuxedo. Moving through the crowd, Arnaud smiles at his guests and seems to be a positive energy moving around the room, although he will tastefully disappear when approached. Some diners have reported seeing a woman in a hat who casually strolls down a hallway before disappearing into a wall where the entrance to a staircase had once stood, no doubt at the time of her earthly tenure. Some believe this ghost to be Arnaud's daughter Germaine, who reportedly also appears in the restaurant's museum area near a display of her Carnival costumes. After hours, the Richelieu Room, the restaurant's bar, is the scene of ghostly well-dressed gentlemen enjoying themselves, although they bring about a noticeable, unexplained drop in the temperature. All of the spirits at Arnaud's are said to be friendly, except for their inadvertent side effect of sometimes surprising the serving staff and causing them to drop their trays.

The **Calcasieu Parish Courthouse** in Lake Charles, Louisiana, was the scene of a sensational courtroom drama in the 1940s with the accused reportedly still in the building, even after being executed. After having three separate trials, Toni Jo Henry became the first and only female to die in Louisiana's electric chair. She was kept during trial in a holding cell in the Calcasieu Courthouse and was executed in the building in 1942. Jailers think Toni Jo's spirit is still on the premises, locking doors, turning on electronic filing systems, and whispering or talking aloud for guards to hear. In the 1940s, Louisiana's electric chair was transported from parish to parish to perform the executions. Thus, the electrocution would be carried out in the courthouse/jail of the locality where the condemned had been convicted. Toni Jo was convicted of cruelly murdering a driver who had given her a lift. She wanted his car so she could help break her boyfriend out of prison where he was being held for murder. After being captured and convicted, the date was set for her execution. Her hair was cut very short to the scalp. As the electric chair did its work, the lights dimmed before growing bright again. Witnesses were overcome by the smell of burning hair and cheap perfume, an odor that is still noticeable when the long-dead Toni Jo allegedly makes her presence known.

There seem to be several denizens of the spirit world who have checked in from beyond the grave at the **Dauphine Orleans Hotel** and its hotel bar, May Bailey's Place, which had been a New Orleans bordello. One of these phantoms is the "Lost Bride," said to be the ghost of a young woman named Millie who was working at May Bailey's as a courtesan. Millie was due to be married but her groom-to-be was shot dead in a gambling dispute the morning of the wedding. The distraught Millie reportedly wore her wedding dress around May's Place while she was alive. Even after her death, Millie is said to continue roaming the Dauphine Orleans, waiting in vain for her erstwhile fiancé. In the hotel ballroom is a ghost known as Jewel, the "Dancing Girl." Described as a young teen, she is said to dance rapidly without her feet touching the ground, both inside the hotel and twirling across the courtyard. Soldiers in military uniforms from the 1800s stalk the grounds by today's hotel pool area and its nearby cottages, perhaps on their way to May Bailey's Place.

Since the 1800s, the **LaLaurie Mansion** in the French Quarter of New Orleans has been known for its hauntings, as well as a particularly grisly form of human ghoulishness. Madame Marie Delphine LaLaurie was a well-respected socialite known for hosting lavish parties in her Creole mansion during the early 1800s. While guests indulged themselves with fine food and drink, unspeakable horrors were contained in another part of the house. When local authorities responded to a kitchen fire in 1834, what they discovered in the attic was far worse: the bodies of chained, tortured, and horribly mutilated slaves. The LaLaurie family fled the country after an outraged mob converged on the house. Soon after, people in New Orleans claimed to hear the phantom screams of her victims emanating from the house at night. In addition, a number of buyers who purchased the mansion were rumored to have been plagued by the ghosts of its tortured souls, usually selling the residence soon after buying it. Whether or not her victims lived on in the spirit world, the infamous murderess LaLaurie was reborn in a sense during 2014 when actress Kathy Bates portrayed her on the FX television series *American Horror Story: Coven*.

With their grounds often draped by eerie-looking Spanish moss, Southern plantation homes are frequently both regal and unnerving. Often they contain the tortured spirits of enslaved people who labored there. **Loyd Hall Plantation** in Cheneyville, Louisiana, is one. William Loyd built Loyd Hall in 1820. With his plantation covering more than six hundred acres that were worked by sixty slaves, he prospered until the Civil War in the 1860s when his work as a double agent led to his being tarred, feathered, and hanged by Union soldiers in front of Loyd Hall. Other tales involve a woman at the home who was so distraught at being left at the altar that she threw herself out of a third-floor window. There was allegedly also an enslaved woman working as a nanny who is reported to have been intentionally poisoned. Ghostly spirits are said not to have left Loyd Hall, staying on to move tableware and play the violin during a full moon. Another notable manifestation is that of a deserter from the Union army who was shot after being discovered in an attic crawl space. His blood allegedly stains the flooring, even after several dozen owners tried to remove the stains—all of them unsuccessfully.

In Natchitoches Parish, **Magnolia Plantation** has been known to "spook" even professional paranormal investigators on TV. While filming one investigation, there were said to be the sounds of chanting from voodoo rituals and tapping noises in a former slave cabin. The spirits of long-dead enslaved people are said to haunt a structure that was used as a hospital, a place where evidence of voodoo has been found. Unexplained lights have been seen as well as the manifestation of a plantation overseer who was killed by Union soldiers when they took over the main house, leaving his phantom spirit to remain in an upstairs bedroom.

It is said that the hauntings at **Myrtles Plantation** in St. Francisville began with an enslaved girl named Chloe who was punished for eavesdropping on the family. As revenge, she baked a poisoned cake. Within hours, three of the family members were dead, including the plantation owner's two children. Chloe was then hung by her fellow slaves, possibly in fear of retribution by their masters if they did not themselves execute the offender who was one of their own. Probably angry with everyone at the plantation, Chloe returned as an apparition whose phantom shape has reportedly been seen in photographs. It has also been rumored that the house was built on top of a former burial ground, so Chloe has to share top billing with the rest of a ghostly cast of characters at Myrtles Plantation.

The entry to **Oak Alley Plantation** in Vacherie, Louisiana, is framed by majestic, ancient live oaks leading to its door. While picturesque, some say they also seem to be pointing with finger-like branches extended to a place where secrets of the past remain. In its day, Oak Alley was said to be the finest home in Louisiana. Construction on the house itself began in 1832, although it is said that the live oaks date from the 1600s. Some say the distinct sound of an invisible horse and carriage can be heard coming up the tree-lined drive. Others claim to have seen a ghostly shape gazing out a window, a woman who some believe is the ghost of the original plantation owner's wife, a proud Creole who loved the mansion and no doubt saw no reason to leave even after death. Witnesses claim to have spotted the apparition of a woman on the mansion's "widow's walk," where the mistress of the house often waited for the first sight of her husband's boat returning up the river from New Orleans. In a macabre postscript, her equally proud daughter suffered an accident, after which she was forced to have her injured leg amputated. The young woman considered herself scarred for life and left home to join a convent. But she had plans to be reunited with her phantom limb in the afterlife: the young woman's amputated leg was put in the family tomb so that when she died, it could be buried with her—as indeed it was.

At Louisiana's **Old State Capitol** building in Baton Rouge, which was built to look like a castle, some politicians may not feel the need to leave office even after being term-limited by death. It is said that noted nineteenth-century legislator Pierre Couvillon suffered a heart attack in the capitol's Senate chamber after a spirited speech about corrupt politicians. Since then, the building has been turned into Louisiana's Museum of Political History. Couvillon's footprints have reportedly appeared in the area that housed the Senate floor, footsteps can be heard in empty hallways, doors open and shut on their own, and visitors have reported the feeling of being watched. One security guard stated that they sometimes see an unexplained shadow or flash of light on their monitors. Another felt a tap on his shoulder while investigating the building's motion detectors going off, indicating someone being on the premises, but no one was behind him or anywhere else in the building, at least no one who was human.

FURTHER READING

Filan, Kenaz. *The New Orleans Voodoo Handbook*. Rochester, VT: Destiny Books, 2011.

Wall, Bennett H., Light Townsend Cummins, Judith Kelleher Schafer, Edward F. Haas, and Michael L. Kurtz. *Louisiana: A History*. 6th ed. Malden, MA: Wiley-Blackwell, 2014.

Ward, Martha. *Voodoo Queen: The Spirited Lives of Marie Laveau*. Jackson: University Press of Mississippi, 2004.

20

Maine

Maine, located in the far northeastern corner of the United States, is known for its jagged, rocky coastline and densely forested interior. It is also familiar to fans of the horror and mystery genres. Griffin (2017) cites mega-bestselling author Stephen King, a lifelong resident of Maine, stating that many of King's books are set in his home state and "several fictional towns have become famous as a result, such as Chamberlain, Chester's Mills, Derry, Haven, and Ludlow" (50). In addition, the long-running TV series, *Murder She Wrote*, set in the fictitious town of Cabot Cove, Maine, has such a high murder rate that even real-life policemen across the country invoke the name of Cabot Cove for an unusual upward homicidal spike in their precinct.

Today's Maine was occupied for thousands of years by Native American tribes like the Kennebec and Penobscot. The first European settlement in the area was undertaken by the French in 1604 on Saint Croix Island. According to Gratwick (2010), in 1607, two expeditions left England, including the future colonists of Jamestown, Virginia. Also leaving England at that time was another expedition led by George Popham ". . . with instructions to establish a colony on the Maine coast. Unfortunately the colony would fail within a year" (19).

Popham's colony was not alone in its lack of success. Various English settlements were established along the coast of Maine in the 1620s, but the cold climate, difficulty in raising crops, and unfriendly relations with Native Americans caused many to fail.

Many historians state that the origin of the name "Maine" came from a region of France. By 1665, the name was documented for English settlements. Through the 1700s, only a few Maine colonies survived to face the American Revolution.

Although they were physically unconnected regions, Maine was part of the Commonwealth of Massachusetts until 1820. That year, residents of Maine voted to become a separate state. Under the Missouri Compromise of 1820, Maine was admitted as the twenty-third state in the Union as a free state, along with Missouri as a slave state, to maintain the balance of power between North and South in the U.S. Senate.

With a nod to trivia, Maine is the only U.S. state with a name of just one syllable. It is also the name of the battleship whose 1898 sinking by an explosion in Havana Harbor precipitated the Spanish-American War.

With its relatively large area and sparse population, many of Maine's residents in the state's interior find themselves few and far between. The costs of road-building between towns outside larger cities like Augusta and Portland were compounded by the fact that many would be impassible during the winter months. Away from the coast, annual inland snowfall averages between 60 and 110 inches. Storms called "Nor'easters" have been known to drop ten or more inches of snow in a single day.

The earliest roads in Maine tended to follow the footpaths of Native Americans, which themselves were often based on trails carved by migratory animals over the centuries. Horseback, sleds, or cross-county skis were often Maine's general modes of travel.

With the coming of transportation innovations in the late nineteenth century, the bicycle sparked a revolution in America's cities and towns. In 1893, the U.S. Department of Agriculture's Office of Road Inquiry was established to look into rural road development in states like Maine, which at the time had mostly dirt roads. It provided funding for a system of paved two-lane highways to be built by state agencies.

The rise of the automobile in the twentieth century led to the need for many more paved roads, state highways, and ultimately America's automotive crown jewel of the 1950s, the interstate highway system, which was initiated by the National Interstate and Defense Highways Act of 1956.

Maine did not lag, having created its State Highway Commission in 1913 with a special eye beginning in the 1920s to keeping Maine's roads open all winter. With those long, dark, isolated stretches of road through dense forests, it was almost inevitable that tales of haunted highways would evolve. In fact, Maine has one more claim to fame: Thomas Verde (2013) states that "America's first documented ghostly encounter occurred in the [Maine] coastal village of Machiasport in 1799" (9) when a ghost was alleged to appear in a house where strange knocking sounds and the disembodied voice of a woman were heard.

Since then, one of the most haunted places in Maine is said to be a section of rural road off U.S. Route 2 called **Route 2A**. It runs through what is known as Haynesville Woods. Before the construction of Interstate 95, U.S. Route 2 was widely used by truck drivers hauling potatoes. The stretch of road is isolated and dangerous, especially in winter, with one sharp curve being almost ninety degrees. Route 2A is the subject of a song recorded by country singer Dick Curless called "A Tombstone Every Mile" in reference to the many fatal accidents that have occurred on this road.

Some of the accidents were said to have been caused by apparitions that suddenly appear, startling unwary drivers. One of the most frequently repeated paranormal experiences is a young woman in white appearing out of nowhere, stumbling along the side of the road. When drivers stop to offer her a ride, she explains that she and her newlywed husband had been in a car accident and need help. Some who have picked her up said they experienced a chilly sensation surrounding the woman. When the driver comes to the end of the Haynesville Woods, the woman has vanished into thin air. Some say the legend is based on a newlywed couple whose auto struck a utility pole, killing the groom instantly. The new bride was said to have freed herself from the car, but froze to death in the snow where she was found.

As some people have pointed out, the master of horror and long-time Maine resident Stephen King had to get his ideas from somewhere.

SOME OTHER REPORTEDLY HAUNTED PLACES IN MAINE

Biddeford's City Theater was originally constructed as a home for two theatrical institutions, an opera house and the seat of city government. The opera house opened in 1860, and welcomed such top-rated actors of the era as Edwin Booth. The entire building was destroyed in a fire during 1894, but the rebuilt opera house opened again in 1896 presenting audience favorites of the day, such as community pageants, dramatic performances by celebrities like the Barrymores, vaudeville, and musical offerings. The latter provided Biddeford's City Theater with its reigning legend of the supernatural. On Halloween Eve in 1904, much-admired soprano songstress Eva Gray collapsed and died after performing a popular song of the day *Goodbye, Little Girl, Goodbye*, with its lyrics including the sad refrain, "Just let me wear /this rose so fair /for I'm marching away to be a soldier." Suddenly, the beautiful thirty-three-year-old Eva collapsed and soon died in her dressing room from heart failure, allegedly with her three-year-old daughter present. Since then, the theater has transitioned from playhouse to silent movie house to "talkies" to decline after the rise of television. In the 1970s, it was used as a storage facility for the city, and even suffered the indignity of having a load of sand dumped into its orchestra section to be used as a horseshoe pit. That may have been too much even for the gentle Eva. Since then, her ghost has allegedly been spotted both in her dressing room and on the staircase, perhaps arranging an otherworldly encore.

The Victorian mansion built in 1874 by a shipbuilder named Captain John McGilvery is today's **Carriage House Inn** at Searsport. In its history, the Carriage House ran the gamut of not only a peaceful retreat for a few guests but it also housed a garrison of Army officers during World War II. With this rich assortment of occupants, it may not be surprising that guests have stated they experienced paranormal activities. One couple said they felt the sensation of someone sitting on the bed with them, waking them both. Later, an apparition appeared in their room, that of a woman in old-fashioned clothing silently combing her long flowing hair. Other guests have heard whispering, music, and unexplained knocking sounds on the door when no one is there. Some witnesses reportedly spotted apparitions in the windows, and have smelled cigar smoke when no one was smoking. There have been reports of feeling they were being followed, especially on the stairs which was said to be the site of a mysterious death. For skeptics who do not credit such reports from humans highly, the owners' dog avoids certain rooms at the inn, refusing to enter them like other rooms, and especially shuns the purportedly haunted staircase.

The **Kennebec Arsenal** in Augusta was constructed to store munitions and to be used by the military following the War of 1812. Among the commandants of the arsenal during its years of military operation, there was Major Robert Anderson, who later became famous for being in command during the siege of Fort Sumter, which lit the powderkeg of the Civil War. By 1901, however, Kennebec Arsenal was no longer needed for military purposes and was transformed into a mental hospital. For the next century, thousands of mentally ill children and adults were brought into the gray granite structure. The facility officially closed in 2004, but today there are tales of horrific treatment suffered by patients who were housed there, as was often the case in the early treatment of mental illness. Some reports claim that scores of people who died in the facility were deposited in unmarked graves. After its closing, there were numerous reports of seeing ghostly apparitions at the building along with unexplained sounds, many of which were said to be eerily reminiscent of the cries of its former residents.

Lake George Regional Park West in Skowhegan was founded in 1992 as pleasant lakeside parkland to be enjoyed by visitors for picnicking, boating, fishing, hiking, and swimming. It has become renowned not only for its rustic loveliness but also reported paranormal activity. In keeping with the park's bucolic surroundings, the supernatural goings-on are noteworthy for being surprisingly agreeable instead of behavior like unpleasantly dark spirits. While some people have witnessed what they called an otherworldly fog and strange apparitions, one of the most frequent claims concerns furniture, objects, and tableware that are arranged at picnic tables for a gathering or event. After being set up as desired, the person may look away momentarily and upon turning back around, the table has been reconfigured into an entirely new formation. The most frequently told tale is about a group of young people who were exploring the woods when they came upon an old deserted cabin. When one child looked through the window, the cabin was seen to contain a dusty old table with chairs randomly stacked around the room. Hearing it was safe, another child decided to walk in, and discovered a clean table with all the chairs perfectly seated around it. Many observers choose to believe it is the park's welcoming spirit inviting them to enter and have fun.

Thomaston was the location of the **Maine State Prison** until 2002 when it was closed after almost two hundred years of housing prisoners. It was established in 1824 as a penitentiary for convicts to serve out their sentences doing hard labor, including those serving life. The maximum security facility also had sections for those found to be mentally ill and a segregation unit for African American prisoners. In its early days, women were also housed at Thomaston. The original layout of the facility had underground cells with one small opening for air, light, and access. Each night, prisoners were lowered into deep holes and brought up in the daytime to labor in the prison's stone quarry. For several decades, prisoners were executed by being hanged at the prison. In 1923, the prison was destroyed by a fire in which many inmates died. When it was rebuilt, the old layout was replaced by two cellblocks that were long narrow hallways containing very small cells, an arrangement that was considered modern for its time. Some of the original underground cells were, however, retained for punishment. In addition to the anguished spirits of convicts who are not believed to have rested in peace, the Thomaston facility may be unusual for housing recycled ghosts. Some equipment used at Thomaston came from an older prison which itself was reported to be haunted. After it was installed, both guards and prisoners reported increased instances of feeling watched by unseen presences, as well as seeing spirits of former inmates at night when the prison is deathly quiet.

The **Mount Hope Cemetery** in Bangor, Maine, was established in 1836. Aside from being the final resting place for about thirty thousand people, it has two significant features. It is only the second burial ground in American to be designed in the "garden cemetery" style, which uses landscaping to create a park-like setting (the first was Mount Auburn Cemetery near Boston, founded in 1831). At about three hundred acres, Mount Hope is not only a place where loved ones are laid to rest, but family and friends can come to pay their respects or simply visit with the departed amidst its pleasant greenery. Mount Hope can claim its own movie credit, serving as the location for the filming of *Pet Sematary* based on the book by Stephen King. It is also the final resting place for countless soldiers who served in a number of America's wars. Even amid Mount Hope's lovely surroundings, visitors report sometimes seeing unexplained shadows, witnessing ghostly figures roaming the grounds, and feeling an overall sense of unease at the cemetery, which happens even when a Stephen King project is not in evidence.

It is said that no trip to Maine would be complete without a visit to Old York, one of the earliest English settlements in the nation. The **Museums of Old York**

Mount Hope Cemetery in Bangor, Maine, established in 1836, is the final resting place for many soldiers who served in America's wars. Visitors to Mount Hope, the location for filming Maine native Stephen King's *Pet Sematary*, sometimes report seeing unexplained shadows and ghostly figures roaming freely. (Nelson P. Jewell/Dreamstime.com)

are nine historic buildings that not only provide a glimpse into three centuries of Maine's history but also might offer a peek into the world of the supernatural. The settlement was one of New England's earliest, with York being incorporated in 1642. Fifty years later, York, in the Maine District, was part of the Massachusetts Bay Colony, which had embarked on a witch hunt in 1692. The witch trials of Salem, Massachusetts, have become the most well-known. In Salem, nineteen people were executed by hanging. Some unlucky residents of York, Maine, did not escape being accused of witchcraft. One York woman was hanged in front of the current museum, which was formerly the town hall. Her aggrieved spirit has apparently never left town. Locals state that it is not unusual to see a ghostly woman they have dubbed "The White Witch" walking alone down the road. At the Museums of Old York, objects have been known to move on their own, doors opening by themselves, and sudden unexplained cold breezes leading people to think it signals the presence of The White Witch. She does not seem to hold a grudge, at least not against innocent schoolchildren, who have reported a nice lady in white asking them to play with her during recess.

When Skowhegan's **Strand Cinema** opened in November 1929, the timing was less than perfect. Silent movies were being replaced by "talkies," and prosperity was being replaced by the effects of the Stock Market crash a month before. The Strand had a seating capacity of one thousand and was forced over the years to undergo numerous renovations. It was broken up into smaller theaters and an apartment unit was even added to the building, which may have been the last straw for a ghostly film fan. When the apartment was being added in 1978, workers were the target of supernatural wrath. Power tools that had been unplugged began working on their own and shocking the user, hand tools were strewn around, and stains were splattered on newly painted walls. Since then, papers and pens have been known to fly off desks, a shadowy apparition is reported to have thrown a piece of balcony ceiling onto the stage, and handprints have been found on the movie screens. There have also been reports of cold spots, unexplained sounds, and a feeling of being held in place on the steps leading down to the basement. Perhaps it is never a good idea to upset a movie fan, even in the spirit world.

FURTHER READING

Gratwick, Harry. *Hidden History of Maine*. Charleston, SC: The History Press, 2010.
Griffin, Nancy. *How Maine Changed the World*. Guilford, CT: Globe Pequot, 2017.
Verde, Thomas. *Maine Ghosts and Legends: 30 Encounters with the Supernatural*. Camden, ME: Down East Books, 2013.

21

Maryland

For thousands of years, today's Maryland was occupied by Native American tribes like the Lenape, Piscataway, and Shawnee. Maryland's seaside location about halfway between the northern and southern colonies made it an appealing place for Europeans to settle in the early years of colonization.

In 1632, King Charles I of England granted a charter to George Calvert, 1st Lord Baltimore. Lord Baltimore proposed the name "Crescentia" for the settlement, a Latin word referring to growth. However, the King proposed another Latin derivative, "Terra Mariae," which translated into Mary Land in honor of his wife, Henrietta Maria, known in England as Queen Mary. The King won, although he later became the first and only English monarch to be beheaded.

Queen Henrietta Maria was Roman Catholic, which made her unpopular during the era's religious strife. Lord Baltimore, a Catholic convert, sought to create a haven in Maryland for Catholics who were being persecuted in England. Often, it is assumed that Maryland was named for a previous Roman Catholic monarch, Mary Tudor, who was so staunch in enforcing Catholicism that she earned the nickname "Bloody Mary." Her reign ended in the mid-1500s, but the deadly religious strife in England continued into the 1600s when Maryland was founded in the name of Henrietta Maria.

Maryland's first colonists arrived in 1634. According to Brugger (1988), Lord Baltimore intended that "Maryland would provide religious asylum" (7). Unlike the Puritans of Massachusetts, who enforced strict Protestant religious conformity, Lord Baltimore envisioned a place where Catholics and Protestants could coexist in peace. Ironically, although Maryland had the largest number of Roman Catholics in the original English colonies, Catholics were still a minority; according to historians, Roman Catholics made up less than 10 percent of the total population.

Maryland's economy was based on its tobacco plantations, which quickly made the new colony profitable. A large number of the early English settlers who arrived in Maryland were indentured servants who were required to serve several years as laborers to pay for their passage from England to the New World.

Soon, Maryland planters found they could reap greater profits if they enlarged their plantations. However, with improved economic conditions in England, the flow of indentured laborers decreased. Maryland planters then imported thousands of enslaved people from Africa, relying on slave labor for the colony's prosperity.

During the 1600s and 1700s, Maryland suffered ongoing strife, both of a religious nature and caused by border skirmishes with the neighboring Pennsylvania colony. Eventually, an agreement divided Maryland and Pennsylvania along what became known as Mason-Dixon Line.

Maryland was one of the original thirteen colonies that joined together in the American Revolution to fight British rule. After independence was won, it became the seventh state admitted to the Union after ratifying the U.S. Constitution in 1788.

In 1790, Maryland donated land along the Potomac River to establish America's new capital city of Washington, D.C. With such close proximity to the federal government, Maryland played a key role in American history in the years to come.

Lying in Southern territory below the Mason-Dixon Line, Maryland was a slave state but it remained in the Union during the Civil War. In April 1861, federal troops were attacked by secessionists as the soldiers marched through Baltimore, Maryland, on their way to Washington, D.C., marking the first bloodshed of the Civil War.

After the war, Maryland was prominent in the rise of the Industrial Revolution, with its waterways and seaports providing convenient transportation both for people and goods. A major factor was Maryland's **Chesapeake and Ohio (C&O) Canal**, which was opened in 1831, and is said by Rubin (2003) to have been hailed as "the 'Great National Project'" (7).

It is difficult for many people today to grasp the extent to which canals were essentially America's "superhighways" in the 1800s. At their most basic level, canals are trenches filled with water. They were often engineering marvels, especially in places with uneven terrain that required locks to raise and lower boats to the next level.

Canal boats provided inexpensive transport that often cut previous costs in half. With the canal system, America's distant frontier communities could be connected with the bustling commerce of the eastern seaboard and from there, ports around the world. Canal boats carried westbound Americans as well as newly arrived immigrants along with the manufactured goods they would need in their new homes. Eastbound, canals were the conduit for raw materials such as the coal, grain, lumber, and stone that fueled the Industrial Revolution.

The C&O Canal carried innumerable people and tons of raw materials until the rise of the railroads in the late 1800s, after which the C&O Canal was abandoned in 1924.

But with so much traffic during its century of operation, it is not surprising that Maryland's C&O Canal would generate its own stock of hauntings, especially among locals with vivid imaginations. After all, as Okonowicz (2007) says, it was Maryland's famed author Edgar Allan Poe "who created the horror genre in fiction" (3).

In the 1800s, canals were America's "superhighways," with Maryland's waterways being a major link for transporting people and goods. The Chesapeake & Ohio (C&O) Canal, which opened in 1831, was considered a great national project. A murdered keeper of locks on the C&O was said to appear as a headless ghost until his murder was avenged. (Cecouchman/Dreamstime.com)

Several local legends are said to have been involved in reports of hauntings at the canal. One tale along the C&O route is the alleged Paw Paw Tunnel's Headless Ghost. A well-liked keeper of the locks near the town of Paw Paw was found brutally murdered, having had his skull crushed in. It was known that the lock-keeper had a collection of unusual rare coins, which was missing. There were no clues, although the boatmen were reminded of the crime whenever they passed through the Paw Paw Tunnel, including some who thought they saw a headless ghost, which they felt was the aggrieved spirit of the murdered lock-keeper. Months later, a group of boatmen were drinking in a local saloon when a stranger offered to buy drinks. When he paid, they recognized a coin from the dead lock-keeper's collection. Roughly searching the stranger, they found the rest. The killer was found guilty and executed. Some think the headless ghost was keeping the story alive until his murder could be avenged.

SOME OTHER REPORTEDLY HAUNTED PLACES IN MARYLAND

The **Baltimore County Almhouse** in Cockeysville was built in 1872 and closed its doors in 1958. It now serves as headquarters for the Baltimore County Historical Society. The facility, essentially a poorhouse, was intended to serve as a home for people who lacked resources of their own. Those unfortunates included the poor, the mentally ill, the elderly, sick people, and children who had no one to care for them. Later, an addition housed prisoners. With all those uneasy spirits, it is not surprising that it has gained a reputation for supernatural activities. Some claims include the disembodied voices of women talking on the unoccupied third floor. Not only have observers claimed to see children's faces looking out the windows, there have been reports of hearing the sounds of children playing and throwing things around the building. It is said that if a person turns a corner quickly after hearing those sounds, the glimpse of a ghostly face might come into view. One ghost even has a name: Anthony Rose. In 1908, the seventy-five-year-old Mr. Rose was admitted as a resident of the almshouse because there was no one to take care of him in his old age. He fell down an elevator shaft to his death, but perhaps there is still no one to care for him because the ghostly spirit of Anthony Rose is said to continue residing at the Almshouse.

Depending on the source, the story of Dr. Samuel Mudd was either a tragic miscarriage of justice against a Good Samaritan who was simply in the wrong place at the wrong time, or it was proper retribution against a conspirator in one of our nation's worst crimes. The alleged haunting of the **Dr. Samuel Mudd House Museum** in Waldorf, Maryland, may offer its own clues. Samuel A. Mudd was the doctor who treated John Wilkes Booth for a broken leg after Booth assassinated President Abraham Lincoln in 1865. Booth incurred the injury by jumping to the stage from Lincoln's balcony box at Ford's Theater. When Booth stopped at Dr. Mudd's house for treatment after riding thirty miles in great pain, the physician had to cut the boot off Booth's swollen leg. The bloody boot had Booth's name inscribed inside the leather, helping to incriminate Mudd, who missed execution by only one vote and was sentenced to life in prison. After several years, due to the tireless efforts of Mudd's wife, the doctor was pardoned and returned home where he may still be in residence. There are stories of seeing the ghosts of both Dr. and Mrs. Mudd around the property. Voices have been heard in unoccupied rooms, and in one incident, electric candles kept turning on in the windows during a Civil War re-enactment. One witness reported feeling someone tugging on his coat before noticing he was the only person anywhere nearby. The most famous of the paranormal reports at the Mudd House is the human-shaped impression routinely discovered on the bed in the room where Booth had stayed, even after the bed is made and remade. Many of the artifacts in the Mudd House were there when Booth made his ill-fated visit, so he may feel comfortable returning there for a nap.

Few figures in American literature capture the imagination like Edgar Allan Poe (1809–1849) who transformed the horror genre. Some sources state that much of his work was inspired by events around him. It is, therefore, not surprising that the **Edgar Allan Poe House Museum** in Baltimore is no stranger to reports of the paranormal. However, it *is* surprising that the spirits who are said to inhabit the house do not include Poe himself. Built around 1830, Poe was residing there when it is presumed he wrote spooky stories like *Berenice* and *Morella*, both of which involve the deterioration and death of a young women who may then return from the grave. Many witnesses have claimed they can sense a high degree of paranormal activity in the house, including a female spirit from the early 1800s who does not seem to be angry or frightening, just a benign energy from the past. Some biographers state that just before the 1847 death of Poe's beloved young wife Virginia, with whom he had lived on and off in Baltimore, she promised she would be his guardian angel after she died. Today, there have been reports that the Poe House Museum is the site of chillingly cold breezes even on the warmest days, guests feeling they have been touched physically when no one else is there, doors and windows inexplicably opening and closing, and the sounds of footsteps, voices, and thumping noises. In a postscript, Virginia's remains were almost lost and Poe was originally buried in an unmarked grave. Today, Poe and his wife are interred in Baltimore, although after Virginia's bones were nearly discarded after an earlier burial, her spirit may feel more comfortably secure at home.

The **Glenn Dale Hospital** in Glenn Dale opened in 1934 as a treatment center for adults and children who suffered from tuberculosis, often called consumption or TB. Before modern antibiotics were developed, tuberculosis relentlessly attacked the lungs, was highly contagious, and was generally a death sentence. When TB in the local area was at its height, Glenn Dale housed about six hundred patients. Although it was designed to provide amenities like fresh air and sunshine, TB carried such a stigma that families refused to tell people that their loved ones were there. The patients often felt—and often were—cast off from society. It is unknown how many died at Glenn Dale where stories circulated about patients undergoing experimental treatments that today might be considered inhumane. By the 1950s, treating TB with antibiotics proved to be effective, and the number of patients at Glenn Dale declined. Evolving into a nursing home in the 1960s, it admitted indigent patients suffering from other types of ailments, eventually closing its doors in 1984. Although other uses have been sought, today Glenn Dale's imposing facility is abandoned, with broken windows, crumbling mortar, and graffiti-scarred walls. Trespassers are discouraged from intruding, but some who entered reported ghostly visions as well as the smell of burning flesh. There have been stories involving the sounds of banging, eerie laughter, strange noises, and yelling from inside.

The **Lord Baltimore Hotel** in Baltimore opened on December 30, 1928. While that was a high point of the Roaring Twenties, within a year the Stock Market crashed and things hit bottom with the Great Depression. Through the years, visitors to the Lord Baltimore have reported encounters with ghosts, as well as a strong feeling of being watched while they sleep. Some say they have felt the sensation of being touched when no one else was around, especially in the elevator. That same elevator has also been known to randomly visit the nineteenth floor when no one pushes the button for that level. Guests who stayed on the nineteenth floor have reported seeing the ghost of a little girl wearing black shoes with a long, cream-colored dress and she carries a red ball. Some guests have complained to the front desk that there was a little girl with a red ball running down the hallway in the middle of the night, while others have seen her crying, screaming, and rocking back and forth. Still other guests have seen the apparitions of two adults on that same nineteenth floor, or else dancing in the ballroom. Local legend has it that one night after a party at the hotel, a married couple who had been ruined in the Stock Market crash jumped to their deaths from the Lord Baltimore. Some say they left their seven-year-old daughter behind, others state they took her with them. In any case, the child has been named Molly and is considered the resident ghost of the Lord Baltimore, always seen with the red ball, which was perhaps a favorite toy. Other manifestations in the hotel include televisions that turn on and off by themselves, as well as TV remotes that move and/or disappear, although in fairness there are very few husbands and wives who have not experienced a vanishing remote in their own homes.

The **Maryland State House** in Annapolis was begun in 1772 and completed in 1797. The imposing domed structure boasts a lightning rod on top which is said to have been made by Benjamin Franklin himself, all of which makes sense because the dome is constructed of wood. The Maryland State House served as the U.S. Capitol from late 1783 to mid-1784, and is still used for legislative purposes. But one of the main draws for the building is the reported appearance of a long-dead construction worker named Thomas Dance (or, according to some, Dence). In 1783, while working on the dome, he fell to his death on the marble floor several stories below. As if that were not cause enough to haunt the building where he died, some say his spirit is aggrieved because of the hardship his family was forced to suffer at the hands of the contractor who employed him. The contractor denied the widow Thomas's unpaid salary and would not return the tools Thomas used so that his sons could continue his work. Thomas is said to be responsible for lights that flash on and off, doors opening and closing, and even blasts of icy cold air that can be strong enough to knock a person down. An apparition is sometimes seen walking on the uppermost levels of the building smoking a pipe, as well as on the outside of the tall dome, a sight which has been startling enough to prompt some concerned observers to report the daredevil to building security.

St. Paul's Cemetery in Chestertown dates back to 1713 and is said to be the site of modern-day supernatural activity. Some of the paranormal events may involve Union and Confederate soldiers buried there who apparently still just cannot get along. But the gravesite at the cemetery with the most alleged paranormal activity is that of notoriously hard-living actress Tallulah Bankhead. It is said that her raspy voice can be heard by lying on the slab and pressing an ear against the stone that covers her grave. Visitors regularly leave beads, tokens, and liquor bottles there. It is possible that even after death, Tallulah still enjoys the attention of fans. It is also possible that her raspy voice is telling visitors to stop leaving litter on her grave.

FURTHER READING

Brugger, Robert. *Maryland: A Middle Temperament, 1634–1980*. Baltimore, MD: Johns Hopkins University Press, 1988.

Okonowicz, Ed. *Haunted Maryland: Ghosts and Strange Phenomena of the Old Line State*. Mechanicsburg, PA: Stackpole Books, 2007.

Rubin, Mary H. *The Chesapeake and Ohio Canal*. Charleston, SC: Arcadia Publishing, 2003.

22

Massachusetts

Massachusetts, one of the original thirteen colonies, is officially termed the Commonwealth of Massachusetts. That designation may have been chosen by Founding Father John Adams in his draft of the Massachusetts Constitution. In the Revolutionary fervor of the late 1700s, a "commonwealth" carried the cachet of being governed by the people rather than a faceless state. In reality, today, it holds no practical implications, having the same position and power as other American states.

It is named after the Massachusett tribe of Native Americans who once inhabited the region. Apart from being commemorated in place names, most of the indigenous people met an unhappy fate after the arrival of Europeans, being decimated by epidemics of diseases like influenza and smallpox.

The first permanent English colonists in New England, sailing on a ship called the *Mayflower*, settled at Plymouth, Massachusetts, in 1620. These "Pilgrims" would go on to become the second successful English colony (after Virginia's Jamestown) in today's United States. The Pilgrims of Plymouth were followed by Puritans who established the Massachusetts Bay Colony in the area of today's city of Boston in 1630.

Puritans believed the Church of England needed to be purified and were harassed by English authorities because of their beliefs. They came to Massachusetts with a goal of establishing what they considered an ideal religious society. Insofar as being "ideal," the concept proved to be defined by a narrow interpretation.

Johnson (2017) states that the main business of most early American settlers was day-to-day survival, adding, "But the leaders of the Massachusetts Bay Colony, in particular, had the wealth to become established fairly early and to turn their attention to matters other than the basic needs of food and shelter" (137). What they turned their attention *to* was culling their own people.

The Massachusetts Bay Colony already dealt harshly with dissenters who voiced religious and/or political disagreements. But a new element would gain notoriety beginning in 1692.

The events that followed in the colonial town of Salem, Massachusetts, were not without precedent. According to Guiley (2011), "The seeds of Salem's history were planted with the first footsteps of colonial settlers upon the land" (6).

Lizzie Borden House

In 1892, the bodies of Andrew and Abby Borden were discovered horrifically bludgeoned in their Fall River home, apparently by "40 whacks" of an ax. The prime suspect was their daughter Lizzie. The Borden case was one of the first in America to unfold in the media spotlight, capturing the nation's attention. Despite allegations that Lizzie had financial motives for the killings, she was acquitted due to lack of physical evidence. In a case worthy of TV's *Cold Justice*, to date, no one has been charged with the murders. Today, the Borden home is a museum and bed-and-breakfast. Visitors can immerse themselves in gruesome crime scene photos and sleep in one of its reportedly haunted rooms, including the one where Abby was killed. Staff and guests maintain that the home is chock-full of paranormal activity, including a woman's apparition in Victorian clothing, cold fingers tapping them on the shoulder, conversations in empty rooms, doors opening and closing, unexplained footsteps, and the sound of a woman softly weeping. Some believe the spirits in the house are those of Abby, Andrew, and Lizzie Borden herself, one of whom reportedly tries to tuck guests into bed at night.

The issue involved people being persecuted for allegations of witchcraft. The practice of "witch hunting" can be traced back to Biblical times for those suspected of black magic and/or heresy. Tens of thousands of documented executions took place in medieval Europe, with historians noting that the vast majority of those executed were women.

Around the time that official witch trials were declining in Europe, witch hunt hysteria in New England reached fever pitch. Twelve women had already been executed in colonial Connecticut and Massachusetts during the 1600s. However, the witch trials that took place in Salem, Massachusetts, during 1692 and 1693 would become the most infamous.

In the **Salem Witch Hunts**, more than two hundred people were accused of witchcraft, nineteen of whom (fourteen women and five men) were executed by hanging. At least half a dozen others died in jail. Some stories of the condemned have become known. One is the eighty-year-old Giles Corey who publicly questioned the proceedings. For that infraction, the frail old man's punishment was to be slowly crushed to death under huge stones over the course of several days.

The backstories of others also often began innocuously. Roach (2013) cites the day when the elderly invalid Rebecca Nurse discovered that someone's pigs had dug up her garden. Infuriated, she confronted a neighbor whose livestock regularly wandered into her yard. Rebecca and the man exchanged heated words. Two weeks later, the neighbor died. Subsequently, the seventy-one-year-old Rebecca was accused of witchcraft and executed by hanging. In 1706, one of the accusers expressed remorse for her falsehoods leading to the death of the innocent Rebecca Nurse, but with that confession coming fourteen years after Rebecca was killed, it was too little, too late.

Before witch hunt hysteria was over, neighbors accused neighbors, friends accused friends, and even some family members accused each other.

The events of Salem in 1692 continue to find themselves embedded in our modern world, with the term "witch hunt" entrenched in American culture. In the

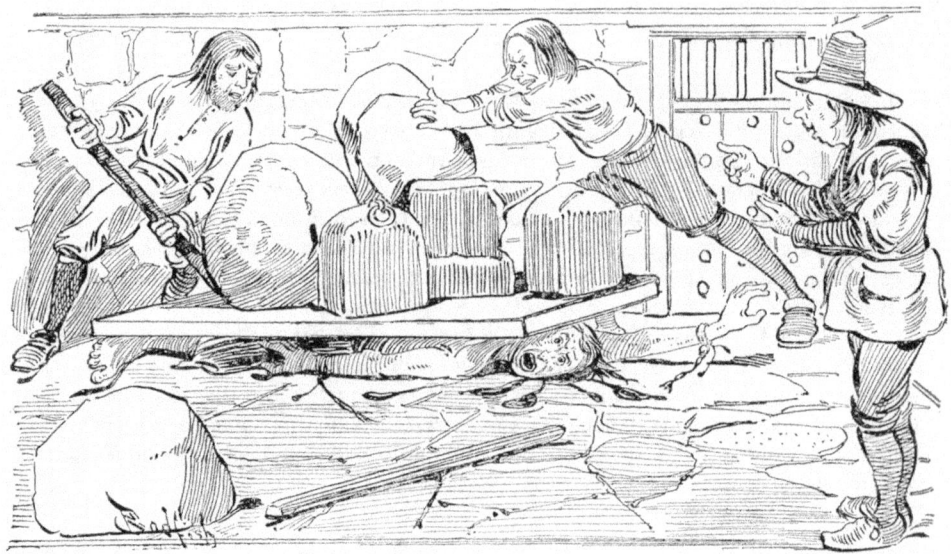

During the witch hunts that were held in Salem, Massachusetts, in 1692–1693, more than 200 men and women were accused of witchcraft. As pictured here, Giles Corey, a frail eighty-year-old man who publicly questioned the executions, was slowly crushed to death. Today, his spirit joins others who are said to haunt the town. (UCSB Collections)

early 1950s, it became synonymous with McCarthyism, named for the Republican senator who accused people of being Communists and traitors with no proof, often destroying lives in the process. One of the accused, playwright Arthur Miller, drew a parallel to Salem in his classic 1953 drama, *The Crucible*. The "witch hunt" terminology is often used derisively in today's world by "accusing the accuser."

In Salem, some say the uneasy spirits of the executed still roam the town. The ghosts of Salem are said to include the elderly Giles Corey who had been crushed to death. With his final tortured breaths, the indomitable old man cursed the town and its sheriff. Corey's ghost is now believed to haunt the Howard Street Cemetery where he was buried in an unmarked grave. His name, however, is memorialized by being inscribed—ironically—on a large flat stone.

Other allegedly haunted sites in Salem include the Joshua Ward House which was built on land belonging to the notorious sheriff who was infamous for his torturous interrogation techniques, including those used on Giles Corey. Several ghosts now are said to haunt the property, including the sheriff himself, the spirit of Giles Corey, and an angry woman with wild black hair, believed to be another witch hunt victim.

The "Witch House" was the home of Judge Jonathan Corwin, who presided over the Salem witch trials and sentenced nineteen people to execution. Today, it is open to the public as a museum, and is the only structure still standing in Salem that has direct ties to the witch hunt. Despite rumors, there is no documentation showing that any interrogations or trials were ever conducted in the Witch House.

Still, the spirits know where it is. Paranormal investigators have reported cold spots, the sound of disembodied voices, and a feeling of being touched by unseen hands. In a particular irony, the foreboding dark gray structure has tall gables that actually resemble witches' hats.

SOME OTHER REPORTEDLY HAUNTED PLACES IN MASSACHUSETTS

Although the name belonging to the ghostly spirit is unknown, without a doubt the classiest paranormal phenomenon in Massachusetts is the **Highwood Ghost** at Tanglewood. For an anonymous entity, it has the distinction of being associated with two of the all-time top names in music: Leonard Bernstein, composer of *West Side Story*, and John Williams, who wrote the music to blockbuster movies like *Star Wars* and *Raiders of the Lost Ark*. Built in 1846, Highwood Manor House is on the campus of Tanglewood, the summer home of the Boston Symphony Orchestra. Tanglewood has long been associated with the annual residency by Bernstein. Williams said he recalled that as they climbed a stairwell at Highwood, Bernstein exclaimed, "This place is haunted." Highwood House, which today contains administrative offices and a dining room, has been the reported site of doors opening and shutting on their own, faucets that mysteriously start running, lights going on by themselves, and various odd noises. On August 19, 2018, the Tanglewood Orchestra performed the world premiere of John Williams's composition *Highwood's Ghost, An Encounter for Cello, Harp and Orchestra* as part of the music festival's annual Leonard Bernstein Memorial Concert. The mood of Williams's musical score is lighthearted, as befits an entity he called a "seemingly very pleasant spirit." The John Williams piece is not nearly as hummable as his *Indiana Jones* theme or Bernstein's *Tonight*, but there aren't too many other poltergeists who have a symphony in their honor associated with two world-class composers.

It is said that the Native American name for Hoosac Mountain meant "forbidden." The **Hoosac Tunnel** in North Adams is a railroad tunnel in the unyielding rock of Hoosac Mountain in the Berkshires. It was begun in 1851 and remained incomplete for twenty-five years because after several incidents workers refused to enter. The tunnel still carries the ominous nickname of "The Bloody Pit." By the time the tunnel was finally finished, about two hundred men had died in explosions, fires, tunnel collapses, and suspicious circumstances. In one incident, a worker set off a nitroglycerine charge before his two coworkers could make it to safety, leaving them buried alive under tons of rock. He vanished and was not seen again until a year later when his body was found strangled, two miles into the tunnel at almost the exact spot where the other two men had been killed. Workers believed he had been executed by their vengeful spirits. Later investigators, including a former Civil War officer, heard the sounds of a man groaning in pain when the tunnel was empty. The combat veteran later stated that he had not been that frightened since the Battle of Shiloh, where he presumably heard the sound of groaning many times. After other catastrophes in the tunnel, workmen claimed to see apparitions of dead miners carrying picks and shovels through a shroud of mist on the snowy mountain, leaving no footprints in the snow.

The **Houghton Mansion** in North Adams was built in 1890 by the prominent Albert Charles Houghton who served as the former mayor of North Adams and owned the town's Arnold Print Works, which was one of the world's leading producers of printed textiles. Mr. Houghton was said to be dedicated to his work, and as an overachiever, may have decided that even death would not slow him down. He is said to be among the spirits that are haunting the Houghton Mansion, which has been called one of the scariest places in New England. Guests have reported hearing disembodied footsteps, voices, and loud knocking when no one else is present. Some have observed flickering lights and seen ghostly shadows, all of which may stem from a family tragedy. In 1914, the Houghtons purchased their first automobile as the "horseless carriage" was coming into vogue. Mr. Houghton, along with his daughter Mary and several friends, went for a drive with their chauffeur at the wheel. Trying to avoid road construction, the car veered off a soft left-hand shoulder, rolling over several times down a steep embankment. Mary Houghton and a friend died, although Mr. Houghton was expected to survive. While Houghton recuperated at home, the distraught driver killed himself. Mr. Houghton died soon after. In later years, the house was used as a Masonic lodge. One of several reported hauntings includes a snowy night when the only two people in the building heard the distinctive sound of a side door opening and closing, followed by the sounds of someone stomping snow off their feet. Investigating the source of the noise, they found no one in the room, no one outside, and no footprints in the snow.

Any site that is called **Spider Gates Cemetery** immediately carries an ominous ring to it. This cemetery in Leicester is named for the distinctive design on its gates. The burial ground's official name is Friends Cemetery that has been in use since 1740 when it was created by a group of Quakers, who are said to have believed the land possessed special powers. Since then, there have been rumors of ghostly sightings, strange noises, and bare circles on the grass where it is believed dark deeds were perpetrated. One of the legends involves the gravesite of Earle Marmaduke who died in 1839. There is indeed a barren circle in the dirt around his grave. As the legend goes, if people walk around Marmaduke's gravestone at midnight ten times (which may explain the barren circle) and say "Marmaduke speak to me," they will be rewarded with the sound of his voice if they kneel down and put their head on the tombstone. A more contemporary tale concerns a photographic team who went to Spider Gates, one of whom lagged behind. When the dawdler dropped her keys in the grass, a man who was described as a skeletal-looking figure accompanied by a female companion seemingly came out of nowhere. Handing the keys back, the man said, "You dropped your keys, ma'am" in what was said to be an old-time New England accent. Before the stunned photographer's eyes, the ghostly duo walked into the marshland and suddenly vanished. Ironically, there was no photographic evidence available of the encounter.

The **Taunton State Hospital** in Taunton, established in 1854, was originally known as the State Lunatic Hospital. Despite that slightly off-putting name, its large pleasant campus offered fresh air and sunlight as part of treating its patients.

In 1975, the main part of the hospital was abandoned, followed by fires and other damage that occurred to the main building over the years. Today the site is considered to be one of the most haunted places in the state, possibly due to the unhappy spirits of thousands of patients over a century, as well as rumors that the basement was used for satanic rituals that involved human sacrifice. It is said that while the hospital was still open, staff would attempt to go into the basement but felt something physically stopping them from reaching that bottom step. There are still said to be unexplained markings on the basement walls which some say is blood. Witnesses claim to have heard moans, cries for help, and unexplained banging sounds. Some have reported seeing strange lights among the trees. Some of the facility's reputation stems from the nature of some of its residents, including serial killer Jane Toppan who, in newspaper reports, admitted taking pleasure in poisoning more than hundred patients and watching them die while working as a nurse. Accused murderer Lizzie Borden was said to talk about being held in the asylum. Actually, she was never admitted, although she was held in the nearby jail. Perhaps "Lunatic Hospital" sounded better to Lizzie than "jail."

The **USS *Salem*** in Quincy today serves as a museum ship open to the public. It was commissioned in 1949 and became the last heavy cruiser to enter service. Today, it is the only one still in existence. The ship was decommissioned in 1959, and although she never saw combat, she did see a number of deaths aboard while serving with distinction as a hospital ship. Another kind of distinction was featured in the 2016 feature film *The Finest Hours*, starring Chris Pine and Casey Affleck, about a real-life daring rescue by the U.S. Coast Guard. But to many, *Salem*'s greatest distinction involves visits by television ghost hunters amid continuing rumors of being haunted. One paranormal investigating group entered the empty wardroom only to encounter a chair tipping over in one corner and a metallic screeching sound in the opposite corner. They then heard the sound of a dentist's drill in that empty section before hearing a moan or wail. They saw what appeared to be someone peeking around the foundation of a gun turret, an apparition that vanished until reappearing in another part of the ship. Other ghostly manifestations are said to wander the decks while a shadowy figure hovers in the machinery room. Secured deck hatches are said to violently bang open and shut, and things generally go bump in the night. Perhaps all of this is to be expected aboard a ship named *Salem*.

FURTHER READING

Guiley, Rosemary Ellen. *Haunted Salem: Strange Phenomena in the Witch City*. Mechanicsburg, PA: Stackpole Books, 2011.

Johnson, Claudia Durst. *Daily Life in Colonial New England*. Santa Barbara, CA: ABC-CLIO, 2017.

Roach, Marilynne K. *Six Women of Salem: The Untold Story of the Accused and Their Accusers in the Salem Witch Trials*. Boston, MA: Da Capo Press, 2013.

23

Michigan

Michigan's name is said to originate from the Native American word "mishigamaa," which refers to a large body of water. This may be an understatement since water is in the state's DNA. Michigan, the only state with two peninsulas, is bound by Lake Erie, Lake Huron, Lake Michigan, and Lake Superior; has the longest freshwater coastline of any state; and contains just under sixty-five thousand inland lakes and ponds.

After thousands of years of being occupied by Native Americans like the Ojibwa tribe, French explorers claimed the region for France in the seventeenth century. A series of wars followed, with the results spurring change of ownership for the region. After France was defeated in the French and Indian War in 1763, the area came under British rule.

When Britain lost the American Revolution, the expanse was ceded to the United States, but stability did not arrive for the Michigan Territory until after the War of 1812. According to Rubenstein and Ziewacz (2014), the War of 1812 proved to be the last time Native Americans fought against whites in Michigan, as well as marked the end of British claims to portions of the territory, adding "Michigan was now open to settlement by families who previously avoided the region because of Indian and British unrest" (62).

Michigan was admitted into the Union as a free state in 1837, the twenty-sixth star on the nation's flag. With its location near the Great Lakes, Michigan soon became an important center of commerce and industry. In the early twentieth century, the state's population exploded when it attracted workers for the automobile industry that centered in Detroit, Michigan.

As the Detroit auto industry boomed, so did a new factor in Michigan's economy: tourism. With the state's wealth of waterways coupled with the ease of automotive transportation, more people could enjoy leisure activities.

The state's numerous islands became popular destinations. While some are populated, the majority of Michigan's islands are small and uninhabited. Most are lovely during warm weather, but in winter, the bare trees and long shadows often bring a feeling of foreboding to isolated islands. Many classic mystery tales are set on remote islands where guests cannot escape.

One of the most poignant spots on Michigan's Mackinac Island is the Drowning Pool where seven women were accused of witchcraft in the 1700s. They were thrown into the pond with heavy rocks tied to their feet. Today, the dead women may haunt the waters as mysterious dark figures floating above the surface, perhaps still proclaiming their innocence. (Paul Lemke/Dreamstime.com)

One of Michigan's most famous islands combines almost every element of a classic ghost story along with an eerie feeling of having gone back in time. **Mackinac Island** (pronounced MAK-in-aw) is located in the Straits of Mackinac between the Upper and Lower Peninsulas. It is less than four square miles in area, and is the most popular tourist destination in the state. Although only a few hundred permanent residents occupy the island after summer is over, a few ghostly inhabitants may never have left.

As Pattskyn (2012) says, it should be no surprise that Mackinac Island is considered haunted: "Even before Europeans arrived in 1634, the island was inhabited by members of the Ojibwa tribe who considered the island to be the home of 'Gitche Manitou' or 'Great Spirit'" (229). Some say Mackinac Island is a huge Native American burial ground. When one of the island's main attractions, the Grand Hotel, was being built in the late 1880s, the legend says construction workers uncovered human remains while digging the hotel's foundation, but there were so many that the workers simply built the hotel on top of them.

Predictably, the Grand Hotel has become known as a hotspot for paranormal activity. But there is an additional element that adds to its general eeriness. In the 1890s, despite nearby Detroit becoming America's car capital, the people of Mackinac Island were dismayed that automobiles startled their horses. They voiced concerns about health and safety amid the rage for the new "horseless carriages." Therefore, at the end of the nineteenth century, the island passed a law banning motor vehicles except for emergency services, a ban that continues to this day.

In addition, as North (2011) says, "about three-quarters of the island remains in its natural state, covered with forests and fields" (14). Given how little the island has changed over the years, it is easy for visitors to feel they have stepped back in time. Perhaps some spirits linger because the island looks just the same as when they knew it.

At the Grand Hotel, where the 1980 movie *Somewhere in Time* was filmed, there have been reports of a malevolent entity with glowing red eyes. A hotel employee working in the hotel's theater reported being rushed by the red-eyed entity hovering above the floor. It knocked him off his feet, and he awoke two days later in a hospital, swearing never to return to the Grand.

Other reported entities at the Grand Hotel appear more benign. Some staffers claimed that a man in a top hat frequents the piano bar, only to suddenly disappear, leaving the lingering scent of a cigar where no one has been smoking. Others have reported a woman in Victorian clothing roaming the halls, and even curling up in bed at night with hotel employees.

Guests and staff have reported phantom footsteps, with doors opening and closing on their own at the Grand. But the Grand Hotel is not the only place on the island where spirits tend to gather.

One of the more poignant is called The Drowning Pool, a twenty-foot drop-off located between Mackinac's downtown area and the Mission Point Resort. The witch hunts in Salem, Massachusetts, were not the only such outbreaks to plague early America. Witch hunting also took place on Mackinac Island in the 1700s and early 1800s. In one case, seven women were accused of witchcraft. In keeping with the conventional wisdom of that time, the fate of the accused witches was to tie heavy rocks to their feet and be thrown into the pond to see if they would float, as witches were believed to do. If they sank, they were not witches.

The good news/bad news was that by drowning, all seven women were proven innocent. They may haunt the waters to this day. Visitors report seeing mysterious shadows and dark figures floating above the surface, perhaps still proclaiming their innocence, or possibly seeking revenge on their accusers.

SOME OTHER REPORTEDLY HAUNTED PLACES IN MICHIGAN

The **Bruce Mansion** in Brown City was built by John G. Bruce in 1876. Within five years, it had gained a local reputation among locals. In 1881, a catastrophic fire destroyed much of the town, but the Bruce Mansion was left standing in perfect condition. Because of that, some called it charmed, but not in a good way. Several owners died in the Bruce Mansion, including one who had a run of bad luck in the 1920s. His wife left him, his fortune was drained, and the house was in foreclosure. Legend says that the man hanged himself in the mansion's tower, and because of the stigma of suicide, no official cause is listed on his death certificate. Today, investigators have claimed to observe frequent apparitions throughout the house and to have recorded electronic voice phenomena. Apparently, there is also a ghostly prankster on the premises who is said to jiggle the handle and try to open the door to the restroom when men are using it, but no one else is around. In addition, there have been reports of growling sounds in the mansion's basement. Witnesses have also reported frequently seeing the ghost of a cat running on the first floor, then disappearing into a particular room every time. It may be that the phantom feline is wisely trying to avoid the ghoulish growling in the basement.

The cornerstone for the **Detroit Masonic Temple** was set in 1922 using what was said to be the same trowel George Washington used to set the cornerstone of the Capitol Building in Washington, D.C. On Thanksgiving Day, 1926, the doors opened for the huge neo-Gothic Detroit Masonic Temple, which remains the largest Masonic temple in the world. Its one thousand–room design was the vision of the aptly named architect George D. Mason who also designed the Grand Hotel on Mackinac Island. Mason was said not only to be obsessed with the details of the building but also added a number of hidden staircases and secret passageways. Mason's presence is literally carved in stone as a kind of impish-looking gargoyle straddling a ledge on the exterior of the building. His presence may also be felt inside the building with people including guests and a night watchman claiming to have seen his ghost. In addition, there are many unexplained cold spots in the building, as well as doors that are said to open and close on their own. In particular, the roof doors have been said to swing open just moments after being locked by the night watchman. Many people report the feeling of being watched while in the building, but perhaps George Mason is still just keeping his eye on his architectural jewel.

Construction on the three-story **Felt Mansion**, located between Holland and Saugatuck, Michigan, began in 1925 for the family of the self-made millionaire Dorr Eugene Felt. With its twenty-five rooms occupying seventeen thousand square feet, including a sweeping ballroom, it was a dream home for Mr. and Mrs. Felt. The property came to be called "Shore Acres" by Mr. Felt who wanted to honor his wife Agnes with a home worthy of her. However, in 1928, only six weeks after moving in, Felt's wife Agnes passed away suddenly. The grieving Mr. Felt followed her in death about eighteen months later. The mansion has gone through various incarnations, including serving as a Catholic seminary, a prison, and a home for cloistered nuns. Today, it has been lovingly restored by the Felt Estate organization as a venue for special events. Reports of hauntings at the Felt Mansion are said to be the benign spirits of Dorr and Agnes Felt whose time in their home was all too short. Shadowy apparitions are said to stroll casually throughout the house, as if taking time to enjoy the dream home that they were unable to do in life. There are reports that the double French doors in Agnes's room open and close on their own. The couple can sometimes be seen dancing in the third floor ballroom, appearing to be friendly and happy to share their home with visitors.

The **Landmark Inn** in Marquette dates to 1917 when construction began, but it was not actually completed until 1930 when it opened as a full service hotel. It has played host to a variety of celebrity guests over the years, from poet Maya Angelou to comedians Abbott and Costello. But the most cherished celebrity guest is a ghostly spirit known as "The Librarian." It is said that in the 1930s, a librarian and a merchant seaman fell in love. They planned to marry after his final cruise that unfortunately turned out to be his *final* cruise. His ship was sunk in a storm on Lake Superior, and the entire crew went down with the ship. When the Librarian finally discovered why her beloved did not return to her, it is said she never recovered from her grief. She could neither work nor eat, dying soon after. Many people have reported seeing the Librarian gazing out of the sixth floor window of the hotel's Lilac Room, which is decorated in lilac, bound for eternity to wait for her missing lover to return from sea. Some people staying in the adjacent lodging have reported that on the side of their guestroom closest to the Lilac Room, they encountered strange static on their cell phones. Speaking of telephones, it is said that the hotel's front desk frequently receives calls from the Lilac Room even when it is unoccupied—at least not by registered guests.

The River Raisin, which flows through southeastern Michigan, was originally named by French settlers as *La Rivière aux Raisins* for the wild grapes growing along its banks since the French word for grape is *raisin*. The **River Raisin National Battlefield Park** in Monroe is the site of a bloody massacre that took place during the War of 1812 and is said to be haunted by the spirits of people who died gruesomely before their time. Although it is little known in American history, River Raisin was the site of one of the biggest battles of the War of 1812. On January 22, 1813, in what is sometimes called the Battle of Frenchtown, 850 American troops at the site were attacked in a predawn raid by a combined force of one thousand British soldiers and Native Americans. After hours of heavy fighting, around three hundred American soldiers were killed outright and hundreds more were wounded. The American general was captured, surrendering what was left of his outnumbered army. The wounded men and the civilians in the nearby settlement were left defenseless and ended up being slaughtered by the Native Americans in what is now known as the River Raisin Massacre. As might be expected in a place of such tragedy, ghostly apparitions have been experienced. Visitors to the forty-acre battlefield park have reported spectral soldiers in uniforms appropriate to American troops in the War of 1812. Some have seen unexplained orbs of light. Photographers are said to have captured shadowy figures in doorways, windows, and on the field. Other people have claimed to hear cries of agony, moans, and the sounds of a heated battle. In a recording by a team of paranormal investigators, a disembodied voice is thought to have said the word *"home,"* possibly wondering if he will ever see it again. Another is thought to say *"breathe,"* possibly wondering if he ever will do it again.

As with many abandoned, decaying mental institutions, the **Traverse City State Hospital** in Traverse City may continue to hold the tortured spirits of a century of inmates who were housed there. Built in 1885, the hospital, also known as Northern Michigan Asylum, admitted about three thousand patients who were accommodated in several buildings. Its first superintendent was progressive for his day, believing that beauty could be used as a form of therapy. He, therefore, strove to establish an atmosphere of tranquility, hoping mental problems would simply vanish. At the hospital, he also abolished the use of straitjackets. When there were outbreaks of influenza, polio, and tuberculosis, the hospital was also used to house those patients along with the mentally ill. But the restless spirits of those who were housed there (and died there) may have remained after the institution closed in 1989. Some visitors have reported experiencing drastic changes in air and energy, feeling unseen forces around them, hearing disembodied voices and footsteps from abandoned areas, and seeing unexplained lights and ghosts, one of which is said to be of a clergyman who allegedly hanged himself in the asylum's chapel, having been driven to suicide by dark spirits. There have been frequent reports of disembodied screams and voices emanating from the empty halls, as well as lights that are said to turn on and off at random despite the fact that the electricity has been disconnected for years. A unique aspect of the hauntings at the Traverse City State Hospital involves what is called the "Hippie Tree" near its grounds. The dead branches of a giant fallen tree are coated with multiple layers of garish neon paint left by various spiritual types, dubbed as "hippies" by the locals. Those would-be mystics allegedly came to meditate beneath the tree to receive visions. Some say a portal to Hell will open beneath its tangled limbs if a person walks around the tree in a certain way. It is said to be a nexus for the unquiet spirits of those that once inhabited the hospital and the madness that haunted them. Many who visit the tree report an overwhelming sense of uneasiness and madness. Others say they can feel the brooding energy that inspired an insane masterpiece painted by a thousand hands. There are no reports of art critics being harmed in the making of Traverse Hospital's psychedelic "Hippie Tree."

FURTHER READING

North, Tom. *Mackinac Island*. Charleston, SC: Arcadia Publishing, 2011.
Pattskyn, Helen. *Ghosthunting Michigan*. Covington, KY: Clerisy Press, 2012.
Rubenstein, Bruce, and Lawrence Ziewacz. *Michigan: A History of the Great Lakes State*. Malden, MA: Wiley-Blackwell, 2014.

24

Minnesota

Minnesota is often called the "Land of 10,000 Lakes," a claim that may sound like the work of an eager Chamber of Commerce. But in keeping with the natural modesty of Minnesotans in general, it is actually an understatement. According to the Minnesota Department of Natural Resources, the state is home to just under twelve thousand lakes that take up an area of 10 acres or more.

That abundance of water was created by huge sheets of ice during the last great glacial period. Vast quantities of rock and soil were scraped from the land by the slowly moving ice, leaving depressions that filled with rainwater to become lakes. The popular Minnesota legend that its lakes were formed by the footprints of Paul Bunyan's giant blue ox Babe has not been conclusively documented.

After the ice moved out of Minnesota, native people found the region a fruitful place to live for thousands of years. When French explorers, fur traders, and missionaries began arriving during the seventeenth century, the Europeans encountered the Dakota and Ojibwe tribes. It is said that the term Minnesota comes from the Dakota words "Mní sóta," meaning "clear blue water." A number of places in the state contain the watery prefix, such as Minnetonka ("big water") and Minnehaha ("curling water" or waterfall).

For decades, much of Minnesota was part of the vast western territory of the American continent that was claimed by France. After the Louisiana Purchase by the United States in 1803, Minnesota was on its way to statehood. According to William E. Lass (2000), "[A] loose assemblage of Yankee lumbermen, fur traders, and other frontier boosters met in 1848 at the Stillwater Convention, which led to the formation of Minnesota Territory" (22), earning Stillwater the reputation of being the birthplace of Minnesota.

Following several reorganizations and the resolution of border issues, today's Minnesota was admitted as the nation's thirty-second state in 1858.

Within a few years of statehood, railroad lines were being constructed across Minnesota with a goal of helping to bring settlers to the sparsely populated region. Amid glowing accounts of unoccupied land ripe for homesteading and farming, a large number of European immigrants arrived in Minnesota during the late 1800s and early 1900s. Many came from Germany and Scandinavia, places where frigid winters were not unknown. Minnesota remains a center of German-American and Scandinavian-American culture.

The standard of living in Minnesota is ranked among the highest in the United States. The people of the state are considered to be among the best educated and wealthiest in the nation. Amid all that scenic and comfortable living, Stansfield (2012) says there are shades of "dark supernatural landscapes in the land of sky-blue waters" (3).

One of the places housing a vestige of the spirit world is no less than the **Minneapolis City Hall** in Minneapolis. In the late 1800s, it was the site of executions of convicted criminals. During that time, as in much of American history, the preferred from of execution was hanging.

If the procedure went well, being suspended by a noose around the neck would ideally break the condemned person's neck in what would be a quick death. It was considered more merciful than such customary medieval forms of execution as beheading, boiling, burning at the stake, and drawing and quartering.

Death by hanging has been utilized as a common method of execution since ancient times, including being cited in Homer's *Odyssey*. Along with capital

Minneapolis City Hall in Minnesota was the location where convicted criminals were executed by hanging. In 1898, the last man to be hanged there suffered a gruesome death for his crime, murdering a man over $14. Today, his apparition is said to appear in the courtroom where he was convicted, the site of his hanging, and even the Mayor's office, perhaps trying to call attention to his plight. (Aliaksandr Nikitsin /Dreamstime.com)

punishment, hanging has also traditionally been a means of suicide. In one account, Matthew 27:1–10 states in the Bible that a remorseful Judas Iscariot committed suicide by hanging himself.

In Mankato, Minnesota, the largest documented mass execution by hanging in the United States took place in 1862 when thirty-eight Sioux had been sentenced to death for their role in the massacre of American settlers. In 1865, the four people convicted by a military tribunal of being involved in the assassination of President Abraham Lincoln, including a lone woman named Mary Surratt, were hanged in Washington, D.C.

Today, various methods of capital punishment, such as lethal injection, have replaced hanging in the United States. In some jurisdictions, if a convict refuses to choose injection, the default method of execution is hanging. At this time, the last person to be executed by hanging in the United States was Billy Bailey, who was executed in Delaware in 1996 for the double murder of an eighty-year-old man and seventy-three-year-old woman.

Although the shape can vary, the hangman's knot is typically a rope coiled around itself, usually thirteen times. Makeshift nooses were frequently used in unlawful vigilante proceedings like lynchings, which are public executions by a mob to punish an alleged offender or to intimidate a group, usually a minority.

The hangman's noose remains a strong cultural symbol. Periodically, nooses are used to menace African American people, especially black students. It is meant to be a throwback to the nooses used in thousands of lynchings. Lynching was the preferred methodology because hangings drew crowds and were easy to photograph, often made into postcards.

Incidentally, the proper past tense of the verb "hang" in its usage as execution is "hanged." An often-used example is that "people are hanged; pictures are hung."

The Minneapolis City Hall is said to be haunted by the ghost of a man who was executed there. In 1898, John Moshik was the last man to be hanged at City Hall. His death was particularly gruesome as the hanging procedure was bungled. It took three long minutes for Moshik to die for his crime, which had been murdering a man over $14. According to Morris and Merk (2012), "Those who have witnessed the ghostly activity in this building claim the ghost is none other than John Moshik himself" (191). The apparition appears in the Mayor's office, the courtroom where Moshik was convicted, and the site of Moshik's hanging. Among the manifestation's antics in the afterlife are rearranging pictures, making attorneys and judges severely ill, and appearing to observers dressed only in his underwear.

SOME OTHER REPORTEDLY HAUNTED PLACES IN MINNESOTA

Dating to 1910, the **Fitzgerald Theater** in Saint Paul was built in memory of Sam Shubert by his surviving brothers, theatrical legends Lee and J.J. Shubert. In 1980, Minnesota Public Radio bought and restored the theater. From 1986 onward, it served as home for the nationally renowned radio program with Garrison

Keillor called *A Prairie Home Companion*, set in the fictitious town of Lake Wobegon. In 1994, the name of the playhouse was changed to the Fitzgerald Theater, after author F. Scott Fitzgerald, a hometown boy who made good. During the restoration, workers found a note signed by a man named Ben, thought to have been a former stagehand who died in the 1940s. As if summoning his spirit, a male entity then began to make his presence known. Unexplained cold spots that weren't there before popped up around the theater, workmen found tools vanishing for a time and reappearing in odd places, and in a near-miss, a large chunk of ceiling plaster plummeted toward workmen from an overhead catwalk. They jumped out of the way, but shining flashlights upward, they saw the dark apparition of a man walking on the catwalk sixty feet above them before suddenly disappearing. Ben may have had a slight drinking problem, with people reporting that they have heard the sound of empty beer bottles being dropped. Sweeter sounds reportedly come from a ghost named Veronica, said to be an actress who died years ago. She loves to sing and entertains staffers who hear her voice echoing in the empty auditorium.

The **First Avenue & 7th St Entry** is a popular nightclub where guests can dance and listen to live music, including such legendary acts through the years as U2 and Prince. The building with its unique rounded front was opened in 1937 as an art deco-style Greyhound Bus Station offering travelers amenities unusual for the time, including air conditioning and shower rooms. Since 1970, First Avenue & 7th St. Entry has not only played host to top-notch musical acts but also a few ghosts of days past. It is said that a young blonde woman in a green jacket committed suicide by hanging herself in the fifth stall of the women's restroom. Some sources say it happened in the 1940s when the woman's boyfriend didn't survive World War II, while others maintain that her suicide did not occur until after the building was converted into a concert venue. Whatever the decade, she apparently replays her unhappy death by appearing to patrons and staff who see a bloated apparition hanging there from a makeshift noose. In other areas of the building such as the V.I.P. Room, DJs have reported hearing strange sounds coming from their headsets. While on the dance floor, people have reported seeing dancing apparitions. It is not unusual that they would be rocking to the music, but these apparitions have been reported as having no legs. Finally, there are tales of a ghost who has been named Slippy who likes to disturb equipment and play pranks, possibly the manifestation of a frustrated roadie.

The building in Saint Paul that now houses the upscale **Forepaugh's Restaurant** was once a stately three-story Victorian mansion built by Joseph Lybrandt Forepaugh for his family. He selected only the finest furnishings and the best domestic servants. One of those was said to be a pretty, cheerful young housemaid named Molly. Apparently, she took her duties in the upstairs bedrooms too seriously, and one day Mrs. Forepaugh is said to have discovered her husband in bed with Molly. Forepaugh ended the affair with the heartbroken Molly who was also pregnant with (presumably) his child. Molly hanged herself, securing a rope around her neck and throwing her body out the window from one of the third floor bedrooms. Later, Forepaugh shot himself. Both he and Molly are said to haunt the restaurant today. While the two of them have been seen walking through the dining areas dressed in Victorian-era clothing, it is the vivacious Molly who is the most active. She is a sociable ghost and seems to enjoy attending weddings and receptions of the sort she would never have in her lifetime. Sources indicate the restaurant has a wedding picture that seems to have captured her image. She can usually be detected by the faint scent of lavender perfume, which she favored. In the basement, lights turn on and off by themselves, and there are unexplained cold spots and strange noises around the building. Sometimes the ghost of Mr. Forepaugh is said to seat himself next to female guests, and sometimes Molly is blamed for smashing glasses, leading to speculation that the two occurrences might be related.

The **Gibbs Farmhouse** in Saint Paul is today operated as a museum of frontier life. Starting by building a log cabin and adding on as their family of five children grew, the Gibbs family lived a happy life there. However, in 1867, nine-year-old Willie Gibbs died of smoke inhalation after fighting a grass fire that threatened the family's house. It is said that his spirit still remains in the family home that he loved. He has been said to remove toys from locked display cases and, like many nine-year-olds, to leave them scattered across the floor for someone else to put away. Cabinet doors are opened and closed by an unseen hand, and an upstairs rocking chair noisily rocks back and forth by itself in an otherwise unoccupied bedroom. Disembodied footsteps have been heard in the kitchen hallway, proceeding up the stairs to the second floor when no one was around. Willie is apparently not shy about being seen, with some witnesses including a night watchman reporting the sight of a child's face peering at them from the windows. One tour guide was sitting on the porch when she glanced in the window to see a boy standing there, looking at her before he disappeared into thin air.

The three-story **Palmer House Hotel** is located in Sauk Center, birthplace of the Nobel Prize-winning author Sinclair Lewis and model for the fictional setting of Lewis's 1920 novel *Main Street*, a depiction of small town America that is not entirely flattering. The hotel's original incarnation was completed in 1863, with various reconstructions and renovations since then. There have been various unexplained occurrences in the building, including the apparition of a young boy who is always described as having green eyes and dirty blonde hair, a ball bouncing down the hallway, disembodied voices, knocking on walls, unexplained temperature changes, and the sound of children playing in the hallways when no children are in the hotel. There have been reports of electrical disturbances, with lights and television sets flickering on and off in guest rooms. One night a guest felt someone's fingers stroking his legs while he slept. Jumping up, he was shocked to find no one there. In addition, there have also been reports that the ghost of author Sinclair Lewis may also be haunting the building: a hotel guest woke up suddenly to see a lanky man standing at the foot of the bed, dressed in clothing from the 1920s. The young Sinclair Lewis worked two summers as a desk clerk at the Palmer House, which turned up in *Main Street* as the "Minniemashie House." Since Lewis left Sauk Center to go to college out of state and lived in big cities, never to return, it is not known why he would choose to spend his afterlife in the kind of small town he satirized, but perhaps he had a change of heart after death.

The **Wabasha Street Caves**, across the Mississippi River from downtown Saint Paul, have had a varied history ranging from glass making to mushroom growing to gangland murdering to disco dancing. Of all these, the one which the caves' alleged ghosts seem to dislike the most is disco. Since 1840, the seven sandstone caves have been useful, first in providing silica for making glass. Then, in the early 1900s, French immigrants found the caves ideal for growing mushrooms, which became a lucrative business. In the prohibition era of the 1920s and 1930s, they were used to hide a whiskey still, store beer kegs, and serve as a popular speakeasy, which was a safe haven not only for consuming illegal alcohol but also as a refuge for criminals evading the law. After prohibition was repealed in 1933, the caves were turned into the Castle Royal nightclub, complete with dance floors, dining rooms, and a bandstand. After World War II, the caves once again were used to grow mushrooms. But during the 1970s, the Castle Royal 2 opened as a venue for disco. During these various incarnations, the caves hosted infamous gangland figures like Ma Baker and John Dillinger, as well as anonymous gangsters who are said to have "rubbed out" three competitors and buried them deep in the caves. Today, supernatural entities seem to feel safe in the caves, and are apparently not afraid to appear in front of living guests. These include the entity of a man wearing a Panama hat strolling around the caves, a ghostly man and woman meeting in the bar at 3:00 a.m., an apparition sitting in the audience while an onstage play is being rehearsed, a woman wandering around the caves as if looking for someone, and three entities of the gunned-down gangsters in prohibition-era clothing enjoying the music. However, during the 1970s era of disco, staff members saw a full-body apparition in gangster attire walk toward them with what they called cold eyes and a hostile demeanor before disappearing into a wall. Perhaps having been exposed to the great jazz musicians of the 1920s, disco was simply not his cup of tea.

FURTHER READING

Lass, William E. *Minnesota: A History*. New York: W. W. Norton, 2000.

Morris, Jeff, and Garett Merk. *Twin Cities Haunted Handbook: 100 Ghostly Places You Can Visit in and Around Minneapolis and St. Paul*. Covington, KY: Clerisy Press, 2012.

Stansfield, Charles, Jr. *Haunted Minnesota: Ghosts and Strange Phenomena of the North Star State*. Mechanicsburg, PA: Stackpole Books, 2012.

25

Mississippi

As might be expected from its name, the state of Mississippi is largely defined by the Mississippi River which forms its western boundary. Settlers are said to have named it after the Native American term "misi-ziibi" or "great river." Today, lovingly restored plantations dot the landscape, but they came at a cost. As Mitchell (2014) says, planters built mansions as symbols of their wealth "and the lifestyle their cotton and slaves enabled them to enjoy" (79).

Living in the region for thousands of years, Native Americans used the river to its best advantage, establishing a trading network that ran from the Gulf Coast up to the Great Lakes. The most prevalent tribes included the Chickasaw and Choctaw, as well as the Biloxi, Natchez, and Yazoo, as reflected in place names.

The first major European expedition to the territory was by Spanish explorer Hernando de Soto who passed through the northeastern part of the state in 1540.

It was not until 1699 that the first European settlement in today's Mississippi was established. Located on the Gulf Coast, it was formed by French colonists under Pierre d'Iberville at Fort Maurepas, also known as Old Biloxi.

In 1716, the French founded Natchez (as Fort Rosalie) on the Mississippi River, which went on to become the region's dominant population center and trading hub.

In the years surrounding the French and Indian War (1754–1763), today's Mississippi was ruled by France, Spain, and Britain. Subsequent to the Revolutionary War (1765–1783), Britain yielded this region to the new United States of America.

In 1817, Mississippi was the twentieth state admitted to the Union. That arrangement lasted less than forty-five years as Mississippi became the second state to secede from the Union in 1861 as one of the founding members of the Confederacy. Following the Northern victory and the reconstruction era, Mississippi rejoined the Union in 1870.

Much of Mississippi reverted to the agricultural economy it had sustained before the war. Plantations and towns were primarily developed along major rivers with access to the transportation routes that carried crops and commercial products. In addition, a heavily traveled land route was the Natchez Trace, which ran between Natchez, Mississippi, and Nashville, Tennessee.

Whether by river transport or overland on the Trace, Natchez was a prime location where business was conducted. Often, that business was transacted in one of the town's taverns.

In their most literal sense, taverns are establishments where people gather to drink alcoholic beverages and be served food. They played a significant role in early American life for colonists coming from Europe where the tradition was strong. In fact, taverns figure in documentation surrounding Jamestown, Virginia, America's earliest colony. Gately (2008) states that some of the people who arrived to populate the colony questioned "their decision to emigrate to a place with 'neither tavern nor beere-house'" (120). It is not known what they had expected to find.

The first recorded tavern was established in Boston, Massachusetts, in 1633, and does not appear to have offended Puritan sensibilities. A great deal of alcohol was consumed in colonial America, often because drinking water could be treacherous. Beer, hard cider, and rum were favorite choices in early American taverns. The result reached the point where Benjamin Franklin printed a "Drinker's Dictionary" in his *Pennsylvania Gazette* in 1737, listing over two hundred slang terms used for drunkenness in Philadelphia.

Taverns catered almost exclusively to males; women were not usually welcomed as fellow drinkers. Other than the tavern's servants, women who entered the premises were presumed to be prostitutes. However, in some colonial towns, almost half the taverns were *operated* by women, especially widows. It was condoned by the town fathers to keep women from having to be supported by public welfare.

To early Americans, taverns were not only a place for food, drink, and companionship but were also essential for learning current crop prices, debating politics, determining betting odds on upcoming horse races, finding business opportunities, hearing newspapers read aloud, playing cards or billiards, and serving as the muster station for militia training exercises. Many taverns also served as the local post office, the county courthouse, and/or the polling place on Election Day.

One such establishment in Natchez, **King's Tavern**, was a hub of community life and one of the town's oldest buildings. After being constructed in the late 1700s, King's Tavern not only served as a recreational and business center but also the town's first post office.

Today, it is a popular restaurant, and its rich history has contributed to the story that it is haunted. According to Alan Brown (2010), "Some of the ghosts that haunt King's Tavern are restless spirits who met a violent end here."

One of those spirits is said to be that of a beautiful sixteen-year-old servant girl named Madeline. According to local legend, Madeline became romantically involved with the tavern's original owner, Richard King, but she disappeared shortly after Mrs. King discovered the affair. Many believe that Mrs. King killed Madeline and hid the corpse behind the tavern's walls.

During work being done in the 1930s, the skeletal remains of three bodies were found hidden in the wall behind the fireplace. Some say they were mummified. The remains were those of two men and one woman. A jeweled dagger was also found with the remains, which was assumed to be a murder weapon. The men were never identified but the woman was believed to be Madeline.

For early Americans, taverns were important community centers. Some also served as the county courthouse as well as a polling place on Election Day. In Mississippi, the rich history of King's Tavern in Natchez, dating to the 1700s, is said to include the ghost of a young servant girl who was killed there, with her body being hidden behind the tavern's walls. (Photo by Nicolas Henderson)

Witnesses have reported seeing a strange reflection that suddenly appears in a mirror as well as feeling unexplained temperature changes. Employees are said to believe it is the unfortunate Madeline who is responsible for the tavern's paranormal activities.

SOME OTHER REPORTEDLY HAUNTED PLACES IN MISSISSIPPI

Chapel of the Cross Cemetery in Madison is the site of paranormal activities such as the organ in the Chapel being heard playing late at night when everyone was gone and the sanctuary was tightly locked. An apparition has been seen wafting through the solid wood front door and the locked iron gate that protects the door. There have also been the sounds of what has been described as manic giggling, and what appears to be a blood stain appearing on the Chapel's stone floor. The accepted tale is that a caretaker who was in charge of the Chapel of the Cross lost his mind and chopped off the head of his wife in the Chapel. After cleaning up the blood as best he could, the caretaker hanged himself from the Chapel's rafters. But the most famous haunting at the Chapel of the Cross Cemetery concerns its role as the final resting place of Henry Gray Vick who was killed in a pre–Civil War duel just days before he was due to be married to Helen Johnstone. Henry was an excellent marksman who fired into the air during the duel, but his opponent did not. After Henry died, it has been documented that his distraught fiancée wore her wedding gown to his funeral, which took place on what had been intended to be their wedding day. During her lifetime, Helen spent hours at his gravesite, crying and talking to his headstone. In her later years, Helen married a minister. The couple built their home, called Mount Helena, on top of what was said to be a Native American burial mound. Helen lived there until she was almost eighty years old. After her death, there have been numerous witnesses who claim to have seen her ghost visiting the grave of her deceased groom-to-be Henry Vick, or sitting on a nearby bench, still clad in her wedding dress and always vanishing when approached. Mount Helena was abandoned for many years, but recently underwent a restoration. There, a play is performed to illustrate the story with descendants playing the roles of their ancestors. According to family members, the first year the play was staged, Helen Johnstone's portrait fell off the wall—on the very day that was the anniversary of the death of Henry Gray Vick.

The **Grand Opera House** in Meridian is said to be one of the most haunted places in Mississippi, but in a good way. The Grand Opera House was built in 1889 by local businessmen from the Marks-Rothenberg family as a site for community entertainment. It succeeded admirably, with reports from the era stating that farmers would stand in the aisles to see the shows. During its heyday, the Grand Opera House welcomed some of the world's leading actors such as Sarah Bernhardt who appeared in *La Tosca*. But the Grand went through the typical lifecycle of such establishments in the twentieth century, including renovation and conversion to motion pictures. In 1927, a legal battle ensued between the owners and a movie chain that rented it and wanted to turn the Grand into office space. According to local historian Dennis Mitchell, during the court case, the theater shut down in 1927 and sat vacant for decades, having a ghostly appearance as if the players had closed up for the night expecting to return in the morning. It has since been restored to its former glory, and may house some of those who never left in 1927. Staff and visitors have heard the sound of a female apparition singing in the opera house. Lights have been known to flicker inexplicably. Paranormal investigators have felt the presence of several benevolent spirits there, capturing photos with orbs of light that when enlarged, appeared to contain the shape of a face. One staff member says that he felt a hand touch his shoulder when he was in the theater, but turned around to find no one there, at least no one living. In any case, at Meridian's Grand Opera House, the show must go on.

Also known as Bellevue and the Pollock House, the **Longfellow House** in Pascagoula was built in 1850 as the home of a slave trader and his wife who were sadistically cruel to the enslaved people who worked at the home. According to local lore, the slaves would be beaten nearly to death, with quite a few later succumbing to their wounds. One, in particular, was said to have been beaten almost to the point of death before being deposited in the nearby woods to die. Today, the property is said to house the spirit of that enslaved servant who is allegedly very angry. He has been reported as being violent, having pushed and slapped witnesses. There are also reports of doors slamming, glasses shattering, items being thrown, and the sound of someone moving around upstairs when no one is there.

One employee not familiar with the home's dark story recalls the feeling of being slapped across the face by an unseen hand, that the slap was loud enough for other people to hear, and that it left a hand print. Although disputed, it has been said that poet Henry Wadsworth Longfellow stayed there and wrote "The Building of the Ship" while a guest. Another poem by Longfellow, entitled "Haunted Houses," might be more applicable:

> All houses wherein men have lived and died / Are haunted houses. Through the open doors,
> The harmless phantoms on their errands glide / With feet that make no sound upon the floors.
> We meet them at the door-way, on the stair / Along the passages they come and go
> Impalpable impressions on the air / A sense of something moving to and fro.

With a name conjuring spooky spirits worthy of Edgar Allan Poe, **McRaven House** in Vicksburg is considered by many to be the most haunted house in Mississippi. McRaven was built around 1797 and received its name from McRaven Street, on which it was located (although later changed to Harrison Street). Its history seems to go back to the time when Native Americans lived in the area, with reports of spotting Native American ghosts on the property. After white families settled in Vicksburg, McRaven originally served as a way station for travelers en route to Nashville, Tennessee, along the Natchez Trace. In 1836, the local sheriff bought the house, but his fifteen-year-old wife died during childbirth in the middle bedroom that same year. The house was purchased by the John Bobb family who enlarged the house in the Greek Revival style. During the 1863 Siege of Vicksburg during the Civil War, McRaven was used as a Confederate camp site and field hospital. The house was battered by cannon blasts from both Union and Confederate armies, but remained standing. In 1864, after Vicksburg had fallen to the Union forces, John Bobb was murdered by Northern soldiers, the first recorded act of violence by Union troops after the Siege. Since then, the apparitions of Civil War soldiers have been spotted in the house, as well as at least five of its subsequent owners who died in the house. One pair of elderly sisters lived like recluses in the house with no utilities or amenities except the telephone, but they at least preserved it to the point where it has been called a "Time Capsule of the South." Today, lamps are known to turn on and off at will, an antebellum shawl is said to give off heat, and ghostly apparitions have appeared, apparently unwilling to leave that comforting time capsule of their past.

The legend of **Stuckey's Bridge** at Enterprise, which was built over the improbably named Chunky River, holds that a man named Stuckey had been an outlaw who had ridden with gang of robbers. Stuckey determined there was an easier way to make a dishonest living by opening an inn near the riverbank. To attract unwary visitors, he would stand outside with a lantern to guide those traveling on the river into coming to his inn. However, once they were asleep, Stuckey would murder his guests, rob them, and throw their bodies into the river at what became the site of the bridge, built in 1850. After the bridge was erected, Stuckey was tried for murder and was hanged from the bridge railing. Today, it is said that the menacing spirit of Stuckey, angry at having been subjected to the same fate as his victims, haunts the bridge. Witnesses have reported seeing him walking with his lantern, apparently in search of new victims. Others have claimed to see him hanging from the bridge as he did on the day of his execution. There are also rumors of hearing a loud splash from beneath the bridge with no apparent source, which is allegedly the echo of Stuckey's body hitting the water after being cut from the noose. In addition, looking in the right spot at the time of the splash is said to result in seeing a glowing spot where his body met the river. It does not help the general spookiness factor that there is a road sign saying "Stuckey Bridge Closed," which might translate into "Enter at Your Own Risk."

At the **Waverly Mansion** in West Point, Mississippi, there is said to be the spirit of a little girl searching for her mother that haunts the property. Originally built in 1852, Waverly had been abandoned for more than fifty years when new owners completely restored it to its former glory. During the renovation, they were sometimes awakened at night by loud noises and strange sounds but never considered ghosts until one afternoon there was the clear sound of a little girl's voice calling "Mama," seemingly out of thin air. It happened again the next afternoon, and repeatedly every day after that. In addition, a definite imprint was discovered on one of the large canopy beds that would be about the size of a three-year-old child. It appeared on the same bed each afternoon, remained there until late in the day, and then would vanish. Mysteriously, one afternoon the little girl's voice was heard for the last time. Instead of sweetly calling as it normally did, it is said that the voice became loud and shrill, yelling "Mama!" five times. The voice never called out again and there were no more indentations on the bed each afternoon. After the renovation was complete, some guests asked the owners if they knew they had a spirit in the house. At that point, the little girl's indention started appearing in the bed again. Although her voice was not heard, she was also seen as a manifestation by the owners, described as being a blond-haired toddler wearing a long, high-necked nightgown who suddenly dissolves into a white mist.

FURTHER READING

Brown, Alan. *Haunted Natchez.* Charleston, SC: The History Press, 2010.

Gately, Iain. *Drink: A Cultural History of Alcohol.* New York: Gotham Books, 2008.

Mitchell, Dennis J. "Grand Opera House of Mississippi." *Mississippi History Now.* 2006. http://www.mshistorynow.mdah.ms.gov/articles/167/grand-opera-house-of-mississippi.

Mitchell, Dennis J. *A New History of Mississippi.* Jackson: University Press of Mississippi, 2014.

26

Missouri

Drained by two of the nation's major rivers, the Missouri and the Mississippi, it is no surprise that the state of Missouri has long been associated with river life.

When European explorers arrived in the seventeenth century, they encountered Osage and Missouria tribes. The French founded Ste. Genevieve in 1735 and St. Louis in 1764. After briefly being ruled by Spain, the United States acquired the region in 1803 as part of the Louisiana Purchase.

Missouri's location on main water routes ensured its important status in transporting goods and people. When it became part of the United States, settlers flocked to the Missouri Territory.

Amid the issue of slavery, Missouri assumed a leading role in the years preceding the Civil War. One significant development was the Missouri Compromise of 1820, in which Maine was admitted to the United States as a free state along with Missouri as a slave state. Thus, the balance of power between Northern and Southern politicians in the U.S. Senate was maintained.

In 1821, Missouri was admitted as the twenty-fourth state, and was the first state entirely west of the Mississippi River to be admitted to the Union. The state's capital was established at Jefferson City, but it was St. Louis that grew dramatically.

Meinig (1995) attributes much of that growth to an incident in the West during 1821 when Mexicans came across a small group of Americans in New Mexico and invited them to come to Santa Fe to trade. "News of this revolutionary openness . . . generated an immediate response in St. Louis" (72). From that time, Missouri played a central role in the westward expansion of the United States. The California Trail, Pony Express, Oregon Trail, and Santa Fe Trail all began in Missouri.

Immigrants from abroad joined American settlers in making their way to the rich lands of Missouri. The state's population grew even more following the Civil War when St. Louis became a business and industrial center.

One particular enterprise was booming. According to Taylor (2012), after the arrival of thousands of German settlers in the 1800s, "beer was the lifeblood of St. Louis for decades" (3). They brought with them a brewing tradition that was centuries old, one that contributed to some of the most basic cultural advances.

DeSalle and Tattersall (2019) state that fermenting grains occurred even before the invention of pottery, adding, "Although pottery might not be entirely essential for making beer in some form, it was certainly a prerequisite for making it in any quantity" (16).

St. Louis, Missouri, became a global center of brewing beer in mass quantities. One of its local businesses, Anheuser-Busch, can trace its origins to 1852. It went on to become the largest brewing company in the world.

A brewery is a business that makes and sells beer. Archaeologists state that some commercial brewing of beer took place at least twenty-five hundred years before the birth of Christ. Ancient Mesopotamian writings describe daily rations of beer and bread to workers.

At first, brewing beer typically took place in the home. Like baking, it was considered "women's work." By the ninth century, farms and monasteries were producing beer on a large scale, not only for their own consumption but so they could sell the excess or barter it as a form of payment. From that time onward, brewing shifted to the domain of men.

In early America, a lot of beer was consumed. Drinking beer was usually safer than drinking local water. Not only could rivers and lakes contain natural pathogens that were harmful to humans, a waterway might also be contaminated if people upstream were using it as a bathroom.

During the Industrial Revolution, beer production expanded to become a major manufacturing sector of American commerce. One of those companies was the Lemp Brewery of St. Louis, with origins going back to 1840.

Johann Adam Lemp was born in Germany. He moved to St. Louis in 1838 where he earned a living by becoming a grocer. However, Lemp soon realized that selling his homemade beer was far more popular and profitable than the sale of groceries.

In 1840, Lemp opened a brewery and trained his son William to take over the business. When Johann Adam Lemp died in 1862, he left a sizable fortune. William Lemp took over the brewery and purchased a larger piece of property for the Lemp Brewery complex in 1864.

Prohibition, the ban on alcoholic beverages in the United States during the 1920s, proved disastrous for many brewers, including the Lemps. Today, the Lemps are known not only for the struggles that took place in their brewery but also in the family home.

With its tragic past, the **Lemp Mansion** in St. Louis is said to be one of the most haunted places in the state. Dating back to the 1860s, the grand Victorian residence was purchased by William Lemp. At first, its thirty-three luxurious rooms provided a happy home for Lemp's family.

However, a series of tragic deaths and suicides followed that sent survivors into an irreversible depression. There are at least four known suicides of family members within the Lemp Mansion.

Along with the decline of the family and the business, the Lemp Mansion itself deteriorated. In 1949, it was sold and became a lower-class boarding house. As if in protest for its reduced state, the hauntings of the Lemp Mansion began. There were reports of burning sensations, cold spots, doors opening and slamming, ghostly knocks, and phantom footsteps in the house to the point where even those looking for a "flop house" refused to stay there.

Fortunately, the Lemp Mansion was renovated into an upscale lodging and restaurant. Even with a loving restoration, there have been reports of glasses flying off the bar, a feeling of being watched, the piano playing by itself, strange sounds, and workmen's tools vanishing. Apparitions have appeared, and if they are the long-dead Lemp family, it can only be hoped that they are happier in death than they were in life.

SOME OTHER REPORTEDLY HAUNTED PLACES IN MISSOURI

Many people do not realize that the wildly popular book and movie *The Exorcist* was based on an actual case that took place in St. Louis. The **Exorcist House** was not in Washington, D.C., as was its fictionalized setting, but on a quiet suburban street in St. Louis. Today, the house is a private residence, although it is said to still be haunted, perhaps tainted by the spirit of an adolescent boy who was alleged to be possessed by Satan. During the 1940s, a boy later designated "Roland Doe" to protect his identity was playing with an Ouija board when he apparently communicated with the dark side. His house began to take on what seemed like a mind of its own, or at least the mind of whatever was possessing it. There were strange sounds like squeaking noises and the echoes of marching feet. Furniture was said to have moved on its own accord, the boy's bed shook, and objects like a vase allegedly levitated and flew around. In more theologically related developments, a picture of Jesus on the wall rattled as if it was being thumped from behind, and a container of holy water smashed to the ground. Priests were called in to perform an exorcism, with one stating that during his encounter with Roland, words like "evil" and "hell" appeared on the boy's body. Even more unsettling for the priest was that Roland broke the clergyman's nose during the procedure. Over the course of several weeks, the ritual of exorcism was performed thirty times. But when it was all over, neither the boy nor the family was troubled again.

The **Governor's Mansion** in Jefferson City has been home to Missouri governors since 1872, with Governor Thomas Crittenden and his family among the first to live there. Their beloved daughter Caroline was born there in 1873, but their happiness was short-lived. The little girl, nicknamed "Carrie," died when she was nine years old after contracting diphtheria. It is said that Governor Crittenden was never the same after her death. When a restoration project for the mansion was underway many years later, there were reports of strange paranormal occurrences in the mansion. One day a workman was performing a project in the attic. When he came downstairs, he asked the housekeeper about the little girl in the white dress who had kept him company by playing in the attic all day while he worked. The housekeeper replied that the current governor had no children, no children lived in the house, and moreover, there was nobody else in the house but him. The workman left without finishing the project and never returned. Since then, there have been reports of objects moving, as well as the mysterious sound of footsteps, soft voices, and waves of laughter that seem to move up and down the stairs. Whether the spirit inside the home is Carrie, she lives on as the inspiration for the playful-looking bronze statue in front of the Governor's Mansion.

The **Jefferson Barracks** Military Post is located on the Mississippi River at Lemay, Missouri, south of St. Louis. From 1826 through 1946, it was an important active U.S. Army installation. Today, it is used as a base for the Army and Air National Guard, and remains the oldest operating U.S. military installation west of the Mississippi River. The adjacent Jefferson Barracks National Cemetery was established in 1866, after the Civil War, in an effort to assemble a formal network of military cemeteries. In the barracks themselves, paranormal activity has been reported at the post headquarters. One night, a soldier spotted an unauthorized light in one of the rooms and went to the window to check. When he looked through the glass, he saw what appeared to be a military officer in nineteenth-century uniform sitting at a desk, writing by candlelight. He suddenly stood up and vanished. At the cemetery, there are two ghosts in old-fashioned uniforms who have been reported as appearing at sundown, acknowledging each other, and then disappearing. Probably the most famous ghost at Jefferson Barracks National Cemetery is the apparition of a toddler who wanders among the headstones, as if lost. This manifestation confuses some people as to why a civilian child would appear at a military cemetery. According to the National Park Service, the first recorded burial at Jefferson Barracks was Eliza Ann Lash, the one-year-old child of an officer stationed there.

The **Jesse James Farm** in Kearney was the home turf of one of America's most notorious outlaw bands, the James Gang, which was led by Frank and Jesse James. The farm was the site of tragedy and violence, making it ripe for hauntings by uneasy spirits. During the Civil War, young Jesse was brutalized by Union soldiers. A half-brother was killed in the farmhouse and their mother lost her right arm by a bomb that was thrown by detectives tracking down Jesse and Frank. After the unarmed Jesse James was killed by a fellow gang member at St. Joseph, Missouri, in 1882, Jesse was originally buried at the family farm. His mother Zerelda (which was also the name of Jesse's wife) placed his gravesite outside her bedroom window so she could see it from her bed. It is said that Zerelda feared that someone would steal her son's body so she had him buried deeper than the standard six feet down. Although Jesse's body was later moved to Mount Olivet Cemetery in Kearney, the original footstone is still at the farm. Jesse's mother wrote his epitaph: "In Loving Memory of my Beloved Son, Murdered by a Traitor and Coward Whose Name is not Worthy to Appear Here." Moving the body did not discourage either tourists or haunted spirits. There have been reports of sounds of disembodied voices, gunshots, and horses' hooves. Lights have been seen moving around in the farmhouse museum after it has been locked up for the night. Staffers report seeing movements that do not register on the security monitoring system, and intense feelings of being watched.

Ravenswood Farm, a grand mansion also known as the Leonard Home, is located at Bunceton, near Boonville. The eclectic Italianate Second Empire-style brick mansion was built in 1880 on more than two thousand acres of land by Captain Charles and Nadine Nelson Leonard. They loved to entertain their friends,

Ravenswood Farm, pictured here, is located near Bunceton, Missouri. Its owners loved to entertain, and after dying, may be the last guests to leave. Visitors report hearing disembodied music and laughter as well as seeing festive lantern lights over the lawn at night, reminiscent of the lavish parties held at Ravenswood in the late 1800s. (Library of Congress)

both inside the house and on its spacious grounds. During the summertime, they would often string lanterns through the trees, hire an orchestra, and invite their guests to dance through the night. Charles Leonard died in 1916, but Nadine lived into late 1935, when she passed away at age eighty-five. But perhaps her spirit never left the home she loved. Visitors have reported hearing a mechanical music sound, although the music box in the home has not worked for years. Phantom footsteps are heard in the hallways, and shadowy figures have been reported on the stairs. Some observers have reported seeing lantern lights bobbing over the lawn at night, accompanied by the sound of music and laughter, all of which are eerily reminiscent of Nadine's beloved lavish summer parties.

Built in 1857, the classical Greek Revival-style **Thespian Hall** in Boonville is the oldest operating theater west of the Appalachians. In its long life, it has served as a playhouse, dance hall, library, movie theater, church, stable, skating rink, and Civil War hospital. The Masons, Odd Fellows, and City Hall occupied the second floor. With all those disparate uses, it is no wonder Thespian Hall is considered to be haunted. It traces its history back to 1838 when leading citizens of Boonville founded an all-male dramatic group called "The Thespian Society," which enjoyed wide community support that was unique in the frontier era. After building the current structure, the good feelings vanished with the coming of the Civil War just four years later. As in the rest of Missouri, Union and Confederate supporters in the town were split. Thespian Hall dodged cannon fire, quartered troops from both sides, and served as a military hospital. The Civil War could not destroy Thespian Hall but the coming of motion pictures almost did. In 1912, the Hall was transitioned into movie house. During the Great Depression, there was a move to demolish Thespian Hall rather than maintain its upkeep, but in 1937, a local preservation group was formed, one of the first of its kind in the state. By then, a large colony of bats was in residence, which added to its spookiness factor. After volunteers worked hard to restore the building, Thespian Hall again served the purpose for which it had been built. Today, ghosts of its past include unexplained ragtime music playing and wig stands in the dressing rooms that turn themselves around to face the mirrors when nobody is nearby. But its main spirit has affectionately been dubbed "Mrs. X" whose apparition was captured in photographs at the theater. With gray hair and wearing an old-fashioned white-collared blouse and dark skirt, she has been identified by a family as their opera-loving grandmother who had passed away. Since then, she has been spotted happily sitting in the audience, enjoying rehearsals.

FURTHER READING

DeSalle, Rob, and Ian Tattersall. *A Natural History of Beer*. New Haven, CT: Yale University Press, 2019.

Meinig, D. W. *The Shaping of America: A Geographical Perspective on 500 Years of History, Vol. 2: Continental America*. New Haven, CT: Yale University Press, 1995.

Taylor, Troy. *Haunted Missouri: Ghosts and Strange Phenomena of the Show Me State*. Mechanicsburg, PA: Stackpole Books, 2012.

27

Montana

As the word suggests, Montana is named for its mountain peaks. Early Spanish explorers called the area Montaña del Norte, or mountainous northern region.

Montana's wide-open spaces range from rugged peaks to vast prairies, from pristine lakes to daunting badlands. With that variety of terrain, the region was rich in wildlife and natural resources, making it attractive for the migrations of indigenous people. According to Enright (2010), as far back as ten thousand years ago, Montana "was a Native American thoroughfare, used to access buffalo-rich prairies" (51).

The land in today's state of Montana east of the Continental Divide in the Rocky Mountains was part of the Louisiana Purchase in 1803. Its land west of the Continental Divide was disputed between the British and United States until the Oregon Treaty was signed in 1846.

Montana was prime real estate. In 1805, the Lewis and Clark expedition put it in the spotlight. According to the Montana Fish, Wildlife and Parks department, the explorers covered more miles within Montana than in any other state, and were beguiled by what Meriwether Lewis called *"seens of visionary inchantment."*

While Lewis may not have had a firm grasp on spelling, he knew he was seeing something special. Soon, American, British, and French fur traders were operating profitably there. However, their voracious quest for fur-bearing animals led to conflicts with the Native Americans who depended on wildlife for their survival. Along with altering native cultural and economic traditions, contact with whites also brought fatal new diseases, for which the Indians had no immunity.

A trading post was established at Fort Raymond in 1807, with the first permanent white settlement in today's Montana being founded at St. Mary's in 1841. Gold was discovered in 1852 and eager prospectors were joined by settlers moving into Montana via the Oregon Trail.

The Montana Territory was created in 1864, joining the Union as the forty-first state in 1889. Settlers poured in throughout the late 1800s, resulting in inevitable conflicts arising with the native people who were already living there.

Donovan (2008) points out that before Montana was part of the United States, one of George Washington's first acts as president was to issue the Proclamation of 1790, which forbade "encroachments on all Indian lands guaranteed by treaty with the new country" (14). However, those well-intentioned sentiments faded as the 1800s progressed.

The Native Americans in Montana were usually moved to reservations, often in remote places far from their ancestral home, with little chance of maintaining the way of life they had honed over thousands of years. For centuries, Indians had depended on the vast herds of bison for survival; now the bison were being destroyed.

Major battles between the U.S. Army and Native Americans in Montana included Red Cloud's War (1866–1868), the Blackfoot Massacre (1870), the Great Sioux War (1876–1877), and the Nez Percé War (1877). Montana's last recorded conflict against Native Americans occurred in 1887 during the Battle of Crow Agency.

But the clash that found its way into the national consciousness for generations to come was Montana's Battle of the Little Bighorn. Also commonly called Custer's Last Stand, it was a fight between the combined forces of Arapaho, Lakota, and Northern Cheyenne Indians against the 7th Cavalry Regiment of the U.S. Army.

The battle took place on June 25 and 26, 1876, along the Little Bighorn River in southeastern Montana. It resulted in the stunning defeat of U.S. forces.

The flamboyant George Armstrong Custer had made a name for himself leading cavalry units in the Civil War. In a footnote to history, Union General Philip Sheridan made a gift of the Appomattox surrender table to Custer as a present for Custer's wife, Elizabeth.

In 1866, after the Civil War, Elizabeth accompanied her husband to the western frontier where Custer commanded the 7th Cavalry. In an effort to subdue Native Americans in the area, Custer ordered the attack on an Indian village despite reports from his scouts that the soldiers had been spotted. He ignored recommendations that his usual tactics should be changed.

Custer and his men were defeated, with many Americans considering it to have been a massacre of more than two hundred soldiers by bloodthirsty savages. Two other units, led by Major Marcus Reno and Captain Frederick Benteen, survived the battle by following different tactics. Reno and Benteen spent the rest of their lives defending their honor.

For decades following the Battle of the Little Bighorn, Elizabeth Custer was an outspoken advocate for her husband. Through her popular books and lectures, she portrayed Custer as a gallant fallen hero, continuing her campaign to burnish his reputation until her death in 1933, just before her ninety-first birthday.

In addition, many Americans were able to visualize a rendition of the battle through countless paintings of "Custer's Last Stand," including one that was mass-distributed by the Anheuser-Busch brewing company.

Today, the site of the conflict can be seen at the **Little Bighorn Battlefield National Monument**, which honors those who fought on both sides. The eeriness of the battlefield, along with what many feel are the uneasy spirits of the dead, have led some people to believe that the site is haunted by the souls of those who died there, as well as survivors like Reno and Benteen, who fought a different kind of battle.

Montana's Battle of the Little Bighorn between Native Americans and the U.S. 7th Cavalry took place in 1876. It was there that George Armstrong Custer's men suffered heavy casualties. At the windswept Little Bighorn Battlefield National Monument, the eeriness of the site has led many to believe they encountered uneasy spirits of the dead who fought on both sides. (Pierre Jean Durieu/Dreamstime.com)

It has been said that the ghosts of Native Americans and soldiers, including Custer himself, have been seen and heard, both on the battleground area and in buildings on the monument grounds. On the battlefield, witnesses have described hearing bugles, frightening screams, rifle shots, and war cries. Some say they've seen riders on horseback and soldiers in uniform. In the buildings, there have been reports of doorknobs twisting, doors opening by themselves, lights suddenly turning off and on, and unexplained footsteps.

According to Stevens (2007), Montana's hauntings may result from life on the frontier which "was rough and frequently dangerous, all too often cut short by accidents or violence" (10). That was especially true for those who died at Montana's Little Bighorn and who may haunt it still.

SOME OTHER REPORTEDLY HAUNTED PLACES IN MONTANA

The **Chico Hot Springs Lodge** at Pray, Montana, close to Yellowstone National Park, was built in 1900 by Bill and Percie Knowles. They operated the hotel with its relaxing springs until Bill passed away in 1910. His wife Percie went on to run the lodge by herself, doing it splendidly until her death in 1941. Some reports suggest she stayed on at the place she loved. Most of the stories revolve around Room 349, where Percie Knowles once resided. It is said the rocking chair in that room always ends up facing the window, no matter how the furniture is arranged. A Bible in the attic is allegedly always open to the same page, and remains eerily free of dust. Over the years, numerous employees and guests have witnessed her specter, joining what has been called "the Percie Club." Two men encountered the manifestation of a woman hovering over a piano in the lounge. Another appearance that was said to be Percie took place when her apparition was witnessed by various guests who thought she was a staff member until she vanished into thin air.

Dating back to 1882, the **Grand Union Hotel** is located in Fort Benton, which is often called the "Birthplace of Montana." With all that history, it's no wonder some spectral spirits have remained behind. The hotel is allegedly home to several ghosts, including a drunken cowboy who rode his horse into the hotel and up its interior staircase. The manager apparently did not feel those antics added to the hotel's ambience; grabbed a gun, he shot and killed the cowboy. Today, people claim to hear the sounds of hoof beats on the hotel staircase and see apparitions of a mounted cowboy in the hallways. There have been reports of strange blue lights that seem to dance across Room 202, and beds that suddenly go from being made to unmade. In addition, there are claims that the ghostly figure of a man in a long, old fashioned-looking coat strolls around the interior of the hotel. Thought to be the manifestation of Charles Rowe, who managed the hotel from 1891 to 1899, he is apparently still keeping an eye on the place, perhaps checking on those unmade beds.

Built by the Great Northern Railway in 1914, the rustic **Many Glacier Hotel** in Glacier National Park is a secluded lodge that in some ways echoes the era in which it was built, having no in-room televisions or air conditioning. It can, however, boast an attraction that other places cannot: active supernatural spirits as permanent guests. One witness saw a woman in a red dress standing in his otherwise unoccupied hotel room. A spectral man in a top hat makes his presence known by walking down the corridors, while other apparitions appear briefly only to vanish into thin air. One ghostly presence likes to have fun by phoning the front desk from inside locked, empty rooms to ask for more towels. But the most well-liked by the staff is a considerate spirit who has been known to make coffee for employees who work early shifts.

A prison that incarcerated inmates for over a century might well be expected to continue housing resident ghosts, and the **Montana Territorial Prison** is no exception. First admitting prisoners in 1871, it served as Montana's correctional facility until the current state prison was constructed in 1979. Known for its overcrowded conditions and insufficient facilities, the old territorial prison was a gruesome place for convicts, with poor food, no heating or cooling, and a reputation for violence. Prisoners and some staff have been killed there, with the most notorious occurrence being a riot in 1959 when the Montana National Guard had to be called in to quell the violence after a prison warden was murdered and several guards and inmates were taken hostage. The riot ended only after the cellblock was fired upon by an antitank bazooka and Thompson submachine gun. The ringleaders died in a murder-suicide, perhaps joining the ghost of a convicted murderer who spent a half century in the prison before dying. Staffers at the Visitors Center claim that guests report hearing eerie sounds, seeing fleeting shadows and strange mists, experiencing sudden coldness, and even a sense of being touched. It is said that paranormal investigation teams who have visited the prison over the years experienced unexplainable activity, with their equipment capturing many of the paranormal phenomena on camera.

The **Philipsburg Opera House**, began life in 1891 as the McDonald Opera House, and over the years has been used as a bank, bottling firm, and livery stable before being restored and returning to its original purpose: entertainment. Along with the performers onstage, theater patrons have described having their hair pulled by invisible hands, feeling inexplicable cold sensations, hearing disembodied footsteps, seeing full-bodied apparitions, and smelling unexplained cigar smoke. Apparitions include a phantom face that materializes inside an empty lighting booth during performances.

The **Pollard Hotel** was constructed in 1893 as the Spofford Hotel and was said to be the first brick building in Red Lodge. Within a decade, Thomas F. Pollard bought the building and expanded it in hopes of attracting more guests, which it does to this day along with ghostly visitors who are not charged for their lodging. Employees and hotel guests have described apparitions including a man dressed in 1920s clothing who is said to spend most of his time near the bar (a very 1920s thing to do). A woman in a yellow dress of undetermined vintage is said to haunt the hallways on the third floor, leaving behind a pleasant, lingering scent of perfume. In third-floor rooms, lights are said to turn on and off by themselves, and guests have reported being overcome by feelings of dizziness and dread.

St. Charles Hall, the oldest building on the campus of Carroll College in Helena is said to be haunted. Construction on the building began in 1909, boasting the distinction of having its cornerstone laid by then-U.S. president William Howard Taft who was on a tour through Montana at the time. Today used as a dormitory, the supernatural activity centers around the men's bathroom on the fourth floor. It is said that in 1964, a popular premed student who was a football star and junior class president blacked out while brushing his teeth. He hit his head on the sink, causing a brain hemorrhage. The student was taken to the hospital but never regained consciousness after surgery, soon dying of pneumonia. After his death, students using that bathroom reported that while brushing their teeth or washing their face, they would glance at the mirror and see a young man with a bloody head wound standing behind them. Turning around quickly, they would find no one else there. After several years of these reports, the bathroom was sealed and locked, as it remains today. There have been rumors of ghostly breathing and scraping sounds coming from inside the locked bathroom, perhaps a youthful spirit trying to get out and enjoy the rest of his college years.

Being called "a town frozen in time," **Virginia City**, Montana, isn't really a ghost town, but it does exemplify what life was like in a Montana mining community during the 1800s. It began life in a somewhat contentious way, having been founded in 1863 by prospectors who called it "Varina" after the wife of Confederate president Jefferson Davis. The local judge who was to sign the town's registration objected to that name, and replaced it with "Virginia." With more gold discoveries, lawlessness ran rampant. As was often the case in the Old West, lawmen were scarce so citizens took things into their own hands as a vigilance committee, or "vigilantes." Bandits, robbers, and other criminals were often hanged by the vigilantes, whose victims may not have been happy about it. After falling into disrepair when the gold dwindled, Virginia City was restored and preserved. Perhaps then the town's lingering spirits felt more at home. One ghost, described as a tall man in a blue Civil War soldier's coat, is said to walk through the town at night enjoying a smoke. Specters of a woman and a young girl have also been seen. At the Bonanza Inn hotel, people state they have been pinched and poked by unseen hands. Doors, drawers, and windows have been said to open and close for no apparent reason, sometimes hastening frightened guests to the check-out desk. In one of the town's residences, a woman named Lucille claimed that a bloody apparition kept materializing in her bathtub. Locals dismissed her story, nicknaming poor Lucille "Loose Wheel." Then the obituary for a former owner of Lucille's home was discovered. It graphically described how that owner had committed suicide by shooting herself in the head while in the bathroom. By the way, Virginia City, Montana, is not to be confused with the real-life town Virginia City, Nevada, where the TV series *Bonanza* was set. Fans ought not to go there either since what is left of the ghost of the fictitious Ponderosa ranch only exists today on a Hollywood back lot.

FURTHER READING

Donovan, James. *A Terrible Glory: Custer and the Little Bighorn—The Last Great Battle of the American West*. New York: Back Bay Books, 2008.

Enright, Kelly. *America's Natural Places: Rocky Mountains and Great Plains*. Santa Barbara, CA: ABC-CLIO, 2010.

Stevens, Karen. *Haunted Montana: A Ghost Hunter's Guide to Haunted Places You Can Visit—IF YOU DARE*! Helena, MT: Riverbend Publishing, 2007.

28

Nebraska

Nebraska, which was admitted as the thirty-seventh state of the Union in 1867, consists largely of the vast treeless prairie known as the Great Plains. Nature provides much of Nebraska's drama. With nothing to stand in their way, fierce thunderstorms and tornadoes race across the landscape in a destructive path. Incessant Chinook winds have been described as so unrelenting that they have driven people mad.

Nebraska was traveled by indigenous people for thousands of years as they migrated across the flat countryside following the great herds of bison that roamed the Plains. There is some debate as to whether Spanish explorer Coronado passed through the region in the 1500s; if so, finding no gold, the conquistador was unimpressed and moved on. However, after trade and settlement by Europeans increased, both Spain and France sought control of the region.

Britain entered the fray in the aftermath of the Seven Years' War (1756–1763) when North America was being divvied up by France and Spain. Then, after America's victory in its War of Independence and the War of 1812, the United States, as the region's new owners, established Nebraska's Fort Atkinson in 1819 as the first U.S. Army post west of the Missouri River.

It took the California Gold Rush of 1848 to stimulate settlement in much of the West. The Kansas-Nebraska Act of 1854 made it official by creating the Kansas and the Nebraska territories. Subsequently, Native American tribes were forced to relinquish their lands and settle on reservations, opening large tracts to development by white Americans and Europeans. Under the Homestead Act of 1862, thousands of settlers migrated into Nebraska to claim free land granted by the federal government. Finding few trees on the prairies, many copied the Native American practice of constructing homes from sod.

The population increased through the 1860s to the point that Nebraska became eligible for statehood in 1867. Still more settlers arrived, finding the vast prairie to be ideal for grazing cattle. Then, agricultural technology brought about inventions like barbed wire, steel plows, and windmills, which encouraged the widespread development of farming. The coming of the railroads brought more people as well as a means to ship farm products to market.

According to Olson and Naugle (2015), "It was estimated that 75,000 permanent settlers entered Nebraska in 1872 and even more in 1873. . . . It was a period of optimism" (208).

However, in 1874, even the most optimistic boosters had to rethink their position with the coming of a plague of Biblical proportions. That year, Nebraska suffered the beginning of a series of cataclysmic infestations by hungry grasshoppers that devoured crops, killed livestock, contaminated water with rotting insect corpses, imperiled trains by making the tracks slick with pestilent bodily oils, and utterly devastated the landscape, with swarms turning the skies black and wiping out livelihoods. Many Nebraskans left the state, never to return.

Others either remained through the devastation or returned to what was left of their homes. Nebraska went on to become a leader in such industries as meatpacking, with many residents moving to urban locales like Lincoln and Omaha.

However, the vast majority of Nebraska towns have fewer than three thousand people, with dozens having a population of less than one thousand. Rural schools have frequently been forced to consolidate. But many Nebraskans have been determined not to lose the identity of their hard-won past. Often, relics that were used by their forebears offer silent testimony to both the hardships and courage of their ancestors by being preserved in museums.

For a state that joined the Union a century after the thirteen original colonies, Nebraska has honored its past by supporting scores of museums. They range alphabetically from Arbor Day Farm in Nebraska City to Wessel's Living History Farm in York. Nebraskan institutions range from art museums and children's museums to the Strategic Air and Space Museum. Along with the Museum of Nebraska History, the Nebraska Museum of Natural and Cultural History, and the Museum of the American Indian, there is a railroad museum, telephone museum, and a museum focusing on military vehicles.

Whatever its format, the purpose of a museum is to collect, preserve, interpret, and display items of artistic, cultural, or scientific significance for the public's education. Simmons (2016) says that objects in a museum's collection "are part of material culture, the physical evidence of cultural practices" (12).

The word "museum" itself is derived from the ancient Greeks denoting a place dedicated to the Muses, which in Greek mythology were the patron divinities of the arts. Along with European landmarks like the Louvre in Paris or London's British Museum, probably the most famous American museum is the Smithsonian in Washington, D.C.

While it may not be able to compete with those world-class centers of learning, Nebraska's **Museum of Shadows** in Plattsmouth has a unique feature: many believe it is haunted.

Dating back to 1880, today's three-story building variously housed a cigar factory, dentist's office, doctor's office, pharmacy, saloon, and brothel. With all of those potential spirits of the past accumulated over almost 150 years, it is no wonder paranormal investigators have claimed to experience the activities of poltergeists with items physically moving on their own, glimpse apparitions, be touched by unseen hands, or hear footsteps, disembodied voices, and other unexplained noises.

Doors at the Museum have been reported as opening and closing on their own, and appliances and power tools have been said to turn on by themselves. But the stars of the Museum's collection are two dolls, Demus and Ayda, which according to the museum's owners are two of the most haunted dolls in the world. There are claims that Ayda was caught by a security footage to be moving and trying to climb out of a box. The doll is said to have been donated to the Museum of Shadows by a family who threw her away, only to discover two years later that the doll returned home to the same spot where they had thrown her away—with her eyes scratched out.

The Museum of Shadows is home to more than one thousand haunted artifacts, with the owner stating that each has a story.

SOME OTHER REPORTEDLY HAUNTED PLACES IN NEBRASKA

The **Alliance Theater** in Alliance, Nebraska, was established in 1938, but it began life as the Charter Hotel in downtown Alliance during 1903. The town itself is fairly isolated, being incorporated during the height of the railroad boom in the late 1880s. Several rail lines converged in Alliance, bringing settlers eager for the 160 acres of free land promised by the federal government under the Homestead Act of 1862. Within the first two months of Alliance being incorporated in 1888, more than two hundred buildings were constructed in the town, hopeful for the kind of success made possible by the railroad. Many of those buildings were destroyed by a series of fires. After the amount of free land available to settlers was increased to 640 acres by federal law in 1904, more residents arrived, sparking another building boom, this time in brick. Today, many brick buildings in downtown Alliance date back to the early 1900s. When hotel trade dwindled, the Alliance Theater was created. Today its resident ghost is said to be an actress named Mary who lost her life in the middle of a performance when a heavy stage light fell and killed her. Theater staffers have claimed her friendly presence remains in the playhouse, with reports of hearing phantom footsteps, feelings of uneasiness, and seeing shadowy figures where none should appear. One report is of the sounds of disembodied footsteps running down the aisles, as if Mary is afraid of missing her entrance.

Antelope Park in Lincoln is a lovely rustic environment in the midst of city life in Lincoln, the state capital. The park contains a field behind the caretaker's house that has reportedly been the site of apparitions that have been spotted walking across the field before suddenly disappearing as they approach the woods on the opposite side. A more disturbing haunt is that of a man who allegedly committed suicide by hanging himself from the swing set in the park's playground space. People have claimed to not only experience an uneasy feeling of being watched in that area and seeing strange shadows nearby but also feel their hair stand on end as if they are being watched.

Today a museum, the Victorian gingerbread-style **Bailey House** in Brownville is the former home of a Civil War officer, Union Captain Benson M. Bailey. The city of Brownville, established in 1854, claims to be the oldest historic frontier river town in the state of Nebraska. When Captain Bailey built his house in 1877, the original site was near the Missouri River, but possibly due to flooding or other reasons, the house was soon disassembled and rebuilt at the current site on Brownville's Main Street. Today, it is said to be haunted by Captain Bailey himself. One account has it that Captain Bailey was poisoned to death by a jealous neighbor. He might have been a crime victim in life but his spirit apparently refuses to be frightened off. Staffers and visitors have reported that doors in the house will not stay closed, and phantom piano music can be heard drifting through the house by dead of night.

Ball Cemetery in Springfield is home to a gravesite dating back to 1869, soon after the Homestead Act of 1862 enticed settlers to hardscrabble stretches of the Western frontier. Today, the cemetery has earned a reputation for being haunted, with apparitions often appearing in the form of a strange mist. People have claimed to hear phantom footsteps on rustling leaves as well as twigs snapping, only to find no one else there. One of the most common reports is being physically touched by the apparition of a tall man. There is also the spirit of a woman who can be heard singing, speaking softly, and laughing after tugging on a visitor's clothes. This friendly spirit from beyond is believed to have been named "Mary Mumford" in her previous life and has been praised for her intelligent hauntings.

Blackbird Hill, the three hundred–foot-high promontory on the Missouri River in Decatur, was not named for its feathered inhabitants, but according to the National Park Service (NPS), received its title in honor of Chief Blackbird, leader of the Omaha tribe. According to NPS, during the Lewis and Clark Expedition, both Meriwether Lewis and William Clark climbed the hill in 1804 to visit the forty-five-foot-tall burial mound of Chief Blackbird, whose ruthlessness was notorious among other tribes as well as white traders. Blackbird's ruthlessness had been no match for the tiny microbes that carried European diseases. Clark wrote that the chief, along with four hundred of his people, died four years earlier from a catastrophic smallpox epidemic that decimated the tribe. Blackbird Hill remained a distinctive landmark for river travelers throughout the 1800s, and developed its own legend of being haunted, not by a vengeful Chief Blackbird, but in a classic story of love gone wrong. The spirit possessing Blackbird Hill is said to be the ghost of a young woman who tried to leave her much-older husband for her true love. Years before, she and the young man had fallen in love, but before they could marry, the young man traveled abroad and was thought to be lost at sea, leaving her heartbroken. After waiting several years, she married the older man. Then her lost love returned, explaining that he had been shipwrecked and unable to contact her. She asked her husband to be released from her wedding vows so she could reunite with her young lover, but the enraged husband attacked her with his hunting knife. The younger man, who had been concealed nearby, saw the husband carried her bleeding body to the top of Blackbird Hill. There, the young man witnessed the husband, still carrying his wife's body, jump into the river beneath them. Today, it is said that every year on October 17, the anniversary of the incident, the woman's chilling screams can be heard echoing around Blackbird Hill.

With a current population of 2,820 residents, the town of Valentine in far northern Nebraska was founded in 1883 when the railroad was extended to that point. Despite its romantic name, it was actually titled for Nebraska representative Edward K. Valentine. Today, it performs a public service in the name of love by participating in an annual program where thousands of pieces of mail flow into its post office so they can be remailed with a special Valentine's Day postmark. The oldest standing building in Valentine, **Centennial Hall**, was built in 1897 when it housed the Valentine Public School. Today, it serves as a museum, and remains the oldest standing high school building in the state of Nebraska. The two-story brick building contains twelve rooms and was used as a school for primary and secondary students in the county. Centennial Hall was opened as a museum in 1978 and was listed on the National Register of Historic Places in 1984; but it also has another distinction: it is said to be haunted by the ghost of a former student who was the victim of a gruesome act. The story goes that in 1944, a girl who attended the school died after someone poisoned the reed on her clarinet. When she began playing the instrument, the undetermined poison took effect and the girl died of a heart attack. No suspect or motive has been documented. Perhaps upset by the lack of justice, after the girl's death, some teachers claimed to see her ghost in the hallways, with her manifestation often accompanied by a feeling of being unwell. After the school was converted into a museum, there have been

The oldest standing building in Valentine, Nebraska, is Centennial Hall, built in 1897 when it housed the Valentine Public School. Today, it is said to be haunted by the ghost of a schoolgirl who was poisoned there in 1944, a crime that is still unsolved. Strange sounds from the former music room where the girl died may suggest her dismay at the lack of justice. (Photo by Ammodramus)

reports of cold spots and the sound of music coming from the school's old music room despite the fact that there have been no musical instruments in the building for years. One of the most common reports is that of a rocking chair on the premises that can be observed to be rocking when no one is in the chair.

The century-old building that houses today's **Platte County Historical Society and Museum** in Columbus contains more than artifacts and memorabilia from Nebraska's history. Inside the building, which was the former Third Ward School, there have been claims of seeing shadow figures walking the halls and hearing the unexplained sound of disembodied voices emanating from empty rooms. Paranormal investigation teams have reported some strange phenomena, such as electromagnetic field disruptions, unexplained shadows, and voices that were audible in recordings. Others have claimed to hear a loud banging noise in the 1857 log cabin that is on the premises, unexplained whistles, and the sound of a young girl talking, as well as an older woman asking, "Can you hear my voice?"

FURTHER READING

Olson, James C., and Ronald Naugle. *History of Nebraska*. Lincoln: University of Nebraska, 2015.

Simmons, John E. *Museums: A History*. Lanham, MD: Rowman and Littlefield, 2016.

29

Nevada

Among its other distinctions, one of the more contentious topics in discussing the state of Nevada is how to pronounce its name. The word itself comes from the Spanish "nevada," meaning "snowy," a reference to the icy peaks of the Sierra Nevada ("snow-covered mountains"). The pronunciation closest to the Spanish word is Nev-AHH-duh. However, most residents of the state, including its legislature, prefer Nev-AAA-duh, with the same short "a" sound as in the word "trap." Some feel that comparison is especially appropriate the closer they get to the gambling dens of Las Vegas.

The state is largely a desert, with nearly three-quarters of Nevadans living in the area around Las Vegas.

Native Americans like the Paiute and Shoshone tribes inhabited the region before European contact. Expeditions by Spanish friars and explorers like Francisco Garcés arrived in the late 1700s. Today's Nevada was annexed by Spain in 1804, becoming a province of Mexico following that country's war of independence in 1821.

The years 1847 and 1848 brought an expanded U.S. presence to Nevada. In 1847, pioneers from the Church of Latter Day Saints (LDS), or Mormons, founded a settlement in what is now Nevada. They called it the State of Deseret, which some people presume is derived from "desert" (of which Nevada has plenty). Actually, "deseret" appears in the Book of Mormon with the usual translation of "honeybee," which was favored as a symbol of industry.

In 1848, following the Mexican War, the United States acquired the region which was made more desirable after the discovery of gold in neighboring California that same year. Wagon trains heading west and the arrival of the railroad brought more people, especially after the discovery of silver in the Comstock Lode near Virginia City, Nevada, in 1859. Even today, Nevada is officially known as the Silver State because of the importance of the precious metal to its economy.

Along with West Virginia, Nevada became one of the two states admitted to the Union during the Civil War. Nevada became the thirty-sixth state in 1864, although it continued to add acreage until 1867. That year, gold was discovered in the Arizona Territory west of the Colorado River, whereupon Nevada absorbed an area that includes most of today's Las Vegas metropolitan district.

During the late 1860s, author Mark Twain lived in Nevada, with an account of those years described in his book *Roughing It* (1872). Twain observed that mining in Nevada led to speculation and immense wealth, adapting a phrase from Shakespeare when he wrote, "To gild refined gold, to paint the lily . . . is wasteful and ridiculous excess."

According to Green (2015), during the state's nineteenth-century mining boom, "Nevada exemplified the Gilded Age" (108), displaying much of what Twain felt was the tendency toward wasteful excess.

In addition, some of Nevada's Gilded Age permissiveness carried into the twentieth century, like the unregulated gambling that was commonplace in its mining towns. In 1931, Nevada's state legislature legalized open gambling along with enacting the nation's most liberal divorce laws. Those amenities came a week after the federal government approved a $50 million construction contract to build today's Hoover Dam near what was then the small Nevada town of **Las Vegas**.

At Las Vegas, Spanish for "the meadows," evidence suggests indigenous people traveled ten thousand years ago. More recent Native Americans like the Anasazi lived there at least two thousand years ago.

In 1829, a Mexican scout named Rafael Rivera arrived in the valley, which featured abundant wild grasses and desert spring waters. Rivera is said to be the first non-Native American to encounter the area of today's Las Vegas. American explorer John C. Frémont arrived in 1844, producing descriptive writings that attracted settlers to the area.

Las Vegas was founded as a city in 1905 when land adjacent to the Union Pacific Railroad tracks was auctioned in what would become the downtown area. In 1911, Las Vegas was officially incorporated.

With legalized gambling and the start of construction on nearby Hoover Dam in 1931, Las Vegas prospered. But it was still a dusty, isolated railroad town. That changed with the coming of an unlikely visionary.

Handsome, charismatic gangland figure Benjamin Siegel was sometimes called "Bugsy" for his sudden, crazed acts of violence, but usually *not* to his face. In the 1930s, Siegel discovered Las Vegas while seeking opportunities for his colleagues in the New York Mob to supply illicit services for construction crews from the Hoover Dam project.

Amid the growth of air travel after World War II ended in 1945, Siegel envisioned Las Vegas, with its legalized gambling, to be the ideal spot for a luxurious hotel with good food and top entertainers. Not only would high-rollers be lured but also thousands of vacationers in America's postwar prosperity.

Siegel's hotel, the Flamingo, opened in 1946, but was not completed. It reopened in 1947, but three months later, Siegel was shot dead in California. Today, between the pool and a wedding chapel at the Flamingo Las Vegas, there is a memorial plaque honoring Siegel.

His vision indeed thrived. Lavish Las Vegas hotels and gambling casinos rose from the desert. The city's tolerance for various forms of adult entertainment earned it the title of Sin City, attracting fun-seekers from all over the world.

In the 1950s and early 1960s, tourists got an extra thrill by being able to view mushroom clouds from nuclear weapons testing at the nearby Nevada Test Site, northwest of Las Vegas. During this time, Las Vegas boasted the nickname "Atomic City," as residents and visitors could excitedly watch the spectacular mushroom clouds, although people were later found to have been exposed to radioactive nuclear fallout in the process.

Las Vegas is also home to the kind of activities associated with being haunted. Writer Paul Papa (2012) quotes TV's History Channel in saying that Las Vegas is a "hot zone of cold spots along with unsettled spirits and well-documented anomalous experiences" (xi).

Among the many examples, one of the most notorious haunts Siegel's Flamingo Hotel. His original investors, alleged to be mobsters, had a tendency to notice when there were mysterious cost overruns. While at the Flamingo, Siegel had stayed in a suite with bulletproof windows and a secret ladder that led from the closet to an underground garage where a getaway car was always waiting. Apparently, Siegel thought he'd be safe in California, but after his investors voiced concerns about the lack of profits, Siegel was found shot to death in Beverly Hills.

However, his ghost is said to prefer Vegas, perhaps proud to see how his vision came to life so spectacularly. His apparition is said to roam the Flamingo, especially near his former suite and the memorial plaque in his honor.

Schumacher (2015) cites the saying, "Las Vegas is a town that will make you pay for your inability to restrain your desires" (19). But perhaps the return on that gamble, after cashing out among the living, is the chance to return in a ghostly form even after all bets are off.

SOME OTHER REPORTEDLY HAUNTED PLACES IN NEVADA

Called one of the Seven Modern Engineering Wonders of the World, the **Hoover Dam**, on the Colorado River just outside Las Vegas, was a construction marvel for its era, or for that matter, any era. It was built between 1931 and 1936 during the Great Depression, not only bringing a significant increase in prosperity to the region but also helping to control floods, produce hydroelectric power, and provide irrigation for the parched landscape. The dam also supports Lake Mead, the largest reservoir by volume in the United States, which offers bountiful recreational opportunities. Constructing the Hoover Dam was the result of a massive effort involving thousands of workers in scorching heat and brutal conditions. Such an enormous concrete structure had never been built before, and some of the techniques were unproven. Many were successful; others were not. The dam opened two years ahead of schedule, but at a cost of more than a hundred lives. Although denied, the legend persists that many fell into the wet concrete during construction and were entombed there. Most of the 112 documented deaths occurred by drowning in the river, falling from great heights, being struck by debris, and running afoul of equipment. Others were officially said to have succumbed to pneumonia, although coworkers alleged the men had actually died from carbon monoxide poisoning while operating vehicles inside the tunnels and that the pneumonia story was promoted to avoid lawsuits. Not only are the spirits of the dead construction workers said to be struggling to find peace in the afterlife by haunting Hoover Dam, the site has become known for the number of people taking their own life by jumping from the dam. Some estimates claim four suicides per year. There have allegedly been reports of sounds of crying and footsteps inside the facility, as well as apparitions of men wearing old-fashioned work clothes, with their spirits perhaps trying to find peace within the engineering marvel they courageously helped to create.

The lovely Italianate **Mackay Mansion** in Virginia City is today a museum and event venue, having served as the home of several of the so-called Silver Kings of Virginia City. It was built in 1859 by a young mine superintendent named George Hearst to be both his residence and the location of a mining office. After what was said to be an initial $400 investment in the rich Comstock mines, George Hearst made a fortune of several million dollars. The mansion's second owner, John Mackay who was born in Ireland and started literally at the bottom as a miner in Virginia City, also made his way up the ladder of success. In the 1870s, Mackay was a rich man who owned the former Hearst Mansion, now known as the Mackay Mansion. Unlike many other dwellings of the Victorian era, it is said that the Mackay Mansion has never been abandoned. It is also said that past residents of the home have remained in the house after death because they loved it so much while they were among the living. Some of the reported apparitions include a former Army officer called the Colonel who liked to sit in the kitchen before his death, and whose spirit may still do so. A female apparition has been seen floating and lingering in favorite spots on the second floor, leading to speculation that she is a former lady of the house. Another female manifestation is clearly a worker bee, making repeated trips up and down the staircase as if trying to finish her chores. Staffers have reported hearing the sound of a little girl playing upstairs when nobody is on the upper floor. A ghostly little girl dressed in white has appeared to guests staying in the bedrooms. But the spirits of the Mackay Mansion also have an ever-popular celebrity connection. According to the Travel Channel, the little girl in white came to visit actor Johnny Depp when he stayed in one of the upstairs bedrooms while filming the 1995 movie, *Dead Man*. Ironically, according to the Internet Movie Database, the movie's plotline involves an accountant who is on the run after murdering a man, encountering a strange Native American who prepares him for his journey into the spiritual world. The manifestation may have been an example of Method Acting at its best.

Built in 1907, the **Mizpah Hotel** in Tonopah once served as a home base for the women who worked there as prostitutes. Today, at least one, called "The Lady in Red," is reported to haunt the building. She is said to be very affectionate and sometimes rubs up against male visitors or runs her fingers through their hair. Occasionally, her manifestation has been seen as half of a ghostly couple, speaking to the apparition of a man who may have been a boyfriend or one of her former clients. It is said that a boyfriend/former client murdered her on the fifth floor of

Like many boom towns, Rhyolite, Nevada, was born in 1904 but was a ghost town by 1916 when the mines played out. Only the shells of its past life remain, like the one seen here. Today, its dusty streets may attract spirits of the dead who reportedly roam there. Rhyolite is sometimes used by movie crews as a stand-in for the collapse of American society in a dystopian future. (Zrfphoto/Dreamstime.com)

the hotel in a jealous rage. Perhaps they have returned to the Mizpah Hotel from the afterlife to try working things out peacefully in a supernatural version of couples counseling.

The ghost town of **Rhyolite**, Nevada, was abandoned as a bustling mining community when the mines played out. The boom town was born in 1904, but was dead by 1916. Today, the scattered shells of a crumbling bank, jail, mercantile store, and train depot are all that remain of Rhyolite's past life. Drawn by the hope of finding gold among the quartz deposits in local mines, prospectors had been drawn to the desert town which sat on the edge of Death Valley. By 1906, Rhyolite was showing the promise of becoming a permanent community, boasting the largest population in the area. According to the National Park Service, the town boomed almost immediately, with buildings springing up everywhere. But the mine closed in 1911, and by 1916, the lights of Rhyolite went out forever, leaving its dusty streets to the spirits of the past who may still roam there. Rhyolite is sometimes said to attract almost as many people in its ghostly form as it did in life. Today, tourists have replaced miners, and movie companies take the place of townsfolk. It is sometimes used as a backdrop not only in Westerns but also in films like the 1987 science-fiction movie *Cherry 2000*, in which the ghost town of Rhyolite was a stand-in for the collapse of American society.

The **Westgate Hotel** in Las Vegas was formerly known as the Las Vegas Hilton, and before that it was the International. Today, among those who check in is perhaps its most sought-after guest: Elvis Presley, or at least the ghost of the King, who died in 1977. In 1956, while he was still alive, Elvis made his first Las Vegas appearance at the New Frontier Hotel, which billed him as "The Atomic Powered Singer" and booked him on the lineup with comedian Shecky Greene and the Freddy Martin Orchestra. That time, both Shecky and Freddy were much better received by Vegas crowds than Elvis. But over the years, that definitely changed. Starting in 1969, Elvis returned annually to the showroom at the International/Hilton, breaking attendance records by attracting millions of fans from around the world, many of whom came year after year. Today, Elvis is apparently repaying the compliment in apparition form by appearing at various places within the hotel, especially near the showroom. Not only can couples get married in Las Vegas with an "Elvis" officiating, but people at Westgate Hotel claim to have seen or heard the manifestation of the real thing. At the Westgate, perhaps Elvis has *not* left the building. Viva Las Vegas.

The hauntings at the **Yellow Jacket Mine** in Silver City bear witness to a deadly fire that tore through the mine in 1869. Most sources agree that the fire killed more than thirty-five miners, but not all of the bodies could be recovered. This is why it is said that spirits of the dead are still haunting the mine. Like most victims of catastrophic events, the miners went to work like every other day. Later that morning, a methane fire broke out at the eight hundred–foot level of the mine, proving uncontrollable. Timbers collapsed, and the fire quickly spread to neighboring shafts. Trapped below, the miners had no chance for escape. Poignantly, families of the miners watched in horror as the mine burned for several days, with their early hopes turning to despair. Although unconfirmed, rumors began to circulate, with some saying the fire was caused by an unattended lantern. But, more darkly, others claimed it was set on purpose by greedy speculators who were trying to crash the market on silver, adding to the troubled feelings of the survivors. Then, stories began to spread that apparitions of the miners were emerging at night. Since then, there have been reports of unexplained lights and blue and white orbs that have been seen near the mine shaft's entrance. There have also been claims that apparitions of miners in work gear walk around the nearby Gold Hill Hotel and Saloon at nighttime. Paranormal activity is said to be the strongest on the anniversary of the fire. Trespassing is not allowed at the now-abandoned mine, although a miner's cabin can be rented by those who wish to be on the lookout for its long-dead former residents.

FURTHER READING

Green, Michael S. *Nevada: A History of the Silver State*. Reno: University of Nevada Press, 2015.

Papa, Paul W. *Haunted Las Vegas: Famous Phantoms, Creepy Casinos, and Gambling Ghosts*. Guilford, CT: Globe Pequot Press, 2012.

Schumacher, Geoff. *Sun, Sin & Suburbia: The History of Modern Las Vegas*. Reno: University of Nevada Press, 2015.

30

New Hampshire

New Hampshire's official nickname is "The Granite State," which refers to the exceptionally hard rock prevalent throughout the region. However, most people are probably more familiar with the New Hampshire state motto that appears on its license plates: "Live Free or Die."

Not only does the motto serve as a catchy title for action movie sequels, it describes what the locals feel is their general character.

Every four years, residents of tiny New Hampshire become VIPs who are much sought-after by national politicians since the state's primary race is the first one in the U.S. presidential election cycle. In this early contest, candidates have been known to figuratively live or die based on the collective wisdom of the Live Free or Die state.

Before the arrival of Europeans, the region was home to Native Americans in the Androscoggin and Pennacook tribes. English explorers visited the area starting in 1600. Permanent settlements like Hilton's Point (present-day Dover) were being established by 1631.

Elting and Elizabeth Morison (1976) state that perhaps the most important feature of the New Hampshire colony "was the little strip of eighteen miles along the sea. Through that small aperture, the first settlers entered the state" (7). Reflecting its British flavor, New Hampshire was named after the English county of Hampshire.

Despite its English heritage, New Hampshire was an early adherent of the American Revolution, even before the war officially started. The only Revolutionary War battle fought in New Hampshire was a raid against the British fort at Portsmouth in 1774 that netted gunpowder and cannons. It holds an honored place in American history. Paul Revere himself alerted the colonists that the fort was about to be reinforced by British troops, and it is said that the captured New Hampshire gunpowder was later used by the Americans at the Battle of Bunker Hill. The skirmish in New Hampshire proved to be among the first shots of the American Revolution, taking place several months before the Battles of Lexington and Concord.

In 1776, New Hampshire was the first of the original thirteen colonies to establish a government independent of Great Britain, and the first to establish its own state constitution. It was one of the colonies signing the Declaration of Independence, and was the ninth state to ratify the U.S. Constitution, the number needed to bring the document into effect.

Even with unquestioned patriotism toward the new American nation, there may still have been some nostalgia in New Hampshire toward its English antecedents in Hampshire. However, it may have been a point of pride that while the highest point in Hampshire is Pilot Hill at a little over nine hundred feet tall, New Hampshire boasts a dozen mountain peaks well over a mile high.

Closer to the ground, some of New Hampshire's rolling hills may have reminded residents of Old England, perhaps thinking that all they needed to look like Britain's Hampshire were a few castles on the hilltops. As Sidney Toy (1985) writes, "some of the most powerful castles of any age or country were built in Great Britain" (153).

Hampshire, England, was—and is—well known for its castles, some of which date back to the early Anglo-Saxon period and the age of King Arthur. Probably the most significant to many people in the twenty-first century is a five thousand–acre estate in Hampshire called Highclere Castle, the place where the television series *Downton Abbey* was filmed.

Across the ocean in America, New Hampshire probably cannot compete with that kind of pedigree, but still has a few castles of its own about which to boast. These include spots like Castle in the Clouds, Castle Anam Cara, Yankee Farmer Castle, Searles Castle, and Windham Castle.

By definition, a castle (from the Latin word "castellum," or a tower stronghold) is the fortified residence of a noble. It is distinct from a palace, which is not fortified, and also different from a fortress, which is not always a private residence. Nobles built castles to control the local area, to provide protection, and to afford a base from which raids could be launched.

Many ancient European castles were originally built out of wooden timbers, but when the enemy began to launch flaming arrows, this design flaw had to be corrected. Today, surviving castles are made of stone.

After the Middle Ages passed into history, some castles in both England and the United States were built to be decorative homes, as well as a statement of the owners' wealth that was literally carved in stone.

Inside their solid walls, some castles are said to be haunted by spirits who cannot or will not leave. **Kimball Castle** in Gilford, New Hampshire, is one of those. Many observers claim that just the sight of Kimball Castle has a spooky aura. It is said that there is a presence in the abandoned structure that is decidedly unwelcoming and leaves no doubt that it wants to be left alone there.

Some of the phenomena that have been reported at Kimball Castle include loud noises and unexplained lights. It is said that several antique clocks which stopped working long ago have occasionally revived themselves. Doors are said to open on their own, and disembodied shadows are said to have been seen.

The castle was built between 1897 and 1899 by railroad executive Benjamin Ames Kimball. He allegedly modeled it after a castle he saw on the Rhine River in

Observers claim that the abandoned Kimball Castle is home to an unwelcoming presence that wants to be left alone within its stone walls. Built in Gilford, New Hampshire, in the late 1800s, it is currently private property. The town ordered the grounds to be fenced to keep trespassers out, or as many say, to keep something else in. (Library of Congress)

Germany. In blending the two motifs, Old Country and New World, local granite was used to build the castle along with materials imported from Europe.

The castle stayed in the family after Kimball died in 1919 until the last remaining direct heir passed away in 1960. With no official owner, the castle was given to the town of Gilford, with the stipulation that the property was to be preserved and not used for commercial development. The site is now private property, and is not open to the public. The town issued an order to the owners to fence the property to keep trespassers out. Or perhaps it is to keep something else *in*.

SOME OTHER REPORTEDLY HAUNTED PLACES IN NEW HAMPSHIRE

The **Amos Blake House Museum** in Fitzwilliam, built in 1837, has become something of a celebrity haunt, being featured on a number of popular paranormal television shows. But one of its resident spirits of the four-legged variety sets it apart from many ghostly places. In 1865, it became the home of the well-respected Amos Blake, who was an attorney, community leader, and state legislator. When Amos died in 1925, his son moved in. However, the son was not known as a pillar of the community as his father had been. Not only was the son considered a "ladies' man," he was what is known today as a hoarder. Amid the piles, there were pathways to move around the house. On the plus side, there were many well-preserved antiques and artifacts from the era of Amos Blake. With a direct link to the past, museum staffers say they often feel that they are not alone. They have heard dancing feet, disembodied voices, and other unexplained sounds as well as seen a shadow person in the corner of a room. Items in the house have moved to other locations by themselves, including old toys that had been placed on the mantle to be displayed only to be found several hours later on the floor, as if they had been played with, although no one else was in the house. One day a staff member was cleaning a section of floor when a small cat approached her, acting as if it wanted to be petted, before suddenly vanishing into thin air. Today, it is said by those in the know that there are eleven spirits in the Amos Blake house, not including the phantom feline. As all cat lovers understand, the latter makes it even more special.

Established in 1877, the **Chase House** in Portsmouth, New Hampshire, was a home for orphaned children. Staff members are said to have heard disembodied footsteps and observed lights and ceiling fans that turn themselves on and off. But the most unsettling for those who work with children is the sight of an apparition resembling a young girl who was said to be living at the home when she hanged herself in her bedroom. Residents sometimes say they have seen her ghostly figure in the hallway who runs away when she is approached, or an apparition of the unfortunate child hanging in the bedroom where she took her own life. There have also been reports of the sound of screaming from inside the room in which she died.

One of the most haunted locales in New Hampshire is a group of nine small islands about seven miles off the coast of Portsmouth called the **Isles of Shoals**. The Isles of Shoals were named by the legendary English explorer Captain John Smith after he sighted them in 1614. Due to their diminutive size, rocky landscape, and remote location, there have been few permanent residents over the centuries. However, the lore surrounding the Isles of Shoals garnered a share of the spotlight for these otherwise isolated spots. The islands have seen their share of deadly shipwrecks, running from the Spanish frigate *Sagunto* (sometimes called the *Concepcion*) in 1813 to the submarine *USSO-9* in 1941. The phantom ship *Isidore*, wrecked in 1842, is still reported to be seen in ghostly form off the Isles of Shoals. With their desolate atmosphere, most of the isles report their own hauntings. For example, the lighthouse at Boon Island is said to be haunted by an unknown spirit who runs up and down the stairs opening and closing doors, as well as what is said to be a sad lady dressed in white who wanders the island. As noted by author Nathaniel Hawthorne in his 1852 journal, Star Island may be haunted by the sight of a ghost and the sounds of her cries, alleged to be a woman who hid with her child from an Indian attack amid several great rocks; when the child began to cry, the terrified woman allegedly killed her baby to keep from giving away their location. Lunging Island may be haunted by the ghost of the pirate Blackbeard as well as one of his many wives. A pale white phantom usually called "Lady-Ghost" is said to be the spirit of a wife who Blackbeard abandoned on the desolate isle and has been observed wandering the island whispering, "He will return." According to some nonromantics, Blackbeard's treasure may be buried there. The ghost of the pirate himself has been spotted, either searching for his treasure or protecting it. Probably the most infamous of the Isles of Shoals has the unappealing name of Smuttynose Island. It was there that the *Sagunto* sank with her crew, and like the *Isidore*, is still said to be visible as a ghost ship in the dead of winter. According to the historical record, Smuttynose Island was the site of a real-life gruesome murder in 1873. In what was called "The Crime of the Century" by newspapers of the era, two young women were butchered, presumably by a man called Louis Wagner. It is said that Wagner's ghost haunts the site, either from remorse or righteous indignation when later evidence pointed to another killer.

Originally constructed in 1842 as the "New Hampshire Asylum for the Insane," a terminology that was changed to Concord's **New Hampshire State Hospital** in 1901, the facility was intended to house the state's mentally ill population. Historically, its conditions were similar to other such institutions at the time, and not in a good way. Reports of abuse, brutality, neglect, and even torture were not uncommon. Patients originally were housed in wards, and underwent experimental surgeries as well as undergoing sterilization. Starting in 1892, after a half century, residential dormitories were constructed to replace the wards. New Hampshire State Hospital closed its doors in 1989 amid allegations about the lack of patient care, with services moved to more modern facilities elsewhere. However, it is said that pain and suffering left a permanent scar on the building. Although the main facility currently lies abandoned, some of the institution's outlying buildings became offices for state departments. Those who visit have reported the sounds of disembodied footsteps and phantom screams. Cold spots are routinely encountered, and objects have been said to be pushed off tables or shelves by unseen hands. Elevators have started working on their own and many visitors are said to have a constant feeling that someone is watching them very closely.

Today, the magnificent **Mount Washington Hotel** in Bretton Woods is one of the last surviving grand hotels in the White Mountains. When it was completed in 1902, the resort was said to be the largest wooden building in New England. It had been the project of a coal and railroad tycoon named Joseph Stickney, who died less than a year after it opened. It would seem that if anyone would haunt the hotel that took him two years to build, it would be Stickney, who had so little time to enjoy it. However, the resident ghost is his wife Carolyn who is known as "The Princess" due to her later marriage to a French nobleman. Staffers and guests have reported seeing the apparition of an elegant lady visiting the dining room where Carolyn had played hostess. It is said that her ghostly presence has been witnessed by so many people that the hotel began leaving Carolyn's traditional seat for her during the evening meal. The shadowy figure of a well-dressed woman has been spotted on the hotel's balcony and captured in photographs. Carolyn's old lodging, Room 314, is said to be particularly active, with guests hearing the disembodied sounds of a woman talking in the dark, feeling as if their hair is played with by unseen hands, detecting the scent of perfume drifting into the room, and seeing the manifestation of a woman sitting on the edge of the bed, quietly brushing her hair. The fireplace is said to start burning on its own, lamps turn on and off by themselves, objects move around the room, and the tub mysteriously fills itself. It may not be surprising that her presence is felt in the room since the original four-poster bed she shared with her husband is still there.

The alleged haunting of the sturdy-looking **Ocean-Born Mary House** in Henniker, New Hampshire, may be something of a misnomer since the woman named Mary for whom it was named never actually lived in the house she is said to haunt. The Scots-Irish Mary Wilson Wallace lived to the ripe age of 94, passing away in 1814 after having been born in 1720 on a ship bound for America. The story goes that during the Atlantic crossing, pirates overtook the ship, threatening to loot and sink it. However, when the pirate captain saw the newborn infant, he agreed to spare the ship if the baby was named after his mother, Mary. The child is reported to have grown up to be a striking woman, over six feet tall, with bright green eyes and red hair. After her husband's death, she moved in with one of her sons but rarely ever visited another son, Robert. It is Robert's home, built in 1760, that still stands and is said to be the site of the haunting. The story of supernatural phenomena was allegedly begun by a later owner of the Robert Wallace house who maintained that a murder had taken place there and that a treasure was buried under the hearthstone. Mary's ghost has been said to haunt the house to protect the hidden treasure, appearing at the door or in the yard in all her red-haired glory as the apparition of a woman dressed in colonial-era clothing. Neither human remains nor a buried treasure at the Ocean-Born Mary House have so far been found.

FURTHER READING

Morison, Elting, and Elizabeth Forbes Morison. *New Hampshire: A History*. Nashville, TN: American Association for State and Local History, 1976.

Toy, Sidney. *Castles: Their Construction and History*. Mineola, NY: Dover Publications, 1985.

31

New Jersey

Sometimes overshadowed by neighboring New York and often the brunt of jokes by late-night comedians, New Jersey is the most densely populated of the fifty states even though its official nickname is "The Garden State."

For almost three thousand years, Native American tribes like the Lenni-Lenape inhabited the region until the arrival of the Dutch in the early 1600s. The Dutch, who concentrated on the economic potential of doing business with the natives, became the first Europeans to lay claim to lands in today's New Jersey under the title of what they called "New Netherland."

Pavonia, the first Dutch colony in the current New Jersey, was established in 1630, eventually becoming the city of Bergen. Lurie and Veit (2018) state that the Dutch were primarily interested in pursuing the fur trade with the Indians, but as so often happened in the New World after contact with the Europeans, "The impact of disease on Native American populations was disastrous" (20). Smallpox, influenza, and malaria decimated local tribes.

In 1664, an English fleet sailed into what is now New York Harbor and took control of Fort Amsterdam, annexing the entire region of New Netherland for Britain. The lands were divided by England's King Charles II, who gave some to his brother, the Duke of York, and some to friends from the island of Jersey, which had remained loyal to the monarch through the English Civil War by giving sanctuary to the King. Thus, the British colonies of New York and New Jersey were christened.

Throughout the colonial era, New Jersey was primarily agricultural, but with its coastline along the Eastern Seaboard, it was also an important shipping port. With fertile land and a tolerant religious policy, more settlers steadily arrived.

Despite origins that grew out of loyalty to the English Crown, New Jersey was one of the thirteen colonies that revolted against British rule during the American Revolution. It was the site of several decisive battles during America's war for independence, including the Battle of Trenton in 1777, commemorated by the iconic painting of *Washington Crossing the Delaware*.

For four months in 1783, Princeton, New Jersey, served as the nation's capital. The Continental Congress was meeting at Princeton when the delegates learned the Treaty of Paris (1783) had been signed, ending the war.

In 1787, New Jersey became the third state to ratify the U.S. Constitution, and it was also the first in the nation to ratify the first ten amendments, called the Bill of Rights.

One of the central figures of the Industrial Revolution established his home base in New Jersey. With a nickname, "The Wizard of Menlo Park" referring to his New Jersey town, inventor Thomas Edison was granted more than a thousand patents while working in the state. A street in Menlo Park was the first in the world to boast electric lighting.

New Jersey prospered in the twentieth century, contributing to the popular culture. The first Miss America Pageant was held in 1921 at Atlantic City, and the first drive-in movie was shown in 1933 at Camden.

During the 1930s, New Jersey also became an important transportation hub for an up-and-coming mode of travel, something that literally went up in flames on a New Jersey airfield.

Before May 6, 1937, an airship was considered something remarkable that carried about a hundred people in luxury, was three city blocks long, and moved eighty miles per hour across the ocean. Most people probably would have said they'd like to travel on one of the miraculous vessels that Botting (2001) describes as "a flying machine resembling a gigantic steel shark with huge fins, the size of an ocean liner" (5).

However, after that day in 1937, those same airships were suddenly transformed in the public opinion into huge, deadly, incendiary devices carrying seven million cubic feet of highly flammable hydrogen where passengers are the last to know they are in the middle of a catastrophe.

The explosive event that changed everything for airships was the *Hindenburg* disaster that took place at **Lakehurst**, New Jersey. Also called dirigibles or zeppelins, one day airships were all the rage in luxury travel, rivaling first-class passage on great ocean liners. The next day, an airship was the horror show that Americans heard on the radio as it burst into flame over Lakehurst. It was captured on film, thanks to Edison's invention of the movie camera, so the *Hindenburg* disaster was replayed constantly in newsreels. Even today, that footage is not only disturbing to watch but also easy to see how it abruptly ended the airship age.

Attempting to dock at New Jersey's Naval Air Station Lakehurst, the German passenger airship *Hindenburg* caught fire and exploded into a massive fireball. There were ninety-seven people aboard, two-thirds of whom somehow escaped the carnage. A ground crew worker also perished as the flaming hulk crashed down from above.

Radio newsman Herbert Morrison was recording an eyewitness account of the landing when the airship detonated before his eyes. Morrison's anguished outcry of "Oh, the humanity!" went down in history.

There have been a number of theories about the cause of the disaster, including fuel leak, lightning, puncture, static electricity, and darkest of all in the days preceding World War II, sabotage. Whatever the cause, in that one cataclysmic

Oh, the humanity! The explosion of the *Hindenburg* took place at Lakehurst, New Jersey, in 1937. Once all the rage in air travel, the disaster abruptly ended the age of airships. Today, Hangar Number 1, which was used as a morgue, still stands, containing what some say are ghostly reverberations of the tragic event. (Nationaal Archief/Spaarnestad Photo)

moment, public confidence was shattered, and the era of the airship came to an abrupt end.

According to Martinelli and Stansfield (2004), while New Jersey "is not as physically large as some, it hosts an impressive number of stories about ghosts" (5). Many of those ghosts are said to reside at Lakehurst.

Today, the site of the *Hindenburg* disaster at Lakehurst is outlined where the skeleton of the airship's gondola crashed. Hangar Number 1, which still stands, was used as a morgue after the catastrophe, and some say there is an eerie sense there of the thirty-six souls who perished. Unexplained sightings, sounds, and incidents within the structure are said to be paranormal reverberations of the tragic event.

Experts say that although the fire consumed the airship in less than a minute, the odds of survival improved depending on where people happened to be at the time. Those who chanced to be deeper inside the ship, such as the passenger cabins or crew quarters, generally perished in the flames. Perhaps it is a sense of irony that keeps their spirits tied to Lakehurst.

SOME OTHER REPORTEDLY HAUNTED PLACES IN NEW JERSEY

The **Burlington County Prison** was built in Mount Holly, New Jersey, during 1811. At the time, Dolley Madison was in the White House and it predated her daring rescue of George Washington's portrait during the War of 1812. Burlington County Prison has seen a lot of history since then, finally closing its doors in 1965 as the oldest continually occupied prison in the United States. Some spirits are said to stubbornly remain, such as Joel Clough who was hanged in 1833 for his alleged murder of one Mary Hamilton when she broke off their engagement. In a pamphlet called *The Confession of Joel Clough*, which is housed in the Library of Congress, the condemned man's statement begins with the phrase that "[with uplifted hands] In the presence of Almighty God, I declare I am innocent." It goes on to say that although he had relatives in New York, none came to visit him in his death row dungeon before his execution. Such a soul might be expected to bear a grudge, and indeed it did. After Clough was hanged, guards and inmates began experiencing unexplained incidents like the sound of disembodied screams, moans, and rattling chains. There were sudden drops in temperature, and construction workers' tools disappeared. Today, the site is a museum where it is said that the most active spot for paranormal incidents is in the basement "death cell."

The **Devil's Tower** in Alpine was said to have been built in 1910 by a wealthy sugar importer, the Spanish-born Manuel Rionda. He intended the hundred-foot-tall stone clock tower at the end of a scenic pathway lined by cedar trees to be a present for his wife Harriet Clarke Rionda. An underground tunnel led from their home to the tower. The story goes that her loving husband provided Harriet with a place where she could relax at the end of the day and enjoy the view all the way to New York City. Once, however, Harriet's view from the tower included the sight of her husband being a bit too loving, this time with another woman. When Harriett died, stories began circulating that Harriet had thrown herself to her death from the top of the tower in despair. It is said that the sound of odd noises and screams can be heard from inside today's locked, sealed-up tower, and if the proper formula is followed, such as circling it a few times, a ghostly apparition will appear, which locals say is Harriet herself. Some people have reported the feeling of being pushed when they are near the tower, and others claim to have seen apparitions in the form of black clouds. It is also said that there have been several attempts to demolish the tower, but each time one or more of the construction workers ended up dying in accidents around the structure, and so it remains standing. Incidentally, this Devil's Tower is not related to the Devil's Tower in Wyoming, which was featured in the movie *Close Encounters of the Third Kind* and predated the New Jersey version by about sixty million years.

Today, it is the Mid-Atlantic Center for the Arts, but when it was built in 1879, the **Emlen Physick Estate** was the largest home in Cape May. It has not been lived in since the last of the Physick family died in the 1930s, but that does not mean it is unoccupied. It is said to be one of the most haunted places in New Jersey. Locals say that due to the spirits of the original occupants, when potential renters or buyers tried to live at the estate, inexplicable occurrences made them think twice and depart. But when the Mid-Atlantic Center bought the property in 1970, restoring it and transforming it into a living museum, the spirits seemed happy to see their former home brought back to its original glory. Some of the spirits may enjoy the sound of music in the home since it has been reported on at least one occasion that visitors touring the home could hear the sound of an old

Victrola playing upstairs, but when they investigated, the music stopped and there was no radio or record player. Emlen Physick, M.D., died in 1916 at age fifty-eight, one year after his mother passed. Although Dr. Physick himself has not made his presence known in his grand old Victorian home, other spirits in residence today are keeping it in the family. His mother Frances is said to exert a strong presence full of residual energy, especially in her second floor bedroom, the home's paranormal hotspot. The spirit of Dr. Physick's energetic, vibrant Aunt Emilie is there along with an invalid aunt, Isabella, who died shortly after the family moved into the mansion. Today, Dr. Physick is buried next to Isabella and Emilie in the Physick family plot in Cape May, but it is unknown why he has apparently declined to join them at home.

The **Grenville Hotel**, a bed and breakfast in Bay Head on the Jersey Shore, has been a vacation hotspot since it opened around 1886. It has also been a hotspot for the paranormal. Employees and guests report regular supernatural activities like hearing the laughter and voices of children when none are nearby, disembodied footsteps, unseen people talking, and objects moving around in the dining room. The third floor is apparently the most haunted, with occupants of Rooms 303 and 304 often reporting the feeling that someone is sitting at the edge of their beds. Some believe the spirits are former owners of the inn, just keeping an eye on things.

As the country's oldest seaside resort, Cape May has hosted city dwellers from Philadelphia and New York who were coming to enjoy the fresh sea air in this Jersey Shore town by the early 1800s. Due to preservation efforts, Cape May is noted for its large number of well-maintained Victorian houses, second only to San Francisco. The **Inn of Cape May** is one of the most popular, owing in large part to its haunted reputation. Guests have heard children bouncing balls in the middle of the night, calling to each other, and playing in the hallway when there are no children on the premises. There have also been claims of hearing adults talking to each other in what was the fifth-floor servants' quarters when the room was empty. Other guests have claimed to see ghostly limbs reaching out to them while they were in bed, including one visitor who spent the rest of the night in the lobby.

The **Hotel Macomber**, also in Cape May, has its own stories to tell, many of them centered on Room 10. The particular lodging was said to be the favorite of a guest who came every year, arriving with a large trunk in order to stay throughout the summer season. She stayed in Room 10, wore large quantities of perfume, and loved to chat. Some say she came to Cape May every summer from the 1930s until her death in the 1970s. After her death, one guest stayed in Room 10, and after dozing off to sleep, heard loud banging on the door. Quickly opening it, there was no one there. After the guest went back to bed, the banging began again a few minutes later, and again there was no one there. Next came the sound of doors opening and slamming closed in the hallway, but she had been told she was the only one on that floor. There have been reports that disembodied voices have been captured on tape in Room 10. After asking if there was anyone else in the room, a woman's voice is alleged to have answered, "We love this bedroom." Right after that, a man's voice is reported to have said something that sounded like, "I'm happy to hear that." In the hotel trade, there is nothing like satisfied guests, even invisible ones.

Now owned by the State of New Jersey and used as a museum, the **Proprietary House** in Perth Amboy, dates back to its completion in 1764. It has certainly seen its share of history, some of it worthy of a television soap opera. It was once the home of the former royal governor of New Jersey, William Franklin, the son of an obscure liaison by his father (and one of the nation's Founding Fathers) Benjamin Franklin. It was William who had assisted Benjamin Franklin in the famed kite experiment of 1752, and it may be William who haunts his former home, with one investigator feeling as though someone was grabbing her neck. Visitors have reported drawers opening on their own, loud noises, and mysterious footsteps. Although born in America, attorney William Franklin was steadfastly loyal to the British throughout the American Revolution and was the last colonial governor of New Jersey. He was imprisoned by the Patriots for several years, but never renounced his loyalty to the Crown, even after America won its war of independence. In 1782, William went into exile and lived in London, England, until his death in 1813, never reconciling with his father. When William died, he was buried in London at the St. Pancras Old Church churchyard. His grave was then lost. Perhaps William's spirit returned to New Jersey's Proprietary House to relive the good old days before it all went bad.

FURTHER READING

Botting, Douglas. *Dr. Eckener's Dream Machine: The Great Zeppelin and the Dawn of Air Travel*. New York: Henry Holt, 2001.

Lurie, Maxine, and Richard Veit, eds. *New Jersey: A History of the Garden State*. New Brunswick, NJ: Rutgers University Press, 2018.

Martinelli, Patricia, and Charles Stansfield Jr. *Haunted New Jersey: Ghosts and Strange Phenomena of the Garden State*. Mechanicsburg, PA: Stackpole Books, 2004.

32

New Mexico

Any place that officially terms itself the "Land of Enchantment" aims high, and New Mexico does not disappoint. Many of its visitors and permanent residents, including celebrities, believe there is something very special about New Mexico; artists say even the light is different there.

Santa Fe, the state's capital, was founded in 1610, a decade before the Pilgrims landed at Plymouth Rock. From its very beginning, Santa Fe flourished. Sanchez and Spude (2013) write that when a trade route from Mexico City was established in 1610, Santa Fe "became the terminus of the trail for the rest of the Spanish colonial period" (43).

The region had been inhabited by Native Americans for thousands of years before European exploration, with the first known inhabitants of New Mexico being members of the Clovis culture about twelve thousand years ago. By the time of European contact in the 1500s, the region was settled by Pueblo people and groups of Hopi, Navajo, and Ute. Today, New Mexico is home to a significant portion of the Navajo Nation.

In the 1540s, Spanish conquistador Coronado led his expeditions around today's American Southwest, known then as New Spain. He was searching for the gold he believed he would find in the mythical Seven Cities of Cibola.

Spanish explorers had hoped to find riches like those of the Aztec (Méxica) Empire, naming the region north of the Rio Grande as "Nuevo México." They ultimately discovered the indigenous people of New Mexico were unrelated to the Aztecs, and were not wealthy, at least not in the way the Spaniards craved.

Today's New Mexico state flag reflects its early antecedents. Often called one of the most distinctive in the nation, it recognizes the region's Spanish origins with the scarlet and gold colors of Spain's Cross of Burgundy, along with an ancient Native American sun symbol.

In the 1800s, New Mexico changed hands a lot. After Mexico won its independence from Spain in 1821, New Mexico became a Mexican territory. At the end of the Mexican War in 1848, New Mexico was annexed by the United States.

In 1853, the United States, planning a transcontinental railroad, acquired more of New Mexico in the Gadsden Purchase. At various points in its long history, New Mexico was also claimed by France, Texas, and the Confederacy, but things settled down after New Mexico was admitted to the Union as the forty-seventh state in 1912.

New Mexico has almost no natural water sources, but that has not slowed it down. The state became home to three Air Force bases, the White Sands Missile Range, and Los Alamos National Laboratory where, in World War II, the top-secret Manhattan Project developed America's atomic bomb. And, of course, starting in the late 1940s, the New Mexico town of Roswell became the nation's epicenter for unidentified flying objects.

In the late twentieth century, Native Americans were authorized by federal law to establish gaming casinos on their reservations, which some feel has brought them the influx of gold Coronado sought to plunder.

Artists and writers have found a creative home in New Mexico, including painter Georgia O'Keeffe who was known for her New Mexico landscapes. The bestselling mystery books by author Tony Hillerman focusing on the Navajo Tribal Police have brought contemporary New Mexico to life for readers around the world.

Hillerman spotlights the challenges of law enforcement in an often unforgiving landscape where a small number of officers have to patrol vast, isolated distances alone. Along with its majestic scenery, New Mexico suffers from many of the ills found in large cities, such as unemployment, illegal drugs, and the abuse of alcohol.

Often, criminals end up going to prison. People charged with crimes might be held in a local jail before their trial, after which they are generally sentenced to state or federal prison. In prison, convicts serve a much longer term, usually years.

Walnut Street Prison in Philadelphia, Pennsylvania, operated from 1773 to 1838, and is considered to be the first prison in the United States. Sing Sing Prison in upstate New York opened in 1826 and is currently operational.

A prison known to many Americans is Attica in upstate New York, which holds prisoners who were often sent there due to disciplinary problems in other facilities. Attica may be best known for the notorious 1971 prison riot that resulted in the deaths of thirty-three convicts along with ten correctional officers and civilian employees.

Prisons are usually secured by armed guards, electrified fencing, guard dogs, iron bars, motion sensors, multiple walls, and roving patrols. They generally house individuals who may be prone to violence, disciplinary problems, and/or mental health issues. Therefore, prisons can be difficult places in which to live or work. Combined with overcrowding, poor food, foul sanitation, violence by prisoners and/or guards, and widespread smuggling of illegal drugs, conditions sometimes lead to rioting.

The **Penitentiary of New Mexico** near Santa Fe may not be as well-known as Attica, but in 1980, it was the site of what has been called the most violent prison riot in the history of the United States.

Over two days, thirty-three inmates were killed and twelve officers were held hostage by prisoners. Fueled by drugs, rioters targeted men who they brutally butchered, dismembered, decapitated, hanged in their cells, and burned alive. More than two hundred inmates were treated for serious injuries.

Today, tours are offered at the now-deserted prison, which is reputedly haunted. There have been reports of unexplained phenomena like ghostly footsteps, unseen voices, prison doors opening and closing on their own, and unexplained shadows. Some have described it as being filled with a kind of force that is an evil energy, while others say the energy is one of sadness and despair.

New Mexico writer Ray John de Aragón (2018) says that, "At one time or another people have believed in ghosts, and they most certainly believe in them now" (9). At least many who tour the Penitentiary of New Mexico seem to.

SOME OTHER REPORTEDLY HAUNTED PLACES IN NEW MEXICO

The **Dawson Cemetery** is located in Dawson, which was once a coal mining town near Cimarron. Throughout the early twentieth century, both the mine and the town prospered. But in 1913, an explosion ripped through the mine, killing more than 250 men, making it one of the worst coal mining disasters in American history. Then, just ten years later, in 1923, another explosion killed 123 men. Even in the face of that adversity, the town did not die. It stood up against disaster but could not fight the economic conditions that forced the mine to close in 1950. Today, virtually all that remains of the town is a cemetery. But the graveyard attracts its own share of visitors, having a reputation of being one of the most haunted places in New Mexico. Some people claim to have seen lights that resemble those on the front of miners' helmets. Others report seeing ghostly apparitions wandering among the tombstones. Although the town disappeared, it may still live on, not only in the sphere of the paranormal but also in the world of show business. The award-winning series *Godless*, shown on Netflix in 2017, is said to have been based in part on the Dawson tragedies. According to the screenwriter, he wanted to create a series about a town that was decimated when all the men were killed, spotlighting the fate of the women after the disaster. Enter Dawson.

The **Dona Ana County Courthouse and Jail** in Las Cruces was put "on the radar" for paranormal enthusiasts after being spotlighted by ghost hunters on national TV. Built in 1937, it is no longer in use, but remains an attraction due to its reputation as a supernatural hotbed. Investigators say they've encountered an unknown, violent entity. In addition, people have spotted shadowy apparitions, heard disembodied voices, witnessed heavy cell doors slamming on their own, feeling cold spots and a sense of being followed, and even being scratched by an invisible hand. According to one story, in the 1950s, a waitress named Mary was found nearby and, accused of being drunk, was brought to the jail. When confined to a cell, she screamed. Just moments later, Mary was found dead with what was called a "horrified look" on her face. Some say her spirit remains in the jail to haunt the place where she was forced to share a cell with unknown demons.

The **Double Eagle Restaurant** is located in Mesilla, New Mexico, near Las Cruces. Mesilla was incorporated in 1848, and holds the distinction of serving during 1861–1862 as the capital of the Confederate Territory of Arizona during the Civil War. On the historic Mesilla Plaza, the Double Eagle Restaurant stands proudly as the 1849 mansion it once was. From its prime location as the Plaza's oldest building, it witnessed the confirmation of the Gadsden Purchase on the Plaza in 1853, as well as the nearby trial of Billy the Kid after being apprehended by Sherriff Pat Garrett. According to the upscale restaurant, newspaper accounts of the era along with other period documents point to the secret romance between the young son of the mansion's owner, Armando, and a beautiful young servant girl named Inez. Upon discovering the affair, the lady of the house was appalled at her son's romance with someone below his aristocratic station. The mother was said to have killed both of the young people as they clung to each other. Although their lives were cut short, the young lovers seem to have reconnected in the afterlife and enjoy having happy people in the restaurant. Instead of being peeved, they are said to have the high spirits of the teenagers they were, breaking glasses, moving tables, turning over chairs, stacking knives outside the kitchen door, whispering the names of employees, and Inez even appearing briefly in ghostly form. Apparently, the young lovers favor a cozy corner spot, so guests are encouraged not to sit in those chairs. Thus, the former residents are not displaced by the intrusion.

The history of **La Fonda** in Santa Fe extends back almost as far as the founding of the city four hundred years ago. The hotel that stands today was built in 1922, but records show that it is built on the site of the city's first inn, located at the end of the Santa Fe Trail when the city was established around 1610. Through the centuries, the hotel has garnered some "spirited" tales. In 1857, it is said that a gambler ran out of luck when a lynch mob dragged him away from the gaming table and hanged him behind the hotel in the space that today is the hotel's enclosed courtyard restaurant. During a leisurely meal *al fresco*, dinner guests have been said to note the shadow of a man swinging from a tree. Ten years later, John P. Slough, chief justice of the Territorial Supreme Court, was shot while relaxing in La Fonda's lobby. Guests have claimed to see the judge, perhaps appalled at this miscarriage of justice, in his signature long black coat, roaming the hotel lobby and hallways. In addition, a young bride, who was said to have been murdered on her wedding night by a jealous ex-lover, reportedly haunts the bridal suite. Finally, visitors to the hotel bar near closing time have been said to encounter the ghost of a cowboy on a barstool next to them, although it is unclear how many late-night margaritas are involved in the sightings.

Santa Fe's **La Posada** hotel encompasses the mansion built by a prosperous merchant Abraham Staab in 1882 for himself and his wife, Julia Schuster Staab. It is said that Julia Staab has never left, though she died in 1896. A La Posada employee is said to have seen a translucent dark-eyed woman with what he called an aura of sadness standing next to a fireplace, wearing a long black gown. Julia's spirit also reportedly appears in mirrors, at the top of the grand staircase, and in a small alcove above the old formal gardens. In addition, Julia Staab has taken the

The history of La Fonda in Santa Fe extends back to the city's founding in 1610. Through the centuries, the hotel has garnered some spirited stories, such as modern-day dinner guests on the outdoor patio seeing the apparition of a nineteenth-century gambler who was hanged from a tree. Other uneasy spirits include a judge and a new bride who were murdered there. (Joe Sohm/Dreamstime.com)

liberty of waking guests who slumber in her former bedroom. She was rumored to have gone mad, retreating to that bedroom until her death at age fifty-two. Julia was reportedly depressed over the loss of a child, and may have experienced severe homesickness after being transported by Abraham from a comfortable life in her German village to a more rugged existence on America's western frontier. Some have speculated that she died from an unintentional—or intentional—overdose of the drug laudanum, with which she may have been self-medicating for her depression. On the other hand, Julia seems to have traveled among Santa Fe's social elite, taking regular walks with Archbishop Jean Baptiste Lamy who resided down the street at the Cathedral of St. Francis of Assisi and is said to have helped her plant the apricot trees on her property. Since then, employees and guests have reported inexplicable incidents like chandeliers swaying, covers wrenched off beds, doors slamming, objects being scattered, and even a feeling of hair being pulled. Perhaps Julia, who wore her dark hair severely coiled, is not a fan of current coiffures.

In the afterlife, Cloudcroft's **Lodge Resort and Spa** may have become the permanent residence of a former chambermaid named Rebecca who is said to have died in the early 1900s. The popular legend is that the lovely Rebecca was exceptionally striking with her flaming red hair, which often seems to be a tip-off regarding events to follow. She reportedly disappeared from her room and was ultimately believed to have been murdered by a jealous lumberjack lover who found her in the arms of another man. There are those who claim that Rebecca still roams the halls of this historic hotel, but in a friendly, mischievous way. Ashtrays have been seen sliding across tabletops, doors open and close by themselves, furniture has been moved, lights turn on and off unassisted, and unexplained fires have suddenly ignited in the fireplace. Some have speculated that Rebecca might be searching for a new boyfriend who hopefully will appreciate her playful nature and not turn out to be an enraged lumberjack.

Built in 1881, the **Luna Mansion** in Los Lunas is said to be the only known Victorian-style structure made of traditional Southwest adobe. Currently, it serves as an upscale restaurant. On the menu is a resident ghost, that of Josefita Otero, who died during renovations to the mansion in 1951, and apparently feels there is unfinished work for her to attend to. The original owner died the same year that the house was completed, so the home passed to his son who only lived at the house for ten years before dying. The mansion passed to Josefita and her husband. She kept herself busy overseeing renovations in the 1920s, and enjoyed the mansion until her death in 1951. In the 1970s, more restorations were needed, and it was then that the ghost of Josefita began to appear. Dressed in attire from the 1920s, she has been described by employees as appearing very life-like. Most often she is seen in an attic storeroom, in two bedrooms on the second floor, and walking to the top of the stairs. There, on the landing, sits an old rocking chair in which she has often been seen slowly rocking. Being approached, she simply stops rocking, stands up, and vanishes. However, Josefita is not the only spirit said to enjoy the Luna Mansion. A former servant, said to have been a groundskeeper, apparently likes to make himself at home in the main house. He has been reported as playing practical jokes on staffers and guests, and being especially friendly to women and children. Wearing old-fashioned clothing, he has been seen by staffers to be sitting on a sofa, as if waiting to be served. When they looked closer, he faded away. Perhaps Josefita gently reminded him his place was outside.

FURTHER READING

de Aragón, Ray John. *Haunted Santa Fe*. Charleston, SC: The History Press, 2018.
Sanchez, Joseph, and Robert L. Spude. *New Mexico: A History*. Norman: University of Oklahoma Press, 2013.

33

New York

When people hear the words "New York," they immediately think of the Big Apple, the iconic island of Manhattan, center of so much that is vital to American culture. However, beyond that urban metropolis, there exists a completely different version of New York, usually called "Upstate." In contrast with New York City's teeming metroplex, the major part of the upstate region is dominated by bucolic farms, forests, lakes, and mountains.

The state of New York was one of the original thirteen colonies, having been named for the Duke of York, the future King James II of England.

Before the arrival of Europeans, New York was inhabited by Native American tribes, including the Algonquin, Iroquois, and Lenape. Most of the region surrounding today's New York Harbor was controlled by the Lenape, who became costars in a saga that has gone down through the ages.

In 1609, the region was visited by Henry Hudson, sailing for the Dutch East India Company. The Dutch established the Hudson River-based colony of New Netherland, including today's New York City which they called New Amsterdam. A document written in 1626 indicates the Dutchmen believed they had purchased Manhattan Island from the Lenape for the equivalent of $24, which everyone seemed to think was a good deal.

However, historians have revised the story. Some believe that like latter-day tourists who "bought" the Brooklyn Bridge, the Dutch "bought" Manhattan from Indians who were just passing through, selling land they did not own. Other historians speculate that from the Indians' point of view, the transaction did not relinquish the island, but simply allowed the Dutch to hunt and fish as trading partners and tenants.

In any case, the point became moot in 1664 when English ships sailed into New York Harbor and seized the colony from the Dutch. Klein (2005) says that during Peter Minuit's administration from 1626 to 1631, the Dutchman's first order of business was to secure Manhattan Island with a fort (30). He did so, but when the British captured what Minuit named Fort Amsterdam, the era of New Netherland ended.

New York, as it was renamed, experienced a split personality during the American Revolution. Many New Yorkers were loyal to the British Crown due to strong commercial and personal links. New York was the only colony *not* to vote for

> *Broadway*
>
> Originally an Indian trail, the midtown portion of New York City's Broadway around Times Square is, to many, the center of the universe. Called the Theater District, hundreds descend on the area each night to see Broadway shows. They may be joined by show folk who are yet to take their final bows. Several theaters on the Great White Way are said to be haunted. The late impresario David Belasco is rumored to haunt the **Belasco Theatre**, built in 1907, where he can be spotted sitting in his old office. At 1923's **Imperial Theatre**, some claim the entity who opens and closes doors is named Fred, but others swear it is the ghost of musical star Ethel Merman, no shrinking violet even in life. Opened in 1903, the **Lyceum Theatre** is the oldest continuously running playhouse on Broadway, but it is reportedly the home of a fairly contemporary ghost, legendary director/choreographer Bob Fosse. Also built in 1903, the **New Amsterdam Theater** is said to be graced by the ghost of beautiful actress Olive Thomas, who died by her own hand in 1920. From the time it was built in 1903, the goal of all vaudevillians was to play **The Palace**. The ghost of acrobat Louis Borsalino is apparently still on the bill there, shrieking and swinging from the rafters, encore after encore. It is fitting that the term theaters all over the world use for the only bare light remaining on in an empty playhouse is called the "ghost light."

independence, although it is said that the rebuff was only because the delegates were not authorized to do so. However, New York did endorse the Declaration of Independence.

About one-third of the battles in the American Revolution took place in New York. The British occupied New York City throughout, making it their military and political base in North America.

When the Treaty of Paris ended the war, there were still English troops in New York City, the final vestiges of British authority in the former thirteen colonies departing in 1783.

In 1788, New York became the eleventh state to ratify the U.S. Constitution. Despite its Loyalist leanings during the war, New York City became the nation's capital under the new Constitution, remaining so until 1790.

From that time, New York began taking its place on the world stage. The Erie Canal, which ran through the state, opened in 1825. The canal linked the Great Lakes to New York City via the Hudson River. From there, the Port of New York connected the city to the world.

According to Cannato (2010), "Nature blessed New York's island empire in many ways, especially with its four-mile-wide harbor sheltered from the rough Atlantic waters" (28). Not only were goods imported and exported by ship, New York's busy harbors also attracted human cargo.

Since the early 1800s, New York City has been the largest port of entry for legal immigration into the United States. It was not until 1890 that the federal government assumed jurisdiction over immigration. Prior to that, the matter had been delegated to the individual states.

In the early days of the republic, new arrivals were welcomed since they could join the unskilled labor force that fueled New York's prosperity as well as that of the new nation. In those days, most immigrants arriving in New York would disembark and disappear into lower Manhattan after docking at the bustling piers. However, in 1847, the state of New York created a board of commissioners to regulate the millions of immigrants who were entering the country.

The first permanent immigration depot in New York was established in 1855 at Castle Garden. But when the federal government took control, it established a central immigration center on **Ellis Island** in New York Harbor.

On January 1, 1892, teenager Annie Moore from Ireland's County Cork was the first immigrant processed at Ellis Island, within sight of the Statue of Liberty. Annie had journeyed across the Atlantic in steerage for almost two weeks. She carried very little with her other than the American Dream.

As a national ethos, the American Dream implies that freedom offers every citizen an equal opportunity for success through hard work and determination. With a public education, it extends hope for upward mobility regardless of social class. The American Dream is what Annie Moore had in common with all the millions who followed, walking in her footsteps at Ellis Island.

More than twelve million immigrants passed through Ellis Island between 1892 and 1954, when it closed. Today, more than a hundred million Americans can trace their ancestry to people who arrived at Ellis Island.

Revai (2005) writes that with all its diversity, "New York has a broad range of supernatural phenomena as well" (2), including the alleged hauntings at Ellis Island.

Along with those whose life took a turn for the better at Ellis Island are those whose hopes for a better life were destroyed there, within sight of paradise.

More than thirty-five hundred people died on Ellis Island, many of whom never made it past the screening process due to illness. About one out of every five arrivals were marked with the dreaded chalk that indicated they suffered from a health problem and had to be taken from their families to hospital wards or isolation rooms. Almost half were children. Some recovered with treatment, some were sent back to their home country, and some died. It was not unknown for immigrants to kill themselves rather than be returned to their home country. Many had nothing to go back to.

Today, the National Park Service welcomes visitors to Ellis Island. Some report hearing the eerie sounds of crying or children's voices when no one else is there. Others experience doors opening and closing on their own, or furniture being moved in empty rooms. Many, especially in the old hospital, report an overwhelming sense of despair.

Most immigrants went on to build new lives. In other cases, rather than return to their birthplace, some anguished spirits remain, knowing that Ellis Island was as close to the American Dream as they would ever get.

SOME OTHER REPORTEDLY HAUNTED PLACES IN NEW YORK

The **Dakota Apartments** are housed in a building with gabled, gothic architecture that simply looks spooky. New York City is known for its famous structures that are recognizable worldwide—the Chrysler Building, Empire State, Flatiron, Saint Patrick's Cathedral—but from the birth of *Rosemary's Baby* to the death of John Lennon, the Dakota is probably its most recognizably prestigious address for the dead as well as the living. Since its opening in 1884, residing at the Dakota remains a sign of wealth and influence. Through the years, purchasing an apartment in the Dakota has been so difficult that some residents were determined to be "carried out" rather than ever sell. Quite a few have died there, and even their ghosts are said to currently remain, including piano maker Charles S. Fischer who died in his apartment in 1905; New York City subway builder John B. McDonald, who died in 1911; and Edward C. Clark, who first envisioned building the Dakota but who died two years prior to its opening, never seeing his creation while he was alive. Before John Lennon was murdered outside the Dakota by a "fan," he claimed to have seen the ghost of a spirit called the "Crying Lady," who is often spotted walking the hallways looking forlorn. Since then, others have reported seeing the ghost of Lennon himself standing at the entrance of the Dakota and surrounded by an ominous-looking light, apparently being another dead Dakota resident who could not bear to leave.

The **Merchant's House Museum**, one of the oldest homes in New York City, was built in 1832. It is reportedly still the residence of long-deceased members of the clan who lived there, the Tredwell family, especially Gertrude Tredwell.

The Dakota apartment building is one of New York City's most prestigious addresses. Since it opened in 1884, purchasing an apartment at the Dakota has been so hard that some residents resolved never to leave, even in death. A spirit called the Crying Lady walks the hallways, while the ghost of John Lennon is said to haunt the entrance to the Dakota where he was murdered. (Luis Estallo/Dreamstime.com)

Gertrude was born in an upstairs bedroom in 1840, never married, and lived her entire life in the home until dying in 1933 at age ninety-three. Today, doors slam, floorboards creak, music comes from a piano that no longer works, and voices are said to be heard in the dead of night when no one else should be in the building. Swirling clouds of mist are said to signify the presence of Gertrude, her father Seabury, and/or brother Samuel. There have been witnesses to unexplained lights and the apparition of a woman in an old-fashioned brown dress moving from room to room. Neighbors have reported seeing a woman who looked like Gertrude run out of the house to scold noisy children on the street. Would-be visitors have been stopped at the front door, being told by a woman in an old-fashioned brown dress that the museum was closed when it was not; upon later gaining entry and seeing her portrait, they recognized her as the long-dead Gertrude.

The **Morris Jumel Mansion** is located at the highest point on Manhattan Island, Washington Heights. That seems appropriate because one of the ghosts said to haunt the mansion is that of George Washington himself, who used the manor house as his headquarters during the Battle of Long Island, also known as the Battle of Brooklyn Heights. There have been reports of his heavy boots pacing in the front room and on the stairs, perhaps contemplating how to win against all odds. The house had been built in pre-Revolutionary days by Colonel Rodger Morris. After the war, the house was purchased by wealthy French wine merchant Stephen Jumel whose wife Eliza had begun life in poverty but seemed to enjoy being the lady of the manor. In present times, there is a report that a group of restless schoolchildren arrived to tour the mansion when a lady in what was called a flimsy purple gown appeared on the balcony and told them to be quiet. Fitting the description of Madame Jumel herself, she then vanished as suddenly as she had appeared. Other witnesses have claimed to see the ghost of a Revolutionary War soldier at the top of the stairs, as well as a young servant girl appearing to be in great distress on the top floor where she had allegedly jumped out the window to her death after becoming romantically involved with a family member. Visitors have also encountered the angry spirit of Madame Jumel's first husband, who accused her of plotting his death, and her angry second husband, Aaron Burr, who died the day their divorce was finalized.

New York City's famed **Washington Square Park** is located in Greenwich Village. While the park, with its iconic arch, has been a trendy gathering spot in current times, it was not so fashionable in the early 1800s when it served other large crowds as a burial ground for about twenty thousand poor New Yorkers and slaves who were buried in paupers' graves. In addition, today's parkland was a veritable dump site for yellow fever victims and criminals, as well as having served in the past as a burial ground for Lenape Indians. In addition, Washington Square Park was the site of public executions that took place at its "Hangman's Elm" through the 1800s and where witnesses today have claimed to see a shadow figure swinging from the tree. Near the site of what had been the gallows, some people have said they felt a cold breeze run through their body even on a hot summer day, and have seen ghostly specters dressed in clothing from the 1700s lurking around before vanishing. Other visitors have noted strange odors, especially after dark, but may have attributed the off-putting aromas to simply being in New York rather than suspecting there are thousands of corpses below their feet.

Outside New York City

No look at the paranormal in New York could omit the **Amityville Horror House**. Located thirty miles outside New York City in the town of Amityville, Long Island, the house is said to be haunted after being the site of a grisly mass murder. From the outside, the private residence is an attractive, upscale-looking Dutch Colonial. However, inside the house, in 1974, a twenty-three-year-old man murdered his parents, brothers, and sister as they slept. The killer later said that he heard voices in the home telling him to murder his family. After a trial in which such disparate elements were brought up as the accused murderer's abuse of heroin and LSD, mental problems, and accusations of the family's alleged mob connections, he received six life sentences which he continues to serve in a New York prison. When another family bought the home after it went vacant for over a year, they reported such phenomena as knives being hurled off kitchen counters, levitations of family members, a red-eyed creature resembling a pig, slime oozing from the walls, and shadowy figures wandering inside the home. Those owners moved out after twenty-eight days. Some community members and an attorney suggested that the family was in debt, aiming to profit from book and movie deals. In the years to follow, the house has been the focus of at least twenty-one movies alone.

Near Cooperstown, New York, home of the National Baseball Hall of Fame, lies **Hyde Hall**, on the grounds of the charmingly named Glimmerglass State Park. Hyde Hall's history goes back to the beginning of its construction in 1817 by the original owner, George Clarke. The ancestral home of the Clarke family was at the town of Hyde in England, and New York's Hyde Hall became what was then the largest private residence in the United States. But instead of enjoying his creation, Clarke died within a year of its completion. However, he has apparently stretched his occupancy into the afterlife. With the house staying in the family for five generations, other long-dead relatives have reportedly also made themselves at home, announcing their presence in the form of apparitions, disembodied footsteps, and assertively pulling sheets off the beds. While each generation seems to have spawned its own ghostly tale, one involves the portrait of Jane "Jennie" Cooper Worthington, whose portrait still graces Hyde Hall's grand dining room. After Jennie's death at age twenty, her husband remarried. It is said that when the second wife removed her predecessor's picture, doors began slamming shut, pots and pans flew around the kitchen, and rattling sounds were heard, all of which halted when Jennie's portrait was returned to its place of honor. Such tales can currently be heard on candlelight ghost tours appropriately called "Hyde & Shriek!"

The **Iron Island Museum** in Buffalo occupies a building that was a former church built in 1883. When the church closed in the 1940s, the structure was later turned into a funeral home. In the year 2000, it was donated to the Iron Island Preservation Society. Soon the building gained a reputation for being haunted, with reports of groaning voices, picture frames moving on their own, and shadow figures roaming around. One of those spirits is said to be Navy and Marine veteran Edgar Zernicke whose cremated remains went unclaimed in the funeral home's basement after he died at age eighty-seven in 1992. His ashes had been placed near the furnace in a quart-sized paint can. When Iron Island Museum was established, its director was determined to discover his identity, contact relatives, and get permission to bury the lost veteran, all of which she did after painstaking effort. She felt the dead veteran's spirit was guiding her to send him on his final mission, which she did. In 2010, there was a memorial at the museum, followed by a military funeral and burial at the national cemetery in Bath, New York. Today, the museum director says Edgar Zernicke's spirit still marches proudly in the museum's hallways, urging her to continue working with lost veterans, which she has done. Mission accomplished.

The Sagamore at Bolton Landing is a grand old hotel on a private island overlooking Lake George in upstate New York. It originally opened in 1883, was burned down by fires in 1893 and 1914, reconstructed in the 1920s, and was expanded to its current configuration in 1930. As students of history will recognize, the year 1930 was not an auspicious one economically. In the midst of the Great Depression, few Americans had money to spend on luxurious lakeside vacations. But The Sagamore continued to thrive for another half century. With another economic downturn, this time in the 1980s, The Sagamore was finally forced to close its doors in 1981. But, just as it rose like a phoenix from multiple fires, The Sagamore did so again. In 1983, a century after the hotel first opened, The Sagamore was purchased and restored to the former grandeur of days gone by. Today, The Sagamore is firmly established as a preferred legacy destination for upscale dining, lodging, and recreation. Many guests appreciate it for its historical provenance. During the 1700s, the region was a hotbed of colonial-era fighting among the British, French, and Native American population. There are reports of claims that The Sagamore was built on Native American burial grounds. Ghosts of more recent personages include a little boy from the 1950s who was reportedly hit by a car while collecting stray golf balls to sell. Today, he is said to haunt the golf course where he enjoys instigating pranks like removing golf balls while they are in play and giggling at the understandably frustrated players. The little boy may have brought friends as there have also been reports of other ghostly children who can be seen not only on the golf course but also giggling in the hotel's hallways. In guest rooms, a woman in white reportedly startles visitors by hovering over them while they sleep, blowing cold air onto their eyelids. Another woman, wearing a blue polka dot dress, strolls casually through hallways and the hotel restaurant. The ghostly specter of a blonde woman reportedly once took the liberty of speaking to a hotel chef, then proceeded to walk right through him. Whether the chef was severely frightened or simply temperamental about having outsiders in his gourmet kitchen, he reportedly quit and never came back. The hotel dining room is the site of quarrels by a ghostly couple who get into a spat. In a rage, the male specter allegedly flings his partner to the floor, at which time she reaches up to him from the carpet, only for them both to fade away. Perhaps they have the good taste to take their differences upstairs since the pair have also been seen in a second-floor guest room. The Sagamore has frequently been named one of the most haunted hotels in the country, on a par with the Stanley Hotel in Estes Park, Colorado, the inspiration for Stephen King's *The Shining*, which, in the spirit world, is high praise indeed.

FURTHER READING

Cannato, Vincent. *American Passage: The History of Ellis Island.* New York: Harper Perennial, 2010.

Klein, Milton, ed. *The Empire State: A History of New York.* Ithaca, NY: Cornell University Press, 2005.

Revai, Cheri. *Haunted New York: Ghosts and Strange Phenomena of the Empire State.* Mechanicsburg, PA: Stackpole Books, 2005.

34

North Carolina

With its long coastline and sheltering islands, North Carolina was home to indigenous people who inhabited the region for about ten thousand years. At the time of European contact, tribes in the North Carolina region included the Cherokee, Pamlico, and Tuscarora.

In the 1500s, Spanish explorers like Juan Pardo tried to establish forts in today's North Carolina to secure a claim to the land for Spain. However, those installations did not survive very long, after which Spain concentrated on its holdings in Florida.

In 1584, England's Queen Elizabeth I granted a charter to Sir Walter Raleigh to colonize land in present-day North Carolina. One became famous not for its survival but because of its disappearance.

North Carolina's "Lost Colony" of Roanoke Island remains one of the greatest unsolved mysteries in American history. It also imparted a name that has rung through the ages: Virginia Dare. Fortson (2016) says on August 18, 1587, Virginia Dare became the first English child to be born in America, adding, however, that "she, along with her parents, would be abandoned on its shores" (36). The infant, along with the 115 colonists, vanished without a trace.

Later attempts at colonization were more successful, with North Carolina becoming one of the original thirteen colonies that formed the basis for today's United States. In 1663, England's King Charles II granted a colonial charter in which he named the new province Carolina in memory of his father, King Charles I (from the Latin "Carolus"). Because of its size, in the early 1700s, the region was split into North Carolina and South Carolina.

As in other colonies, when more Europeans arrived in North Carolina, disease ran rampant among the Native Americans who had no immunity to epidemics like smallpox, decimating their tribes.

In 1776, North Carolina's delegates signed the Declaration of Independence, with a majority of its residents supporting the American Revolution. In 1789, North Carolina became the twelfth state to ratify the Constitution.

In the early 1800s, cotton and tobacco became the foundation for North Carolina's growth and prosperity based on a plantation system that operated on slave labor.

With the coming of the Civil War, North Carolina was the last of the Confederate states to declare secession from the Union. The war took its toll: more than twenty thousand North Carolina men were killed in battle, the most of any state in the Confederacy. An additional twenty-one thousand died of disease.

After the war, like the rest of the former Confederate states, North Carolina struggled to emerge from the devastation. Agriculture was still an important element of its economy, especially inland. A large segment of its population moved away from the coast due to the continual threat of pirate raids, which had been present since the region's earliest settlement.

Piracy is violent robbery inflicted on a ship or a coastal area by seagoing outlaws. The pirates' goal is to steal whatever will enrich them.

Pirates were hardly new. The documentation of piracy goes back to the ancient Aegean and Mediterranean civilizations. In the New World, especially the Caribbean, what has become known as the classic era of piracy lasted from the mid-1600s to the early 1800s.

As European powers established colonies and/or plundered the natives, a lot of trade went back and forth by boat across the Atlantic. With gold being shipped regularly to Europe from the New World, it appeared to pirates there was a fortune that was theirs for the taking.

The ever-increasing volume and value of shipping attracted more seagoing bandits who usually sailed with skilled, charismatic captains. Some of the most famous pirate chieftains were Jean Lafitte, Calico Jack Rackham, Bartholomew Roberts, and the most infamous of all: **Blackbeard**.

The exploits of Englishman Edward Teach, also called Edward Thatch or Thache but known by most as Blackbeard during the early 1700s, became the stuff of legend. According to Brooks (2015), the absence of a known past allowed later chroniclers to "produce a more exciting and colorful account of pirates and their exploits" (2). Brooks maintains that while the real "Edward Thache faded into the background" (2), the notorious pirate stepped forward to capture the public's imagination for four centuries after his death.

It is known that Blackbeard's crew pillaged the West Indies and the east coast of Britain's American colonies. Capturing a large French merchant vessel, he renamed her the *Queen Anne's Revenge* and equipped the ship with forty cannons.

As if his massive weaponry was not enough, Blackbeard's appearance was designed to strike terror. He had a waist-length beard and thick black hair in which he reportedly tied slow-burning cannon fuses to surround his face with a miasma of smoke and fire, making him look like a terrifying demonic creature.

To discourage resistance, Blackbeard let his prey know who was pursuing them by raising his distinctive pirate flag. Sherry (1986) says Blackbeard personalized his own variation in addition to the standard skull-and-crossbones motif, the classic Jolly Roger: "Blackbeard also used a skeleton, but added a bleeding heart" (97).

In 1718, Blackbeard is said to have purposely run the *Queen Anne's Revenge* aground at Beaufort Inlet, North Carolina, boarding a smaller ship. Blackbeard believed he had been granted a pardon but was ambushed and killed at North

Carolina's Ocracoke Island. Today, isolated Ocracoke is said to be haunted by the demonic—and no doubt highly annoyed—dark spirit of Blackbeard.

At what is currently called Teach's Hole on Ocracoke, much of this alleged paranormal activity takes place. Although it is known as a hotspot for paranormal pirate doings, to some, even the supernatural does not approach the scariness of actual events. When ships of the British Royal Navy battled Blackbeard and his crew there in 1718, it turned into bloody, hand-to-hand combat. Blackbeard is reported to have suffered twenty-five pistol, sword, and dagger wounds until he was finally subdued by being decapitated.

The British captain then hung Blackbeard's head by his hair from the bow of the English ship. Sailing to various ports in North Carolina, it was meant to serve as a warning to other would-be outlaws. Ultimately, the severed head was impaled on a stake at the entrance to the harbor in Hampton, Virginia, as a cautionary symbol before being taken back to London, where Blackbeard's head vanished.

Today, the pirate's ghost is said to haunt the land near where he was killed in such a bloody manner. There have been numerous reports of witnesses encountering the apparition of Blackbeard skulking along the shoreline, presumably looking for his missing head.

At North Carolina's Ocracoke Island, legendary pirate Blackbeard was finally subdued by being decapitated. In 1718, Blackbeard is said to have purposely run his ship aground, believing he had received a pardon. However, he was ambushed and killed at Ocracoke. Today, Blackbeard's angry apparition is said to stalk the shore, presumably looking for his severed head. (Library of Congress)

SOME OTHER REPORTEDLY HAUNTED PLACES IN NORTH CAROLINA

The **Attmore-Oliver House** in New Bern has allegedly been the scene of a ghostly presence who quietly goes about her business with a typical Southern charm. The home was originally built in 1790 and for over almost 250 years, it served as the residence of only a few prominent New Bern families. The paranormal activities are said to stem from the feisty spirit of the last private owner. Often called a "character" who was used to having her own way, Miss Mary Oliver was born in the Attmore-Oliver house before the Civil War. She ran the family insurance business from the home where she lived for almost a century before she died in 1951 at age ninety-one. She was childless and the last of her line. Therefore, she may not have felt any great need to leave home, overseeing it as a ghostly spirit. Staffers from the New Bern Historical Society say that occasionally the door opens for no apparent reason. During a professional paranormal investigation, investigators documented orbs and energy fields, with supernatural activity at its strongest in the attic. Some have said that when they enter that space, they can feel the hair standing up on the back of their necks.

When the **Biltmore Estate** in Asheville was officially opened to friends and family in 1895, its thirty-five bedrooms, forty-three bathrooms, and sixty-five fireplaces took up over four acres of floor space. The owner who built it wasn't worried about cost overruns. His name was George Vanderbilt, heir to one of America's largest fortunes. With all that money, he may have felt he could do exactly what he wanted to do, including never leaving Biltmore after he died. When it was completed, the Biltmore Estate was the largest privately owned home in the United States, and remains so today. In one more instance of how "the rich are different," Biltmore was intended not to serve as a primary residence—that was a mansion in New York City—but to be a *vacation* home. In 1886, age twenty-six, he had traveled to Asheville with his mother and fell in love with the mountainous region. He proceeded to buy one hundred twenty-five thousand acres of it for his estate, and built a private railway line to bring his family and friends to Biltmore's grounds. However, even with all that outdoor space, when in residence there, Vanderbilt spent a lot of his time in the home's library. It was his special habit to retreat into the library when he saw a storm approaching. Today, staffers and visitors claim to have seen a shadowy figure in the library, usually when the skies are darkened by an oncoming storm. It was up to his wife Edith to trek down the long hallways to the library to summon George when it was time to join his guests for dinner. Today, when touring Biltmore, many people passing through the library have reported hearing a woman's voice whisper the name "George." In addition, employees and visitors to Biltmore have reportedly heard the sounds of clinking glasses, laughter, and music from now-empty rooms, as well as splashing from a swimming pool that has long been drained. The old adage may be true that "you can't take it with you," but in the case of the ultra-rich, it may also be that even in the afterlife, you don't have to leave it behind.

The **Carolina Inn** at Chapel Hill continues playing host to one of its renowned permanent residents even after he has been long dead. Dr. William Picard Jacocks was a noted physician with a global reputation for his groundbreaking work in the eradication of public health problems like hookworm. His work took him from his home in Chapel Hill across the globe to places like Ceylon (currently Sri Lanka) where he waged successful medical battles against cholera, malaria, smallpox, and plague. He was said to be a kind, gentle man with a great sense of humor. Born in 1877, his life spanned two world wars as he traveled the globe. In 1948, after returning to Chapel Hill, he coordinated programs for the North Carolina State Board of Health, making the Carolina Inn his home. When he passed away in 1965 at age eighty-eight, he maintained his vigorous lifestyle, or more accurately, *after* life style. Staffers at the Carolina Inn say that there is a friendly spirit who enjoys playing jokes on those who stay in Room 256, Dr. Jacocks's lodging for seventeen years before his passing. Guests who have stayed in his old room have claimed incidents like the curtains being pulled wide open after having been closed the night before, and the bath mat being rumpled as if someone had gotten out of the shower recently. Sometimes there is a distinct aroma of flowers in the room, especially in the morning, and a strange, loud "whizzing" sound. The apparition of what has been described as a well-dressed, "portly" man roams the halls wearing a long blue coat over a black suit topped by a knit hat. As he passes, he rattles doorknobs to see if they are locked before moving to the next door. If a guest answers the door, he quickly scurries away. It is said that sometimes this mischievous spirit has enjoyed locking guests out of his former room, requiring a maintenance worker to gain access. This was thought to have been solved when the Carolina Inn installed electronic door locks, but the lock to Room 256 still occasionally manages to jam. Dr. Jacocks might appreciate the wit behind naming an offer to stay in his old lodging the *Room with a Boo!* package.

The **Carolina Theatre** in Greensboro has set the stage for visits from apparitions, including a little boy whose house used to be on the same property and who enjoys childish pranks, such as removing a lone chair from the stack in which they had been placed, or tossing a bolt across the stage to hit a worker in the foot while he was the only one (human variety) there. Another alleged ghost is that of a steelworker who was killed after falling from a beam during the construction of the theater but remains on the job by showing up in his work clothes and walking through the lobby in front of a theater employee before suddenly vanishing. But the most famous is the spirit of a woman who nearly burned the building to the ground in 1981. Although she is sometimes called Melba Frey, her name was cited as Melvaleene Reva Ferguson in newspaper accounts of her destructive deed. She was said to be mentally disturbed and homeless. After watching a movie at the theater, she apparently hid behind the seats at closing time before climbing a stairwell to the balcony and starting a fire. The blaze, which consumed much of the balcony and lobby, also consumed the lady, whose body was found by firefighters. According to theater staff, it took several years to repair and reopen the playhouse. Now, her apparition is said to haunt the area in which she died. She has been seen during rehearsals walking back and forth across the mezzanine level holding a bundle before suddenly disappearing into a wall. It is said that sometimes she jiggles the handles of one of the storage closets and flips the folding seats up and down. It should be mentioned that the Carolina Theatre opened in 1927—on Halloween night.

It would seem that even the state's chief executive is not immune from ghostly doings, at least at the **Executive Mansion** in Raleigh for the North Carolina governor. The paranormal activity is attributed to Daniel Gould Fowle who was the governor of North Carolina from 1889 until his death, which took place at the Governor's Mansion in 1891. Fowle was known as a headstrong, colorful character who had opposed secession, but still volunteered in the Civil War. He joined as a private in the North Carolina militia, was soon appointed major in the commissary branch, and later rose to the rank of lieutenant colonel in an infantry regiment, as well as adjutant general of North Carolina's militia unit, ranking as senior officer. After the war, he was voted into office as governor in 1888, and was the first governor to live in the executive residence. He was also the first to die there, after promoting programs like protecting farmers and advocating education for women. The mansion's original bed was made to Fowle's specifications, and was the place where he died while still in office. When Bob Scott took office as governor in 1970, he replaced the massive wooden bed in the second-floor bedroom of the mansion with a modern, king-sized bed. Fowle's old bed was moved to a room on the third floor. However, soon afterward, Governor Scott began to be awakened at night by a strange rapping sound coming from the wall where the original headboard had been. The rapping continued for several years, throughout the rest of Scott's administration. The Scott family nicknamed the spirit, "Governor Fowle's Ghost." When a new administration moved in during 1973, Scott's successor apparently decided that the politic thing to do was to move the old bed back down to its original location. After doing so, the weird phenomenon ceased.

FURTHER READING

Brooks, Baylus. *Blackbeard Reconsidered*. Raleigh: North Carolina Office of Archives and History, 2015.

Fortson, Ben. *A Nutshell History of North Carolina*. Charleston, SC: The History Press, 2016.

Sherry, Frank. *Raiders and Rebels: A History of the Golden Age of Piracy*. New York: Harper Perennial, 1986.

35

North Dakota

In general, North Dakota is considered to be a friendly, affable place that for many years has had one of the lowest crime rates in the country. There does seem to be one sore spot, however, concerning North Dakota's neighbor to the south. In 1889, when it came time to declare statehood for North and South Dakota, the rivalry between the two presented a dilemma: which would be admitted to the Union first?

To solve the predicament without alienating any potential voters, then-President Benjamin Harrison ordered the enabling documents for statehood to be shuffled and placed so he could sign them without knowing which was which. Therefore, North and South Dakota joined the Union simultaneously on November 2, 1889, as the thirty-ninth and fortieth states with no one actually knowing which of the two was admitted first.

However, the alphabet ultimately reigned supreme. Since North Dakota appears alphabetically before South Dakota, the statehood proclamation for North Dakota was published first in the government's record of statutes.

North Dakota had been home to Native Americans for thousands of years before the coming of Europeans. When white explorers arrived, they encountered tribes like the Crow, Lakota, and Mandan.

The first documented white man to reach the area was a French Canadian trader named Pierre Gaultier, Sieur de La Vérendrye. In 1738, he led an exploration party but was primarily interested in trading with Mandan villages.

North Dakota was included in the Louisiana Purchase of 1803. Fur traders and trappers from Canada had been coming to the area for over a half century before the arrival of Lewis and Clark. Their cross-country expedition traversed the region in the winter of 1804–1805 when they built Fort Mandan near present-day Washburn, North Dakota.

During both the outbound and return journeys, the two-year Lewis and Clark expedition spent more than two hundred days in North Dakota. On the return trip in August of 1806, North Dakota was the place where the Native American guide Sacajawea was returned to her home.

The Dakota Territory was settled by white people only sparsely until the late 1800s when the railroads opened up the region. Land in the Dakotas was promoted to Easterners and Europeans as being ideal for agriculture. After statehood in 1889, a large number of immigrants, especially Germans and Scandinavians, were attracted to the region. Some raised cattle while many others became wheat farmers.

The good news was that since both wheat and cattle require large tracts of land, there was plenty of it in North Dakota. The bad news was that the huge distances between homesteads, often no more than sod houses, led to extreme isolation.

According to Risjord (2013), improvements in farm technology allowed homesteaders on the prairie to subsist, but nothing could help ease the drudgery and isolation of frontier life. "Farmers' wives in particular often suffered from loneliness and despair. They seldom left the house and might have gone months or even years without seeing another woman" (142).

There was even a name for it: "Prairie Madness." It afflicted settlers on the Great Plains, especially those who had come from cities or towns, and, in particular, women. The harsh living conditions and extreme isolation led to the risk of mental breakdown like depression and withdrawal. In some males, it could lead to violence against others, especially their wives and children, while some women were drawn to suicide, or violence against themselves.

There are cases about farm wives going insane after years of isolation and being taken by their husbands to the state hospital. Even with conditions being what they were in early mental hospitals, those may have been the lucky ones; healthcare facilities in the region were usually few and far between.

According to Risse (1999), "From its earliest days, Christianity demanded that all of its adherents aid needy and sick people" (72). The history of hospitals predated that. The earliest documented institutions attempting to provide cures can be traced to the temples of ancient Egypt. In classical Greece, shrines were dedicated to the healer god Asclepius, becoming centers of medical advice. When Christianity was accepted by the Roman Empire, construction of a hospital in every cathedral town followed the First Council of Nicaea's decree in the year 325.

In England, after the dissolution of the monasteries by King Henry VIII in 1540, support for hospitals began to evolve from the church exclusively to more secular means. In Tudor times, citizens had to petition for hospitals to be endowed by the Crown. Later, British hospitals were funded by businesses like banks or by wealthy individuals.

The concept of public hospitals spread in England's American colonies. New York City's Bellevue Hospital, founded in 1736, is called the oldest public hospital in the United States, tracing its origins to the city's almshouse. With the city's purchase of Belle Vue farm, the land where yellow fever victims had been quarantined, the facility was formally named Bellevue Hospital.

The Pennsylvania Hospital in Philadelphia was founded in 1751 by Benjamin Franklin and Dr. Thomas Bond. With a charter from King George III, New York Hospital was founded in 1771, making it the third oldest.

St. Joseph's Hospital was originally built in 1911 in Dickinson, North Dakota. Some stories have earned St. Joseph's the reputation of being haunted. It is said that call buttons are activated in empty rooms, disembodied voices are heard in the cafeteria, and the elevator runs up and down by itself to the morgue, where there are reports of unexplained laughter. (Boston Public Library, Tichnor Brothers collection #80686)

Being settled much later, hospitals in North Dakota have a shorter history than those of the original thirteen colonies. The North Dakota State Hospital was founded in 1885, predating statehood.

In Dickinson, North Dakota, the original forty-room **St. Joseph's Hospital** was built in 1911. Sisters of Mercy of the Holy Cross came to Dickinson to staff the St. Joseph's Hospital. In 2014, the older St. Joseph's Hospital was closed and a new hospital was opened about a mile away.

The new facility may have taken one element of the old hospital with it. Being under the auspices of the Catholic Church, it is not encouraged to discuss issues attributed to the supernatural, such as apparitions, demons, and disembodied spirits. But some stories have earned St. Joseph's Hospital the reputation of being one of the most haunted places in North Dakota.

There are stories of call buttons being activated from empty rooms, doors opening by themselves, the elevator to the morgue running up and down by itself, and moaning and disembodied voices in the cafeteria. On the cheerier side, there are reports of unexplained laughter in the basement.

SOME OTHER REPORTEDLY HAUNTED PLACES IN NORTH DAKOTA

The **Children's Museum at Yunker Farm** in Fargo is housed in an 1876 red brick farmhouse. One visitor who apparently prefers to stay after closing time is the alleged ghost of Elizabeth Yunker who loved children in life and continues to be a warm, inviting spirit in the afterlife. She is said not to try scaring the children, going out of her way to make them feel welcome. Even when visitors have gone and staff members are by themselves, it has been said they feel a friendly, unseen presence keeping them company. Doors and windows open and close for no particular reason, and the elevator button is pushed by unseen hands, going up to the second floor where a lot of children's activities take place. This friendly spirit also enjoys the ground-level exhibits from the time when she lived. John and Elizabeth Yunker raised their ten children at the farm, so large groups of young people at the homestead are basically standard operating procedure. Mrs. Yunker lived through the 1930s, and apparently turning the former family home into an interactive children's museum has pleased her so much that she has stayed behind to help.

The **Custer House** at Fort Abraham Lincoln in Mandan represents a more domesticated side to the legend of frontier Indian fighter George Armstrong Custer and the massacre at Montana's Little Bighorn. In 1866, after Custer had made a name of himself during the Civil War, his beloved wife Elizabeth accompanied him to the Dakota frontier where Custer commanded the 7th Cavalry. They built the two-story home in 1874 to impress others, as befitted the commanding officer and the Colonel's Lady. In addition to providing large rooms where Custer could meet with his staff, Elizabeth Custer desired a home that could provide her with a sense of the civilized life she had left behind. She also understood her duty to entertain other officers' wives using the house for social events. After Custer's death at the Little Bighorn in 1876, Elizabeth Custer continued to burnish her husband's reputation. Although they only lived at the Custer House in Mandan for two years, perhaps her spirit continues to dwell there in the place where she last saw her husband ride away. Elizabeth Custer died in 1933, a year after the structures at Fort Abraham Lincoln began to be to be rebuilt by the Civilian Conservation Corps during Franklin Roosevelt's presidency. Today, the Fort Abraham Lincoln Foundation oversees the historic buildings on that site. At her old home, Mrs. Custer apparently continues to take on the hostessing responsibilities of being an officer's wife. Since she kept a meticulous inventory of the home's furnishings, the restored house is full of family pictures, period furniture, personal artifacts, and even Mrs. Custer's favorite curtains. Today, amid her familiar surroundings at the Custer House, doors open and close on their own, lights regularly flicker on and off, and visitors have reported hearing disembodied voices. Some have claimed to see the apparition of Mrs. Custer wearing her black mourning dress. There have also been reports of cold spots, disembodied voices, moaning, wailing sounds, and wispy images that are seen only for a split second. Some feel those entities may be the wives of Custer's officers, perhaps reliving the moment in 1876 when they received news of the death of their loved ones as they sat together with Mrs. Custer. With her responsibilities at home continuing into the afterlife, even the tireless Mrs. Custer may need to occasionally rest a bit. It has been reported that in an upstairs room, a bed that was neatly made when everyone left and locked up at closing time was found to have the indentation of a human form on it when the Custer House was opened the next morning.

In the town of Harvey, North Dakota, the **Harvey Public Library** was built where the residence of Jacob and Sophia Eberlein Bentz once stood. Many say that because of that particular location, the library is one of the most haunted places in North Dakota. In 1931, as she slept, Sophia was bludgeoned to death by her husband, Jacob. Sophia was the forty-one-year-old mother of two daughters. After her first husband's death, Sophia had married Bentz. According to a newspaper article from 1931, Jacob Bentz later said that he and Sophia had quarreled. After she went to sleep, he struck her several times with a hammer. Some sources speculate that she was able to survive the violent act for a short time. Instead of seeking help for his dying wife, Jacob Bentz busied himself by trying to clean up the scene of the murder. There was blood on the bedding, on the floor, and splattered on the wall. After his cleaning efforts, he attempted to make Sophia's death look like a car accident. After staging the scene, he initially told investigators that he and Sophia were on a business trip early that morning, with Sophia driving the car. He claimed she ran off the road and the car caught fire in the ensuing wreck. He added that he had valiantly attempted to save Sophia from the flames, but could not. However, when Sophia's daughter came home for the funeral, she discovered bloodstains in the bedroom of the small frame house, which she reported to the police. Jacob Bentz was arrested. He admitted to the murder and was sentenced to life in prison, where he died in 1944. In 1990, the town's new library was built on the site where the Jacob and Sophia Bentz house had stood. According to locals, the librarian's office is built directly over the spot where the bedroom had been. Today, librarians report cold chills, a door that relocks itself after being opened, lights blinking on and off, an entryway light staying on even after the light switch was turned off, and a heavy cart filled with books that allegedly moved by itself to block a doorway. There have even been reports of computer glitches in which the screen goes blank, erasing what was written there and replaced with the single letter "S." Perhaps these are no coincidences since the library opened on the anniversary of Sophia's funeral.

The sweet-sounding **Medora Fudge and Ice Cream Depot** in Medora may seem like an unlikely place to be haunted, but it is said that there is one ghost who visits the shop as an apparition only one day a year, reportedly on her birthday. There are strange noises and unnatural cold spots (even for an ice cream shop) all year, but the manifestation only appears on her special day when presumably she takes time to check out the Flavor of the Month.

FURTHER READING

Risjord, Norman. *Dakota: The Story of the Northern Plains.* Lincoln: University of Nebraska Press, 2013.

Risse, Guenter. *Mending Bodies, Saving Souls: A History of Hospitals.* New York: Oxford University Press, 1999.

36

Ohio

The state of Ohio takes its name from the Ohio River, whose name, in turn, is said to have originated from the Seneca word "ohi:yo," meaning "great river." Often considered part of America's heartland, seven U.S. presidents were born in Ohio: Garfield, Grant, Harding, Hayes, McKinley, Taft, and Benjamin Harrison, son of President William Henry Harrison who moved to Ohio as a young man. This makes Ohio second only to Virginia, which can boast of being the birthplace of eight U.S. presidents.

French explorers entered today's region of Ohio in the 1700s to set up trading posts where they could deal in furs with the indigenous people there. The Frenchmen encountered Native American tribes like the Iroquois and Algonquin, although archeological evidence points to both ancient Clovis and Folsom people in the Ohio Valley as early as thirteen thousand years before the birth of Christ.

After the defeat of France in the French and Indian War (1754–1763), Britain took control of the Ohio region, which was then considered the frontier, called the Northwest Territory. After the American colonists won the War of Independence in 1783, Britain relinquished its claims to Ohio, granting the region to the United States. With a rapidly growing population, in 1803, Ohio became the seventeenth state admitted to the Union. With the issue of slavery a contentious one in the new nation, Ohio entered as a free state.

Slavery had been banned in the Ohio territory under a clause in the Northwest Ordinance of 1787. Kern and Wilson (2014) state that the 1787 ban overruled a provision in a 1784 version of the Ordinance that would have allowed it. They cite this clause as a major factor "In making slavery a regional, rather than a national, institution" (105), adding, "Had the Virginians and Kentuckians, who were some of the earliest settlers of Ohio, been able to take their slaves with them, the history of Ohio and the United States might have been very different" (106).

Ohio held an important position during the Civil War (1861–1865). Along with Ohio's railroads, the Ohio River was vital for moving troops and supplies. The state's industrial output provided a large portion of the materials the North needed to fight the war.

In 1863, Ohio also played a role in Morgan's Raid, a diversionary attack by Confederate General John Hunt Morgan that was meant to draw Northern troops away from battlefields in the South. Morgan's Raid ended in northern Ohio, after which he was forced to surrender when his troops could not escape back to the South. About two thousand Confederate prisoners were taken. Before that happened, around twenty-five hundred much-needed horses were stolen in Ohio, where more than four thousand homes and businesses were raided for supplies. Though perhaps not a military success, Morgan's Raid spread terror in Ohio and cost its taxpayers hundreds of thousands of dollars in damages.

Morgan and six senior officers were taken to the Ohio State Penitentiary in Columbus. Remarkably, they tunneled their way out and took a train to Cincinnati, where they crossed the Ohio River to safety.

During the war, Ohio contributed more soldiers per capita than any other state in the Union, losing almost thirty-five thousand men who died in the conflict.

Two national cemeteries in Ohio, Dayton National Cemetery in Dayton and Woodland Cemetery Soldiers' Lot in Cleveland, were established to inter her war dead. Prior to that, in Ohio, as elsewhere, the deceased were usually laid to rest at churchyards or in family plots. However, there was also another type of burial ground for less fortunate people: the potter's field.

A potter's field, also called a pauper's grave or common grave, was traditionally a site for the burial of unknown or indigent people. The term "potter's field" is of Biblical origin. In the New Testament, Matthew 27:3–27:8 refer to the thirty pieces of silver returned by the remorseful Judas. That money was used to acquire a piece of land in which to bury strangers, criminals, and the poor. Before being used as a burial ground, the land had literally been a place where potters collected clay for the production of ceramics. The name "potter's field" endured.

The term and the tradition continued through the Middle Ages and into European colonization of North America. Meltsner (2012) says, "The Elizabethan Poor Law of 1601, promulgated just 19 years before the *Mayflower* landed, would become the standard means" of dealing with the destitute in the English colonies (7).

Some paupers' graveyards were eventually repurposed. New York City's Bryant Park, Madison Square Park, and Washington Square Park were all originally potter's fields. Portions of Chicago's Lincoln Park, which originated as Chicago City Cemetery in the mid-1840s, included a potter's field where about twenty thousand burials took place.

In Ohio, the **Cincinnati Music Hall** was built over a nineteenth-century potter's field whose inhabitants were either offended or delighted that their final resting place was transformed into a concert venue. Today, the Music Hall, which is home to the Cincinnati Symphony Orchestra and Cincinnati Pops, may also provide ghost-in-residence status to those who have given it the reputation as one of America's most haunted places.

Cincinnati's Music Hall was completed in 1878. The land on which it was built already came with its own history. In 1818, the city of Cincinnati purchased the land to establish what was called the Commercial Hospital and Lunatic Asylum.

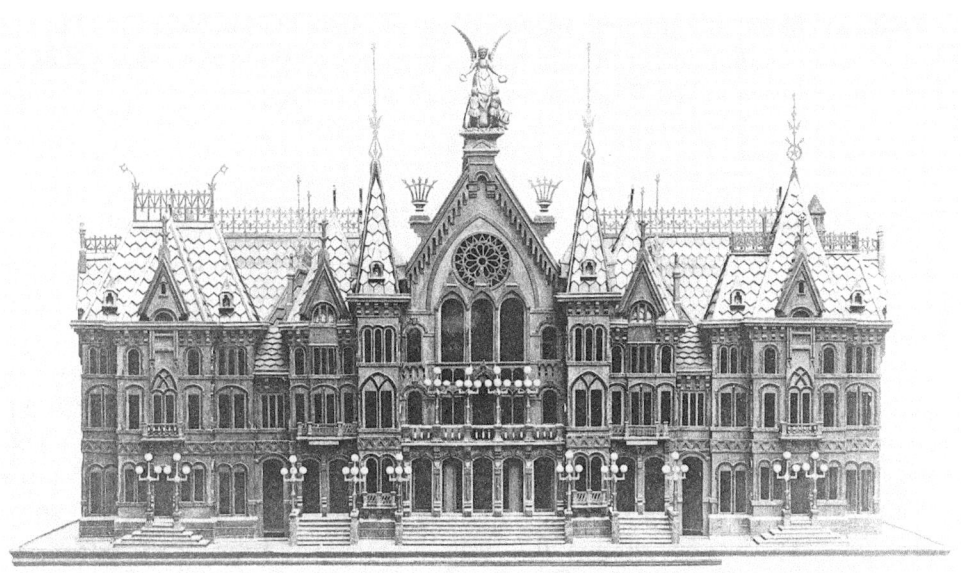

Ohio's Cincinnati Music Hall was built over a nineteenth-century potter's field. Also called a common grave, it was traditionally a site for the burial of unknown or indigent people. Today, some spirits are said to frequent the music hall, either offended or delighted that their unsung resting place was transformed into a top-notch concert venue. (Library of Congress)

After locals demanded that what they called the "pest house" be moved further out of town, the land was used to bury victims of an 1832 cholera epidemic as well as the city's poor. More complaints from nearby property owners led to the site being converted into a park in 1859. Exposition buildings were erected and used until 1876 when it was turned over to the Music Hall Association.

By that time, the hauntings at the site were already well known. In addition to the alleged spirits of paupers buried in the potter's field, there was said to be an even more grisly source of hauntings. In 1838, boilers on the steamboat *Moselle*, sailing from Cincinnati to St. Louis, exploded. Newspaper accounts claim that human corpses and burned body parts from 150 passengers were strewn across the city, with bodies falling through the roofs of houses. The remains of the unrecognizable victims were gathered for burial at the potter's field site.

Later, when a canal was being cut through an area of the potter's field, about a hundred skeletons were encountered. Excavations in 1927 uncovered three coffins that were said to be reburied beneath the Music Hall. During an expansion later that same year, another sixty-five graves were found, and were also reburied at the site, earning that side of the Music Hall the nickname "Valley of Death."

In 1988, another construction project uncovered more than two hundred pounds of adult and children's bones that were encased in concrete. Those remains are said to have become part of an anthropological study at the University of Cincinnati.

In addition to the thumping of unseen footsteps, there have been reports of loud rapping on the ceiling, under the floor, and on doors and windows. These ghostly sounds are presumably not from the orchestra's percussion section.

SOME OTHER REPORTEDLY HAUNTED PLACES IN OHIO

The **Ceely Rose House** in Lucas, Ohio, is located on land that is now part of the Malabar Farm State Park. Its history dates back more than a century when a horrific crime that took place there in 1896 still haunts it today. Celia "Ceely" Rose was described as unattractive, "silly," and a slow learner. In her late teens, she developed a crush on a neighbor boy. After deciding she was going to marry him, Ceely was determined to circumvent any familial disapproval. She did so by poisoning the breakfast cottage cheese of her mother, father, and brother. All three died, and suspicion fell on Ceely. In the days before forensics helped to solve crimes, the authorities simply asked a friend to talk with Ceely, who confessed. Ceely was tried on three counts of murder; in each case, she was found not guilty by reason of insanity. Ceely Rose became one of the first patients at the new Lima State Hospital for the Criminally Insane. When she died there in 1934, no one claimed the body. Ceely was buried in the hospital graveyard, although many say her spirit returned to haunt her old family home. There have been reports of hearing ghostly voices and seeing a young woman wandering the hallways or peering out a window. On some nights, people have claimed to see an apparition that looked like Ceely walking outside the house, perhaps in search of the neighbor boy she loved and lost, along with everyone else in her life.

The **House of Wills** is an imposing thirty-four-room mansion in Cleveland built in 1898 and used as a funeral home and alleged satanic meeting place. It is said to be haunted by spirits from beyond. With its multifaceted backstory, it may be easy to see why. The building began life as a German social club, and was later turned into a hospital for immigrants. A prominent African American businessman, John Walter Wills, bought the property in 1942 to use as a funeral home. Wills owned one of the oldest and most successful black businesses in Cleveland, with his mortuary company reportedly the largest black funeral home in the state. His vision also included the House of Wills serving as living quarters and eventually a civil rights organizational headquarters. Many of the building's rooms were embellished with designs reminiscent of ancient Egypt and classical Greece, with lavish woodwork and art-deco detailing, all of which give it an otherworldly atmosphere. After Wills himself died there in 1971, his family sold it. The magnificent structure fell victim to vandalism and disrepair. It was slated for demolition, with the land to be turned into a parking lot, when it was purchased by a local artist and alleged satanist. Today, the House of Wills is rumored to be one of the most haunted sites in Cleveland, led by the ghost of Walter Wills himself. There have been reports of disembodied voices in empty rooms, an apparition staring down into the street from a second-floor window, shadowy figures moving from room to room before suddenly disappearing, and a spectral man in a suit quietly making his presence known in the casket room.

The **Lorain Palace Theater** opened in 1928 in Lorain, Ohio, near Cleveland, and was the first movie theater in the state to show talking pictures. After the 1940s, the theater gradually suffered the same decline as other entertainment palaces of the era until it was lovingly restored by a local group. Not only has it gained the reputation of being haunted it can also boast of a starring role in a documentary. Titled *Ghosts of the Palace*, the 2017 film chronicles the Lorain Palace Theater's haunted history. According to locals, most people are aware of its panorama of the paranormal. One investigator told the local newspaper that there are so many spirits there, he couldn't even count them all. Ghosts are said to roam the aisles and hallways of the Palace. One witness claimed to have seen a black cloud hovering in the art-deco lobby one night. Some of the spirits are said to be the victims of a deadly tornado that destroyed much of Lorain in 1924. The disembodied voice of one was allegedly heard to say "My body flew." An investigator claimed to encounter the spirit of a man named Ed, who said he had worked at the shipyard, which was directly behind the Palace. The spectral Ed claimed he had been murdered by being pushed down stairs. Perhaps his spirit sensed a comfortable home at the Lorain Palace, which is one of the few establishments feeling the need to officially state that the décor above the proscenium is *not* coffin lids.

The Gothic-looking **Ohio State Reformatory** in Mansfield is now a state historical site. It may be even more famous by serving as the location for the 1994 film, *The Shawshank Redemption*, which was based on a novella by master of the macabre Stephen King. It is hard to look at the cavernous institution without sensing that Mr. King would be proud. Visitors have reported hearing strange noises, seeing unexplained shadows, detecting the sound of conversations, and experiencing feelings of anger, dread, and sadness, all of which are to be expected at a place with so much of all three within its walls. The cornerstone was laid in 1886, and was an operational prison until 1981, almost a century later. Death, disease, and violence were common. A teenage boy is believed to haunt the basement, where he was reportedly beaten to death. The ghosts of a former prison superintendent and his wife are said to carry on disembodied conversations in the superintendent's former office. At various places around the facility, shadowy manifestations appear along with unseen voices, footsteps, and the feeling of not being alone. In an attic area, a paranormal investigator was said to have been so spooked that he left and refused to go back. With all the alleged murders and suicides that took place in the cellblocks, visitors have experienced what they say were overwhelming feelings of death and despair, especially in solitary confinement where many men were said to have taken their own lives while locked up alone.

The **Stivers School for the Arts** in Dayton traces its history back to its construction 1908, but its haunted history appears to have begun with the death of a teacher named Mary Tyler. In the 1920s, she was found dead, floating fully clothed in the school's basement pool, with a locket in one hand and a broken pointer in the other. She was reportedly romantically involved with a student who was a senior at the time of her death. Authorities believed the unnamed student tore his picture out of the teacher's locket to avoid suspicion. He is said to have disappeared after her body was found and was never seen again. The school eventually covered over the pool, building a classroom on top of it. The area where the pool was is currently used for storage, with a trapdoor leading down to it. However, Mary Tyler allegedly does not need trapdoors or any other entrance. Her ghostly figure has been spotted levitating over the abandoned pool area along with floating around the tunnels in the lower levels, banging on pipes and wailing loudly. In the classroom built over the pool, students have reported flickering lights, objects disappearing, and sudden temperature changes. Stivers School for the Arts may not only be a creative center but also a hub for haunts.

FURTHER READING

Kern, Kevin, and Gregory S. Wilson. *Ohio: A History of the Buckeye State*. Malden, MA: Wiley-Blackwell, 2014.

Meltsner, Heli. *The Poorhouses of Massachusetts: A Cultural and Architectural History*. Jefferson, NC: McFarland, 2012.

37

Oklahoma

The name "Oklahoma" is said to be derived from the Choctaw words "okla" and "humma," meaning "red people." Those people would prove to be an integral part of Oklahoma's history.

Spanish conquistador Coronado traveled through the state in 1541, but French explorers claimed the region in the 1700s. That lasted until 1803, when all French territory west of the Mississippi River was sold to the United States in the Louisiana Purchase. Throughout this period, Osage and Quapaw people inhabited today's eastern Oklahoma, while Apache, Comanche, and Kiowa entered the region from the west.

From 1819 to 1828, the land currently known as Oklahoma was part of the Arkansas Territory. Following the Indian Removal Act of 1830, tens of thousands of Cherokee and Choctaw people were forcibly removed from their homes in other parts of the country by the U.S. Army and expelled to Oklahoma, enduring what became known as the "Trail of Tears."

Perhaps with the memory of blue-coated federal soldiers fresh in their minds, all of what were called the Five Civilized Tribes in Oklahoma (Cherokee, Chickasaw, Choctaw, Creek, and Seminole nations) sided with the Confederacy during the American Civil War. At that time, most of what is now the state of Oklahoma was designated as the Indian Territory, an unorganized region. It was the scene of seven officially recognized battles.

After the war, in which the Confederacy did not emerge victorious, Texas cattle ranchers drove their herds through Indian Territory on their way to Kansas railheads. By 1881, four of five major frontier cattle trails cut through today's Oklahoma. Some whites began settling illegally in Indian Territory.

In 1887, the increased presence of white settlers prompted the U.S. Congress to pass the Dawes Act, which established allotments including land appropriated by the federal government and the ever-expanding railroads.

That led to an event called the Oklahoma Land Rush in 1889, in which certain parts of the Oklahoma Territory were opened to settlement starting at a precise time and available on a first-come, first-served basis. Some broke the rules by crossing the border sooner than the official opening and were called "sooners," leading to the state's official nickname.

In 1907, Oklahoma Territory and Indian Territory were merged into Oklahoma, which became the forty-sixth state to join the Union.

It was a landlocked state, but billions of gallons of fresh water were captured underground in rock formations known as aquifers, which to many was more precious than any other commodity. That was until something even more desirable, at least to some, was discovered in what Baird and Goble (2011) call "the creative processes that turned ancient swamps into petroleum and natural gas" (5).

A great deal of the "black gold" happened to lie beneath land owned by Native Americans. In the 1920s, major oil deposits were found on property belonging to Osage Indians, spurring incursions by whites who gained control by means that included murdering oil-rich Osage people. It is said that those events led in large part to the creation of the Federal Bureau of Investigation (FBI).

Prior to the authority of the FBI, Indian Territory was guarded from 1824 until 1888 by Fort Gibson in Muskogee County. When it was constructed, Fort Gibson was farther west than any other military post in the United States. Today, the fort site is managed by the Oklahoma Historical Society.

Fort Gibson National Cemetery lies nearby. It is there that a particular haunting is said to take place, one that underscores a little-known chapter of American history. At the cemetery, witnesses have claimed to see the apparition of a young soldier, weeping and pacing around a tombstone that seems out of place. Among the graves in the military cemetery is one stone that reads "Vivia Thomas, January 7, 1870."

It is said that one of the troopers at the fort was actually a woman. She had told her story of how she passed as a male soldier to a chaplain before she died. Vivia Thomas of Boston reportedly fell in love with a young Army officer who eventually left Vivia to join his regiment at Fort Gibson. Vivia cut her hair, dressed in men's clothing, and, reaching Indian Territory, enlisted at Fort Gibson. After her lover was killed (some say by Vivia herself), she began visiting his gravesite where she wept for her lost love. One night, she froze to death on the grave where she was found the next morning. As the body was prepared for burial, her gender was discovered, and today Vivia's spirit remains to haunt the Fort Gibson cemetery. Many dismiss the story as implausible, but documentation now shows that there were more women soldiers disguised as men in the 1800s than were previously thought. It was especially the case during the Civil War when combat troops were needed on both sides.

Abbott (2015) states that the medical examination would usually consist of a doctor checking the trigger finger of recruits (to prove they could shoot) and asking each if he was "in pretty good health" (12). According to Abbott, a doctor marked one of them, Frank Thompson, fit to serve in the war, but "Frank Thompson was really Emma Edmondson, and had been posing as a man for two years" (13).

Emma was not alone. Documentation has substantiated women Civil War soldiers like Sarah Rosetta Wakeman. Under the name "Private Lyons Wakeman," she died during the war and is buried in Louisiana's Chalmette National

Cemetery. Through letters and other documentation, it has been substantiated that the body in the grave is Rosetta Wakeman.

Another, Frances Clayton (or Clalin), disguised herself as "Jack Williams" to fight for the Union in the Missouri artillery and was wounded in battle, but was able to keep her gender undetected.

"Albert Cashier" fought in about forty battles alongside the Illinois infantry until the end of the war. Cashier was awarded a pension and lived in an Illinois soldiers' home. In 1913, a doctor discovered that Albert Cashier, living life as a man, was a woman. The aged Cashier, whose original name was Jennie Hodgers, was sent to an insane asylum, dying soon after. Jennie was buried under the name Albert Cashier, wearing her carefully preserved Union Army uniform. Fellow veterans insisted that the burial include military honors.

Sarah Edmonds Seelye was known as "Franklin Flint Thompson" while serving in the Michigan infantry. She is the only known woman to receive a veteran's pension after the Civil War based on letters of support from her fellow soldiers.

Most female soldiers were lower-class girls with bleak futures. They came from farms and factories. The Union Army provided regular wages of $13 a month, more than triple what they could earn elsewhere. Even with its hardships, army life had more to offer. It is said that hundreds of unknown women may have risked death or injury to live the life they wanted by serving their country.

Generally, their gender was detected if they were wounded, got sick, or were taken prisoner. In one case, a "male" soldier from New Jersey who had been promoted for bravery in battle was discovered a month later on giving birth to a baby.

Women found to be serving among the troops were accused of being prostitutes, homosexuals, or insane. When discovered, some were sent home, but others were put in prison or a mental asylum.

If the story of Vivia Thomas is true, she, like them, was a bold woman whose spirit could not be held down, even in the afterlife.

SOME OTHER REPORTEDLY HAUNTED PLACES IN OKLAHOMA

Cain's Ballroom in Tulsa has been offering a good time to music lovers since 1924. Apparently, there are spirits whose enjoyment of the club continues even after death. Cain's Ballroom was the site of the first regular radio broadcast by the legendary country-western band Bob Wills and His Texas Playboys; today the venue is nicknamed "Home of Bob Wills." That may be more literal than figurative since Cain's Ballroom is reportedly haunted by the ghost of Bob Wills who died in 1975. After the building was refurbished in 1976, Cain's Ballroom has seen performances by such acts as Death Cab for Cutie, Ted Nugent, Van Halen, and the Ramones. Thus, it is considered a local hotspot for live music. There have been claims that, along paranormal lines, it is also a hotspot for cold spots. Orbs of light have allegedly been caught in photos, and lights have been known to turn on and off on their own. There have also been reports of disembodied voices, feelings of

In Tulsa, Oklahoma, Cain's Ballroom has been offering a good time to music lovers since 1924. It is reportedly haunted by the ghost of legendary musician Bob Wills. Orbs of light have allegedly been caught in photos, there have been reports of disembodied voices, and a shadow person has been observed disappearing through a closed door. (Frank Manno/Dreamstime.com)

being watched, full-body apparitions, and mysterious giggling and singing. A shadow person has been seen moving from the entrance to the bar area to the far end of the bar before disappearing through a closed door.

The **Cherokee Strip Museum** in Alva began life as a hospital. After opening its doors in 1932, it served as a local healthcare center serving the community. While the hospital did not have a particularly bad record, it is felt that much of the haunting today may be the result of the spirits of those who were lost during unsuccessful operations. The top two floors of the building have been bricked up, which seems to have concentrated all its lingering spirits on the lower floor. The hauntings are said to have begun shortly after the building was renovated and opened as a museum. People have reported strange lights and shadows moving around in the building at night, and reportedly there is a mysterious blood spot on the floor that cannot be washed away. There are sudden cold spots, strange orbs, and the sounds of an unexplainable ghostly whispering that seems to be coming from unoccupied parts of the building. The supernatural star seems to be an old player piano that starts to play on its own, but only when there is no one in the room. Those checking on it find only an empty space. The museum is home to pioneer exhibits and collections of Native American art and artifacts. On display among its forty exhibit spaces are an old school room, drug store, and kitchen from the area's past. If those are not enough to make visitors feel they are being watched, there is also an array of vintage (some say "primitive") medical instruments plus—what else?—an embalming table.

The **Constantine Theater** in Pawhuska, Oklahoma, first operated as the Pawhuska House Hotel in the 1880s. In 1911, a Greek immigrant named C. C. Constantine transformed the site into an opera house where notable singers like Enrico Caruso performed. The building was abandoned in the 1970s, but a group of Pawhuska citizens restored the structure. They may have captured the spirit of the past since it is said a century later, the ghost of Enrico Caruso still haunts the theater. The Constantine Theater currently presents plays, classic films, and musical shows. Staffers and audience members have reported hearing the sound of doors opening and closing, unseen footsteps going up and down the stairs, and even a mist seen drifting in the crawlspace beneath the stage. When paranormal investigators set up their equipment, a recording seemed to reveal the sound of a gunshot, followed by a gasp and laborious breathing, and a male whisper that sounded like, "Where is she?" Those could be bits of stagecraft from a melodrama that closed decades ago. But in the theater's balcony, it is said that a certain apparition has pride of place. The ghost is described as a beautiful young woman in an old-fashioned dress who some claim is Sappho Constantine Brown, the owner's daughter, and who presumably can sit anywhere she wants, dead or alive.

The **Fort Washita Historic Site** at Durant may be the current home of the ghost of a long-dead woman called "Aunt Jane" whose apparition roams the grounds. Built in 1842, the frontier fort was used until 1865. Confederate troops held the post until the end of the Civil War when they burned most of the remaining structures. It was never reoccupied by the U.S. military. It is currently owned by the Oklahoma Historical Society, with living history programs conducted on its grounds. Another regular on the grounds is said to be Aunt Jane who was murdered by thieves when she refused to tell them where her money was hidden. In the struggle, Aunt Jane was beheaded. Her scattered remains were buried at Fort Washita. Some say her gold was also buried on the grounds and her headless ghost, dressed in a white gown, is still looking for it. Treasure hunters have heard the story as well, but some have reported that they have felt her presence to the extent that she kept them from digging, as if holding on to their tools and not letting them break ground. It is said that after the fort was abandoned, a family moved into a remaining structure with their thirty-two dogs. The first night after they moved in, all of the dogs disappeared. After rounding them up the next day, they were brought home—only to be gone again the next morning. The family got the hint and moved away. Today, living history guests who stay in one of the restored cabins often report feeling as if they were being suffocated in their sleep. One re-enactor placed her period-appropriate corset on a chair and locked the door before bed, only to find all the laboriously threaded corset strings gone the next morning, never to be found again. Some people say the manifestation only exhibits hostility toward women. Apparently dogs are not too popular with the entity either.

The **Gilcrease Museum** in Tulsa is home to one of the nation's most renowned collections of Native American artwork, oil paintings, and artifacts of the

American West. The extensive collection was lovingly gathered by a millionaire philanthropist who was apparently so fond of the items that he decided not to leave them, even after death. Thomas Gilcrease made a fortune in the Oklahoma oil industry and amassed a notable collection. When he died in 1962, he was given a funeral service that included traditional Native American rituals, befitting his Creek Indian heritage. His remains were entombed in a mausoleum on the grounds of his estate, which became the Gilcrease Museum to provide a home for his collection. Today, the generous oil man seems to enjoy a stroll along the museum's garden pathways, which were a particular favorite of his in life. He apparently also welcomes other spirits on his former property, including ghostly children, an unseen woman who likes to sing, and the sound of men arguing. Strange whispers have been heard in the dark, doors mysteriously slam, loud banging noises seem to come from the second floor of the unoccupied museum, temperatures fluctuate, unexplainable technical malfunctions occur, and items mysteriously disappear only to emerge later in unlikely places. Some estimate that there could be as many as seven different spirits remaining the property. The good news is that except possibly for the argumentative men, the spirits seem to be harmless, lingering at the Gilcrease simply because they like it there. The bad news is that according to some sources, the sight of the late Mr. Gilcrease and the sensation of other spirits has unnerved guards at night to an extent that there is an unusually high turnover rate among the security staff.

FURTHER READING

Abbott, Karen. *Liar, Temptress, Soldier, Spy: Four Women Undercover in the Civil War.* New York: Harper Perennial, 2015.

Baird, W. David, and Danney Goble. *Oklahoma: A History.* Norman: University of Oklahoma Press, 2011.

38

Oregon

Today's state of Oregon, in the Pacific Northwest region of the nation, boasts some of the country's most spectacular scenery, as well as some of its most notorious haunted places. According to Andy Weeks (2014), "In many respects, Oregon, with its long and active history, seems to be the perfect place for ghosts" (10).

In centuries past, Native American tribes like the Chinook, Klamath, Nez Perce, and Shasta tribes called the future state of Oregon their home. There were mapping expeditions by French and Spanish explorers during the seventeenth and eighteenth centuries. The Lewis and Clark expedition of 1805–1806 established a presence there for the newly created United States.

Starting in 1842, the Oregon Trail brought settlers to the region, and in 1859, Oregon was admitted to the Union as the thirty-third state. Railroads connected Oregon to the rest of the nation in the late 1800s, bringing more settlers and those who saw business opportunities in marketing the state's furs and lumber.

If, as Weeks said, Oregon seems to be the perfect place for ghosts, the most haunted city in that state would no doubt be Portland. Although roses bloom in Portland throughout the year due to its moderate climate, it is the city's shady underground that harbors one of the state's most notoriously haunted sites: the **Shanghai Tunnels**. Running beneath a large portion of Portland, their history is mired in the sinister act that today would be called human trafficking.

According to Mark Strecker (2014), "The word 'shanghai'—kidnapping and forcing a man to serve on board a merchant ship–first appeared in print in 1872" (4). Although it may not have been publicized with a specific name, the practice itself was initiated much earlier than that, often involving the use of drugs, liquor, intimidation, trickery, and violence. Shanghaiing also preyed on women by forcing them into slavery and prostitution, both foreign and domestic.

Shanghai, a major port city in China, was a prime destination of many cargo ships. Although the term "shanghaiing" became popular in the late 1800s, the act itself was not new. "Impressment," or pressing men into service on military ships, had been a common practice. The British Navy's impressment of Americans was a major justification for the War of 1812.

By the 1850s, kidnappers known as "crimps" could earn large amounts of money by providing crews for whalers or merchant ships. The rate per head was almost $900 in today's dollars. One crimp named Laflin is reported to have kept an account book showing that in only four years of his fifty-year career, he trafficked more than six thousand victims. Thus, shanghaiing was a lucrative pursuit in the underworld. In Portland's tunnels, that was literally the case.

Ships docking at West Coast cities like Portland often found experienced sailors abandoning ship *en masse* to become prospectors in the California Gold Rush that started in 1849, then again in the Klondike Gold Rush from 1896 to 1899 in Alaska. Ship captains needed anyone who could help hoist the massive sails.

Sometimes the process worked in reverse, as hungry, naïve, unsuccessful prospectors made their way back to West Coast cities looking for any kind of work and, in their desperation, found the cheapest food and lodging near the waterfront. More and more souls were added to the grisly contents of Portland's Shanghai Tunnels in the twentieth century.

In the age before steamships, Portland was notorious for shanghaiing. No seafaring knowledge was required to raise and lower huge canvas sails. Any civilian was fair game. Some men, like house painters looking for work, made the mistake of accepting a drink in a bar from someone posing as a prospective employer before waking up on a ship bound for Asia. Similarly, women looking for housekeeping jobs could also be seized and trafficked.

Both male and female crimps operated boarding houses, casinos, saloons, and similar businesses that supplied victims. After being clubbed or drugged into unconsciousness, usually with opium-laced liquor, victims in Portland were dragged into underground tunnels before being loaded on ships, often waking up hours or days later when they were already far out to sea.

After at least a year aboard ship, some men might be handed back to the crimp for a cut of the profit in the victim's resale. With the law on the side of ship owners and captains, men who were able to escape found themselves charged with desertion. When women's usefulness was over, they often simply disappeared.

Shanghaiing was an "open secret." Some law enforcement officials were said to look the other way or profited from bribery by the crimps. Corrupt politicians could benefit not only from kickbacks but also by crimps who supplied dazed victims on Election Day to vote at one polling place after another. Thus, laws were rarely passed to end the human trafficking that was taking place.

In addition, most victims of shanghaiing were not literate enough to record their plight, and few members of the general public knew or cared about their fate. Ultimately, shanghaiing sailors was curtailed by the rise of the steamship, which required a trained crew.

Before that happened, Portland's tunnels continued being used for their horrific purpose. Many of the victims died in the city's Shanghai Tunnels before they could be moved onto ships. Sometimes death was due to their head injuries after being knocked unconscious or from consuming drinks that were heavily dosed with drugs. The souls of these victims are said to be haunting the Shanghai Tunnels.

After the decline of shanghaiing, there were reports of disembodied screams and agonized voices in the dark recesses beneath the city. Today, tours are available of Portland's Shanghai Tunnels, which are said to be haunted by the aggrieved spirits of captives whose lives tragically ended there.

SOME OTHER REPORTEDLY HAUNTED PLACES IN OREGON

In addition to being a historic music venue, Portland's **Crystal Ballroom** has also been known as one of the most haunted places in Portland. At the Crystal Ballroom building, which dates back to 1914 and is listed on the National Register of Historic Places, there have been numerous reports of strange occurrences on the property that are generally believed to be the hauntings of several different spirits. But this ghostly energy appears to be happy. During the Depression years of the 1930s, the ballroom's owner held upbeat, family oriented events like dances to keep people's spirits up. During segregation, black schools held their proms there. In the 1960s, the Crystal Ballroom offered some of the best in rock music as well as rhythm and blues, featuring acts like James Brown, Marvin Gaye, Buffalo Springfield, the Grateful Dead, and Ike & Tina Turner. Today, after a performance has ended and audience members have gone home, the remaining performers and staff often hear disembodied voices and laughter from large groups of people, as well as phantom footsteps on the wooden floors. There have also been reports of the elevator going up and down of its own accord when no one else is in the building. Ghostly apparitions have also been seen walking in and out of rooms before abruptly disappearing. This is one place where there has traditionally been a lot of upbeat musical energy, housing happy sprits who enjoy the chance to come out when the building is quiet and closed to the earthly public.

Sometimes movie patrons remain in the theater to catch the next show, but the ghosts that appear to haunt Portland's **Hollywood Theatre** have been hanging around for almost a century. Built in 1926 as a vaudeville theater and "picture palace," it seated fifteen hundred people in luxurious surroundings. Even its entrance façade, described as a combination of Byzantine, Rococo, and Spanish Colonial Revival, was designed to capture attention. Over the years the theater was reconfigured, but continues to show movies. It also has some loyal guests who seem to enjoy spending their afterlife with fellow film fans. There have been detailed reports from moviegoers that bear a remarkable similarity to each other: the spirit of a well-dressed, middle-aged man roaming the upstairs lobby, a ghostly woman sitting quietly in the back row of the theater, and a misty, transparent figure that passed by an onlooker before dissolving into a wall. Some people have reported being tapped on their back or shoulder by a male ghost who also whispers unintelligible words in their ears; while startling, most feel it was done in jest. There is also a poignant story that the spirit of a young blonde female, wearing high heels and nervously smoking a cigarette while pacing upstairs hallways, is waiting eternally for her husband to meet her, not knowing he was killed in an automobile accident on the way. All reports indicate the spirits are friendly and benevolent. Some show folk lament that the movies killed vaudeville, but at Portland's Hollywood Theatre, vaudeville—or at least its fans—may have never died.

Dating back to the 1920s and located in Oregon's Union County, the **Hot Lake Hotel** was named for the thermal spring-fed lake on the property. In the early twentieth century, it served as a luxury resort and sanitarium, advertising the medicinal attributes of the hotel's mineral water. It was the first known commercial building in the world to utilize geothermal energy as its primary heat source, drawing visitors from around the nation. However, a massive fire destroyed much of the hotel in 1934. Subsequently, the remainder of the property was used for various purposes, such as an insane asylum, a nurses' training school during World War II, and a retirement home. A number of people died on the property, including a nurse who perished after falling into scalding hot springs, an employee who killed himself in an operating room, and several suicides by the residents of the sanitarium. There have been reports of disembodied crying and screaming coming from the hospital's surgical room. Rocking chairs reportedly moved on their own and a piano played by itself. Although it was added to the National Register of Historic Places in 1979, the dilapidated building stood abandoned from 1991 to 2002. In 2001, it was featured on the television series *The Scariest Places on Earth*. Today, it is utilized as a bed and breakfast, museum, and spa.

Because of its attachment to Portland's infamous Shanghai Tunnels (above), **Kell's Irish Restaurant & Pub** is often cited as one of the city's most haunted places. One of the most active spots is said to be Kell's Cigar Room, a space in the basement that leads directly into one of the Shanghai Tunnels, which can be viewed by visitors. Many of the bars and restaurants around Portland's Old Town were connected to the Shanghai Tunnels, making it convenient for "crimps" to drug the drinks of unsuspecting men and women, dragging them straight into the tunnels. Kell's bills itself as "a Northwest Tradition since 1983," and was not in existence when the actual human trafficking via shanghaiing was at its height. Like many establishments in Old Town, it supplanted previous buildings. In addition, there are other hauntings reported at Kell's: a piano that has been known to play by itself, the sound of heavy breathing in an empty room, chairs being rearranged, televisions that turn on by themselves, and people feeling someone brushing past them when nobody is around. The owner of Kell's claims to have seen a face (not his own) appearing in the mirror. Kell's Cigar Room is reportedly haunted by the spirit of a firefighter named David Campbell, the first Portland fireman to die in the line of duty. He is said to appear in full firefighter gear, and is most often seen by those who have some sort of connection to firefighting.

Multnomah County Poor Farm, now called **McMenamin's Edgefield**, was built in Troutdale during 1911. The large property variously operated as a poorhouse, reform school, and sanitarium, as well as an institution for the mentally challenged, the disabled, and the elderly. The facility was often overcrowded. Disease and death were commonplace, and there are said to be countless unmarked graves on the grounds. It currently operates as a luxurious hotel, restaurant, and winery. Visitors have frequently reported manifestations of spirits, such as hearing a woman's voice reciting nursery rhymes, the unexplained sound of children crying in a wing that was once an infirmary, and sightings of a woman dressed in white wandering around the property. A lot of activity has been reported in Room 215, and on the entire second and third floor, as well as around the winery which previously served as the poorhouse infirmary. An employee reported seeing a woman's apparition carrying keys, walking by, and then simply vanishing. There have also been claims of a ghostly dog waking guests in the middle of the night by putting its cold nose on their faces.

Old Town Pizza was once known as the Merchant Hotel. This Portland site is reportedly haunted by a ghost named Nina, a girl who was murdered by being thrown down the elevator shaft of the building in the late 1800s. Nina has been reported to observe diners while they eat, signaling her arrival as a spirit with faintly wafting perfume and giving people the feeling of an unseen presence behind them. The restless soul of Nina, who was sold into slavery as a prostitute and tried to escape her fate by informing on the brothelkeepers, has reportedly been seen wandering the basement and main floor wearing a black dress. Some employees have felt her tap them on the shoulder. Nina may not be alone. Staff members have also seen a lady in white heading downstairs after hours. When they follow what looks like a customer to let her know the building is closed, she vanishes. The dining room sits in the original hotel lobby which was often the last sight unsuspecting victims saw before meeting their fate in the grisly Shanghai Tunnels.

Old Town Pizza in Portland, Oregon, is reportedly haunted by the ghost of a restless soul named Nina, who was murdered in the late 1800s by being thrown down the building's elevator shaft. In addition, the dining room sits in the original hotel lobby that was often the last sight unwary victims saw before meeting their grim fate in the city's subterranean Shanghai Tunnels. (Erik Lattwein/Dreamstime.com)

At the **Pittock Mansion** in Portland, it is obvious that Henry and Georgiana Pittock put a lot of love into building the French Renaissance-style château as their home in 1909. However, they only had a few years to enjoy it: Georgiana died in 1918 and Henry in 1919. They may have loved their home so much that they declined to leave. The mansion opened to the public in 1965 and remains a community landmark. Disembodied voices have been heard, items have been mysteriously moved around the building, and windows have opened and closed by themselves. Visitors reported feeling an unseen presence following them around the mansion, which was believed to be Henry Pittock escorting them like a good host. Other reports include Henry's portrait moving around the mansion unaided and seeing the reflection of an older lady, believed to be Georgiana, in the glass of a painting. Georgiana's apparition has also been felt in the basement, keeping people company. An avid gardener, the aroma of roses inside the home is believed to mean that Georgiana is present. The mansion even became a movie star, being featured in the 1977 film *First Love*, 1982's *Unhinged*, *The Haunting of Sarah Hardy* in 1989, and 1993's *Body of Evidence* with Madonna. Today, the historic Pittock Mansion serves as a museum as its ghostly former residents may venture back into this world, perhaps trying to relive memories, watch over their home, or catch a glimpse of Madonna.

The White Eagle Saloon in Portland opened in 1905. Today, it is a bar and hotel that is reportedly haunted by a woman who was murdered there when the building functioned as a brothel and opium den, the ghosts of a former call girl named Rose, and the spirit of a pre-Prohibition bartender named Sam, as well as the anguished souls of innocent victims who were trapped in the notorious Shanghai Tunnels that run under much of Old Town Portland. In its early days, the White Eagle was renowned for the violent brawls that took place there, earning the nickname "Bucket of Blood." While most spirits there are not harmful to others, on one occasion, a waitress reported being pushed down the stairs by some unseen force that left her bruised but not bloody. In another case, a patron reported being locked in the restroom for fifteen minutes, only to find that the door had no lock on it. Some guests at the eleven-room White Eagle Hotel, located directly above the saloon, reported their bed moving up and down, the water in the sink running on its own, and being awakened by the feeling of something tickling their toes.

FURTHER READING

Strecker, Mark. *Shanghaiing Sailors: A Maritime History of Forced Labor, 1849–1915*. Jefferson, NC: McFarland & Company, 2014.

Weeks, Andy. *Haunted Oregon: Ghosts and Strange Phenomena of the Beaver State*. Mechanicsburg, PA: Stackpole Books, 2014.

39

Pennsylvania

Officially designated as the Commonwealth of Pennsylvania, the state is rich in American history. It is considered by many to have been the nation's birthplace since Philadelphia, Pennsylvania, was the site where both the Declaration of Independence and the U.S. Constitution were created.

Before its discovery by Europeans, Pennsylvania had been inhabited by Native American people for more than ten thousand years. By 1600, tribes living in Pennsylvania included the Shawnee, Susquehannocks, and the Lenni Lenape, also known as the Delaware.

The Dutch began colonization of the region in the 1630s by establishing the Zwaanendael Colony. In 1638, Sweden established the New Sweden Colony, claiming parts of present-day Pennsylvania, although not many colonists settled there.

In early 1664, England's King Charles II gave the Duke of York a land grant incorporating parts of today's Pennsylvania, which conflicted with claims in the area by the Dutch New Netherland colony. Later in 1664, the British conquered New Netherland. Although there were some skirmishes over areas of present-day Pennsylvania, ultimately the British prevailed.

In 1681, King Charles II issued yet another land grant, this time to the Quaker William Penn as repayment of a debt. The King named it Pennsylvania, or "Penn's Woods."

William Penn established a colonial government that provided freedom of religious conviction. He also set out to deal fairly with the Native Americans, offering them equal rights under English law. Penn signed a peace treaty with Tammany, leader of the Delaware tribe, which began a long period of nonviolent relations with the local Indians.

Another innovative act by the Pennsylvania colony was issuing its own paper money beginning in 1764 due to a shortage of gold and silver. The iconic Pennsylvanian, Benjamin Franklin, helped to create this currency and regulate its use to avoid inflation, which supported the colony's prosperity.

Philadelphia was a particular success story. Klein and Hoogenboom (1998) note that in one year alone, sixty ships docked at Philadelphia, "bringing thousands of settlers to swell this rapidly growing town and take up land in the interior" (25). Central location, general prosperity, peaceful relations with the natives, and religious toleration all contributed to making Pennsylvania a key part of the thirteen original colonies.

In 1787, Pennsylvania was second only to Delaware in ratifying the U.S. Constitution. Not only did the Continental Congress produce the Declaration of Independence and the Constitution in Philadelphia, but the rapidly growing city also served as the nation's capital for Presidents George Washington and John Adams from 1790 to 1800.

The state continued to prosper in the 1800s. In 1859, near the Pennsylvania town of Titusville, the first commercially drilled oil well was a success, leading to the earliest major oil boom in U.S. history. In the twentieth century, Pennsylvania's economy centered on steel production and industrial manufacturing that utilized not only Pennsylvania's rich underground supply of petroleum but also its coal.

With the expansion of mining for coal and drilling for oil, Pennsylvania has seen its share of environmental calamities. These events were not confined to oil and coal, with Pennsylvania also being the site of the notorious Three Mile Island nuclear power plant incident in 1979. However, there is one environmental disaster in the state that has taken on legendary proportions.

In 1856, anthracite coal mines opened in the Pennsylvania town of **Centralia**. Mining was expanded as the arrival of the railroad connected Centralia with important markets. But after the Stock Market crash in 1929, some mining companies shut down operations in Centralia, leading to "bootleg miners" who continued digging in idle mines without safety precautions, often causing tunnels to collapse.

In 1962, the population of the Centralia area is said to have been about two thousand people. Before Memorial Day of that year, sources say there was an attempt to clean up the town landfill, located in an abandoned strip-mine pit. The dump sat near a local cemetery, and it is said the authorities wanted to tidy things up for Memorial Day ceremonies. As they had done in the past, volunteer firefighters set the dump on fire in a controlled burn.

However, the flames ignited a seam of coal that runs beneath the land. The fire burned down into the labyrinth of abandoned coal mines under Centralia. The inferno could not be extinguished. It never went out, and is not expected to do so for at least 250 more years.

Today, noxious gases and smoke from the smoldering coal-fed fires spew from the many openings in the ground, giving the town an otherworldly appearance that some say resembles the gates of Hell.

At the very least, Centralia is a ghost town. With the underground fire burning for over a half century now, the groundwater is heated to boiling temperatures, causing steam to rise from the earth. Therefore, in addition to smoke and gas escaping from every fissure in the ground, the steam gives Centralia a misty, unsettling appearance that seems to emanate from a fiery lair.

Centralia, Pennsylvania, lies atop a rich vein of coal. In 1962, the local dump was set on fire in a controlled burn. However, the flames ignited a seam of coal running below town that will not burn itself out for at least 250 years. Today, with smoke spewing from the abandoned graffiti-covered highway near the deserted town, some say it looks like the haunted road to Hell. (Kris Snopek/Dreamstime.com)

The ghostliness of Centralia is magnified by the lack of human inhabitants or even vegetation. Residents were evacuated, and their homes destroyed. Of the nearly two thousand Centralia residents who were there when the mines caught fire, only a few are said to still remain, determined to live in their doomed town until they die.

Some did not have that choice. David Dekok (2010) cites one Centralia family who "thought about moving but realized it would bankrupt them. Besides, they preferred to fight for their home, which they had worked hard to make nice" (113).

But with the fire having burned nonstop for thirty years, carbon monoxide reached dangerous levels in remaining homes. Smoke poured from the ground, the earth's surface glowed red, and even pumping gas took on potentially deadly proportions since the fire heated the underground gas tanks. A twelve-year-old boy tumbled into a pit when the backyard of his grandmother's home collapsed, coming perilously close to death before being rescued.

A mandatory evacuation was ordered in 1992 by the government, using eminent domain and condemnation proceedings to remove residents who had not voluntarily sold their properties to the state.

The Centralia mine fire has left the town a "dead zone" where large patches of ground are devoid of trees and any plant life. With the underground fire heating the soil to such high temperatures, tree roots die, vegetation withers, and noxious fumes kill the rest.

Even the four-lane highway near town has been closed down as the massive fire caused gaping sinkholes spewing fumes that are emitted from its cracked, fractured asphalt surface.

In the now-abandoned Centralia, broken sidewalks, steps leading to nowhere, and street signs where there are no streets give the impression to many that some paranormal force has driven everyone away. Only the three cemeteries seem to be occupied. With such a ghastly, ghostly appearance, it is no surprise that many people feel Centralia is haunted.

SOME OTHER REPORTEDLY HAUNTED PLACES IN PENNSYLVANIA

Philadelphia's **Eastern State Penitentiary** is a menacing-looking Gothic style prison that opened in 1829. It was the first in the United States to implement solitary confinement, a punishment that is still debated today. At Eastern State, prisoners languished in dank, gloomy underground stone cells with virtually no human contact. They had no exercise, no light, no toilet, and precious little air and food. Any time they were moved out of their cell, hoods were placed over their heads. The theory was that this would give them plenty of time for introspective thought about the error of their criminal ways. In reality, men went mad with emotional anguish that some maintained was comparable to physical torture. There was no shortage of that either, including the water bath, in which inmates were dunked then hung out on a wall in winter until ice formed on the skin. In the "mad chair," inmates were bound so tightly that circulation was cut off, often necessitating amputations. There were others too grisly to relate. When the prison closed in 1971, after almost 150 years and about 70,000 prisoners, it is believed that the ghosts of tormented inmates were unable to rest easy. Today, tours of the crumbling facility with its looming high stone walls are offered for the daring. Throughout the abandoned cellblocks, there have been reports of apparitions wandering the corridors and the sound of furtive whispers along with cackling laughter and wailing cries. Cellblock 12 is said to be the site's most haunted location, featuring a mass gathering of shadow figures. Cellblock 6 is allegedly the home of shadowy forms that dart across the walls, while Cellblock 4 is known for visions of ghostly faces. Keeping an eye on things is the tower that is reputed to be haunted by the ghost of a former guard.

The **First Bank of the United States** in Philadelphia is reportedly haunted by the ghost of Alexander Hamilton himself. After the American Revolution was won, Hamilton, the first Secretary of the Treasury, believed a national bank would stabilize the new nation's credit and improve handling the financial business of the U.S. government under its newly enacted Constitution. Always a man with a keen eye for detail, the ghost of Alexander Hamilton may be keeping an eye on his financial creation, the First Bank of the United States, even though it has been closed for several decades. Hamilton was never a slacker. As one of America's Founding Fathers as well as the originator of the nation's financial system, he interpreted the U.S. Constitution for the general public through his writings, created the U.S. Coast Guard, established a system of tariffs to promote America's fledgling economy, and was active in ending the legality of the international slave trade. Along the way, he made powerful enemies, including Vice President Aaron Burr. In 1804, Burr challenged Hamilton to a duel in which Hamilton was mortally wounded, dying the next day. Today, in addition to being the darling of Broadway in the musical *Hamilton*, it would seem that Hamilton has the last laugh by staking a ghostly claim to the majestic building that housed his First Bank.

Although little known, Philadelphia's **Fort Mifflin** is sometimes called "The Fort that Saved America." It was built by the British in 1771 to protect what was then the wealthy English colonial city of Philadelphia. But when the American Revolution began, George Washington recognized the importance of disrupting the British army's supply route. After Fort Mifflin was taken by the Americans, Washington ordered the garrison at the little fort to "hold to the last extremity," no easy feat as they faced off against the mightiest army and navy of the time. When the British surrounded Fort Mifflin, about forty young American soldiers spiked the cannons and set fire to the fort before the enemy could prevail. Fort Mifflin never actually surrendered, giving Washington time to escape and regroup at the patriots' winter camp in Valley Forge, Pennsylvania. Today, Fort Mifflin is said to be haunted by the ghosts of stalwart colonial soldiers, still hanging tough. One particular soldier, said to be named Amos, has reportedly been seen on numerous occasions cleaning his gun by the artillery shed. A ghostly lamplighter strolls around the soldiers' barracks, and a faceless ghost has been seen at the fortified gun enclosures. There have also been disembodied sounds like those emanating from the blacksmith shop and a screaming lady in the officers' quarters.

The peaceful town of **Gettysburg**, Pennsylvania, is also home to one of the most historic, most significant, and most bloody battles of the American Civil War. Today, Gettysburg is said to be among the ghostliest locations in Pennsylvania, with the spirits of both Union and Confederate soldiers still battling it out from the Great Beyond. Between July 1 and July 3, 1863, more than fifty-one thousand Americans were reported killed, wounded, or missing. In addition, skirmishes took place virtually throughout the town. When Northern forces retreated on the first day of the battle, they poured into the community of Gettysburg, establishing themselves on the relative safety of Cemetery Hill. Many were killed there, with their bodies left where they fell in the July heat awaiting burial. According to some sources, townsfolk were only able to walk the streets after the battle with scented handkerchiefs pressed to their faces to combat the horrible smell of death. Today, it is said that wafting aromas of peppermint and vanilla can still be detected. At Devil's Den, a natural rock formation on the grounds of the battlefield, visitors have reported hearing sounds of drums and gunshots as well as sightings of a barefoot, shabbily dressed man who tries holding their hand. The Jennie Wade House marks the home where a twenty-year-old girl was killed when a sniper's musket ball smashed through the door of her house, with Jennie's ghost still in residence. A hotbed of paranormal activity is the battlefield's Little Round Top. There, one of the most prevalent stories involves Civil War re-enactors working as extras on the film *Gettysburg*. They claim to have encountered a man in the uniform of a Union soldier, whom they assumed worked on the movie. Before disappearing, he passed them some ammunition which they presumed were blanks but later realized were musket rounds dating back to the Civil War, in pristine condition. With the bloody back-and-forth of the Battle of Gettysburg over three long days, it may be that the restless souls of the soldiers who fought and died there may be unwilling to admit that the battle has ended or that time has moved on.

While Philadelphia can allegedly boast the ghostly presence of Alexander Hamilton, the **Logan Inn** at New Hope may be the supernatural lodging of Hamilton's nemesis, Aaron Burr. Said to be one of the five oldest inns in America, the Logan is a restored 1727 colonial inn and tavern where Burr is said to have enjoyed food and drink during his lifetime. Burr owned a home in New Hope, so it may be that after his disgrace, that would be the spot where his spirit would return. Burr, a lawyer and politician, served as the third vice president of the United States between 1801 and 1805, during President Thomas Jefferson's first term. Before that, Burr had served as a Continental Army officer in the American Revolution, was appointed New York State Attorney General, and was elected to the New York State Assembly and U.S. Senate. But during the last full year of his single term as vice president, Burr killed his political rival Alexander Hamilton in a historic duel in 1804. Burr was never tried for the illegal duel, but Hamilton's death ended Burr's political career. Burr traveled west seeking new opportunities, but his activities eventually led to his arrest on charges of treason. He fled overseas, returning to the United States where he died an obscure death in 1836. There are claims that the ghost of Aaron Burr still visits the Logan Inn where it is said he stopped briefly after the ill-fated duel with Hamilton. At that point, Burr did not know how far he would fall from grace. Windows at the inn have been known to throw themselves open in the middle of the night. Perhaps it is Burr reliving his earlier glory days. He may also be manifested as the apparition of a soldier in Revolutionary War attire who wanders around the inn, especially the dining room and the bar.

FURTHER READING

Dekok, David. *Fire Underground: The Ongoing Tragedy of the Centralia Mine Fire.* Guilford, CT: Globe Pequot, 2010.

Klein, Philip, and Ari Hoogenboom. *A History of Pennsylvania.* University Park: Penn State University Press, 1998.

40

Rhode Island

In the first place, Rhode Island is not actually an island. In addition, according to its government website, while Rhode Island may be the smallest state in the United States, it also has the longest official name: "State of Rhode Island and Providence Plantations," derived from the merger of several colonial settlements.

Some say the word "Rhode" in the state's name evolves from an account by Dutch explorer Adriaen Block who sailed past the area in the early 1600s and described it as having a reddish appearance, or "rodlich" in the Dutch language of the seventeenth century, a coloring that might have been due to red autumn foliage.

In 1636, residents of the Massachusetts Bay Colony like Roger Williams were banished over religious views. They settled in the area of today's Providence, Rhode Island. The colony became known as a place of religious freedom where all were welcome. In 1638, after conferring with Williams, other religious dissenters like Anne Hutchinson settled in Rhode Island.

McLoughlin (1986) quotes the Puritan minister Cotton Mather as calling Hutchinson an "American Jezebel" (18). Within a few years of moving to Rhode Island, there were threats of Massachusetts taking over Rhode Island, compelling Hutchinson to move totally outside the Puritan reach. She and her followers migrated again, this time to the Dutch colony of New Netherland, today's Manhattan, in a settlement where she was murdered by hostile Indians.

Today's Brown University in Providence was founded in 1764 as the College in the English Colony of Rhode Island and Providence Plantations. It was the first colonial college to accept students regardless of their religious affiliation.

Rhode Island was in the forefront as events led to the American Revolution (1775–1783). In 1772, a year before the Boston Tea Party, a group of Providence residents attacked and burned a British revenue ship for enforcing unpopular trade regulations.

On May 4, 1776, two months before the Declaration of Independence was created, Rhode Island was the first of the thirteen colonies to renounce its allegiance to the British Crown. During the Revolution, the English occupied Newport,

Rhode Island, starting in 1776. But after sinking some of their own ships to avoid capture and thereby blocking the harbor, the British abandoned Newport in 1779.

After the Americans won the Revolution, Rhode Island further asserted the independent spirit that had led to its founding by becoming the last of the thirteen colonies to ratify the U.S. Constitution. It did not do so until 1790 (others had preceded it three years earlier) when it received assurances that a Bill of Rights would become part of the Constitution.

During the American Civil War (1861–1865), Rhode Island was the first in the Union to send troops in response to President Abraham Lincoln's request for help from the states. By that time, Rhode Island had become heavily invested in the Industrial Revolution, utilizing its manufacturing capability to supply the Union with materials the North needed to win the war.

After the Civil War, the wealth Rhode Island accrued through industrialization mirrored much of the nation as a whole, allowing a number of cities in Rhode Island to prosper. For example, Davis (2011) states that after the Revolutionary War, Newport, Rhode Island, had fallen "into an economic depression that paralyzed the city for several decades" (18). However, in the era of the Industrial Revolution that followed the Civil War, Newport would bounce back in a very big way.

Rhode Island boasts the nickname "The Ocean State" for its hundreds of miles of picturesque shoreline. In the late 1800s, Newport Harbor, in particular, became known for the many pleasure boats docked there. Mark Twain labeled the era as the "Gilded Age" in the sense of "gilding the lily," an unnecessarily extravagant display of opulence. Rhode Island, and Newport in particular, attracted the Gilded Age millionaires who built grand "summer cottages" by the sea. They did their best to impress and out-do each other, exactly as they did the rest of the year at their New York City mansions.

In the twentieth century, many of the legendary Newport mansions opened for tourists, offering a glimpse into the lives of America's ultra-rich. In the later years of the twentieth century, Rhode Island became known not only for the extravagance of millionaires but also for the activities of local organized crime. However, crime—especially murder—was not limited to recent times.

Murder is defined as the unlawful killing of another human without a justification like self-defense. Premeditated murder involves malice aforethought, meaning conscious intent. Some interpretations of the Bible's Book of Genesis consider Cain to be the original murderer for slaying his brother, Abel.

In 1630, a colonist named John Billington, who had traveled to the New World aboard the *Mayflower*, was one of the original Pilgrims who landed at Plymouth Rock. Billington is also said to be the first colonist convicted of murder in America. After making powerful enemies and being accused of shooting another colonist, Billington is reportedly the first European to be executed by the state in the New World.

Two centuries later, another New England murder may have spurred supernatural repercussions in Rhode Island. The **Sprague Mansion** in Cranston, Rhode Island, was the home of wealthy industrialist Amasa Sprague. The family was prominent, but their wealth could not buy happiness.

Amasa's son, William Sprague IV, was not only rich but also became Rhode Island's youngest governor at the age of twenty-nine, additionally serving as a Civil War general and U.S. senator. William IV married Kate Chase, the daughter of Salmon P. Chase, chief justice of the U.S. Supreme Court. Kate Chase Sprague was considered to be the most beautiful and popular belle in Washington, but her marriage to Sprague was an unhappy one that eventually led to their divorce, socially disastrous at the time. Their son Willie Sprague committed suicide at age twenty-five; in his parting note, he blamed his father for his life's failures. Willie's mother, the once glittering and now miserable Kate Chase, died alone and destitute at age fifty-eight.

A crime that rocked both the family and their Rhode Island community led to developments that would echo into the twenty-first century. In 1843, William IV's father Amasa Sprague was found bludgeoned to death within sight of the Sprague Mansion. John Gordon, an Irish immigrant, was found guilty of the murder and sentenced to death. In 1845, John Gordon was hanged at the Rhode Island State Prison yard, where the Providence Place Mall now stands.

A public outcry followed Gordon's execution, which many said had been due to anti-Catholic bias. In 1852, legislation abolished capital punishment in Rhode Island, making Gordon the last person executed in the state. In 2011, Gordon was pardoned posthumously based on evidence that later came to light proving his innocence.

However, the spirits of the dead have been known to hold a grudge. Today, the Sprague Mansion is reportedly the site of manifestations including disembodied footsteps, flickering lights, strange orbs, and filmy white apparitions.

Some candidates for the source of the hauntings include the murdered Amasa Sprague, the unhappy Kate Chase Sprague, her son Willie who committed suicide, and the first William Sprague who died after a bone lodged in his throat at breakfast.

It might also be the ghost of John Gordon haunting the mansion of his accusers, indignant not only at being wrongfully convicted and hanged but also having the site of his execution turned into a shopping mall.

SOME OTHER REPORTEDLY HAUNTED PLACES IN RHODE ISLAND

The seventy-room **Breakers Mansion** in Newport was built in 1893 by the ultra-wealthy family of Cornelius Vanderbilt II as a "summer cottage," as a respite from life at their New York City mansion. Today, his wife Alice Gwynne Vanderbilt is said to maintain her role as family matriarch with her commanding presence at The Breakers even after her death in 1934. The mansion is open for public tours, although one floor is kept private for use by the family. Some say Alice Vanderbilt is keeping an eye on her property, others claim it is a place she might feel comfortable in the afterlife since her family was an object lesson on how money cannot buy happiness. Her first child died at five years old. The eldest son died at age twenty-two from typhoid fever. Another son was disinherited for

Elaborate mansions like The Breakers in Newport, Rhode Island, were built by the wealthy during the late 1800s. Quaintly called "summer cottages," they served as a respite from life at their New York City mansions. Today, Alice Gwynne Vanderbilt is said to maintain her role as matriarch with her commanding presence at The Breakers even after her death in 1934. (Lequint/Dreamstime.com)

marrying a woman of whom his parents did not approve. The third son was a source of pride but died on the *Lusitania* after the passenger liner was torpedoed by Germans in World War I. The fourth son died at age forty-five, which some said was due to hard-living. After Alice's passing in 1934, The Breakers was opened for public tours in 1948 to benefit the Preservation Society of Newport County. It is likely that the identifiable apparition reported by staff and visitors at the mansion belongs to Alice Vanderbilt where her unseen presence is said to be watching over things. She may be an indomitable but benign spirit who is happy to see her beloved residence being well cared for, as well as still being enjoyed by her descendants and awestruck guests. Alice may simply feel happily at home after death, having experienced pain and loss even in a privileged life.

The gravesite of the nineteen-year-old Mercy Brown at **Chestnut Hill Cemetery** in Exeter is considered by some to be the best-known haunted place in Rhode Island. Today, flowers and trinkets adorn her tombstone, showing her grave more "mercy" than the namesake Mercy received at the time of her death in 1892. Several members of the Brown family had died from tuberculosis, which was nothing unusual since the disease was highly contagious. When Mercy died, following her mother and sister, the ground was frozen so her body was kept in an aboveground vault until it could be interred. But instead of suspecting the infectious illness, some feared that supernatural powers were at work. When multiple members of the same family became ill, it was believed that the deceased returned as vampires to claim the lives of their loved ones. When Mercy's brother became sick, people suspected the foul doings of a vampire. The bodies of the dead family members were exhumed for examination. The mother and sister had decomposed, but Mercy's body had not—more than likely because her remains were stored at freezing temperatures for two months. Mercy's heart and liver were cut out and burned, which would supposedly end her alleged vampire activity. Because her brother was also ill, the ashes of Mercy's heart and liver were mixed into tea that was given to him to drink, supposedly to ward off his vampire sister. The brother soon died of tuberculosis. What was left of Mercy was buried in the cemetery, but some say the desecration of her body disturbed the resting of her soul. Today, many believe that the ghost of Mercy Brown haunts Chestnut Hill Cemetery, claiming to see Mercy's ghost walking at night. There have been reports of strange noises around the gravesite as well as orbs of light. Some who have been standing at her tombstone report being pushed away from the spot with extreme force. Considering what happened to Mercy's body, she might be trying to be left alone.

The **Providence Athenaeum** is a library that was a hotspot for such luminaries of the supernatural as H. P. Lovecraft and Edgar Allan Poe, so it is not unusual for paranormal cold spots to be attributed to their hauntingly macabre presence. Today's Providence Athenaeum was founded in 1836, the same year Poe married his thirteen-year-old cousin, Virginia, who died of tuberculosis in 1847. In Providence, the poet and spiritualist Sarah Helen Whitman was a fan of Poe's writing. Whitman had a heart condition that she treated with ether which she breathed in through her handkerchief. She had a fondness for wearing all black, set off by a cheery coffin-shaped charm around her neck. Whitman was, in short, Poe's kind of woman. After Virginia's death, Poe and Whitman exchanged letters until he proposed marriage. One of their meeting places was the Athenaeum where Whitman accepted his proposal on the condition that he would remain sober until their wedding day. He promised, but that particular vow lasted only briefly. While Whitman was visiting the Providence Athenaeum, she is said to have received an anonymous letter informing her that Poe was drinking heavily again, leading to an abrupt end of their relationship in December 1848. Poe died mysteriously in October 1849 after wandering the streets of Baltimore in a delirious state. Whitman is said to have summoned his spirit to the Athenaeum. Years later, the story goes that when a man was found sleeping on the Athenaeum steps and was asked to move, he yelled, "The Conqueror Worm!" (the title of one of Poe's poems about mortality) before vanishing into thin air. Since then, there have been reports of a figure resembling Poe dressed in black, sitting on the steps of the Athenaeum where he and Whitman had played out their gothic-attired love story. Some claim to have witnessed his apparition walking along the street in front of the Athenaeum, as well as inside a room at the library itself where portraits of Poe and Whitman are displayed. Not surprisingly, when approached, the manifestation is said to look melancholy before quickly vanishing. The Providence Athenaeum was also favored by horror writer H. P. Lovecraft who wrote in the 1920s that Poe was his "God of Fiction." Therefore, it seems fitting that the ghost of Providence native Lovecraft, author of such tales as "The Rats in the Walls," would join his literary idol in haunting the Athenaeum.

According to the Library of Congress, **Slater Mill** in Pawtucket was an early landmark in the Industrial Revolution, being founded in 1790. Some call it the birthplace of the Industrial Revolution in America, with Samuel Slater bringing new manufacturing technologies from Britain to start the first U.S. cotton mill. It was also an early landmark in the practice of industrial child labor. In the past, it had not been unknown for children to work on the family farm. However, in the mills, children worked long hours to the point of exhaustion and did some of the most dangerous jobs amid the deafening machinery. There were no workplace safety laws or regulations against child labor. Reportedly, the first nine employees of Samuel Slater were five girls and four boys under the age of twelve. Some came from the local poorhouse and source of cheap labor. Their small bodies operated the unforgiving machines that opened and slammed shut constantly, continuing to run even if an arm, a leg, or an entire body was crushed inside. Today, Slater Mill is operated as a National Historic Site. In addition to tourists, it is said to be the haunt of small dark figures whose shadows move about the building. There have been sounds of screaming and strange voices, sometimes described as the past crying out to be heard. One alleged childlike ghost says hello and giggles, but others are not so companionable. Once, during a tour, a spike was propelled by an invisible force off the blacksmith's bench. On another occasion, a set of crutches on display was said by a local TV station to have flown out at a guest before scattering on the floor.

FURTHER READING

Davis, Deborah. *Gilded: How Newport Became America's Richest Resort*. Hoboken, NJ: Wiley, 2011.

McLoughlin, William. *Rhode Island: A History*. New York: W. W. Norton & Company, 1986.

41

South Carolina

South Carolina is often described as a mystical place, which may largely result from its geography. Along with its Low Country on the coast, inland cities like the state's capital, Columbia, were founded on sand hills that according to Brown (2010) "form part of an ancient beach dating back to a time when the land was covered by oceans" (3). With foreboding swamps in the region, some say much of the state's eerie quality dates back to prehistoric times.

Archaeologists have found evidence of human activity in today's South Carolina from about forty thousand years ago. When Europeans began arriving in the sixteenth century, Native American tribes in the region included the Catawba and Cherokee. Several tribes lived inland but also spent pleasant summers on the coast where they cultivated crops along with harvesting fish and oysters.

The Spanish were the first Europeans to arrive. In 1526, Spaniard Lucas Ayllón landed near today's Georgetown, South Carolina, establishing the San Miguel de Guadalupe colony. Although soon abandoned, it is said to be the first European settlement in what is now the continental United States, predating St. Augustine, Florida, which was founded in 1565.

Ayllón reportedly brought the first African slaves to today's United States. According to Bass and Poole (2009), Ayllón's settlement also became the site of the first North American slave revolt: "African slaves and native people banded together against the Spanish who abandoned the settlement the following year" (207).

During the next century, England established the Province of Carolina in 1629, consisting of the region that is now North Carolina and South Carolina. Like its immediate neighbor to the north, South Carolina was named for England's King Charles I, with "Carolus" being Latin for Charles.

The city of Charleston, South Carolina, was founded in 1670, honoring King Charles II. English settlers built rice plantations in South Carolina's Low Country, with labor being forced on African slaves.

Further west in the Carolina Province, small farmers displaced Native American tribes. In 1729, North and South Carolina were split into two separate entities.

By the coming of the American Revolution, South Carolina was one of the richest of the thirteen original English colonies. It also became a battleground during the Revolution, with a large portion of all combat taking place in South Carolina, more so than in most other states.

After victory, South Carolina joined the other original colonies in ratifying the U.S. Constitution. In 1788, it became the eighth state to join the Union.

In the years between the Revolution and the Civil War, South Carolina's prosperity and population grew. In 1800, its capital, Columbia, was connected to Charleston by the Santee Canal, one of the first such waterways in the United States.

Although South Carolina was one of the thirteen original colonies that joined the Union, it was also the first state to vote in favor of seceding from that same Union, which it did in December, 1860. In doing so, it became the state where America's Civil War is said to have begun. Fort Sumter in the harbor at Charleston was shelled by Confederate forces on April 12–13, 1861, after South Carolina seceded and the federal troops stationed at the fort refused to leave.

The Civil War proved disastrous for South Carolina. The war ruined the economy of the state, which lost almost one-third of its white male population. In addition, many white landowners abandoned their plantations, leaving about ten thousand slaves behind. Toward the end of the war in 1865, troops under Union General William Tecumseh Sherman marched through the Carolinas in a crushing swath of devastation. During the postwar reconstruction era, South Carolina suffered much of the same impoverishment as the rest of the defeated South.

Malnutrition and sickness were prevalent. In South Carolina, as elsewhere in the world, one of the most feared and deadly illnesses was the bacterial disease, tuberculosis (TB).

TB fatally attacks the lungs with symptoms of active TB including a chronic cough (usually accompanied with blood) and extreme weight loss. The disease was often called "consumption" due to the weight loss that made it appear as though the body itself was being consumed.

Historically, tuberculosis was often associated with vampires. It was observed that when one member of a family withered and died from the disease, others would follow. People believed this was caused by the dead TB victim draining life from the other family members.

By 1946, the masses were able to retire their garlic and wooden stakes when the development of antibiotics became an effective treatment for tuberculosis. However, before modern medicine isolated a cure, treatment for TB patients often depended not only on their socioeconomic status but also on their gender.

According to Rothman (1995), males were often advised to leave their home to travel to places with fresh air in search of recovery. But "women, insofar as possible, were expected to restore [their] health within the family and in ways consistent with their domestic responsibilities" (23). Since TB is a highly contagious disease spread through the air, the result for the family was often inevitable.

TB was so commonly fatal in the 1800s that it inspired tragic cultural themes. In a series of six paintings called *The Sick Child*, Edvard Munch (who also painted

The Scream) depicts his bedridden sister dying of TB as an older woman mourns at her side; his mother also died of the disease.

TB and its related themes became associated with composer Frédéric Chopin, poets like John Keats, Edgar Allan Poe, and Percy Bysshe Shelley, and writers including Charlotte Brontë, Franz Kafka, and Robert Louis Stevenson. TB was also the centerpiece of such iconic operas as *La Bohème* and *La Traviata* as well as the classic Greta Garbo film, *Camille*.

In the early twentieth century, TB facilities for the middle and upper classes generally offered good care. The infected poor were directed to sanitariums that sometimes resembled prisons.

In South Carolina, the **Greenville Tuberculosis Hospital** in Greenville treated hundreds of patients suffering from TB between its opening in 1930 and the early 1950s when it shut down. Many died there. After it closed, people exploring the old building claimed to hear footsteps in the empty hallways as well as screams and sobs.

The former hospital sat abandoned until a fire ravaged the building in 2002. Today, the popular Herdklotz Park stands where the hospital once did. It is named for a former county councilman because of his interest in outdoor recreation for the area. There is signage that refers to the history of the Tuberculosis Hospital, but some say that is not all remaining of the old building.

Especially at night, people have reported hearing banging, screaming, and unseen bells that clang. Some visitors claim to have seen shadows flashing through the darkness as well as shadowy apparitions that are said to sometimes enter nearby homes. Locals report puddles that turn blood-red after a rain, suggesting the phenomenon might be a manifestation of patients who died at the TB hospital from the bloody disease.

SOME OTHER REPORTEDLY HAUNTED PLACES IN SOUTH CAROLINA

Dating from 1736, the historic **Dock Street Theatre** in Charleston is said be one of the first theaters in America, with some qualifying it by stating that while it may not have been the very first theater in the thirteen colonies, it was the first building in America built exclusively to be used for theatrical performances. Statements regarding its past are muddled as it experienced several incarnations because of disasters like fires and wartime depredations, including the time the building was used as a lodging. When it was the Planter's Hotel, it is said to be the place where Charleston's famed Planter's Punch was first introduced. What no one seems to dispute is Dock Street Theatre's reputation for being haunted. Some witnesses who have passed the theater at night claim to have seen what look like the ghosts of lost souls gazing out from the windows of the darkened playhouse. There are two ghostly spirits who are said to haunt the building. In its heyday during the early 1800s, the Planter's Hotel became known as one of Charleston's preeminent locations. Wealthy out-of-town Carolina planters, for whom the lodging was named, flocked to the city for the horse racing season, on which fortunes were made and lost. The Planter's Hotel was also known to play host to theatrical groups, one of which starred an actor named Junius Brutus Booth, father of the presidential assassin John Wilkes Booth. The story is that the elder Booth stayed at the Planter's Hotel around 1838 and for some reason had an altercation with the hotel manager that led to Booth attacking and almost killing the other man. After the Civil War, the building declined before being reborn into the theater. Today, the ghost of Nettie Dickerson may be in residence. She is said to have been a beautiful country girl who came to Charleston in hopes of finding a husband, but at age twenty-five, she was considered too old and too lower class to attract a suitor. With her meager savings, she bought a bright red dress and entered prostitution to make a living. One night during a storm, Nettie, distraught at her circumstances, went out to the hotel balcony where she was killed by lightning. Today, the site is the Dock Street Theatre where Nettie's dramatic story should be right at home.

Folly Beach was used as a Union Army field hospital where many wounded soldiers were sent subsequent to the battles at the nearby Fort Wagner in 1863. The wounded men included members of the famed 54th Massachusetts Volunteer Infantry Regiment, the first military unit consisting of black soldiers to be assembled in the North during the Civil War. Many of the casualties were found to have been mutilated, and were buried on this barrier island in shallow graves. Over the years, hurricanes and heavy storms have uncovered some of these unmarked gravesites. In 1987, the remains of fourteen unknown soldiers were uncovered on the island; twelve of these were missing their skulls and other body parts. Folly Beach seems to have been a haven for hauntings since the arrival of Europeans in the early 1600s. Local Native American tribes were virtually wiped out, in large part due to European diseases like influenza, measles and smallpox for which the Indians had no immunity. It is said their spirits haunt the island. During the 1700s, pirates, who may have included the fearsome Blackbeard himself, sought to hide out among its coves and use it as a base of operations for pillaging. One of the most unsettling Folly Beach stories occurred in 1832 when the ship *Amelia* wrecked off the coast near the island. More than a hundred passengers survived but were cast ashore on Folly Beach and were left to fend for themselves amid rumors that cholera had broken out among the survivors. It is said that the ghostly spirits of those who died while stranded on Folly Beach haunt the island to this day.

The "Grey Man" is the most famous ghost from **Pawleys Island**. This apparition is said to appear just before a catastrophic storm hits the island, warning people to flee for their lives. He is spotted walking along the beach wearing grey clothes and will sometimes speak to people, but in other cases, simply appears in front of them before vanishing. No one is quite certain who the man was, but most locals have a "Grey Man" story of their own. The ghost of Alice Flagg is also said to appear at Pawleys Island. She was the sister of a wealthy man who disapproved of her romance with a young suitor beneath their social class. After Alice's brother discovered she wore her beloved's ring on a ribbon around the neck, he tore it off and threw it away. The broken-hearted girl soon died from malaria, and is buried under a flat stone that simply says "Alice." Some witnesses state that Alice's specter can be seen at the graveyard with her hand on her chest, appearing to search for something.

At **White Point Gardens** in Charleston, also known as The Battery, the lovely grounds are said to be haunted by the spirits of numerous pirates who were hanged here. Today it is reported that their ghosts roam the gardens searching for their executioners in order to take revenge. In the 1700s, Charleston was one of the four busiest ports in America, with untold wealth entering and leaving its harbor. It was, therefore, an attractive target for pirates. One of the most notorious found it unnecessary to expend a single cannonball. In 1718, Edward Teach, better known as Blackbeard, blockaded Charleston Harbor and took over the city. He commandeered a ship that had many prominent citizens aboard, and sent a letter to the Royal Governor claiming he would slay them all if he did not receive certain supplies (which some said were for venereal disease). The Royal Governor complied and Blackbeard did not execute his prisoners, although he robbed them of their money, valuables, and even their clothes. In addition, Blackbeard had a friend among pirate captains named Stede Bonnet who had been born into wealth but decided to try being a pirate after becoming unhappy in his marriage. Bonnet was known as the "The Gentleman Pirate" for his degree of civility. Sadly, he lacked the vocational skills for piracy, eventually joining forces with Blackbeard. However, most of Bonnet's men jumped ship to team up with the more charismatic and skillful Blackbeard. Bonnet struck out on his own, but when he was pursued by authorities, his ship ran aground at the Cape Fear River. Before he would ever

The grounds of White Point Gardens in Charleston, South Carolina, are said to be haunted by the angry spirits of pirates from the 1700s who were hanged there. It is reported that their manifestations roam the gardens seeking revenge on long-dead executioners. Visitors claim to have seen ghostly faces peering back at them from the gallows tree and to hear terrifying screams echoing in the air at night. (James Kirkikis /Dreamstime.com)

surrender, Bonnet planned to blow up the boat with gunpowder that was aboard, but that plan was vetoed by his remaining crew. They were captured and shipped in chains to Charleston. His men were hanged at White Point, but before Bonnet could be executed, he tried to escape wearing a dress, disguised as a woman. When he was recaptured, Bonnet wrote to the Royal Governor, begging for mercy and promising to have his own arms and legs cut off as assurance that he would never again commit piracy. Remarkably, the governor delayed Bonnet's execution seven times. But on December 10, 1718, Stede Bonnet was led to the gallows at White Point where he died an agonizing death by strangulation since the rope did not cleanly break his neck. Like his men, Bonnet's body was kept on display, swinging from the gallows, until being tossed into the marshes. It is said that today their souls continue to haunt the park. Visitors claim to have witnessed ghostly faces peering back at them from within the gallows tree. Some have reported a manifestation hanging from an old oak. Terrifying screams have been said to echo in the air at night. Legend also has it that when people stand at Water Street and glance down, they can still spot the grotesque faces of executed pirates staring back at them beneath the surface of the water.

FURTHER READING

Bass, Jack, and W. Scott Poole. *The Palmetto State: The Making of South Carolina.* Columbia: University of South Carolina Press, 2009.

Brown, Alan. *Haunted South Carolina: Ghosts and Strange Phenomena of the Palmetto State.* Mechanicsburg, PA: Stackpole Books, 2010.

Rothman, Sheila M. *Living in the Shadow of Death: Tuberculosis and the Social Experience of Illness in American History.* Baltimore, MD: Johns Hopkins University Press, 1995.

42

South Dakota

According to Tennant (2017), "South Dakota's history cannot be told without including the Lakota, Dakota, and Nakota people from whom the state gets its name, meaning 'friend'" (9). That friendship would be strained with the passage of time, resulting in one of the most storied conflicts in American history, the Wounded Knee Massacre in 1890, which took place on South Dakota's Lakota Pine Ridge Indian Reservation.

The region of today's Dakotas was populated by indigenous people for thousands of years. By the late 1800s, when many European and American settlers arrived, the Sioux were the dominant tribe.

Forming the southern part of the Dakota Territory, South Dakota sought statehood in 1889. Because of the rivalry with neighboring North Dakota, the enabling documents for statehood were shuffled so then-President Benjamin Harrison could sign them without knowing which was which. Therefore, North and South Dakota joined the Union simultaneously on November 2, 1889, as the thirty-ninth and fortieth states.

South Dakota can claim one of the most iconic features of the American landscape. Within the Black Hills, sacred to the Sioux, stands Mount Rushmore with its images of four U.S. presidents that were carved into the mountainside from 1927 to 1941.

European contact with the Dakota region began in 1743, when brothers François and Louis-Joseph Gaultier de La Vérendrye explored the region. They left a marker plate on a hill near the site of today's Pierre, South Dakota, claiming the region for France as part of Louisiana. As such, Dakota fell under Spanish control between 1762 and 1802, but reverted briefly to France, until it was bought by the United States in 1803 as part of the Louisiana Purchase.

Permanent American settlement in the region followed the opening of a fur trading post at the present-day Fort Pierre in 1817. The U.S. Army established a presence in the Dakota Territory at frontier forts, and U.S. government officials signed treaties with the Sioux marking the division between Native American land and that of the United States.

With the rise of the railroads, settlers arrived steadily in South Dakota. But a watershed event occurred in 1874 with a military expedition led by George Armstrong Custer. It was an unlawful incursion onto land that had been granted to the Lakota Sioux. Worse, Custer's expedition discovered gold.

The Sioux declined to grant either land on the Sioux reservation or mining rights to the Americans. But when news about the gold got out, prospectors poured into the Black Hills illegally. On its part, the U.S. government did not uphold the treaties to stop the flow of miners and settlers. Predictably, conflict ensued.

There was a special attraction for miners to flood into the area despite it being on Sioux land. Ames (2004) says the Black Hills were riddled with "easy placer gold found in relatively shallow deposits of gravel and sand, so no expensive equipment or elaborate mining was required to get at it" (5).

During this Black Hills Gold Rush, a settlement called **Deadwood** began illegally on sacred land that had been granted to the Lakota Sioux. It was named by the early settlers after the dead trees found in a nearby gulch. In the raw, lawless, get-rich-quick atmosphere of the era, the population of Deadwood quickly soared to about five thousand. In early 1876, frontiersmen Charlie and Steve Utter led a wagon train to Deadwood that carried the gamblers and prostitutes who were accurately predicted to become profitable.

Between 1876 and 1879, Deadwood was a boom town. It attracted such larger-than-life figures of the Old West as Wyatt Earp, Calamity Jane, and James Butler "Wild Bill" Hickok.

Like many of his compatriots, Hickok had a wide-ranging past that included stints as an actor, gambler, gunfighter, lawman, scout, soldier, and spy. There were

Deadwood, South Dakota, began illegally on sacred land granted to the Sioux. In the late 1800s, Deadwood was a raw, lawless boom town, attracting Old West icons like Calamity Jane and Wild Bill Hickok who were buried there. Visitors claim to feel ghostly eyes watching them, suggesting that Deadwood's deceased residents may not be resting in peace. (Thomas Carlson/Dreamstime.com)

other endeavors that were said to be fabricated either by Hickok himself or "dime novelists" hoping to sell their pulp fiction. What is certain is that in 1876, Hickok was shot and killed while playing poker in a Deadwood saloon, murdered by a disgruntled fellow gambler. The cards Hickok was playing at the time—eights and aces—have become known as the dead man's hand.

Pulp fiction of the era promoted the exploits, real or imagined, of Deadwood denizens like Hickok and Calamity Jane. "Deadwood Dick" was a fictional character in a series of stories by Edward Lytton Wheeler that were published between 1877 and 1897.

Deadwood, therefore, became widely known as a flamboyant, lawless town. But the easy placer gold began to run out by 1879, and expensive deep mining was needed to extract the ore. Prospectors pulled up stakes and scattered elsewhere.

Al Swearengen, who controlled the local opium trade, ran a saloon that burned down in a fire that devastated the town of Deadwood in 1879. Along with Swearengen's saloon, the 1879 fire destroyed more than three hundred buildings in Deadwood and wiped out a number of residents as their possessions went up in flames. Many departed to start over someplace else.

Since then, the entire town has been designated a National Historic Landmark. Its remaining buildings are said to be prime examples of frontier architecture from the late 1800s.

The heyday of Deadwood, South Dakota, has been depicted in many books, films, and television shows. It became a cultural icon with the HBO television series *Deadwood* that ran on cable from 2004 to 2006. The program was especially noted for its authentic look and feel, as well as actor Ian McShane's portrayal of the amoral Al Swearengen.

Today, as a place with a colorful past that has been captured in time, the town of Deadwood is a popular tourist destination. As Shadley and Wennes say, "Walk down Main Street, and you can feel the energy of an earlier time" (11).

Part of that energy may be derived from spirits from the past who continue to call the town home. There are a few places that are said to be especially popular with the dead of Deadwood. At the restored Adams House, built in 1893, former owner W.E. Adams died of a stroke. When his wife reported encountering Adams's spirit from the afterlife, she closed up the house and moved out, but his spirit stayed behind.

The Bullock Hotel is said to remain the lodging of its original owner Seth Bullock, the first sheriff of Deadwood, who passed away in 1919, but apparitions and orbs seem to indicate that he never left. Glassware and dishes are said to be hurled around, and in the Bullock Hotel's basement, staff have claimed to hear the piano playing on its own.

At the Fairmont Hotel, there is a room that was the scene of a violent murder. People have reported encountering an evil presence, having objects thrown at them, and a woman's apparition pacing the floor.

Deadwood's Mount Moriah Cemetery is the current resting place of Seth Bullock, Calamity Jane, and Wild Bill Hickok, but based on reports by visitors of feeling ghostly eyes watching them, those colorful characters may not be resting at all.

SOME OTHER REPORTEDLY HAUNTED PLACES IN SOUTH DAKOTA

With a name like **Devil's Gulch**, it is not surprising that the ravine in Garretson, South Dakota, might have paranormal connections. It is said to be haunted by the ghosts of two lovers who died there, reportedly in each other's arms. The tale is that in the late 1800s, a young woman named Nellie Harding was kidnapped by renegades. Her fiancé gave chase and caught up with the band at Devil's Gulch. He managed to shoot most of her abductors, but both he and Nellie were killed in the crossfire. Since then, visitors to the Gulch have reported hearing moans and screams, as well as seeing an apparition of the lovers. Devil's Gulch is also known for another story that some feel is a bit far-fetched, even for legendary outlaw Jesse James. There is signage at what is now called Devil's Gulch Park stating that James was trying to evade a posse in 1876 after his gang tried to rob a bank in Northfield, Minnesota. Despite what many say is an impossibility, the plaque states that James spurred his horse to jump the gorge, which is almost twenty feet wide. By doing so, locals say, he evaded capture and escaped to Missouri. Cynics are of the opinion that with Devil's Gulch being just a half-mile long, Jesse could have just ridden around it.

South Dakota is not generally known for its castles, but what was originally a thirty-room, three-story Queen Anne–style mansion in Aberdeen is popularly known by the name **Easton's Castle**. It was constructed in 1889 by banker C. A. Bliss, who had the home's wooden exterior reputedly painted emerald green. After banker Bliss ironically encountered financial problems, another banker, Carroll Francis Easton, obtained the house in 1893. It was Easton who covered the exterior in yellow bricks. Both decorating choices would prove significant for American popular culture. The ghost stories began during the years when it is said that Easton's adult son became reclusive. Since then, there have been reports of hauntings by the ghost of the first Mrs. Easton, a family housekeeper, and an alleged phantom who chases people while wielding a knife. But it was a real-life guest who attended parties at Easton's Castle who may have been inspired to secure its place in immortality. Author L. Frank Baum who wrote *The Wonderful Wizard of Oz*, published in 1900, lived in Aberdeen from 1888 until 1891. Baum wrote items in the local newspaper praising the mansion's unique features. Some say he drew inspiration from the fantastical emerald (later yellow brick) house on the prairie. It was not Kansas, but it was home.

The **Homestake Opera House** in Lead, South Dakota, is said to be among the state's most haunted places. It is also connected to an iconic American film that many say is the best of all time, 1941's *Citizen Kane*. Homestake Opera House was built in in 1914 by Phoebe Hearst, owner of the Homestake Gold Mine. Mrs. Hearst was the mother of William Randolph Hearst who became a media tycoon and was said to be the model for the movie's fictional Charles Foster Kane. Mrs. Hearst's husband was a successful miner who struck it rich, and she put some of the profits into philanthropic acts. Homestake Opera House is prominently situated on the town's Main Street. In addition to a one thousand–seat theater, the performing arts venue and recreation center boasted a billiards room, bowling alley, library, social hall, and even a heated indoor swimming pool. It is still operational today, presenting concerts, cultural events, and educational programs. It also seems to be the site of paranormal events, such as disembodied voices, vanishing files, and full body apparitions. During the 1919 influenza epidemic, flu patients were housed there; with the high mortality rate, some died there. When a paranormal investigating team went to the pool area, one was hit by a rock that none of the others said they threw. On the stage area, they also captured what sounded like a phantom voice saying, "I'm right here," and in the dressing room, "Here I am, right here," and "Get out!" Could it be a supernatural phantom of the opera?

When the **Hotel Alex Johnson** in Rapid City opened in 1928, it was hailed amid great fanfare as "The Showplace of the West." The owner was Alex Johnson. As one might expect in an establishment he named for himself, Alex Johnson may never have left the premises, even after his death in 1938. In one room, a young couple reported hearing phantom music and the feeling of being choked. In another room, guests sometimes get out of a nice warm shower only to find the chilling words "help me" scrawled on the fogged-up mirror.

At the **Old Minnehaha Courthouse Museum** in Sioux Falls, staffers and visitors have reported hearing someone fall down the stairs, but when they rush to help the unfortunate accident victim, there is nobody around. There have been sounds of disembodied voices, odd whispers, and phantom footsteps moving from room to room. The Old Minnehaha Courthouse was completed in 1890 and served as the county courthouse until 1962, during which time it was the site of life-and-death decisions by judges and juries, often concerning vicious criminals. Apparently, it also inspired loyalty among former employees. Some visitors report they have felt a sudden blast of cold air that quickly disappears, followed by the sight of an elderly man sweeping the floor of one of the courtrooms who then vanishes if he is approached, just like the icy air.

The alleged ghost at the **Orpheum Theatre** in Sioux Falls even has a name: "Larry." The historic playhouse was built in 1913 but it was not until it was sold to the Sioux Falls Community Playhouse in 1954 that Larry made his first guest appearance. The story is that the new owners stumbled on an old, ornate casket in the theater's boiler room, but when they returned to remove the coffin, it was gone. Since then, it is said that strange, random objects appear and disappear at will. Some speculate that Larry might have been a construction worker who was killed while the theater was being built, a stage hand who died during a vaudeville show, or as most people want to believe, an actor who was having an affair with a married woman and was killed by the jealous husband in the theater's balcony. This latter theory carried some weight after the time an actor was rehearsing his role onstage and spotted the figure of a man in the balcony who was bathed in an odd pulsating blue-green light and was pointing at him. The actor then felt a blast of cold air. Arriving at the theater the next day, the actor was onstage in a dress rehearsal when a sandbag from atop the stage fell on him, knocking him unconscious. The stage crew took special precautions to make sure such gear was secured, but on opening night, another sandbag fell on the actor, again rendering him unconscious. In another instance, a technical director was sweeping the stage to prepare for a children's theater production rehearsal the next day. While sweeping, he heard a sound behind him. Looking down, he saw an old tintype picture that looked like those produced in the 1890s. The person in the photo was a bearded man with rosy cheeks. The employee turned on all the stage lights and called out to see if anyone else was in the theater who might have dropped the tintype. Hearing no response, he put the mystery picture up on the theater's light board for safekeeping. At that point, the employee reportedly felt a cloud of icy coldness settle over him and quickly left the empty building. The tintype remained on the light board for some time before it mysteriously vanished. Today, the Orpheum Theater presents dozens of events annually, including concerts, plays, private parties, school functions, and other community events. About 100,000 patrons are said to visit each year. Perhaps, counting Larry, the number is 100,001.

FURTHER READING

Ames, John Edwards. *The Real Deadwood: True Life Histories of Wild Bill Hickok, Calamity Jane, Outlaw Towns, and Other Characters of the Lawless West*. New York: Chamberlain Bros. Publishing, 2004.

Shadley, Mark, and Josh Wennes. *Haunted Deadwood: A True Wild West Ghost Town*. Charleston, SC: The History Press, 2012.

Tennant, Brad. *On This Day in South Dakota History*. Charleston, SC: The History Press, 2017.

43

Tennessee

Today's Tennessee is rooted in the Watauga Association pact of 1772, an early attempt to establish their own democratic government by frontier Americans. Virginia's British royal governor called the Watauga Association a dangerous example of Americans forming a government independent of the English Crown. America's Declaration of Independence was not signed until 1776 in Philadelphia, Pennsylvania, earning Tennesseans the right to boast that from Independence to Elvis, *their* state was ahead of the cultural curve.

The first recorded visit to Tennessee by Europeans was an expedition in 1540 led by Spanish explorer Hernando de Soto. In 1567, another Spaniard, Juan Pardo, recorded the name of an Indian village in the region as "Tanasqui," which is said by some to have evolved to the state's current name.

Settlers from the South Carolina colony established a presence in Tennessee near Fort Loudoun in 1756. It was the westernmost British outpost up to that time. As more white colonists moved into the area, the Native American population was driven out by force. The displaced tribes included the Chickasaw, Choctaw, and Cherokee.

During the American Revolution, a frontier fort on the banks of Tennessee's Watauga River served as a staging area for colonial soldiers. From there, patriots engaged the British Army, defeating the enemy at the Battle of King's Mountain.

In 1784, a year after the colonists won the Revolution, several counties in today's East Tennessee attempted to break off to form the State of Franklin. However, by 1789, it was clear that their efforts to join the Union as a new state were failing, and the State of Franklin ceased to exist.

Even though it was generally considered to be the wild frontier by established residents of the thirteen original colonies, Tennessee developed at a remarkable pace in the years between the Revolution and the Civil War. Its economy, culture, and population grew. During these years, according to Bergeron (2007), "Tennesseans cast off their frontier status [and] steered their state out of the national backwaters" (92).

In 1796, Tennessee was admitted to the Union as the sixteenth state. With the coming of the Civil War in 1861, Tennessee was the last state to leave the Union and join the Confederacy. It was also the first state to be readmitted to the Union when the war was over. Numerous major Civil War battles were fought in Tennessee, including the bloody clash at Shiloh in 1862.

According to the *Tennessee Encyclopedia*, in 1860, before the war, there were more than two hundred seventy-five thousand enslaved people held in Tennessee. In 1863, when President Abraham Lincoln issued the Emancipation Proclamation, Tennessee was largely under Union control. Since the decree did not specifically name Tennessee as being in rebellion against the United States, the Proclamation did not free any slaves there.

The late 1800s brought reconstruction, followed by the "Jim Crow" era of institutionalized discrimination against African Americans. The Tennessee legislature passed restrictive laws that kept many blacks on the same plantations as before the war.

Plantations were an important part of the economy of the South since the beginning of colonization. According to Matrana (2009), in 1619, enslaved Africans were introduced to augment indentured laborers in the English colonies, "although slavery was not fully codified until 1661. Even during these first few decades, plantations flourished" (2).

Huge fortunes were made. With fertile soil and mild climate in the South, white-owned plantations mushroomed before the Civil War. They depended on slave labor to toil in the fields for such cash crops as cotton, sugarcane, and tobacco.

In the antebellum era before the Civil War, many Southern plantations held hundreds of slaves in bondage. The large, elegant mansions of planters were symbolic of their wealth. Many were built by the labor of enslaved people who themselves lived in small, primitive cabins.

During the Civil War, many plantation mansions in the South were burned or looted by Union soldiers. In Tennessee, a few survived and today are listed on the National Register of Historic Places. These include Beechwood Hall, Belle Meade, Brabson's Ferry Plantation, Carnton, Davies Manor, Fairvue, The Hermitage, Northcutt Plantation, Rose Glen, Ramsey House, and White Plains. One of them, the improbably named Rattle and Snap, was allegedly won in a game of chance called "rattle and snap," similar to modern dice or craps.

Along with illustrating the elegant lifestyle of the antebellum planter class, many of those plantation homes are said to contain more than artifacts from the past. According to Brown (2009), amid such colorful supernatural tales as a half-human, half-feline creature called a Wampus Cat who is said to roam the state, "some of Tennessee's most moving ghost stories focus on personal misfortunes" (2).

That is certainly true of **Wheatlands Plantation** in Sevierville, said to be haunted due to its long history full of murder, death, and destruction.

After the Chandler family's original farmhouse burned in 1823, claiming the lives of four children, John Chandler built the present Wheatlands plantation house on the site. Among the hauntings at the mansion today is that of what is reportedly called a child-like spirit in the basement.

Spirits may also have moved into the big house from a mass grave on the property, which is said to hold the remains of Revolutionary War soldiers as well as twenty-eight Cherokees who were killed fighting encroaching settlers in 1780 at the Battle of Boyd's Creek, which runs along the property. It is also said that the mass grave contains the remains of about seventy African slaves who were held in bondage at Wheatlands, never to leave, even in death.

The spirits of two women who lived in the house are said to haunt the staircase. One reportedly had a heart attack on the stairs in 1888, with the other breaking her neck in a fall in 1932.

Some of the walls and floorboards of the mansion are said to be stained with blood after one of the last owners from the Chandler family was killed by his son. The father was reportedly enraged over ownership of Wheatlands passing to his son rather than himself. When the father allegedly attacked his offspring, the son stabbed him with an iron poker. Today, it is claimed that bloodstains from the incident can still be seen in the parlor of Wheatlands, even after the floorboards have been thoroughly cleaned and even sanded down to remove them.

SOME OTHER REPORTEDLY HAUNTED PLACES IN TENNESSEE

No look at the supernatural in Tennessee would be complete without a mention of the **Bell Witch**. This malicious spirit is reportedly that of Kate Batts, a malevolent neighbor of John Bell who was said to have a mean disposition in life and apparently even more so in death. The Bell Witch was so named because in the early 1800s, her evil spirit was said to have murdered John Bell and tormented the Bell family with poltergeists at their farmhouse near the town of Adams. At one point, the reputed terror was said to be so intense that even the ultra-macho president Andrew Jackson refused to stay in the Bell house overnight. According to the legend, the paranormal activity was most intense from 1817 to 1821 when the Bell family was attacked by an entity that was sometimes invisible and sometimes a shape-shifter. Today, the Bell Witch is said to haunt a cave next to John Bell's farm, reportedly making the cave one of the most haunted places in Tennessee. Some reported activity in the cave includes the sound of rattling chains and unexplained knocking. The story of the Bell Witch was documented in 1894 with the publication of *An Authenticated History of the Bell Witch* by newspaper editor Martin V. Ingram, which was reportedly based on an 1846 manuscript entitled, "Our Family Trouble," written by Richard Williams Bell. Today, the cave is open to visitors who wish to buy a ticket. Curiosity-seekers may also wish to investigate the hauntings through the magic of movies. Horror films based on the Bell Witch include *The Bell Witch Haunting* (2004), *An American Haunting* (2005), *Bell Witch: The Movie* (2007), *The Bell Witch Legend* (2008), and *The Bell Witch Haunting* (2013). The most famous was the immensely popular *Blair Witch Project* of 1999, in which the witch's name was presumably changed to avoid ghostly lawsuits, which can sometimes be a worse fate than being haunted.

Carnton Plantation in Franklin, Tennessee, holds the unusual distinction of having a porch that overlooks a graveyard where almost fifteen hundred bodies are buried. Before the Civil War, Carnton had been a peaceful home for the John and Caroline McGavock family. Built in 1826, the mansion played host to dignitaries like Sam Houston and Andrew Jackson. However, in 1864, the bloody Battle of Franklin turned Carnton into a war zone. As the battle wore on, hundreds of soldiers were brought inside the house where clothing was torn up for bandages. The parlor was turned into a field hospital, with bodies of dead men stacked like kindling wood at the back of the house. When the battle was over, a mass grave was dug for 1,481 Confederate dead. The bodies of Union casualties were left in Franklin, but later retrieved. The McGavock Confederate Cemetery, donated by the family as a permanent resting place, is the largest privately owned military cemetery in the United States, being maintained by the United Daughters of the Confederacy. Some spirits of the dead are alleged to continue their wartime service by haunting the site. Visitors to Carnton sometimes report seeing ghostly Confederates roaming the grounds, astonished to discover that the figures are not part of any modern re-enactment. The most famous ghost is said to be a restless soldier who has been seen marching the perimeter of the yard, as well as walking through the house to the back porch where so many of his fellow soldiers had been stacked. Witnesses report the sound of heavy boots accompanying his wandering. He has been joined at the house by the spirit of a beautiful woman with long dark hair believed to be Caroline McGavock herself. In addition, there have been sightings of a woman believed to be a former cook whose head allegedly appears in a photo showing her apparition hovering in the hallway, perhaps trying to inform the long-dead family and guests that dinner is served.

Dating back to 1921, when another theater, the Grand Opera House, sat on the spot, the **Orpheum Theatre** in Memphis was able to overcome a variety of adversities, ranging from bankruptcies, devastating fires, and the decay of downtown Memphis to the threat of demolition to make way for an office complex. Today's 1928 incarnation, called one of the South's finest theaters, welcomes thousands of people each year to a number of events, including an ambitious schedule of touring Broadway shows. Among the theatergoers is said to be the spirit of a twelve-year-old girl named Mary who had been excitedly dashing across the street in front of the Grand Opera House when she was killed in a motor vehicle accident. Apparently, she has been determined to patronize the theater ever since. She is often seen in a balcony seat, although when she gets restless, is sometimes heard giggling while running up and down the aisles. It is reported that while touring with *The King and I*, actor Yul Brenner witnessed Mary sitting quietly in the balcony, clothed in her Sunday best, a 1920s-style white dress. Cast members from *Fiddler on the Roof* also claimed to see Mary sitting in the same balcony seat so often that they reportedly held a séance to communicate with the theater-loving child. Mary also seems to enjoy music, having been spotted during an organ concert. A group reportedly saw the apparition of a young girl in an old-fashioned white dress who was dancing in the lobby before vanishing into thin air as they watched. Employees have reported feeling a cold, eerie presence around them even though no manifestation appears. One worker described it as a sensation like

Among today's playgoers at the Orpheum Theatre in Memphis, Tennessee, is said to be the spirit of a twelve-year-old girl named Mary who was excitedly dashing across the street in the 1920s toward the building when she was killed in a motor vehicle accident. Today, she welcomes Broadway touring companies, making her presence known all around the playhouse she loved. (Daniel Schreurs/Dreamstime.com)

getting into a bathtub of cold water. Perhaps peeved at that unappealing description, Mary apparently took a set of tools and put them in the toilet. Staffers have seen a theater door fly open to the outside, and then shut all by itself. In a more helpful incident, a repairman was working on the Orpheum's famed ninety-year-old "Mighty Wurlitzer" organ, which refused to cooperate with his repair efforts. Frustrated, he decided to take a break. After locking up, he went out to get coffee. Returning to the malfunctioning musical machine in the empty theater, he was shocked to discover the problem had somehow been fixed. If it was Mary who did the trick, she is a remarkably talented young lady who is happy with her home in the afterlife at the Orpheum.

In the 1970s, developers bulldozed an area along the Harpeth River while working on a housing development in Pegram, Tennessee. In the process, they impacted the **Pegram Family Cemetery**. Small houses on concrete slabs were built there. The developers sold soil and other materials from the graveyard site as fill dirt around town. Within a few years, the Harpeth River uncharacteristically rose over thirty feet. Homeowners whose houses were built above the graveyard awoke to find not only floodwater in their yards but also coffins. One belonged to a member of the family for whom the cemetery, as well as the town, was named. Like other Pegram family members before her, dating back to 1866, Carrie Pegram Heath served as the town's postmaster. She was born in 1876 and died in 1953 before reappearing on the lawn of a subdivision. It is said that the areas receiving the cemetery landfill have now fallen victim to hauntings by the spirits of the disgruntled dead. The river now regularly floods. After Carrie Pegram Heath was reburied, a flood in 2010 resulted in her coffin re-emerging. Some townsfolk judge that the developers had not taken very good care of their honored dead, allegedly building right on top of them. It is said that some homeowners have claimed to see tombstones appearing and disappearing in their gardens. Fires that have been extinguished mysteriously restart themselves several times, including the one that destroyed Pegram's only grocery store. Trains seem to stall with some regularity on the town's tracks, blocking subdivision residents from going to school or work since there is only one way in or out. The town's sewer system is reportedly trouble-prone, and quite understandably, either due to faulty sewers or angry spirits, there is an overall atmosphere of malice and unrest in the air.

The **Rotherwood Mansion** in Kingsport was built in 1818 by Frederick Ross whose daughter Rowena was well-liked in the community but faced a life of despair. On her wedding day, her groom-to-be drowned in the nearby Holston River. She became reclusive, but married another young man who died of yellow fever within the first year of their marriage. Trying again a third time, she married and joyously gave birth to a baby, but the child soon died. After that, Rowena drowned herself in the same river as her first love had. Her apparition, called the "Lady in White," has been spotted wandering along the riverbank at the homestead where she had longed to find happiness.

FURTHER READING

Bergeron, Paul H. *Tennesseans and Their History*. Knoxville: University of Tennessee Press, 2007.

Brown, Alan. *Haunted Tennessee: Ghosts and Strange Phenomena of the Volunteer State*. Mechanicsburg, PA: Stackpole Books, 2009.

Goodstein, Anita S. "Slavery." *Tennessee Encyclopedia*. October 8, 2017. https://tennesseeencyclopedia.net/entries/slavery

Matrana, Marc. *Lost Plantations of the South*. Oxford: University Press of Mississippi, 2009.

44

Texas

Texas is nicknamed "The Lone Star State" to pay homage to its former status as an independent country. It is enormous in size (the largest state in the continental United States), and boasts a storied history that rivals many nations. The expression, "Texas—It's Like A Whole Other Country" has been adopted by the state's tourism industry. In fact, if Texas were today a sovereign nation, according to the World Bank it would boast the tenth largest economy in the world, higher than Australia, Sweden, or Switzerland.

The term "six flags over Texas" is more than an amusement park. It stands for the six nations that controlled all or part of the current state of Texas. They were Spain (starting in 1520, sporadically to 1821), France (1685–1690), Mexico (1821–1836), and the independent Republic of Texas (1836–1845). Texas became the twenty-eighth state of the Union in 1845 but joined the Confederate States of America (1861–1865). After the Civil War, Texas rejoined the Union, where it remains today.

The first residents of Texas were Native American tribes like the Apache, Caddo, and Comanche. Many sources attribute the name "Texas" to origins as a Caddo word, "táysha," or "friend." In Spanish, it evolved into "Tejas" (pronounced TAY-hoss) and later as "Texas."

But, as in other areas of the New World, friendship often came at a premium as centuries of Native American habitation came under threat. Referring to the Spanish conquistadors of the 1500s, Fehrenbach (2000) says, "a new and powerful invader burst into the American Southwest" (19).

Most sources agree that the first European to see Texas was Spanish explorer Alonso Álvarez de Pineda in 1520. Although Álvarez de Pineda claimed the area that is now Texas for Spain, the region was essentially ignored for more than 150 years.

Its initial permanent settlement by Europeans occurred as a result of a perceived threat by France. In 1685, René-Robert Cavelier, Sieur de La Salle established a French colony near Matagorda Bay, dividing the territory of New Spain in the west and Spanish Florida to the east. The first Spanish-speaking settlers grouped around the San Antonio River in 1718 when a mission and fort were established.

By the early 1800s, there was still confusion as to the spelling of the region's name. However, whether called Tejas or Texas, its mythology was known across the United States. With its wide open spaces, lawmen were few and far between. Texas became known as a place to disappear and start over. It was reputed to harbor outlaws and escapees from their past. The expression "Gone To Texas" (often simply abbreviated as "GTT") was something people scrawled on their abandoned houses. During the financial Panic of 1819, when Texas was a province controlled by Spain, many left the United States and moved to Texas to escape their debts. In subsequent years, Texas remained extremely popular among debtors.

The need for some sort of law enforcement over the vast distances in Texas gave rise to one of the most storied organizations in America, the Texas Rangers. The Rangers were unofficially created by Stephen F. Austin, the "Father of Texas," in 1823. Austin issued a call to arms as needed to protect settlers who were steadily arriving in Texas. A permanent body of Texas Rangers was created in 1835, with authority to range statewide. This contrasted with the attempt at local law enforcement used when Texas was a province of Spain: the presidio system.

A presidio was a fortified base in lands controlled by Spain. The term is derived from the Latin word *"praesidium"* referring to a military district where the Romans literally presided. Moorhead (1975) notes that garrisoned frontier fortifications date back to the wars of ancient times, so "When the Spanish presidio came into being, it was neither novel in concept or basic characteristics" (3).

In Spanish territories of the New World, these fortresses were built to protect against threats like pirates, hostile Indians, and rival colonists. After Mexico's independence from Spain, Mexican soldiers garrisoned Spain's former presidios. Catholic missions were usually established at the presidios to convert local Native Americans to Christianity.

In Texas, the presidio/mission system sometimes led to the establishment of permanent settlements. Presidio San Antonio de Bexar was founded in 1718, forming the groundwork for today's city of San Antonio. The Presidio Nuestra Señora de Loreto de la Bahía, usually known as Presidio La Bahia, was opened in 1749 near today's Goliad, Texas. Presidio de la Junta de los Ríos Norte y Conchos was founded in 1760, with today's nearby town of Presidio, Texas, simply adopting the first word.

In the early 1800s, demographics in Texas were changing along with political developments. In 1825, Texas had about thirty-five hundred people, most of them claiming Mexican descent. By 1834, less than ten years later, the region's inhabitants (often calling themselves "Tejanos" or "Texians") had grown to almost thirty-eight thousand people, with only seven thousand eight hundred of Mexican descent, a clear minority.

Beginning in 1834, the "Texian Army" was organized to fight for independence from Mexico. Mexican president Antonio López de Santa Anna personally led Mexico's army, intending to stop the Texian revolt. Often the Texians would utilize former Spanish missions and presidios as a base of operations, and just as often they became a battleground.

In 1836, soon after The Alamo, another massacre of Texian defenders took place at Presidio La Bahia in Goliad, Texas. The Goliad massacre further galvanized the Texians' resolve to fight, ultimately winning their freedom. The spirits of her defenders are said to make today's reconstructed presidio at Goliad, pictured here, one of the most haunted places in Texas. (Wilsilver77/Dreamstime.com)

One of these took place in San Antonio between February 23 and March 6, 1836. After a two-week siege, Santa Anna's forces overwhelmed Texian forces at the Battle of the Alamo. The Mexicans overran the Alamo mission, killing its defenders and giving rise to a new spirit of rebellion in Texas with the cry of "Remember the Alamo!"

Three weeks later, on March 27, 1836, another massacre of Texian defenders by the Mexicans took place at **Presidio La Bahia** in Goliad, Texas.

After the Alamo, Santa Anna's army continued its advance across Texas. Following the Battle of Coleto on March 19–20, 1836, more than four hundred Texian soldiers and their wounded were taken by the Mexicans as prisoners to Goliad, where they were held at the presidio.

On Palm Sunday, March 27, 1836, the Texians were marched out of the presidio. Following Santa Anna's orders, Mexican soldiers began shooting the men point blank. Any wounded survivors were killed with bayonets. Although arguably not as well-known as the Alamo, the Goliad massacre further galvanized the Texians' resolve to fight and ultimately to win their freedom.

As recounted by Brown (2008), the massacre of Texian patriots at the Goliad presidio would "not only fuel the drive for Texas independence, but it still resonates today in the fort where they died" (58).

With so much pain, despair and death, one of the most haunted places in Texas is said to be today's reconstructed presidio at Goliad. It was named a National Historic Landmark in 1967, and currently operates as a museum that is open to the public. There have been frequent reports of seeing ghostly apparitions of massacre victims, as well as hearing the cries and screams of injured men emanating from the presidio at night.

SOME OTHER REPORTEDLY HAUNTED PLACES IN TEXAS

With a name like the **Devil's Backbone**, there is almost certainly going to be some supernatural element. This limestone ridge that cuts through the Texas Hill Country in the central part of the state seems to attract strange phenomena that have become well-known in the region. The Devil's Backbone is allegedly haunted by Native American ghosts, an especially strong apparition of Confederate soldiers on horseback, and the spirit of a wolf that can reportedly possess a human. The Devil's Backbone rises above the Texas Hill Country, which was the scene of many horrific acts of violence by both white settlers and Native Americans, particularly the Comanche who were known as masters of torture. Each atrocity by one group brought about an even more appalling act of revenge by the other, which, in turn, spawned a worse act of reprisal, and so on. Along the Devil's Backbone, the tormented spirits of those who died a ghastly death are said to roam, hoping to find peace. There is also the story of a ranch foreman who was awakened by the sound of horses' hooves thundering past his cabin loud enough to shake the structure. When he went to find out what caused the commotion, he claimed to see the ghosts of at least twenty men on horseback who appeared to be Confederate soldiers. In another report, several young men were hiking along the Devil's Backbone when one of them saw the vision of a wolf who jumped at him, but the friends did not see any animal. The friends noticed that the man who claimed to have been attacked grew very cold. After they went home, the man seemed to be possessed, speaking in a deeper voice than usual and talking about Indian massacres. Suddenly, a gust of wind strong enough to open the back door blew through the room. At that point, the man returned to his normal self.

Reminiscent of the Gilded Age, the **Hotel Galvez** with its majestic turrets is one of the oldest lodgings on Galveston Island and is also said to be one of the most haunted places in Texas. Built in 1911, the huge, stately hotel quickly attracted clientele, including businessmen, celebrities, and socialites. What is more remarkable is that it was opened just a few years after the Great Hurricane of 1900 that wiped out Galveston Island. With a storm surge over fifteen feet high that inundated the entire town, it was the deadliest natural disaster in U.S. history. Every house on the island sustained damage, but even worse, untold thousands died. Burial was impossible. About fifty African American men were forced to work at gunpoint. They were given whiskey to dull the horror of gathering the dead, loading them on a barge, and dumping them in the Gulf of Mexico. However, currents washed many corpses back onto the beach, where they were destroyed in funeral pyres that burned night and day for weeks. The spirits of the dead may still haunt the island. Some ghosts prefer the Hotel Galvez. On the fifth floor, the sudden unexplained scent of gardenias signals the arrival of the "Lovelorn Lady," who hanged herself at the hotel when her husband was lost at sea. When she is allegedly present, there are sudden cold breezes, the sound of doors slamming, and lights and televisions turning on or off by themselves. In the turrets of the Hotel Galvez, odd lights have been reported, even when the turrets were being renovated and there was neither a power source nor access for people with candles or flashlights. Some wonder if the ghostly lights are beckoning the dead who were dumped at sea to return home.

Some spirits who have been reported at the **Jefferson Hotel** in Jefferson, Texas, are said to have a bit of a naughty streak, being known to sometimes throw things at guests and lock them in their rooms. Other reports of paranormal activity include cold spots, disembodied voices and footsteps running down the hall, the sound of children laughing when none are nearby, knocking on the walls in the middle of the night, and strange shadows that appear for no apparent reason. The town of Jefferson is located where ancient Caddo Indians built their communities. There are tales of Caddo spirits whispering through the mysterious-looking cypress trees at the nearby bayou called Caddo Lake, named for those long-departed people. At the Jefferson Hotel, guests in Room 5 reported their young son awakening them repeatedly in the middle of the night because he said a man in a long coat and high boots would not go away. Each time they investigated, no one was seen. Other witnesses claimed to see a thick white cloud surrounding the apparition of a young woman with long blonde hair. A ninety-year-old man who said he did not believe in ghosts was unable to sleep one night and went out into the hallway to stretch his legs. There, he saw a blonde woman floating down the stairs smiling at him, only to disappear before she reached the bottom. After ninety years, he is said to have re-evaluated his position on ghosts after that. Television crews who try to film inside the hotel have experienced malfunctions in areas of the building, ranging from cameras not working to tape recorders turning on and off by themselves. The stories of hauntings at the Jefferson Hotel have been so numerous that it keeps a journal called the Book of the Dead, which has been compiled by guests describing ghostly encounters.

The **Littlefield House** in Austin may look like a regal fairytale castle but is a royally haunted spot. It stands on the campus of the University of Texas (UT), where the home's former owners are revered for their generosity and kindness during their lifetime. The mansion was built in 1893 for Civil War veteran George Littlefield and his wife Alice. They had met while in college, with higher education being somewhat unusual for their time. After the Civil War, George became a successful businessman, and they apparently had a happy marriage. At one point, George Littlefield had a cedar tree plus its native soil imported from the Himalayas as a gift for his wife. After digging a hole to excavate the existing dirt and replace it with Himalayan soil, the tree was planted on the grounds of the Littlefield house where it still stands today. George and Alice Littlefield were well-liked and said to have loved young people. They had two children, but each child died in infancy. The Littlefields reached out to their extended family, paying for the college educations of all twelve nephews and seventeen nieces. However, when she was sixty-six years old, Alice Littlefield developed an unexplained "nervous condition," in which she became obsessed with the fear that she would be kidnapped and her husband would be murdered, sometimes running and screaming, needing to be restrained. For eight years, George Littlefield cared for her at their home with the help of round-the-clock nurses. After George died of pneumonia, Alice's nervous condition improved, which some said resulted from the fact that her husband's safety was no longer a concern. Apart from visiting with relatives, she spent little time in public until her death in 1935 at age eighty-eight. She left her home to UT where it is used for university events. Alice may have remained onsite to serve as hostess. Her apparition is said to wander upstairs and sometimes she is reported to be heard playing her piano to entertain modern-day guests. Sometimes, however, her spirit seems to be dragged back to the years when she was ill, as there have been reports of frightened screaming and the sound of footsteps running on the staircase. Witnesses often report seeing her face peering through the windows of Littlefield House, perhaps keeping an eye on the university and its students. Inside the house, people have claimed to feel a ghostly presence walking through the halls of the home on a regular basis. When people get closer to the source, they are said to feel oddly cold but recognize that it is only Alice's protective spirit.

FURTHER READING

Brown, Alan. *Haunted Texas: Ghosts and Strange Phenomena of the Lone Star State.* Mechanicsburg, PA: Stackpole Books, 2008.

Fehrenbach, T. R. *Lone Star: A History of Texas and the Texans.* Boston, MA: Da Capo Press, 2000.

Moorhead, Max. *The Presidio: Bastion of the Spanish Borderlands.* Norman: University of Oklahoma Press, 1975.

The World Bank. *GDP 1960–2017 (Current US$).* 2019. https://data.worldbank.org/indicator/NY.GDP.MKTP.CD

45

Utah

Many people believe the name "Utah" is derived from the Ute tribe of Native Americans, with the approximate meaning, "people of the mountains." For other sources, the name of the state actually comes from an Apache word "yuttahih," referring to those who are "higher up." In any case, it was ultimately Anglicized into "Utah."

For thousands of years before the arrival of Europeans, ancestral Puebloans lived in what is now known as Utah. Those people excavated their homes in the mountains before disappearing from the region around the 1400s.

After their departure, tribes like the Navajo, Paiute, Shoshone, and Ute appeared. They were the area's inhabitants when European explorers arrived.

The southern part of today's Utah was traversed by Spanish conquistador Francisco Vásquez de Coronado in 1540 during his continuing quest to find the legendary Seven Cities of Gold. Failing to find anything that glittered, Coronado kept going.

Spaniards made a few perfunctory explorations into what they considered part of Spanish territory, but were not interested in colonizing the area since it was basically a waterless desert. When Mexico gained its independence from Spain in 1821, the region became part of the Mexican territory of Alta ("upper") California.

Various trappers and traders explored parts of Utah in the early 1800s, with many establishing trading posts in the area near the Great Salt Lake. But during the mid-1800s, Utah's destiny changed dramatically.

Reaching the Salt Lake Valley in 1847, Brigham Young led a group of the faithful from The Church of Jesus Christ of Latter Day Saints (LDS), sometimes called Mormons. Over the next several decades, more than seventy thousand Mormon pioneers crossed the plains to settle in Utah. In the arid desert landscape where even its major water feature was full of salt, the Mormons felt it was a place where they could practice their religion without the kind of harassment they had experienced elsewhere.

Today, almost two-thirds of Utah's population is reported to belong to the church of Latter Day Saints, making it the only state with an overwhelming majority belonging to a single denomination. The world headquarters of the LDS Church is located in Salt Lake City.

For the first few years, Brigham Young and the early settlers in Utah struggled to survive. They called it Deseret, which some people think is a reference to the desert landscape but reportedly was found in the Book of Mormon as an ancient word for "honeybee," symbolizing industriousness and productivity.

When the first Mormon settlers arrived in 1847, Utah belonged to Mexico. After the Mexican War in 1848, the Southwest, including California and New Mexico, became U.S. territory. When California and New Mexico took steps to apply for statehood, settlers in today's Utah envisioned a state of Deseret. Instead, in 1850, the Utah Territory was created, which was smaller than the proposed state of Deseret. Utah did not become the forty-fifth state admitted to the Union until 1896.

The Utah Territory did, however, take a significant place in American history. Salt Lake City was designated as the territorial capital in 1856. Just five years later, in 1861, Salt Lake City became the final link of the first transcontinental telegraph. Along with Abraham Lincoln and other officials, Brigham Young was among the first to send a message.

Before the end of the 1860s, Utah was to play a vital role in the future growth of the United States. On May 10, 1869, the first transcontinental railroad was completed at Promontory Summit, Utah Territory, near the Great Salt Lake, when the final spike was driven into the track. The coast-to-coast rail system revolutionized the settlement and prosperity of the West. It made transporting passengers and goods from one side of the American continent to the other faster, safer, and more economical.

However, it came with a high cost of human lives. The backbreaking manual labor to build the bridges, tunnels, and track in the West was done primarily by thousands of imported Chinese workers. According to Stone (2013), "Comprising nearly 90 percent of the workforce and working 12-hour shifts, [the Chinese] laid eighteen hundred miles of roadbed through the country's most rugged terrain" (52). White workers were given free room and board, while the Chinese had to purchase theirs. They were strangers, stranded in a strange land, and their white superiors boasted that there was no danger of strikes among them.

Tunnels were dug through the mountains by using dangerous nitroglycerine explosives, often causing fatal accidents. It is unknown how many Chinese laborers gave their lives to build America's transcontinental railroad, and whose spirits may haunt the lonely wilderness where they died.

The first half of the twentieth century brought about the golden age of American rail travel. Nationwide, people discovered Utah's natural beauty through its majestic national parks like Bryce Canyon and Zion.

The burgeoning technology of motion pictures exposed the world to the iconic, almost otherworldly landscape of Utah's Monument Valley. As Alexander (2003) notes, "John Ford used this marvelous scenery for the 1939 movie classic *Stagecoach* and numerous filmmakers have followed suit" (15). Ford alone shot nine movies there. Others have included everything from *The Searchers* to *Easy Rider*, from *2001: A Space Odyssey* to *Jurassic World: Fallen Kingdom*. Even TV's

Doctor Who landed there, marking the first time the show's principal photography was shot on location in America.

Rail travel made it possible for Americans from coast-to-coast to visit Utah for those natural wonders, as well as its ski resorts which gained popularity in the first half of the twentieth century. In 1910, Salt Lake City's elegant **Rio Grande Depot** was constructed to accommodate rail passengers. It also reflected the state's growth and success that had been the vision of the original settlers of Deseret.

Between its opening in 1910 and the decline of American rail travel that began in the late 1940s, the Rio Grande Depot bustled with the kind of activity reminiscent of the honeybees that Mormon settlers adopted as their symbol. Along with being a hub for passengers and freight, the Rio Grande Depot was also a staging area for soldiers shipping out on troop trains during World War I and World War II.

With the rise of affordable air travel and automobiles, the Rio Grande Depot went into decline. Between 1986 and 1999, it served as Salt Lake City's Amtrak station, but by 1999 Amtrak relocated, permanently removing the tracks near the Depot. Today, the Rio Grande Depot is home to the Division of Utah State History and the Utah Department of Heritage & Arts. But even before the building's transformation, ghostly doings were noted. Starting around 1940, the apparition of a beautiful, black-haired woman wearing an old-fashioned purple dress was seen around the station, especially its ladies' lounge and the Rio Grande Cafe. It is said that she had been struck by a train as she frantically searched for her engagement ring on the tracks, where her fiancé had thrown it after a quarrel.

Staffers have also reported feeling and hearing what is said to be the presence of a restless spirit who walks the balcony and first floor lobby area. Some say it might be the remorseful ex-fiancé who had acted so rashly.

SOME OTHER REPORTEDLY HAUNTED PLACES IN UTAH

The **Ben Lomond Hotel** in Ogden has had several incarnations during its lifetime, both as a hotel and as a permanent residence for long-term guests. It may also be a permanent residence for long-term guests of the ghostly variety. Replacing a previous hotel in 1927, the Ben Lomond had a feature that was extremely attractive to entrepreneurs during the prohibition era: an underground tunnel. In the past, some downtown areas across America had a tunnel beneath the streets so business could be conducted even during inclement weather. For many, most of the underground activity was perfectly legitimate, like moving supplies or boxes of files. In the case of the Ben Lomond, it is said that visitors arriving by train, especially VIPs, could be escorted directly to the hotel. During prohibition in some towns, it is also said that alcohol could be smuggled along with drugs and female companions. Upstairs at the Ben Lomond, there are spirits other than alcohol. The eleventh floor is said to be particularly active among the dead. In one room, a lady drowned in the bathtub on her wedding night in circumstances that are still unknown. Her son, presumably by a previous marriage, came to collect her belongings, staying in the room next door. He was reportedly overcome with despair and took his own life. Both mother and son are said to be haunting the

The Ben Lomond Hotel in Ogden, Utah, may be a permanent residence for long-term ghostly guests. In one room, a lady drowned in the bathtub on her wedding night in unknown circumstances. Today, guests report the water in the room's tub running by itself, and some have described the feeling of being pushed under the water by an unseen force. (Cesar Robles/Dreamstime.com)

hotel. Guests report the water in the room's tub running by itself, and some have described the feeling of being pushed under the water by an unseen force. Some have reported a man's disembodied voice in the room, as well as the sight of physical apparitions. The scent of lilac perfume, as favored by the dead woman, is often detected, seeming to indicate her presence. In addition, there are reports from the front desk that calls are received from the woman's former room, but when the call is answered, the line is dead.

Salt Lake City's **Capitol Theatre** has apparently attracted a theater-lover who refuses to leave when the house lights go up. The spirit is believed to be of a teenage usher who died in a fire at the theater in 1949. Like many teens, the ghostly spirit enjoys playing a good joke on people. A security guard reported hearing a voice behind him when no one was there. Walking down to the basement to investigate, the guard noticed it smelled of smoke, although there wasn't any fire. A theater manager has also reported feeling the ghostly teen's presence, which seems to be particularly active during performances of *The Nutcracker*. One opening night of a *Nutcracker* performance, the stage lights would not turn on. All equipment and power sources were found to work fine. The manager walked onstage and yelled for the ghost to *turn the lights on!* They came on immediately. At least the teen spirit at the Capitol Theatre seems to respect authority.

The oldest part of the **Devereaux Mansion** in Salt Lake City dates back to 1857 when it was built for a pioneering member of the LDS Church. The Devereaux house was listed on the National Register of Historic Places in 1971. It was renovated before opening as a restaurant and event venue, but apparently at least two ghostly spirits in residence consider every day to be an event of the supernatural kind. One apparition is that of a young girl who seems to enjoy playing tricks on the kitchen staff by rattling pots and pans. She has also been known to sit at the top of the staircase at night, as if watching a ghostly party of adults below. She cheerily waves to people before vanishing, if approached. Illuminating those ghostly parties may be the reason for the phenomenon of lights in the mansion repeatedly turning on throughout the night, although they are just as repeatedly turned off. From a tall office building nearby, the figures of people are reportedly seen walking past the windows of the Devereaux Mansion at night when the house should have been empty. Apparently, the manifestations play favorites. When some guards try their passkeys, the keys will not work. However, if the spirits like a certain guard, that person's keys *will* work. It would appear that in death as in life, it all depends on "who you know."

The **McCune Mansion** in Salt Lake City was built in 1901 by railroad magnate Alfred McCune and his wife Elizabeth. More than a century later, it is still the site of weddings and other celebrations of gracious living. The venue's stated mission is to provide the atmosphere of a historic treasure embodying superb taste and service. It also seems to provide a taste of the supernatural. Pots rattle in the kitchen, with some flying off their hooks. This is said to be the ghostly spirit of Mrs. McCune, keeping the staff on their toes. Disembodied voices can also be heard, and unexplained cold spots can be felt. Doors open and close at will, and doors that were unlocked are found locked, even when they have no locking mechanism. A regular apparition is that of a young girl who strongly resembles a child in the portrait hanging on the wall of the mansion. Wearing a long, flowing white gown, the little girl has been seen walking into and out of the mirror, which hangs on the first floor. Her footprints have been found in several rooms, all seeming to start and end in the middle of each room, without entering or exiting. Apparently, enjoying the festive atmosphere of weddings, her misty presence has sometimes been caught on film while her manifestation has been reported as dancing and giggling. The child was perhaps a would-be party planner before the career existed since items that have been professionally arranged for an event the next day have been found to be reorganized overnight when no one was in the building. In addition, some say that Elizabeth McCune reserved a small hidden room for musicians to play at her dinner parties so the performers would be heard but not seen as their music wafted in the air throughout the house. Today, chamber music can sometimes be heard emanating from the walls of the mansion when no one is present. Hopefully, Mrs. McCune's dedicated musicians are not still there.

The **Mountain Meadows Massacre** site at Veyo, Utah, marks the event that happened in 1857 when more than 120 settlers were murdered by what is said to have been Mormon militia. According to the *Encyclopedia of Arkansas*, in April 1857, about 120–150 settlers, mostly from Arkansas, started a journey westward toward what they hoped would be a better life in California. Before they had any hope of doing so, they stopped to rest on a plateau pleasantly known as Mountain Meadows in southern Utah where there was water and fresh grass. Most sources agree that as the party made its way into Utah Territory, the Mormons did not receive the travelers hospitably, refusing to trade with them. This hostility was said to have been based partly on the death of a Mormon leader in Arkansas a few months before. On September 7, 1857, the travelers were attacked by a group of Indians and/or what was said to have been Mormons dressed as Indians. All the settlers were killed except for seventeen children who were taken into Mormon homes. Beyond this outline of what are taken to be facts, little can be agreed upon, ranging from the number of victims to who was responsible. Sources report that people who came upon the site after the massacre claimed that the bodies of the travelers had been left unburied and were scavenged by wild animals. Today, there is a monument at Mountain Meadows in memory of those who died in the assault. In 2011, the site was designated as a National Historic Landmark, and is said to be one of the most haunted places in Utah. Visitors report experiencing an overwhelming wave of sadness and hearing ghostly cries carried on the wind, said to be of the victims whose bodies did not rest in peace.

FURTHER READING

Alexander, Thomas. *Utah, the Right Place*. Layton, UT: Gibbs Smith, 2003.

Finck, James. "Mountain Meadows Massacre." *Encyclopedia of Arkansas*. Last accessed June 25, 2018. http://www.encyclopediaofarkansas.net/encyclopedia/entry-detail.aspx?entryID=129

Stone, Eileen Hallet. *Hidden History of Utah*. Charleston, SC: The History Press, 2013.

46

Vermont

Many people have a warm place in their hearts for Vermont due to its status as the leading producer of maple syrup in the United States. It also boasts a proud history of progressive ideas, being an early adherent of the abolition of slavery. Vermont was an early supporter of public education as well as guaranteeing women's right to vote. It has also been one of a handful of states that were sovereign republics before joining the Union, and still retains much of its independent spirit.

Some say that spirit is due to the geography of the land, in which the Green Mountains form what resembles a rocky spine running the length of Vermont, north to south, down the middle of the state like a backbone.

Vermont's history also had a hand in its development, like two fault lines rubbing against each other. According to Klyza and Trombulak (2015), "Vermont came under French influence from the north and British influence from the south" (52).

Before then, indigenous peoples like the Mohawk occupied much of the territory of today's Vermont. The first European presence is thought to have been France's Jacques Cartier in 1535. In 1609, fellow French explorer Samuel de Champlain claimed Vermont as part of New France. French settlers erected Fort Sainte Anne in 1666, creating the first European settlement in Vermont.

In 1763, after France's defeat in the French and Indian War, the territory was ceded to Great Britain. However, the French left something of themselves behind in the name of today's state of Vermont with its first known use in 1777. In French, "les monts verts," roughly the equivalent of "the green mountains," became "Vermont."

In 1770, a Vermonter named Ethan Allen recruited his brothers and cousins to serve as an informal militia unit known as the Green Mountain Boys to protect local settlers. In 1775, with the coming of the American Revolution, the Green Mountain Boys gained fame by joining a force from Connecticut in capturing the British fort at Ticonderoga, New York. That brigade was led by American officer Benedict Arnold (before he switched sides).

In 1777, a group of settlers established what they called the Vermont Republic. Never having been one of the thirteen original colonies, Vermont was an independent territory during the American Revolution.

After the war ended in 1783, more newcomers arrived in Vermont. Various land claims by former colonies like Massachusetts, New Hampshire, and New York were resolved. At this time, the independent republic of Vermont issued its own coinage and operated its own postal service.

But soon, Vermont was ready to join the newly formed United States. It was the first to join the Union after the original thirteen colonies, being admitted as the fourteenth state in 1791. Along with California, Hawaii, and Texas, Vermont was one of the only four current U.S. states that were previously sovereign republics.

In its constitution, the Vermont Republic had abolished slavery, at least in a partial form, before any of the other states. During the mid-nineteenth century, Vermont was a stronghold of abolitionist sentiment. Many Vermonters provided refuge for escaped slaves fleeing to Canada as part of the Underground Railroad.

Vermont sent many men to fight for the Union in the Civil War, and boasts an interesting piece of historical trivia. The St. Albans Raid in St. Albans, Vermont, took place in 1864. It was an unofficial incursion from Canada by twenty-one Confederates who wished to rob banks for much-needed money and trick the Union Army into diverting troops to defend the northern border. Although an engagement at West Point, Ohio, is considered to be the northernmost point reached by an officially organized Confederate military body, the rogue St. Albans raid in Vermont is held to be the northernmost land action of the Civil War.

That was not the only distinction held by Vermont during the Civil War years. Its early constitution had specified support of public schools, indicating a statewide priority set on education. Dorn (2017) notes that after Vermont residents elected Justin Morrill to Congress in 1854, "the junior representative wasted no time in acting on an issue of particular interest to him—the establishment of agricultural colleges" (85).

The Morrill Act of 1862 was signed into law by President Abraham Lincoln during the Civil War. Considering all the other matters Lincoln was forced to deal with at the time, he too must have felt the plan had merit for the future of the nation. Under the Morrill Land Grant Colleges Act, each state was to use the proceeds from the sale of federal lands to set up "land grant colleges" specializing in agriculture and engineering.

Commenting on the land grant colleges founded as the result of the 1862 Morrill Act, according to Gleason (2010), there are approximately seventy such institutions in the United States. "Among them are some of our finest universities: the Universities of California, Illinois, Wisconsin, Minnesota, and Arizona, along with Purdue, Ohio State, Penn State, and Michigan State Universities" (n.p.).

In the colonial era, religious denominations established most early colleges to train ministers. They were modeled after England's Oxford and Cambridge. In America, Harvard College was founded by the Massachusetts Bay colonial legislature in 1636, and named for an early benefactor.

In 1693, the College of William and Mary was founded in Virginia, created by a charter issued by England's King William III and Queen Mary II. Yale College was founded in 1701. It was originally located at Saybrook, Connecticut, but was relocated to New Haven in 1716.

With an interest in education since its founding, it is not surprising that Vermont was ahead of the curve. The **University of Vermont** (UVM) was founded as a private college in 1791, the same year Vermont became a state. In 1865, the school merged with Vermont Agricultural College, chartered in 1864 under the Morrill Land Grant Colleges Act. The resulting institution of higher learning emerged as the University of Vermont and State Agricultural College.

For most of America's early history, women were not permitted at institutions of higher learning. However, in 1837, Ohio's pioneering Oberlin College admitted four women, becoming the first "coeducational" college. In 1871, the University of Vermont admitted two women as students.

According to UVM, it was the first American college to have a charter declaring it would not give preference to any religious sect or denomination.

Over the years, the University of Vermont prospered and grew. The result of some of that growth has been the need to purchase nearby homes for renovation into campus buildings. Some of those homes may have brought the spirits of the departed who lived in them before they became college material.

One of these properties is today's college Counseling Center, which was once the home of Captain John Nabb. Staff members at the Counseling Center say that Captain Nabb enjoys making his presence known by knocking things over and slamming doors and windows.

The nearby Public Relations building is said to be haunted by a former owner who has embarked on his own public relations campaign by making various banging noises all over the house.

SOME OTHER REPORTEDLY HAUNTED PLACES IN VERMONT

The **Brattleboro Retreat** in Brattleboro was founded in 1834 with the best of intentions. Its various structures, spread over hundreds of acres, were built through the 1930s, and most remain in use today. It was created through a bequest specifically to be used as a mental health facility, in itself an idea that was ahead of its time in an era when mental problems were considered shameful aberrations. Even more advanced was the institution's philosophy of the humane treatment of patients. Patients were treated with dignity and respect. The Retreat emphasized fresh air, exercise, good meals, and a caring environment. It also placed an emphasis on physical labor which was intended to improve mental health by providing stability and a meaningful endeavor. One of these projects was the Brattleboro Retreat Tower. It was built in 1887 by a group of patients. The large stone tower was meant to provide a scenic overlook of the asylum grounds. However, as some roads are paved by good intentions, the tower was soon utilized in ways other than observing pretty scenery. A number of patients climbed its spiral staircase to the top of the tower in order to commit suicide by leaping onto a rocky cliff below. Although it is currently closed, witnesses report seeing ghostly figures jumping from the tower, vanishing from sight before they hit the ground. At another area of the Retreat—the cemetery—visitors have been said to sense an ominous presence marked by strong feelings of uneasiness. Some of the tombstones are in poor condition, dating back to the 1800s. Many of the graves are marked with only numbers or "Unknown." Visitors have reported seeing fleeting shadow figures that are always just out of sight.

Construction began on Manchester's **Equinox Golf Resort and Spa** in 1769, even before America was an independent nation. Over the centuries, it has boasted its share of U.S. history, attracting guests like Presidents Ulysses S. Grant, Benjamin Harrison, William Howard Taft, and Theodore Roosevelt. However, reports of hauntings at the Equinox do not concern those illustrious men but one of the most controversial women in American history, the wife of Abraham Lincoln. Although today she is usually called Mary Todd Lincoln, during her lifetime she preferred simply Mary Lincoln. During the summer of 1864, life in Washington D.C. was unpleasant due to both the pressures of the Civil War and the city's oppressive heat. Having lost her beloved son Willie two years earlier, Mrs. Lincoln visited the Equinox with her two remaining children. The eldest, Robert Lincoln, liked it so much he later built a magnificent estate called Hildene nearby in Manchester, which is where he died in 1926. Mary Lincoln also enjoyed the resort and made reservations for the following year, with plans to visit the Equinox again with her husband in the summer of 1865. A special suite was constructed to honor a presidential visit that tragically never took place. Abraham Lincoln was assassinated on April 14, 1865 before he could visit Vermont with Mary. Since then, Mary Lincoln's spirit may have returned alone to a place where she was happy. Guests and staff have reported seeing her apparition, sometimes accompanied by one of her children, with her ghost appearing and quickly vanishing. Some have claimed to hear whispers and feel an unexplained cold chill pass through them. Others said that items in their guestroom mysteriously moved to different spots than where they were left, as well as people being awakened in the middle of the night by lights in the room coming on by themselves.

The ghost town of West Castleton on **Lake Bomoseen** has been abandoned since the 1930s. In its heyday during the late 1800s, it was a busy industrial community full of Irish immigrants employed at the town's slate quarries. After work, many enjoyed visiting a tavern on the opposite shore by crossing the two thousand–acre Lake Bomoseen. One night, three men set out across Lake Bomoseen in a rowboat but never reached the tavern nor were they ever seen again. Their empty boat was found the next morning, floating on the calm surface of the lake. Despite a thorough search, their bodies were never found. Today, people claim that on a dark night, a ghostly empty rowboat can be seen drifting silently across the lake with the calm surface undisturbed by any oars rippling the water. Other doings on Lake Bomoseen concern today's lonely Neshobe Island in the middle of the lake. In the 1920s, its rustic isolation attracted literary critic Alexander Woollcott who purchased it as a quiet place to work. Sometimes celebrity friends would visit, including Laurence Olivier, Vivien Leigh, Walt Disney, and Harpo Marx of the comedic Marx Brothers. Soon there were reports by boaters hoping to glimpse a celebrity that a horrible paranormal creature rushed out of the

In its heyday during the late 1800s, Vermont's Lake Bomoseen was the site of a busy community. Some residents enjoyed visiting a tavern on the opposite shore by crossing in a rowboat. One group never reached the tavern, nor were they ever seen again. Today, people claim that on a dark night, a ghostly empty rowboat can be seen drifting silently across the lake. (Library of Congress)

woods, scaring them off. The story is that Marx would cake his naked body with mud, put on a red wig, and run from the woods screaming. The island was not haunted by a rumored supernatural creature, just Harpo.

Located on the village green in Fair Haven, Vermont, the **Marble Mansion Inn** was built in 1867 by businessman Ira C. Allen, who was related to Revolutionary War hero Ethan Allen. In 1893, the house was wired for power and became the first house in Fair Haven to have electricity. The three-story mansion was constructed entirely of gleaming marble. It changed hands a number of times during the decades, first passing from family members and other owners to serve as their private residence, and later as a luxurious inn where each room is different. Along with unique designs, the Marble Mansion may provide the rooms with a resident ghost. Guests have reported being awakened by an eerie feeling in the night to see the apparition of a man dressed in a gray suit standing over the bed. He is said to be a former owner who died there. There have also been reports of a woman who haunts the basement, as well as children who run through the halls when no children are registered.

The **Vermont Police Academy** in Pittsford was formerly a state hospital for tuberculosis (TB) patients. Among the State Police recruits may be ghostly remnants of the facility's past. Until the mid-twentieth century, sanitariums were the usual response for TB, housing victims of what was then an often-fatal illness. Some facilities were better than others, often dictated by the families' ability to pay. In the early 1900s, Pittsford gained the reputation of having the most sunshine of any town in Vermont, earning the nickname "Vermont's Sunshine Village." In 1907, a large tract of land was purchased by a wealthy family with the purpose of building a TB facility. The patients got plenty of fresh air, sunshine, exercise, and healthy food in the lovely mountainous setting. Some who might have survived in those surroundings succumbed to questionable treatments, such as removing ribs with saws, inserting inflated balloons into infected lungs, and weighing the patient's chest down with heavy sandbags to allegedly strengthen the lungs. One of its unique features was a "Preventorium" that generally catered to children from underprivileged families. The poor were not considered intelligent enough to prevent a child from getting sick, as opposed to the wealthy who were assumed to know enough not to cough on them. With the rise of antibiotic treatments, the complex was sealed up until 1971 when it was converted into a basic training facility for State Police officers. Renamed the Robert H. Wood Jr. Criminal Justice and Fire Service Training Center of Vermont, it is currently home to a sixteen-week training program. The facility may still be haunted by one of the nurses named Mary who contracted TB while working there. With old call buttons still in the rooms of the recruits, it is said that if a button is pushed, the ghost of Nurse Mary will stop by to check on the occupant during the night.

FURTHER READING

Dorn, Charles. *For the Common Good: A New History of Higher Education in America.* Ithaca, NY: Cornell University Press, 2017.

Gleason, Bill. "World-Class Greatness at a Land-Grant University Near You?" *Chronicle of Higher Education*, September 26, 2010. https://www.chronicle.com/article/World-Class-Greatness-at-a/124591

Klyza, Christopher, and Stephen Trombulak. *The Story of Vermont: A Natural and Cultural History.* 2nd ed. Lebanon, NH: University Press of New England, 2015.

47

Virginia

Officially called the Commonwealth of Virginia, the nickname "Old Dominion" is sometimes used due to Virginia's status as the first permanent English colony established in mainland North America. The Virginia General Assembly is the oldest continuous law-making body in the New World. Virginia is also referred to as "Mother of Presidents," with eight chief executives being born there, more U.S. presidents than any other state.

Thousands of years before that, indigenous people called today's Virginia home. In 1570, just before the first Europeans arrived on its shores, a number of Native American tribes merged under Chief Powhatan to strengthen their trading position. Powhatan controlled more than thirty tribes who lived in about 150 settlements and shared the Algonquian language. By the time Europeans arrived, the Native American population in Virginia's coastal region was almost fourteen thousand.

Spaniards founded a mission on the Virginia Peninsula in 1570, but the following year, the small group was massacred by hostile Indians. Spanish forces sailed to the site and killed about two dozen Native Americans in retaliation.

In 1583, Queen Elizabeth I of England granted Walter Raleigh a charter to plant a colony north of Spain's Florida territory. In 1584, Raleigh sent an expedition to explore the area he named Virginia. The name is usually said to refer to Elizabeth's unmarried status as the "Virgin Queen."

It took a few years to be financed, but in 1607, the first permanent English settlement was established. Called Jamestown in honor of England's King James I, it was located near the coast on the James River, not far from today's Williamsburg. Life in the colony was difficult and dangerous. Many died during what was called the Starving Time in 1609. About half of the early settlers died.

For the remainder, there was a powerful incentive to persist. According to Wallenstein (2014), "The combination of tobacco and servants supplied the menu for a settler society that could work, even at enormous cost and under continued uncertainty" (33). In 1619, the same year that the colonists elected their own legislature, the House of Burgesses, the first African forced laborers were brought to Jamestown.

At first, the Africans labored as indentured servants, able to gain their freedom after certain conditions were met. But the system soon changed to a lifetime of slavery for the Africans *and* their descendants. In Virginia statutes starting in 1661, slavery was not only officially condoned but was made hereditary based on the status of the mother.

In 1776, along with England's other colonies, Virginia declared independence from British rule. A number of prominent Virginians played important roles before, during, and after the Revolution, including Patrick Henry, Thomas Jefferson, James Madison, and George Washington.

Virginia ratified the Constitution of the United States in 1788, becoming the tenth state in the Union. It seceded from that same Union in 1861 to join the Confederate States of America, which chose Richmond, Virginia, as its capital. Fewer than 150 miles separated Richmond from the Union capital of Washington, D.C.

As the Civil War began, Virginian Robert E. Lee took command of Confederate forces. During the war, more battles were fought in Virginia than anywhere else.

Virginia was also the setting for events that are considered to be among the first and the last of the conflict. Near the Civil War's beginning, the family home of Wilmer McLean in Manassas, Virginia, was in the line of fire at the First Battle of Bull Run. Seeking safety, they moved to Appomattox, Virginia. There, McLean's house was where Robert E. Lee surrendered to General Ulysses S. Grant. McLean is said to have stated that the war began in his front yard and ended in his parlor.

In addition to the First and Second Bull Run, major Civil War battles in Virginia include Chancellorsville, Fredericksburg, Hampton Roads, Petersburg, and the concluding battle at Appomattox Court House. Amid all that bloodshed, the battle that many historians cite as one of bloodiest, not just in the Civil War but in all of American history, was Virginia's Battle of Cold Harbor.

It was fought near Mechanicsville, Virginia, from May 31 to June 12, 1864. Later, as Davis (2014) points out, Union General Ulysses S. Grant said in his memoirs, "I have always regretted that last assault on Cold Harbor was ever made" (97). Even Grant admitted that no advantage whatsoever was gained to compensate for the heavy losses.

Even the land at Cold Harbor was unforgiving. Trench warfare in the difficult terrain was a hot, miserable experience for both sides since the dugouts were cramped with both the living and the dead. Food and water were scarce. Dehydrated men fought on empty stomachs. After two weeks of fighting, the Confederates had lost forty-five hundred men. Union casualties were estimated to be almost thirteen thousand.

Along with Gettysburg in Pennsylvania, Virginia's **Cold Harbor Battlefield Park** near Richmond today ranks as one of the most haunted places in the United States. Visitors and residents who live nearby claim to have heard and felt the phantom thunder of artillery fire. Some have heard cries from unseen men, and others have heard the ghostly pounding of horses' hooves, many of which were also slaughtered on the battlefield. In addition, the distinct smell of burned gunpowder

Many visitors to Virginia's Cold Harbor Battlefield Park near Richmond claim to hear the phantom thunder of artillery fire, to be overcome by a devastating sense of pain, and to see the apparitions of Civil War–era soldiers. Many of the dead could never be identified and may haunt it today, with their spirits among the most restless of all. (Library of Congress)

is joined by a dense, unexplainable fog that vanishes as quickly as it appears. Many visitors claim to have been overcome by a devastating sense of anguish and pain, and there have been reports of seeing the apparitions of soldiers.

At the Cold Harbor Cemetery, there are monuments to the dead by individual states like Pennsylvania and New York. Since many of the men killed in the battle could not be identified, there is also a Tomb of the Unknown Soldier. But for some of the men who died at Cold Harbor and may haunt it still, there are those whose spirits may be the most restless of all.

Photography was just being popularized during the Civil War. For the first time, Americans across the country could see both the gallantry and the carnage on battlefields far from home. Civil War photographers made frequent trips to the two-week battle at Cold Harbor, both during and after the conflict. One particular photo has become burned in the memory of those who see it. According to Nesbitt (2012), "It seems the burial crews at Cold Harbor were not as efficient as the [dead] soldiers would have wished" (168). A famous photograph at the Library of Congress shows skeletons thrown haphazardly onto a flat stretcher, with skulls visible, as well as a leg with an intact shoe and pants-leg still attached.

In addition to the sad skeletal remains of soldiers who were never properly buried, much of the seventy-five hundred–acre battlefield where they lay has been taken over for commercial and residential use. It is reported that by 2007, only about three hundred acres remained.

With their final resting place, such as it is, being paved over, some historians point out that while we might call the deceased "soldiers," many were teenage boys just off the farm, somebody's son or father or husband. Many lives were shattered at the bloody battle where even Ulysses S. Grant had regrets. The photo of those skulls might be symbolic of the spirits that still haunt Cold Harbor.

SOME OTHER REPORTEDLY HAUNTED PLACES IN VIRGINIA

The **Boxwood Inn B&B** at Newport was originally built for Simon Reid Curtis and Nannie Cooke Curtis. If it is indeed haunted, it can boast of one of the most friendly, helpful spirits in the paranormal universe. When the twenty-one-room mansion was being restored in 1995, its new owner broke a fingernail while working on the renovation and, although she was alone in the house, exclaimed aloud that she needed an emery board. Turning around, she saw a bright, clean nail file sitting in the middle of the dust-covered floor. Apparently amused, the lady voiced her appreciation and added that she could also use $100. She soon felt something stick to her shoe, and retrieving it, discovered it was a gold tooth filling, which she sold to a local pawnshop for $100. The kindly spirit is said to be Nannie Curtis who is happy to see her former home restored to its former glory and may simply be offering to pitch in and help.

Edgewood Plantation was built in 1850 when it was known as Berkeley Plantation. Today, the resident spirit of the restored bed-and-breakfast is said to be the apparition of Elizabeth "Lizzie" Rowland, who lived in the home during the Civil War. Her name remains etched on the window pane of an upstairs bedroom as she waited for her beloved fiancé to return from the Civil War. Like so many of the young men who went off to fight, he never returned. It is said Lizzie died of a broken heart after waiting for years, never knowing when or where he disappeared. Lizzie Rowland passed away in 1870, five years after the war ended. Lizzie's manifestation reportedly walks the halls of Edgewood, lost and broken-hearted, on her way to wait at an upstairs window where she is doomed to keep waiting in vain.

The known history of the land beneath the **Ferry Plantation House** in Virginia Beach can be traced back to 1636 when it served as the landing for a ferry-boat serving the Lynnhaven River. The property had many owners and served multiple uses, including as a courthouse, post office, and school, in addition to being a plantation home. Being repurposed repeatedly, it may not be surprising that today it is said to be haunted by almost a dozen ghosts. Along with Native American spirits from a tribe that was reportedly wiped out by Powhatan, one of the most regularly encountered is a male manifestation who is described as being very talkative. The spirit of a slave named Henry is said to be looking for vengeance, while Sally Rebecca Walke's ghost cries grief-stricken tears over the death of her lover. The "Lady in White" replays her death from a broken neck after tumbling down the stairs, while victims of an 1810 shipwreck also seek safe harbor. But the most poignant tale of its hauntings is the story of the so-called Witch of Pungo, who was one of the only people convicted of witchcraft in Virginia. This apparition is said to wander the grounds of the Ferry Plantation after being tried nearby. Grace White Sherwood was a farmer and midwife who was convicted of being a witch in 1706. She was beautiful, wore pants instead of a long dress, and practiced healing through herbal remedies. Bad weather, crop failures, and dead livestock were routinely blamed on Grace. After a neighbor woman suffered a miscarriage, Grace was accused of being responsible. Grace underwent the fate of accused witches, the ordeal by water. She bobbed to the surface, "proving" she was a witch, and was seized from the water by a mob. Grace is said to have spent almost eight years behind bars, presumably while her fate was being debated. She died before her name could be cleared. According to local residents, a strange moving light, reportedly her restless spirit, still appears over the spot at Witch Duck Bay where she was thrown into the water. Some locals have reported seeing the apparition of a woman with long, wet hair walking along the banks of the river at night. In 2006, Grace received an informal pardon by Virginia's governor to officially restore her good name, but for Grace, it may have been too little and too late—by three hundred years.

An area of Williamsburg known as "The Bloody Ravine" was part of a Civil War battlefield, and it is there that the **Fort Magruder Hotel** is built. Not surprisingly, the spirits of the dead may have checked in. Fort Magruder was the name given to a thirty-foot high earthen fortification on the road between the historic Virginia communities of Yorktown and Williamsburg. In 1862, Confederate Colonel John B. Magruder's command was sent to occupy and defend the earthworks, which had been built early in the war during the spring of 1861. The hotel was built in 1971 on the site of the fortification, which was the focus of an intense battle that raged for two days. Cavalry horses and infantry troops were slogging through the mud before they engaged in combat with the other side. The Battle of Williamsburg, also known as the Battle of Fort Magruder, saw the clash of about forty thousand Federals and thirty-two thousand Confederates. When the smoke cleared, more than twenty-two hundred Union troops and almost two thousand Confederates had lost their lives for a result that most historians call "inconclusive." Today, it is said that apparitions of rain-soaked soldiers can be seen behind their fortifications, while flashes of gunfire spark through the trees. It is said that ghostly manifestations appear at the Fort Magruder Hotel where a collection of Civil War artifacts are displayed. They were found during construction of the hotel, and range from swords and musket balls to uniform buttons and a Union Army belt buckle. Paranormal activity at the hotel may be caused by soldiers who feel welcome where they are honored. One female guest is said to have had her sleep interrupted by a red-haired Confederate soldier perched upon her bed. In the hotel's lobby and lounge, employees have reported ghostly figures walking through windows, doors mysteriously becoming unlocked, and broken glass being scattered all over the floor.

The **Staunton Train Depot** in the town of Staunton has seen its share of paranormal activities. In 1864, several people perished when the depot was burned down by Union soldiers, and may still haunt it. Some say ghosts of mental patients from a nearby asylum wander to the station in hopes of escaping the hospital's brutal conditions. Perhaps the most poignant ghost is that of a would-be singer named Myrtle Ruth Knox. Amid great hopes for her musical career, she had recently joined an opera company. On the night of April 26, 1890, the seventeen-year-old Knox was aboard a train that was scheduled to stop at Staunton. Even today, the tracks approaching Staunton twist and turn, dropping about eighty feet in elevation before reaching the station. The engineer of Knox's train later said the brakeman applied pressure to the brakes, but nothing happened. The engineer lost control of the train, and as its speed increased on the downgrade, its wheels slid off the track. Sleepy passengers were thrown around the railcars. After a few moments, the train slammed into the Staunton Train Depot, causing the building to collapse completely. Debris from the demolished station toppled over an entire sleeper car. Unfortunately, that was where the young Miss Knox was in her compartment. One of her legs was nearly severed, and a three-foot section of sharp wood pierced the length of the other leg. Another shard sliced her femoral artery. She died from the uncontrollable bleeding that gushed from her wounds. A number of people are believed to have died in the accident, but it is the spirit of Miss Knox that is said to haunt the depot. It was the place where her journey, her dreams, and her young life were cut short.

FURTHER READING

Davis, Daniel, and Phillip Greenwalt. *Hurricane from the Heavens: The Battle of Cold Harbor.* El Dorado Hills, CA: Savas Beatie, 2014.

Library of Congress. *Cold Harbor, Va. African Americans Collecting Bones of Soldiers Killed in the Battle*, 1865 April. https://www.loc.gov/item/2018666599

Nesbitt, Mark. *Civil War Ghost Trails.* Mechanicsburg, PA: Stackpole Books, 2012.

Wallenstein, Peter. *Cradle of America: A History of Virginia.* Lawrence: University Press of Kansas, 2014.

48

Washington

Officially termed the State of Washington, the "Evergreen State" was named for the first president of the United States, George Washington, but not without a kind of confusion that persists to this day. In 1853, a new territory in the Pacific Northwest was to be named "Columbia" for the Columbia River, but a U.S. congressman found the terminology too similar to the District of Columbia. The name "Washington" replaced the territorial title, with apparently little thought to the fact that the nation's capital also contained the word "Washington."

During the statehood process in 1889, some residents proposed the name to be "Tacoma," but Washington remains the only U.S. state named after a president. To distinguish it from Washington, D.C., the nation's capital where the naming hubbub took place, the state of Washington is sometimes referred to as Washington State.

Washington appears to have been the home of one of the nation's first residents, with the remains of Kennewick Man being discovered in Kennewick, Washington. The prehistoric individual in question was about nine thousand years old, with his skeleton being one of the oldest and most complete ever found.

Although Kennewick Man survived in skeletal form for almost ten thousand years, many of his descendants were not so lucky. When Europeans arrived in the late 1700s, Native American tribes in today's Washington State included the Cayuse, Okanogan, Spokane, and Yakama. Today, their legacy survives in names of many places. A smallpox epidemic in the 1770s devastated the Native American population, and as for those few who were left to welcome the 1800s, Ritter (2003) notes, "Missionaries and settlers began to arrive in the 1830s and 1840s [bringing] typhus, measles and dysentery" (25).

The first documented European to land on the Washington coast was a Spanish captain, Don Bruno de Heceta in 1775. He claimed it for the Spaniards, who proclaimed the Pacific Ocean to be a "Spanish lake," with everything that touched it belonging to Spain.

English fur trader Charles William Barkley arrived in 1787, leading to a series of disputes between Britain and Spain that ultimately put an end to Spanish claims to the region by the early 1800s. Traders began to settle in today's Washington from Britain, Russia, and the new nation of the United States. The Lewis and Clark Expedition entered the state of Washington in 1805.

More disputes over the territory would ensue between Britain and the United States, but ultimately, in 1889, Washington became the forty-second state to join the Union.

The state prospered through its lumber industry and becoming a leading producer of apples, shipping them around the country. Being known for apples became somewhat ironic when Apple Computer's competitor Microsoft moved its headquarters to Washington in 1979. Today, the Microsoft campus at Redmond, Washington, is said to employ between thirty thousand and forty thousand people.

In a further irony, a number of hydroelectric dams were constructed along the Columbia River during the Great Depression of the 1930s to produce electricity. The Grand Coulee Dam near Spokane is currently the largest concrete structure in the United States. Having all that power did not prevent an incident in 1938 when the radio program *War of the Worlds*, about a Martian invasion, sent Americans into a panic. In a poorly timed coincidence, a chance explosion at the town power plant in Concrete, Washington, during the broadcast knocked out the area's electricity. Convinced that the Martians had landed, many of the one thousand residents of Concrete ran away in a panic, hiding in the mountains.

Some of the residents of Concrete may have thought the universe had gone mad. But madness was not something to be taken lightly. Andrew Scull (2015) underscores the fact that few diseases were more dreaded than madness, no matter one's station in life: "When the last king of North America, George III, sensed that he was losing his reason, he insisted to anyone who would listen" (189) that he was just nervous, not mad.

Perhaps that was because through much of history, the "treatment" of mental health issues was the stuff of nightmares. One of the more so-called humane practices was dunking the afflicted person in cold water. At the other end of the temperature scale, some were burned at the stake as witches.

By the time of George III's reign in the 1700s, the "lunatic asylum" was coming into vogue. Its reputation was such that even George, at the top of the socioeconomic ladder, feared being committed to one, even though he would be someone seemingly assured of gentle treatment.

The feeling among the men who declared themselves experts in the field of mental illness was that institutionalization was the correct solution to treat people considered "mad." It also locked them safely away, removing the stigma that would attach to their family due to the patient's condition.

The first known facility for the mentally ill in America was created in Philadelphia. A portion of The Pennsylvania Hospital, founded by the Religious Society of Friends, was set apart for the mentally ill, with the first patients being admitted in 1752.

The first institution specifically for the mentally ill was incorporated in Williamsburg, Virginia. Named the Hospital for Persons of Insane and Disordered Minds, it admitted its first patients in 1773.

Sadly, many mental asylums descended into bedlam. Well into the twentieth century, some practices included electroshock treatments, ice water baths, lobotomies (sometimes with an icepick), strenuous physical labor, or its polar opposite, being forced to sit in a straight-backed chair for up to twelve hours without talking or moving. Patients in overcrowded conditions were routinely shackled, immobilized in straightjackets, and sometimes beaten, raped, or forced to lie naked in their own excrement.

Women were sometimes institutionalized for having strong opinions or not being submissive to the males who were in charge of them, such as a husband, father, brother, or in the case of Mary Lincoln, widow of the assassinated president Abraham Lincoln, a son.

In 1887, a twenty-three-year-old newspaper reporter for Joseph Pulitzer's *New York World* who called herself Nellie Bly (pen name for Elizabeth Cochran Seaman) had herself committed to the Blackwell's Island Insane Asylum in New York City. She hoped to investigate conditions there, which she experienced first-hand. Most are too gruesome to detail. She was one of the lucky ones, having the full weight of Pulitzer and the *New York World* to win her release after only ten days. Bly's account was published in the newspaper and in the book *Ten Days in a Mad-House*, prompting a move toward reforms.

It is no wonder that some former mental hospitals are said to be haunted by the ghosts of those who were not lucky enough to be released except by death. Washington's **Northern State Mental Hospital** in Sedro-Woolley admitted the

Washington's Northern State Mental Hospital in Sedro-Woolley utilized electroshock treatments, lobotomies, and strenuous physical labor. Many are said to have died there amid pervasive despair, and some may never have left even after death. There are reports of disembodied screams, plus apparitions including a little girl with a red ball and a nurse hanging from a noose. (Saveri0/Dreamstime.com)

mentally ill from 1912 to 1976. It was one of the facilities that utilized electroshock treatments, lobotomies, and strenuous physical labor. Many are said to have died there amid the pervasive despair, and some have never left even after death. There are reports of cold spots, disembodied screams, and eerie shadow figures. Apparitions run from a little girl with a red ball to a nurse hanging from a noose.

SOME OTHER REPORTEDLY HAUNTED PLACES IN WASHINGTON

The **Fort Vancouver National Historic Site** at Vancouver, Washington, dates back to 1824 when it was established by the British as a fur trading outpost. Today, more than two million archeological exhibits on display by the National Park Service (NPS) tell the story of the area going back to the time before contact was made by Europeans. Native American tribes such as the Chinooks, Clackamas, and Multnomah lived there before the Hudson's Bay Company built its fur trading business on the land. According to the NPS, Fort Vancouver was essentially the colonial capital of the Pacific Northwest, supporting a multiethnic village of six hundred to one thousand residents. They included Hawaiian men who worked in the agricultural fields and sawmills of the company's operations. In 1849, Fort Vancouver became the administrative and military headquarters for the U.S. Army overseeing settlement of the Oregon Territory. As the American military presence grew, the Hudson's Bay Company departed in 1862 leaving the fort to expand. Part of its expansion covered what many say was a graveyard from the colonial past. The twenty-one stately houses built for officers stood proudly until the Army officially moved out and they were allowed to deteriorate. It is said that the spirits of past occupants took offense at seeing their former homes become so run down. They may have remained behind when the buildings were listed on the National List of Historic Places in order to supervise the restoration. One of the mansions on Officers' Row was the home of Ulysses S. Grant, who was stationed there in the 1850s. Today, this building houses the Grant House Folk Art Center and seems especially attractive to the spirit world. Some of the strange phenomena there include cold spots, disembodied footsteps, doors opening or closing by themselves, a feeling of being touched by unseen hands, and telephones ringing when they are completely unplugged. Located in a state that loves its coffee, the spirits also seem to enjoy the brew. One entity, nicknamed Sully, likes to sit in the cafe drinking coffee. Other entities have been reported to help themselves to freshly made coffee, so the accommodating staffers have learned to make extra.

The fifteen hundred–seat **Mount Baker Theatre** opened to entertain the community of Bellingham in 1927. It was built as a luxurious movie palace with an exotic Spanish Moorish design that was meant to transport the town's patrons to another time and place. For the supernatural spirits said to inhabit the landmarked building, the opposite may also be true: they come from another time and place to visit the theater. In general, many structures are said to become haunted after years of use, sometimes being repurposed to serve different needs. But the Mount Baker Theatre has allegedly been haunted ever since it first opened its doors in the

Roaring Twenties. Some of the phenomena over the years are said to have been recorded, such as balls of light, cold spots, disembodied voices, unexplained noises, and various apparitions. One ghost is said to be that of a young woman whose home was bulldozed to make way for the theater's construction. If that entity is haunting her old homestead, she may be the same friendly ghost who is called Judy. For years, there have been reports at the theater that Judy tends to develop a crush on male projectionists and ushers working at the theater. When she focuses on the object of her affections, the man will hear his name called out across the stage. Sometimes the man might feel a ghostly touch on his back and shoulders. It is not known if Judy was responsible for a trick that was played on theater staff when the safe in a former office was found closed and locked. No one knew the combination. After many years the room was being cleaned for renovation, whereupon the safe was suddenly discovered wide open.

The **Oxford Saloon** in Snohomish began life as a grocery store from the time it was built in 1890 until 1910 when it became the Oxford Saloon. The structure has been said to see its share of violence over the years, although it must be assumed there was not as much bloodshed among the grocery shelves as in the barroom. It is reported that ten people died there, including the murder of a policeman named Henry who was a regular at the saloon and may have worked as a bouncer when he was off duty. It is said that Henry was stabbed, rolling down the stairs to the basement as he died. He may still be a public servant in spirit form. Staffers report that at the end of one evening, a musician went down to the basement to get cleaned up, and upon coming back upstairs, complimented the management on a particularly nice bartender downstairs. Apparently, the genial barman had shared the history of the building in fascinating detail. The manager was forced to declare that, being responsible for locking up, he was the only one left in the building—no barmen downstairs. The musician left, guitar in hand, never coming back. On the upper floors there are said to be the apparitions of a man in a bowler hat and two female spirits. One is said to be Amelia, a young woman who was found dead in a closet on the premises after being forced into prostitution by a madam named Kathleen. Another is Kathleen, the madam herself. This manifestation has been described as an older woman dressed in purple. Kathleen's grisly death is reported as having been by decapitation in the claw-footed bathtub that is still upstairs. Unfortunately, the phantom bartender, who was so generous with details of the building's past, apparently did not see fit to include the details of how Kathleen lost her head.

The facility in Olalla originally called The Institute of Natural Therapeutics is usually known today as **Starvation Heights Sanitarium.** The term "starvation" was not a figure of speech. According to *Smithsonian.com,* the patients were literally starved to death—and paid a lot to do it. Starvation Heights Sanitarium was operated in the early 1900s by a woman who called herself "Dr." Linda Hazzard. Her methodology was hazardous indeed. She had neither a medical degree nor much in the way of formal training. However, she was able to be licensed by the state of Washington as a "fasting specialist." That was not entirely unusual, since even today, many people believe in periodic fasting as a way to good health. However, Hazzard's methods were extreme, deadly, and involved a big element of greed. In her 1908 book, *Fasting for the Cure of Disease*, Hazzard wrote that the key to good health was to let the digestive system "rest" through fasting. Patients came to the sanitarium for minor ailments. Based on its promotional material, they expected a healthy routine that would include supporting their supervised fast with a nutritious broth made of fresh vegetables. After paying a substantial fee, what they got was an occasional small serving of a weak, unappetizing substance later said to have been watered-down canned tomato soup. Patients' systems were "flushed" with harsh daily enemas that could last for hours, verbal abuse, and "massages" that were later said to be closer to beatings. An estimated forty patients or more died while in captivity. Hazzard would rob them of valuables, yank out any gold teeth, and compel them when they were in a delirious, weakened state to make her the beneficiary in their wills, which Hazzard was also known to forge if the patient was not compliant. The exact death count remains unknown because the bodies were quickly incinerated within the sanitarium. In 1911, Hazzard was ultimately convicted of her crimes, herself dying a few years later. The building burned in 1935, and today, its foundation can be seen along with the gruesome incinerator, a seven-foot-tall concrete tower that may contain the spirits of the dead who roam the ruins, sometimes seen as starving figures stumbling through the woods.

FURTHER READING

Lovejoy, Bess. "The Doctor Who Starved Her Patients to Death." *Smithsonian.com*, October 28, 2014. https://www.smithsonianmag.com/history/doctor-who-starved-her-patients-death-180953158

Ritter, Harry. *Washington's History, Revised Edition: The People, Land, and Events of the Far Northwest*. Portland, OR: WestWinds Press, 2003.

Scull, Andrew. *Madness in Civilization: A Cultural History of Insanity, from the Bible to Freud, from the Madhouse to Modern Medicine*. Princeton, NJ: Princeton University Press, 2015.

49

West Virginia

The story of West Virginia has been shaped by two forces: its mountainous terrain and the American Civil War. When it was part of the state of Virginia, the economy of the western region was completely different from the eastern Tidewater. Instead of elegant plantation estates and the sophisticated society of coastal cities, western residents of the state tended to live in small isolated communities in the mountain valleys.

The rocky soil in the west made it impossible to build huge, profitable plantations that depended on slave labor as in the east. Therefore, while a portion of the residents in today's West Virginia held slaves, most were small farmers who thought of themselves as "mountaineers."

When the Civil War began in 1861, the state of Virginia seceded from the Union. That same year, a group of delegates from some counties in northwestern Virginia decided to break away. West Virginia became an independent state following the Wheeling Conventions of 1861.

West Virginia was admitted to the Union in 1863 as the thirty-fifth state. It was the only one to be formed by separating from a Confederate state, and was the first to separate from any state since Maine split from Massachusetts in 1820. Along with Nevada, West Virginia was also one of the only two states admitted to the Union during the Civil War.

Even prior to that, its history was not without episodes of strife. In the 1670s, a powerful Native American tribe of Iroquois drove out other Indian communities from the region to preserve their land as a hunting ground.

From 1607 to 1776, England considered the area of today's West Virginia to be part of its Virginia Colony. In the early 1700s, German settlers from Pennsylvania founded New Mecklenburg, today called Shepherdstown, West Virginia. Other settlers followed.

Around 1750, a survey team composed mainly of Virginians explored the area of the current West Virginia, proposing a fourteenth American colony to be established with the name of "Vandalia." It did not come to be. Then, in 1776, with the coming of the American Revolution, the movement to create a new state in the region was revived. This time the petition to Congress called it "Westsylvania." It also did not come to pass.

Between 1776 and 1863, the United States considered this area to be the western part of the state of Virginia. However, residents of western Virginia grew increasingly dissatisfied with their situation, feeling the state's government was dominated by wealthy planters from the east. The coming of the Civil War brought things to a boiling point.

When those who they considered to be the planter elite of eastern Virginia voted to secede from the Union in 1861, residents of western counties created a separate government. This time, the U.S. Congress saw the value in adding a new state to the Union. Possible names included Allegheny, Augusta, Columbia, Kanawha, New Virginia, Vandalia (again), Western Virginia, and ultimately West Virginia.

West Virginia sent about an equal number of soldiers to both the Union and Confederate armies, about 22,000–25,000 each. This made for a difficult atmosphere in the state. As Snell (2011) points out, West Virginians were "regularly fighting against each other, in some cases, neighbors against neighbors and families against themselves" (189).

When the war was finally over in 1865, West Virginia was among the states that most needed to forget the recent past and move on to the future. After so much wartime deprivation, they were ready for some fun. One place they found it was at an amusement park.

As opposed to fairs and traveling carnivals, an amusement park is a permanent place that is set aside to offer attractions such as games, rides, and other entertainment, usually for the whole family. In the 1800s, amusement parks in America were a relatively recent development. According to Silverman (2019), "the oldest continuously-running park in the world is Bakken, in Klampenborg, Denmark, which has been gladding crowds since 1583" (11), while in America, "the nation's oldest amusement park is Bristol, Connecticut's 1846 Lake Compounce" (11).

During the late 1800s, there was a wave of industrial innovation in the United States that created mechanical rides like the steam-powered carousel. In addition, the nation's amusement parks were highly influenced by the World Columbian Exposition of 1893 in Chicago. The site was ablaze with new electric lights, earning it the name "The White City." It merged amusements, engineering, and even education as it aimed to entertain the masses. A new feature at the White City called the "midway" contained rides, concessions, and diversions, such as penny arcades, games of chance, shooting galleries, and a variety of shows.

The World Columbian Exposition opened on May 1, 1893, and only ran until October 30 of that same year. But it set the template for the burgeoning growth of amusement parks across the nation.

In the Gilded Age of the 1890s, most of the United States had recovered from the Civil War. Average Americans enjoyed more leisure and higher wages than at any time in the past. They loved the new technology of the age which brought improved transportation to get to the parks, as well as exciting new rides like roller coasters, which they found highly entertaining.

In Brooklyn, New York, just outside New York City, amusement parks mushroomed at Coney Island: Sea Lion Park in 1895, Steeplechase Park in 1897, Luna Park in 1903, and Dreamland in 1904. By 1910, Coney Island was such a success that on some days, it could attract a million people.

The 1920s were a golden age for amusement parks as they sprang up across the country. However, the Great Depression of the 1930s and World War II in the 1940s saw their decline. By the 1950s, many of the older parks closed. Some, with their facilities made primarily of wood, burned to the ground. Others would be demolished to make way for postwar development and suburban housing.

Those that remained faced a new challenge. According to Swick (2017), "The 1960s saw changes in American culture and interests" (258). Television was the prime source of entertainment, and California's dazzling Disneyland, which opened in 1955, made older amusement parks seem outdated. In 1964, Coney Island's Steeplechase Park, which was once the superstar of amusement parks, closed.

Amusement parks in West Virginia followed a similar pattern. **Lake Shawnee Amusement Park** in Mercer County opened in 1927 during the "Golden Age." It closed for good in 1966. The park had been built on land where there had been a bloody conflict between white settlers and Shawnee Indians. Three of the settlers' children were kidnapped and killed, which some said left a curse on the land.

The now-abandoned Lake Shawnee Amusement Park in West Virginia enjoyed a golden age in the 1920s. Today considered one of the most haunted places in West Virginia, at least a half-dozen people died in accidents at the park. Near the swings where a little girl was killed, witnesses have claimed to see the ghost of a child with her pink dress covered in blood. (Edward Lange/Dreamstime.com)

In addition to its past history, at least a half-dozen people died in accidents at the park. The abandoned remains of Lake Shawnee Amusement Park are now considered one of the most haunted places in West Virginia. Witnesses have reported seeing the apparition of a man as well as a little boy who drowned in the park's swimming pond. Others claim to hear the sound of wooden swings creaking. Those swings were the place where a little girl in a pink ruffled dress was killed when a truck backed into the path of the swing. Today, witnesses have claimed to see the ghost of a little girl in pink, with her dress covered in blood.

SOME OTHER REPORTEDLY HAUNTED PLACES IN WEST VIRGINIA

The **Droop Mountain Battlefield** in Pocahontas County commemorates the final significant battle fought in West Virginia during the Civil War. On November 6, 1863, Union troops under General William Averell were victorious over the Confederates, driving them south into what is now Virginia. The fight lasted all day, much of it in hand-to-hand combat. The best estimate of the number of men who were killed during the battle or succumbed to wounds is at least seventy-eight men (forty-five Union soldiers and thirty-three Confederates). The site became Droop Mountain Battlefield State Park as a memorial to those who lost their lives here. Since then, visitors have reported a variety of paranormal occurrences, including the sounds of a battle and galloping horses, as well as the screams of the combatants. Sightings include the apparitions of fighting men and one report of an exhausted-looking Civil War soldier slumped against a tree. Another report came from a logger who stopped at Droop Mountain State Park to camp for the night near the small cemetery that contains the graves of Confederate soldiers. He claims to have heard the sound of rustling leaves on a windless night. Looking up, he saw a manifestation floating past, that of a Confederate soldier who was headless. The apparition was possibly the spirit of one of the many casualties during the Civil War by cannon fire, which often decapitated men when struck by hurtling cannon balls.

The town of **Harpers Ferry** is well-known not only for its historical significance but also for its alleged hauntings. Harpers Ferry (which according to the West Virginia Tourism Office has no apostrophe in its name) can trace its origins back to 1733 when a ferry service was established across the Potomac River. The community held strategic importance from the beginning, being located at the spot where the Potomac and Shenandoah Rivers meet. It can boast of two prestigious designations, with the lower part town being the Harpers Ferry National Historical Park and the other being the separate Harpers Ferry Historic District. Many of the buildings date back to the 1800s, but its significance in American history goes beyond the landmark status of its architecture. Harpers Ferry is best known as the place where abolitionist John Brown attempted to raid the town's arsenal in 1859, planning to use the weapons to help free slaves. After being captured by troops under a young Army officer named Robert E. Lee, John Brown was hanged for treason. During the Civil War, the town was held at different times by both Union and Confederate troops. It is no wonder the whole town is said to be haunted. The most common report is hearing ghostly strains of military fife and drum music, which is said to signal the presence of some phantom army marching past. Civilian spirits include some who value etiquette. At a museum, the manager reported often hearing footsteps and children's voices. Usually, she said good morning to them when she opened the museum each day. One day she forgot to speak, and the audio on one of her displays came alive by itself. As soon as she realized what she had done and offered a belated greeting, the sound stopped.

Lewisburg is a West Virginia town where the entire historic district is said to be haunted instead of just one building. At one spot, visitors say that at night they hear moaning, screams, and cries of pain coming from the Old Stone Church. Since the building had been used as a Civil War hospital, the ghostly sounds are thought to be the spirits of wounded soldiers. At the General Lewis Inn, the town's most famous spirit is said to be the ghost of a lady named Zona Heaster Shue who was killed by her husband in 1897. Zona's spirit attained lasting fame by helping to convict the sinister spouse who brutally murdered her, a man by the name of Erasmus Stribbling Trout Shue. Initially, there were no suspects, and Zona Shue's death was thought to be from natural causes. According to the local legend, Zona appeared to her mother, Mrs. Heaster, in a dream four weeks after the funeral. The ghost allegedly appeared first as a bright light, then slowly formed and filled the air with a chill. The apparition said that Shue was a cruel, abusive man who had attacked Zona. To demonstrate that the husband had broken her neck, the ghostly specter turned her head around until it was facing backward. The spirit is said to have visited Mrs. Heaster for four nights in a row. Authorities reopened the case and found Zona's husband guilty of murder. Mrs. Heaster's claims were used in court and helped to convict her son-in-law. The state of West Virginia erected a state historical marker near the cemetery where Zona Shue is buried, stating ". . . her spirit appeared to her mother to describe how she was killed by her husband. . . . Only known case in which testimony from a ghost helped convict a murderer."

The **Trans-Allegheny Lunatic Asylum** in Weston opened for patients in 1864. At first, it appeared to be a humane environment where fresh air, sunlight, and a pleasant-looking building were intended to serve as a healing environment. Steadily, however, things went downhill. Part of the problem was overcrowding. It is said that by the 1950s, when it was still in use, the facility designed for 250 people housed almost ten times that many patients in vastly overcrowded conditions. Many had to sleep in shifts so the bed could be reused. Part of the problem was that people were confined not only for what would today be called mental health issues but also for conditions ranging from alcoholism to women's change of life. Patients were physically restrained by being shackled as well as being subjected to electroshock therapy and lobotomies that were performed with an icepick, which usually left them in a vegetative state. It is believed that hundreds of patients died during the asylum's lifespan of more than a century, which ended in 1994 due to reforms in mental health treatment and the deterioration of the building. Today, it appears that the spirits of many who died there are still confined within its walls. Along with seeing apparitions walking through walls and orbs of light moving rapidly down the hallways, visitors have reported the sound of a voice saying "Get out!" in a ward where several patients had committed suicide and another patient had been stabbed to death. Objects are said to move, including those that are apparently thrown at male guests by a ghost named Ruth, who was said to hate men while she was alive and used to throw things at them. Now, in her ghostly form, Ruth is still apparently none too fond of males, retaining her reputation for throwing things at them. Hysterical laughter has been heard emanating from empty rooms. But of all the manifestations at the Trans-Allegheny Lunatic Asylum, one is particularly poignant. It is said to be of a young girl called Lily who was born when her mother gave birth to her while at the asylum. Apparently, having no other family members who would take her in, Lily died at age nine after spending every day of her short life confined within the stone walls of the asylum. Perhaps knowing no other home, Lily is said to appear there wearing a white dress. She reportedly plays with a ball by rolling it along the floor and to play music on a phantom music box. The manifestation of Lily is also said to talk, but the most unnerving sound she makes is to giggle in a way that witnesses who experienced it have described as both sweet and horrifying at the same time.

FURTHER READING

Silverman, Stephen. *The Amusement Park: 900 Years of Thrills and Spills, and the Dreamers and Schemers Who Built Them.* New York: Black Dog & Leventhal, 2019.

Snell, Mark. *West Virginia and the Civil War: Mountaineers Are Always Free.* Charleston, SC: The History Press, 2011.

Swick, Gerald. *West Virginia Histories: Unique People, Unusual Events, and the Occasional Ghost.* Nashville, TN: Grave Distractions Publications, 2017.

50

Wisconsin

Popularly known as "America's Dairyland," Wisconsin is honored both by those who love eating cheese and those who love wearing it. Fans of the state's Green Bay Packers NFL football team support the players by wearing big yellow "cheesehead" hats.

As with so many states, the name Wisconsin is derived from a Native American word, in this case, one that was given to today's Wisconsin River. Tribes that lived in the area included the Kickapoo, Ojibwa, Pottawatomie, and Winnebago. After 1673, when French explorer Jacques Marquette became the first European to reach the Wisconsin River, writers in France transcribed the word from his journal as "Ouisconsin." Hordes of English speakers arrived in the early 1800s, after which the legislature of Wisconsin Territory anglicized it, making the current spelling official in 1845.

Following the journey of exploration by Marquette and Louis Jolliet, Frenchmen established some fur trading posts in Wisconsin, but not much in the way of permanent settlements. Britain won control of the region in 1763 following France's defeat in the French and Indian War.

At first, like the French before them, the British were interested in little but the fur trade. The British remained in control of the Wisconsin region until after the War of 1812 when victorious America established its presence there. After the discovery of rich deposits of lead, mining replaced fur trading, soon supplemented by wheat farming.

Formally created as the Wisconsin Territory in 1836, the completion of the Erie Canal and other transportation routes boosted the population of settlers in Wisconsin enough for statehood to be attained in 1848 when Wisconsin entered the Union as its thirtieth state. After the Civil War ended in 1865, farmers in Wisconsin shifted from wheat to dairy production, which they found more profitable.

In the twentieth century, Wisconsin's scenery stimulated a new growth sector of the economy: tourism. Much of the attraction was the state's abundance of waterways that made it appealing for people to escape the concrete canyons of nearby mid-American cities like Chicago, Detroit, and Milwaukee. According to Janik (2010), in Wisconsin, "One can stand on a ridge between two streams, one headed for the icy waters of the North Atlantic and the other for the sultry swamps around New Orleans" (6). In addition to its many rivers, Wisconsin's breezy lakefronts drew thousands of tourists trying to beat the heat each summer.

In the late nineteenth and early twentieth century, for the first time in U.S. history, average Americans enjoyed an increased degree of prosperity and leisure allowing them to escape the stifling temperatures in the city. It is difficult for many people today to grasp what the world was like before the advent of air conditioning. It was especially brutal in large cities where the heat was trapped, radiating in waves off asphalt. Many average people saved all year to afford a vacation in the mountains, while others checked into a resort hotel or rented a summer house where they could enjoy cool ocean air or lakeside breezes.

However, rich denizens of the Gilded Age had the time and money to enjoy summer lodgings whenever they wanted, for as long as they wanted—no rentals for them. Just as they strove to out-build and out-do each other with their mansions in town, they focused on impressing their friends by constructing elaborate summer homes.

Newport, Rhode Island, was a bastion of these massive vacation palaces (which the wealthy called "cottages"). Among those still standing in Newport are McAuley Hall (built in 1882), Ochre Court and Marble House (both 1892), The Elms and Vernon Court (both 1901), Rosecliff (1902), and perhaps the best-known summer "cottage" of all, The Breakers, built by the Vanderbilt family in 1895, still attracting scores of tourists each year.

Wisconsin, with its breezy lakes and waterways, also attracted moguls to build summer homes. One of the most legendary is **Summerwind**.

Sometimes known as the Lamont Mansion, Summerwind was built on the shores of West Bay Lake near Land O'Lakes, Wisconsin. In 1916, businessman Robert Lamont purchased a fishing lodge that stood there and embarked on remodeling that is said to have taken two years to complete. Thus, it became the place to beat the heat for Lamont and his family. They had even more incentive to find a place to escape to after Lamont accepted the position of U.S. Secretary of Commerce under President Herbert Hoover. Lamont took office in March of 1929, just a few months before the devastating Stock Market crash. He left the post in 1932, with Lamont's tenure as secretary of commerce falling solidly in the Great Depression, often considered the worst possible time for commerce in American history.

One local legend is that Lamont fired a pistol in the house one night at what he thought was a either an intruder or a ghost. In either case, he allegedly became so unsettled that he and his family abandoned the house.

The property passed through a number of owners before the family of Arnold and Ginger Hinshaw bought it in the early 1970s. Following their purchase, another oft-told tale is that the Hinshaws and their children were so disturbed by alleged hauntings that Arnold suffered a nervous breakdown and Ginger attempted suicide.

Godfrey (2010) describes Summerwind as brooding next to the chilly, lapping waters of the lake, "sheltering not only a succession of human residents but also dancing ghosts, a bat colony, and even a boarded-up corpse" (6).

The Hinshaw family reported vague shapes and shadows flickering down the hallways, as well as the sounds of mumbled voices in darkened, empty rooms that would stop when anyone walked in to check. Most alarming to them was said to be the ghost of the woman who floated rhythmically back and forth past the French doors that led to the dining room.

Part of the home's reputation was that it certainly seemed to engender stories of its haunting. It did not help matters when it turned out to be Ginger Hinshaw's father Raymond Bober, who disseminated stories of the supernatural at Summerwind.

In 1979, writing under the pen name "Wolfgang Von Bober," he wrote a book called *The Carver Effect: A Paranormal Experience*, in which he claimed the mansion was haunted by eighteenth-century explorer Jonathan Carver. There was indeed a man named Carver who claimed to have explored part of Wisconsin in the 1760s. However, Carver's claims were not recognized by the authorities. In 1778, Carver published a book called *Travels Through the Interior Parts of North America in the Years 1766, 1767, and 1768*. Following his death, some of Carver's heirs claimed that he had obtained a land grant from Sioux Indians for a large area of Wisconsin during his expedition, although the grant was not found legally valid and was later called a fraud.

According to the "Wolfgang Von Bober" narrative, Summerwind was abandoned due to alleged supernatural activity. Bober reported seeing a ghost that he believed was Jonathan Carver. He cited shadow figures, strange unexplained noises, and the discovery of human remains behind a secret door in one of the closets. Bober also stated that the family could not get workers to enter the home to do remodeling work because of its fearsome reputation, such as rooms having the power to change shape and dimensions at will.

In 1986, the house was said to be purchased by investors who had plans for the structure. However, during a severe storm in 1988, Summerwind was struck by lightning and burned to the ground. Today, only the foundations and stone chimneys remain. Yet, Summerwind still has the power to capture the imagination. People claim that they have seen ghosts and heard disembodied voices in the ruins where lovely Summerwind used to proudly stand.

SOME OTHER REPORTEDLY HAUNTED PLACES IN WISCONSIN

At the **Dartford Cemetery** in Green Lake, Wisconsin, there have been reports of various paranormal events, including orbs of light, shadowy figures, and unexplained sounds. One phenomenon occurs when visitors attempt to sit on top of a particular mausoleum. Anyone who does so is said to be pushed off by the ghost of a child who is buried there. There have also been apparitions of Civil War soldiers marching through the cemetery, but probably the supernatural being who is most widely known at the graveyard has the memorable name of Chief Highknocker. His name is said to be derived from the stovepipe hat that he always wore. On his tombstone, the dates of his birth and death, 1820–1911, are listed. It is said that when he died, he was the last chief of his tribe in the area. The legend is that he drowned in 1911 when he attempted to swim across a river while making his way to Green Lake, which was considered to be a sacred location by the Native Americans. If Chief Highknocker made the pilgrimage in 1911 and died trying to reach his destination, he did so when he was ninety-one years old. His tombstone is carved with the unsettling image of a man said to be Highknocker himself, with the gravesite marked by a moss-covered boulder taken from the lake that has his name and date of death. Today, there are reports at the cemetery of a Native American apparition in ceremonial dress. For reasons perhaps known only to himself, this spirit is said to make mysterious scratches on the headstones of fellow graveyard residents.

The **Grand Opera House** in Oshkosh was built in 1883. Like many playhouses of its age, the Grand went through various incarnations depending on the public's taste in entertainment at the time. When it opened, opera appealed to the community. Soon, touring plays were presented at the Grand by traveling troupes of actors (known as "troupers"). In the first part of the twentieth century, vaudeville was in vogue. Finally, motion pictures replaced them all. The Grand Opera House went through all those phases, and until the advent of movies, it attracted top-notch live performers, including Enrico Caruso, Mark Twain, the Marx Brothers, and the legendary Harry Houdini, who many assumed was an exotic East European, but who actually grew up as Erik Weisz in the nearby All-American town of Appleton, Wisconsin. Even with all that star power, the most well-known apparition who is said to haunt the theater is its long-dead stage manager, Percy Keene. There have been reports of a man in the balcony wearing a white shirt and small round glasses, along with a friendly smile, whose description matched that of Percy. Others have seen the same face looking out of an upstairs window as they passed the building. There have been reports of doors slamming for no apparent reason, lights turning on and off, mysterious footsteps being heard, and temperature drops along with the sight of a glowing image and strange orange-tinted mists hovering on the stage. One actor reported walking suddenly into a dressing room one night, only to come face-to-face with another occupant: the apparition of a man in turn-of-the-century clothing who was holding a playbill from a show that was performed in 1895.

The pleasant-sounding **Maribel Caves Hotel** in Maribel, Wisconsin, has acquired a less attractive nickname: Hotel Hell. It was constructed from limestone blocks in a style resembling a medieval castle or fortress. The hotel was built on the site of the original health spa in 1900, attracting thousands of guests through the years who sought to be invigorated by the waters of Maribel Springs. However, as the hotel's fortunes rose and fell with the times, it was operated by various owners. Some reported strange occurrences, including the mysterious death of one owner's daughter. Business was affected as the hotel gained the reputation of being haunted by angry spirits. There were tales of apparitions, floating objects, unsettling feelings, and people being touched by unseen hands. During a time when the hotel was closed, rumors began circulating that a coven of witches used the empty building. Its reputation grew darker with allegations that the witches had opened a portal to Hell, allowing dark entities to dominate the structure. If

Maribel Caves Hotel in Maribel, Wisconsin, has acquired a less attractive nickname: Hotel Hell. Its sinister reputation grew with allegations that witches opened a portal to Hell, allowing dark entities to dominate the structure. Angry shrieking spirits are said to haunt the now-abandoned ruins, including the ghostly apparition of a man who looms over the bare bones of the building. (Rhbabiak13/Dreamstime.com)

there were indeed dark spirits that came from "down below," perhaps they grew homesick for its eternal hellfire. With no known cause, the building was engulfed in flames in 1985, reducing it to rubble with only its limestone skeleton remaining. With its gutted, eerie appearance, it was then that the "Hotel Hell" name really took hold. There have been reports of the ghostly apparition of a man who looms over the bones of the building. Sometimes he is said to appear where windows used to be, always facing outward. Strange voices and startling shrieks are said to be heard from the basement area. Some claim that rocks and other objects on the premises move on their own. Others have claimed the sensation of feeling cold hands pressed on their back when they walk around the ruins. Visitors were discouraged from dropping by when the remains of the structurally unsound building were almost leveled by a tornado. Like some businesses that never quite seem to be a success, the Maribel Caves Hotel has seen its share of hard luck.

Wealthy Charles F. Pfister of Milwaukee was an extremely successful banker, financier, and newspaper publisher. He also strove to fulfill his father's vision of building the greatest hotel in the city. Milwaukee's lavish **Pfister Hotel** opened in 1893, boasting the latest Gilded Age amenities, such as electricity throughout the hotel, fireproofing, and thermostat controls in each room. The state's Republican convention filled the hotel to capacity in 1894 after which word of the lodging's regal elegance and deluxe service spread far and wide. Charles Pfister lived for many years in one of hotel's suites, personally overseeing its progress as the Pfister Hotel became known as the "Grand Hotel of the West." He guided the hotel as it became the preferred location for political functions and official events. It also attracted upscale businessmen, celebrities, and visiting dignitaries, including U.S. presidents since the age of William McKinley. To some people, however, presidential visits take a distant second place compared to stopovers by professional baseball and basketball teams when they are in town. According to the Major League Baseball website, pro ballplayers have reported a wide range of paranormal activity when they stayed in the hotel. The supernatural antics reached the point that one year, some players refused to stay there for "away" games after reporting suspicious occurrences. These included apparitions with physical features very similar to Charles Pfister himself, apparently still keeping an eye on things. There were also reports of air conditioning and television sets switching on and off by themselves, the sound of disembodied voices, unexplained electrical glitches, and objects being moved and manipulated. One player kept hearing someone knocking on his door, but found no one there when he looked. Another was startled to see his iPod switch on by itself, vibrate wildly, and bounce itself to the edge of the table. When the athlete put the device back where it belonged, it began doing the same thing again. Yet, another baseball player took appropriate action: after being awakened by pounding noises from behind his headboard, he was so rattled that he took a bat with him to bed for protection.

FURTHER READING

Clair, Michael. "The Most Frightening Haunted Baseball Stories from Milwaukee's Pfister Hotel." *Cut4 by MLB.com*, October 20, 2018. https://www.mlb.com/cut4/haunted-baseball-stories-from-pfister-hotel-c298043052

Godfrey, Linda S. *Haunted Wisconsin: Ghosts and Strange Phenomena of the Badger State*. Mechanicsburg, PA: Stackpole Books, 2010.

Janik, Erika. *A Short History of Wisconsin*. Madison: Wisconsin Historical Society Press, 2010.

51

Wyoming

Referring to the state of Wyoming, Larson (1990) quotes a popular postwar journalist and author in stating, "'Here is America, high, naked and exposed,' observed John Gunther in *Inside USA*" (1). It is said there are few places in the country that have the feel of the Old West quite like Wyoming. With rugged mountains and vast prairies, the landscape often lends itself to a feeling of isolation that can be both beautiful and unsettling. Along with Alaska, Wyoming is one of the least densely populated states in the Union.

Before the arrival of Europeans, today's Wyoming had room enough in those same wide open spaces for a number of Native American tribes, including Arapaho, Crow, Lakota, and Shoshone, among others. Like much of the West, the region would come under the control of various nations in the eighteenth and nineteenth centuries. Parts of Wyoming were claimed by Spain and later by Mexico as part of Alta California. At the end of the Mexican War in 1848, the area was ceded to the victorious United States.

The name applied to the "Wyoming Territory" after the Civil War was, like many, originally a derivation from a Native American term. However, it was already widely known by many Americans in the early 1800s. The Wyoming Valley in Pennsylvania was popularized in an 1809 poem called *Gertrude of Wyoming: A Pennsylvanian Tale* by Thomas Campbell. The poem was based on the Battle of Wyoming in 1778 during the American Revolution.

After the Civil War, the expansion of the railroad throughout the American West brought increasing numbers of people to the Wyoming Territory, especially those who wanted to try their hand at mining. But mining was often a boom-and-bust proposition. Permanent residents were scattered and sparse. This led to a significant historical development for the future of women's rights.

Wyoming, like several other western territories, did not have a large population. In particular, there were very few women, who were seen as essential for the kind of permanent settlement that was needed for eventual statehood. Historians suggest that to attract more of a family friendly female element to what was considered the Wild Frontier, the Wyoming Territory extended voting rights to women in 1869, the first in the nation to do so. Those same rights were in place when Wyoming was admitted into the Union as the forty-fourth state in 1890. Therefore, by 1920, when American women received the right to vote nationwide, the female population of Wyoming had already been voting for half a century.

It is an unfortunate irony that with its history of human rights, Wyoming was embroiled in what many historians consider to be one of the worst human rights violations in America's history: the internment of Japanese Americans during World War II.

On February 19, 1942, shortly after Japan attacked Pearl Harbor in Hawaii, U.S. president Franklin Roosevelt authorized the forced incarceration of Japanese Americans for reasons involving what was said to be national security amid fears of sabotage. Although it was initially also said to be for their own protection to avoid revenge by angry crowds, many Japanese American internees noted that the guns in the guard towers were pointed inside—at them—not potential mobs outside the gates.

Of about one hundred twenty thousand people of Japanese ancestry who were taken from their homes, almost two-thirds were U.S. citizens. The criteria for internment was said by one of the relocation program's directors to be "one drop of Japanese blood," including orphaned infants who had been adopted by American families.

Most internees had been West Coast residents, who were taken to remote regions of the interior. The isolated relocation camps were located at Poston and Gila River (both in Arizona); Rohwer and Jerome (both in Arkansas); Manzanar and Tule Lake (both in desolate areas of inland California); Granada, Colorado; Minidoka, Idaho; Topaz, Utah; and Heart Mountain, Wyoming.

The internees were taken from their homes by soldiers and were told to sell their houses, possessions, and businesses within days. Some were sold for pennies on the dollar; others simply had to be abandoned. Even beloved pets had to be left behind. Each person could bring with them only what they could carry. They did not know where they were being taken, how they would be treated, or how long they would be gone.

Heart Mountain was similar to the other internment facilities for Japanese Americans, having more than ten thousand people incarcerated there. Upon arrival at the camps, which were enclosed by barbed wire, the people were housed in tarpaper barracks. Food was poor, and there was inadequate medical care. None of the barracks had bathrooms or running water. There were communal mess halls and latrines. Wood burning stoves were eventually installed in the barracks to provide some level of heat in the winter.

According to Steven Bingo's history of Heart Mountain Relocation Center, guard towers were situated at strategic points and staffed by military personnel. The camp had a segregated administrative area that included a military police section in addition to a segregated residential section for white personnel.

American citizens among the internees petitioned for what they considered to be their constitutional rights. However, this met with little, if any, success. In 1943, Wyoming's legislature passed a bill denying American citizens interned at Heart Mountain Internment Camp the right to vote. Holscher (2014) says that the legislation may seem shocking in retrospect, "although probably not as shocking as internment" (56).

Shock was an emotion felt by many internees, especially by the American citizens among them, along with worry, depression, shame, and a sense of helplessness and dislocation. The enforced idleness, loss of purpose, and harsh living conditions added to their anguish. About two thousand died from disease while in camp while others are said to have killed themselves.

Worry among internees increased when many of their sons who were born with American citizenship left the camps when they volunteered or were drafted to serve in the U.S. military. An estimated thirty-three thousand Japanese Americans served in the military during the World War II era. About eight hundred were killed in action. One of these "Nisei" regiments, the 442nd Infantry, became the most decorated unit in U.S. military history. Another Japanese American battalion, the 522nd Field Artillery, liberated the Nazi concentration camp at Dachau.

Even after the war was over in 1945, many lives among the Japanese American internees at camps in America remained shattered. When they were freed, many, especially the elderly, had no place to go. They were forcibly put on trains and buses back to where they had originally been removed, where nothing awaited them. Some committed suicide.

With the trauma experienced by many people who were incarcerated at Heart Mountain, it is said to be one of the most haunted places in Wyoming. Their anguished spirits may still remain. Today, the **Heart Mountain Interpretive Center** illustrates the heartbreak many suffered during their years of confinement. Visitors often say they experience a chilling, uneasy feeling while there, especially after dark. Nighttime is said to be when alleged shadow people come out. There have been reports of cold spots, phantom footsteps, and unexplained noises in the building.

A unique element of the alleged hauntings at the Heart Mountain Interpretive Center is one that is often reported by daytime visitors who say they felt a friendly spirit guiding them around the grounds. Some might say that perhaps kindness, even as embodied by a friendly ghost, might be considered a step in the right direction.

SOME OTHER REPORTEDLY HAUNTED PLACES IN WYOMING

At the **Fort Laramie Historical Site** in Fort Laramie, Wyoming, visitors often report phantom footsteps and doors that open by themselves, possibly manifestations of the hundreds of soldiers who called it home. Fort Laramie was founded in 1849 as a military post when Indian attacks on westbound settlers became more common. By 1850, a fur trading post was added to the fort. Its most well-known ghost is neither a soldier nor a trader. Called the "Lady in Green," she was the daughter of the agent in charge of the trading post. She loved to ride horses, but knowing the dangers on the frontier, her father ordered her to never leave the compound without an escort. One day, she slipped away on a big black horse. She never returned. Her father and men from the fort searched, but no sign of her was ever found. Today, her ghost is said to appear wearing a long, green riding dress and a veiled hat, riding a big black stallion. Inside the fort are said to be other spirits, including those inside the captain's quarters where doors open by themselves, disembodied footsteps are heard, and lights can be seen inside even though it has no electricity. Another spirit is thought to be a cavalry officer who walks through the building, sometimes telling people in a ghostly whisper to "be quiet." Sometimes early in the morning at the cavalry barracks, the sound of heavy boots can be heard around the time soldiers would have turned out for reveille more than a hundred years ago.

The **Historic Plains Hotel** in Cheyenne is said to be haunted by the ghosts of three people who met a sudden, violent end in a deadly love triangle. Built in 1911, the hotel was known for its elegance. With guest rooms having thick velvety carpets and amenities not usually found on the prairie, it was the preferred destination for businessmen, military officers, and honeymoon couples. Soon after its opening, one pair of newlyweds staying at the hotel apparently got into an argument on their wedding night. The groom left their room to go down to the hotel bar. After a while, his bride went to look for him. She saw him leave the bar with another woman, said to be a local lady of the evening. The bride followed them to the woman's fourth floor bedroom. Bursting in, the bride shot her new husband and the other woman, then shot herself. Today, there are three entities who are said to be the cast of characters in that tragic story. A female entity, who has been dubbed "Rosie," is reportedly seen wandering the hotel wearing a blue gown, emanating an aura of mourning and regret. A male entity who may be the unfaithful husband is said to roam the hotel dressed formally in a long black coat of early 1900s vintage, black boots, and a white shirt with decorative silver buttons—just right for a groom of the era. Along with seeing these apparitions, witnesses report doors and windows opening or closing by themselves. Housekeeping staff report hearing crying coming from the empty room that had been the honeymoon couple's. The third member of this triangle manifests herself as a female spirit wearing a short red dress with white lace. Apparently, she harbors a grudge against new brides. Staffers report that one Halloween, two mannequins were dressed as a bride and groom. One staffer saw the apparition of a woman standing next to the mannequins when suddenly the bride mannequin toppled over, with the apparition vanishing into thin air.

The **Irma Hotel** in Cody, Wyoming, is known for its pedigree by having been built in 1902 by the legendary Buffalo Bill Cody. The hotel was named for Buffalo Bill's daughter Irma Louise Cody. Perhaps to keep an eye on her namesake, Irma is said to be haunting the property. Room 16 of the hotel is where Irma Cody Garlow lived before she died of pneumonia brought about by an attack of influenza in 1918 when she was thirty-five years old. Her death took place just a few days after the same illness took the life of her husband, hotel manager Fred Garlow. She had outlived her famous father by only one year. Today, there are rumors that her spirit appears in the Irma Hotel as a mysterious woman in white, roaming the hallways at night. However, her spirit seems most at home in Room 16, the "Irma Suite," where she used to live. An apparition matching her description appears to guests who have reported her sitting in a rocking chair in the corner of the room. Room 35 is also no stranger to the supernatural world. Visitors staying in that guestroom over the years have reported disturbances like their clothing being moved in the middle of the night, as well as water in the bathroom turning on and off by itself. Historic photos and pictures on the wall of Room 35 are found lying on the floor in places where they would not have fallen naturally from their hook. In Room 35, guests have reported seeing a ghost that appears to be a soldier in a cavalry uniform. He carries a sword, but in something of a departure for cavalry officers, he appears to be missing the lower half of his body. Needless to say, Room 20, the "Colonel Cody Suite," has been the site of high-energy paranormal readings by investigative teams that have been ascribed to visits from Buffalo Bill Cody. Some employees have said they've seen Cody wandering the hallways late at night. There have also been reports of hearing spurs jangle in the bar when there was no one there. During his lifetime, Cody organized panoramic extravaganzas with a cast of hundreds that toured the world. Therefore, there is no reason why he shouldn't keep an eye on his hotel after death.

It is said that Buffalo Bill's Irma Hotel (above) attracted visitors like Annie Oakley and Calamity Jane. But at the **Occidental Hotel** in the town of Buffalo, some of the guests who checked in included showman Buffalo Bill himself, as well as outlaws Butch Cassidy and the Sundance Kid. Built in 1880, the Occidental was located near the Bozeman Trail. It became a popular place to stop off in the Old West, once serving as a saloon and brothel. Today, it is said to be haunted by the spirit of a girl whose mother was a prostitute who worked there in the late 1800s. The daughter is said to have died of cholera in the building when she was a small child. Near the room where she died, guests report seeing the apparition of a young girl with long dark hair, wearing a flowing white gown. While it

Buffalo Bill's Occidental Hotel attracted visitors like Annie Oakley and Calamity Jane to the town of Buffalo. Today, it is said to be haunted by the spirit of a girl whose mother was a prostitute working there in the late 1800s. Near the room where the child died of cholera, guests report seeing the apparition of a young girl with long dark hair, wearing a flowing white gown. (Library of Congress)

has been alleged that she moves furniture around and is responsible for various unexplained ghostly sounds, she has also been known to tap guests on the shoulder while they are sitting in the bar, after which the guests claim to have heard her laughing.

The **Wyoming Territorial Prison** in Laramie was built in 1872 and was known for housing criminals with light sentences. Its inmates had usually been convicted of offenses ranging from theft to manslaughter. With convicted murderers confined to another facility, there were no reported executions at the Wyoming Territorial Prison. Nor were there reports of inmates being killed by guards, other inmates, or poor care. As a young man in 1894, outlaw Butch Cassidy spent eighteen months there for stealing. Although he was not rehabilitated, there is currently an exhibit in his honor at the restored state historic site. The spirit who is said to haunt the prison is not Butch, but an individual named Julius Greenwelch, who not only spent his prison time constructively but is also the only known death to occur there, in his case, of a heart attack. Greenwelch traveled around Wyoming selling the cigars he made but was convicted of killing his wife when he found her in the arms of another man. He was sent to the Wyoming Territorial Prison after being convicted of second degree murder. Being a good salesman, Greenwelch apparently convinced prison officials to allow him to set up a cigar-making operation as a kind of fundraising venture for the prison. However, after only a few years in operation, he died of a sudden heart attack. The small prison closed in 1903 but was restored as a museum in 1989. Greenwelch's cell was removed to make room for a doorway, which may have affronted him. His apparition is said to appear in the space where his old cell used to be. In addition, Greenwelch may have held workmen responsible for eliminating his cell since they occasionally find hammers, drills, and saws to be missing, especially if they are making too much noise. Needless to say, Greenwelch's manifestations are almost always accompanied by the unmistakable scent of cigar smoke.

FURTHER READING

Bingo, Steven. "A Brief History of Heart Mountain Relocation Center." *Wyoming History*, November 8, 2014. https://www.wyohistory.org/encyclopedia/brief-history-heart-mountain-relocation-center

Holscher, Patrick T. *On This Day in Wyoming History*. Charleston, SC: The History Press, 2014.

Larson, T. A. *History of Wyoming, Second Edition*. Lincoln: University of Nebraska Press, 1990.

Appendix: Ghost Tour Road Trips by Region

These are suggestions, organized alphabetically by state, for "Ghost Tour Road Trips." They are listed according to geographic regions of the United States as defined by the U.S. Census Bureau. Websites are listed for the main historical haunted spots described in this book. These online resources will provide more information, directions, days and hours of operation, special events, and whether open to the public. Happy Haunting!

EASTERN UNITED STATES

New England States

Connecticut: Remington Arms, http://www.damnedct.com/remington-arms-bridgeport

Maine: U.S. Route 2A, https://maineanencyclopedia.com/tag/u-s-route-2a

Massachusetts: Salem, https://www.salem.org

New Hampshire: Kimball Castle, http://www.lakesregionchamber.org

Rhode Island: Sprague Mansion, https://www.cranstonhistoricalsociety.org/sprague-mansion

Vermont: University of Vermont, https://www.uvm.edu

Mid-Atlantic States

New Jersey: Lakehurst, https://www.nps.gov/articles/hangar-no-1-lakehurst-naval-air-station.htm

New York: Ellis Island, https://www.nps.gov/elis/index.htm

Pennsylvania: Centralia, https://www.centraliapa.org

South Atlantic States

Delaware: Deer Park Inn, http://www.deerparktavern.com/Home

District of Columbia: Ford's Theatre, https://www.fords.org

Florida: St. Augustine Lighthouse, http://www.staugustinelighthouse.com

Georgia: Bonaventure Cemetery, http://www.bonaventurehistorical.org

Maryland: Chesapeake and Ohio Canal, https://www.nps.gov/choh/index.htm

North Carolina: Ocracoke Island, https://www.outerbanks.com/ocracoke.html

South Carolina: Greenville Tuberculosis Hospital, https://www.goupstate.com/news/20000823/history-of-the-old-tuberculosis-hospital

Virginia: Cold Harbor Battlefield, https://www.nps.gov/rich/learn/historyculture/cold-harbor.htm

West Virginia: Lake Shawnee Amusement Park, https://visitmercercounty.com/lakeshawnee

CENTRAL UNITED STATES

East South Central States

Alabama: Sloss Furnaces, https://www.slossfurnaces.com
Kentucky: Buffalo Trace, https://www.buffalotracedistillery.com
Mississippi: King's Tavern, http://www.kingstavernnatchez.com
Tennessee: Wheatlands, http://visitsevierville.com

East North Central States

Illinois: Robinson Woods, http://fpdcc.com/robinson-woods

Indiana: Edna Collings Bridge, https://goputnam.com/things-to-do-putnam-county/page/2

Michigan: Mackinac Island, https://www.mackinacisland.org

Ohio: Cincinnati Music Hall, https://www.cincinnatiarts.org/music-hall

Wisconsin: Summerwind, Land O'Lakes, https://golandolakeswi.com

West South Central States

Arkansas: Crescent Hotel, https://www.crescent-hotel.com

Louisiana: Marie Laveau Gravesite, Saint Louis Cemetery No. 1, https://www.atlasobscura.com/places/marie-laveaus-tomb

Oklahoma: Fort Gibson Historic Site, https://www.okhistory.org/sites/fortgibson

Texas: Goliad Presidio, https://presidiolabahia.org

West North Central States

Iowa: Squirrel Cage Jail, https://www.thehistoricalsociety.org/museums/squirrel-cage-jail.html

Appendix: Ghost Tour Road Trips by Region

Kansas: Hutchinson Library, http://www.hutchpl.org

Minnesota: Minneapolis City Hall, http://www.ci.minneapolis.mn.us/hpc/landmarks/hpc_landmarks_4th_st_s_315_minneapolis_city_hall

Missouri: Lemp Brewery, http://www.lempmansion.com/history.htm

Nebraska: Museum of Shadows, https://www.museumofshadows.com

North Dakota: St. Joseph's Hospital, https://dickinson58601.com/2017/04/14/old-st-josephs-hospital-in-dickinson-the-most-haunted-place-in-north-dakota

South Dakota: Deadwood, https://www.deadwood.com

WESTERN UNITED STATES

Mountain States

Arizona: Vulture Mine, http://www.vultureminetours.com

Colorado: Stanley Hotel, https://www.stanleyhotel.com

Idaho: Shoshone Ice Caves, http://www.shoshoneicecaves.com/home.html

Montana: Little Bighorn Battlefield, https://www.nps.gov/libi/index.htm

Nevada: Las Vegas, https://www.lasvegasnevada.gov

New Mexico: Santa Fe Prison, http://www.santafeghostandhistorytours.com/SantaFePrison-GhostTour-.html

Utah: Rio Grande Depot, Salt Lake City, https://www.visitsaltlake.com/listing/rio-grande-depot-utah-state-historical-society/55168

Wyoming: Heart Mountain Relocation Center, http://www.heartmountain.org

Pacific States

California: Donner Memorial State Park, http://www.parks.ca.gov/?page_id=503

Oregon: Shanghai Tunnels, http://www.shanghaitunnels.info

Washington: Northern State Mental Hospital, https://www.onlyinyourstate.com/washington/asylum-wa

Bibliography

INTRODUCTION

Argie, Theresa, and Eric Olsen. *America's Most Haunted: The Secrets of Famous Paranormal Places*. New York: Berkley Books, 2014.

Buckley, Christopher. *But Enough about You*. New York: Simon & Schuster, 2014.

Hawthorne, Nathaniel with introduction from Mary Oliver. *Mosses from an Old Manse*. New York: The Modern Library, 2007. Kindle edition.

Sagan, Carl. *The Demon-Haunted World: Science as a Candle in the Dark*. New York: Ballantine Books, 1997.

Shermer, Michael. *The Believing Brain: From Ghosts and Gods to Politics and Conspiracies—How We Construct Beliefs and Reinforce Them as Truths*. New York: St. Martin's Griffin, 2012.

ALABAMA

Sloss Furnaces National Historic Landmark. Accessed February 28, 2020. https://www.slossfurnaces.com

Windham, Kathryn Tucker, and Margaret Gillis Figh. *Thirteen Alabama Ghosts and Jeffrey*. Tuscaloosa: University Alabama Press, 2016.

ALASKA

Borneman, Walter. *Alaska: Saga of a Bold Land—From Russian Fur Traders to the Gold Rush, Extraordinary Railroads, World War II, the Oil Boom, and the Fight Over ANWR*. New York: HarperCollins, 2003.

Naske, Claus, and Herman Slotnick. *Alaska: A History*. Norman: University of Oklahoma Press, 2014.

Ritter, Harry. *Alaska's History: The People, Land, and Events of the North Country*. Portland, OR: Alaska Northwest Books, 1993.

ARIZONA

Blair, Robert. *Tales of the Superstitions: The Origins of the Lost Dutchman's Legend*. Tempe: Arizona Historical Foundation, 1975.

Eppinga, Jane. *Unsolved Arizona: A Puzzling History of Murder, Mayhem & Mystery*. Charleston, SC: History Press, 2015.

Sheridan Thomas E. *Arizona: A History*. Tucson: University of Arizona Press, 2012.

ARKANSAS

Anderson, Layne. *Haunted Legends of Arkansas: Thirteen Historic Sites in the (Super) Natural State*. Little Rock, AR: Plum Street Publishers, 2016.

Hendricks, Nancy. "Taking the Waters." In *Popular Fads and Crazes through American History*. Santa Barbara, CA: Greenwood, 2018.

Steed, Bud. *Haunted Northwest Arkansas*. Charleston, SC: History Press, 2017.

CALIFORNIA

Brown, Dee. *The American West*. New York: Scribner, 2010.

Hoover, Mildred, and Hero Rensch. *Historic Spots in California*. 4th ed. Palo Alto, CA: Stanford University Press, 1990.

Ignoffo, Mary Jo. *Captive of the Labyrinth: Sarah L. Winchester, Heiress to the Rifle Fortune*. Columbia: University of Missouri Press, 2012.

Krist, Gary. *The Mirage Factory: Illusion, Imagination, and the Invention of Los Angeles*. New York: Crown, 2018.

Maxtone-Graham, John. *The Only Way to Cross*. New York: Collier Books, 1972.

May, Antoinette. *Haunted Houses of California: A Ghostly Guide to Haunted Houses and Wandering Spirits*. San Carlos, CA: Wide World Publishing, 2006.

Ogden, Tom. *Haunted Hollywood: Tinseltown Terrors, Filmdom Phantoms, and Movieland Mayhem*. Lanham, MD: Globe Pequot Press, 2015.

Starr, Kevin. *California: A History*. New York: Modern Library, 2007.

Stewart, George R. *The California Trail: An Epic with Many Heroes*. New York: McGraw-Hill, 1962.

Wallis, Michael. *The Best Land under Heaven: The Donner Party in the Age of Manifest Destiny*. New York: W. W. Norton, 2017.

Wellman, Gregory L. *History of Alcatraz Island, 1853–2008*. Charleston, SC: Arcadia Publishing, 2008.

COLORADO

Baker, Dennis. *Ghosts of Colorado*. Atglen, PA: Schiffer Publishing, 2008.

Dallas, Sandra. *Colorado Ghost Towns and Mining Camps*. Norman: University of Oklahoma Press, 1988.

Gallagher, Jolie Anderson. *A Wild West History of Frontier Colorado: Pioneers, Gunslingers and Cattle Kings on the Eastern Plains*. Charleston, SC: The History Press, 2011.

Lamb, Kailyn. *Ghosthunting Colorado*. Covington, KY: Clerisy Press, 2016.

Stansfield, Charles. *Haunted Colorado: Ghosts and Strange Phenomena of the Centennial State*. Mechanicsburg, PA: Stackpole Books, 2011.

CONNECTICUT

Boynton, Cynthia Wolfe. *Connecticut Witch Trials: The First Panic in the New World*. Charleston, SC: The History Press, 2014.

D'Agostino, Thomas, and Arlene Nicholson. *Connecticut Ghost Stories and Legends*. Charleston, SC: The History Press, 2011.

Roth, David Morris. *Connecticut: A History*. New York: W. W. Norton, 1979.

DELAWARE

Benson, Barbara Ellen. *The Delaware Adventure*. Layton, UT: Gibbs Smith, 2006.

Duffy, Jim. *Eastern Shore Road Trips: 27 One-Day Adventures on Delmarva*. Cambridge, MD: Secrets of the Eastern Shore Guides, 2016.

Guice, John. *By His Own Hand?: The Mysterious Death of Meriwether Lewis*. Norman: University of Oklahoma Press, 2011.

Sandoval-Strausz, Andrew. *Hotel: An American History*. New Haven, CT: Yale University Press, 2008.

DISTRICT OF COLUMBIA

Anderson, Brian, and Ford's Theatre Society. *Ford's Theatre*. Charleston, SC: Arcadia Publishing, 2014.

Bordewich, Fergus. *Washington: The Making of the American Capital*. New York: HarperCollins, 2008.

Dickey, J. D. *Empire of Mud: The Secret History of Washington, DC*. Guilford, CT: Lyons Press, 2015.

Wilmeth, Don, and Christopher Bigsby, eds. *The Cambridge History of American Theatre*. New York: Cambridge University Press, 1998.

FLORIDA

Clark, James C. *Hidden History of Florida*. Charleston, SC: The History Press, 2015.

Jones, Ray, and Bruce Roberts. *American Lighthouses: A Comprehensive Guide to Exploring Our National Coastal Treasures*. Guilford, CT: Globe Pequot Press, 2012.

Lower, Catherine, and Cynthia Thuma. *Haunted Florida: Ghosts and Strange Phenomena of the Sunshine State*. Mechanicsburg, PA: Stackpole Books, 2008.

GEORGIA

Dunn, Ryan. *Savannah's Afterlife: True Tales of a Paranormal Investigator*. Atglen, PA: Schiffer Publishing, 2015.

Eggener, Keith. *Cemeteries*. New York: Norton, 2010.

Meyers, Christopher, and David Williams. *Georgia: A Brief History*. Macon, GA: Mercer University Press, 2012.

HAWAII

Daley, Jason. "Five Things to Know about Liliuokalani, the Last Queen of Hawaii." *Smithsonian.com*, November 20, 2017. https://www.smithsonianmag.com/smart-news/five-things-know-about-liliuokalani-last-queen-hawaii-180967155/

Daws, Gavan. *Holy Man: Father Damien of Molokai*. Honolulu: University of Hawaii Press, 1984.

Queen Liliuokalani. *Hawaii's Story by Hawaii's Queen*. Honolulu, HI: Hui Hanai, 2013.

Thompson, Judi. *Supernatural Hawaii*. Atglen, PA: Schiffer Publishing, 2009.

IDAHO

Derig, Betty. *Roadside History of Idaho*. Missoula, MT: Mountain Press, 1996.

Robinson, Russell. *The Story of the Shoshone Indian Ice Caves*. Shoshone, ID: Shoshone Indian Ice Caves Pamphlet, 1978.

Schwantes, Carlos Arnaldo. *In Mountain Shadows: A History of Idaho*. Lincoln: University of Nebraska Press, 1991.

Weeks, Andy. *Haunted Idaho: Ghosts and Strange Phenomena of the Gem State*. Mechanicsburg, PA: Stackpole Books, 2013.

ILLINOIS

Banash, Stan. *Roadside History of Illinois*. Missoula, MT: Mountain Press, 2013.

Johnson, Raymond. *Chicago History: The Stranger Side*. Atglen, PA: Schiffer Publishing, 2014.

Jonnes, Jill. *Urban Forests: A Natural History of Trees and People in the American Cityscape*. New York: Penguin Books, 2016.

Kleen, Michael. *Haunting Illinois: A Tourist's Guide to the Weird and Wild Places of the Prairie State*. Holt, MI: Thunder Bay Press, 2014.

INDIANA

Madison, James H. *The Indiana Way: A State History*. Bloomington: Indiana University Press, 1990.

Miller, Terry, and Ronald G. Knapp. *America's Covered Bridges: Practical Crossings, Nostalgic Icons*. North Clarendon, VT: Tuttle Publishing, 2017.

Willis, Wanda Lou. *Haunted Hoosier Trails: A Guide to Indiana's Famous Folklore and Spooky Sites*. Covington, KY: Clerisy Press, 2004.

IOWA

Lewis, Chad, and Terry Fisk. *The Iowa Road Guide to Haunted Locations*. Eau Clair, WI: Unexplained Research Publishing, 2007.

Worley, Robert. *American Prisons and Jails: An Encyclopedia of Controversies and Trends*. Santa Barbara, CA: ABC-CLIO, 2018.

KANSAS

Coopers, Beth. *Ghosts of Kansas*. Atglen, PA: Schiffer Publishing, 2010.
Jones, Theodore. *Carnegie Libraries Across America: A Public Legacy*. Hoboken, NJ: Wiley, 1997.
Kells, Stuart. *The Library: A Catalogue of Wonders*. Berkeley, CA: Counterpoint, 2017.
Pollard, Justin, and Howard Reid. *The Rise and Fall of Alexandria: Birthplace of the Modern World*. New York: Penguin Books, 2007.
Zink, Adrian. *Hidden History of Kansas*. Charleston SC: The History Press, 2017.

KENTUCKY

Cecil, Sam K. *Bourbon: The Evolution of Kentucky Whiskey*. New York: Turner; 2010.
Klotter, James, and Craig Thompson Friend. *A New History of Kentucky*. Lexington: University Press of Kentucky, 2018.
Slaughter, Thomas P. *The Whiskey Rebellion: Frontier Epilogue to the American Revolution*. New York: Simon & Schuster, 2010.

LOUISIANA

Allured, Janet, and Michael S. Martin. *Louisiana Legacies: Readings in the History of the Pelican State*. Malden, MA: Wiley-Blackwell, 2013.
Long, Carolyn Morrow. *The Tomb of Marie Laveau in St. Louis Cemetery No. 1*. New Orleans, LA: Left Hand Press, 2016.
Taylor, Troy. *Haunted New Orleans: History & Hauntings of the Crescent City*. Charleston, SC: The History Press, 2010.

MAINE

Stansfield, Charles. *Haunted Maine: Ghosts and Strange Phenomena of the Pine Tree State*. Mechanicsburg, PA: Stackpole Books, 2007.
Woodard, Colin. *The Lobster Coast: Rebels, Rusticators, and the Struggle for a Forgotten Frontier*. New York: Penguin Books, 2005.

MARYLAND

Chappelle, Susan. *Maryland: A History*. Baltimore, MD: Johns Hopkins University Press, 1986.

High, Mike. *The C&O Canal Companion*. Baltimore, MD: Johns Hopkins University Press, 2001.
Shaw, Ronald E. *Canals for a Nation: The Canal Era in the United States, 1790–1860*. Lexington: The University Press of Kentucky, 2014.

MASSACHUSETTS

Brown, Richard D. *Massachusetts: A Concise History*. Amherst: University of Massachusetts Press, 2000.
D'Agostino, Thomas. *Haunted Massachusetts*. Atglen, PA: Schiffer Publishing, 2007.
Roach, Marilynne K. *The Salem Witch Trials: A Day-by-Day Chronicle of a Community under Siege*. Lanham, MD: Taylor Trade Publishing, 2004.

MICHIGAN

Barber, Sally. *Myths and Mysteries of Michigan*. Guilford, CT: Globe Pequot Press, 2011.
Sonnenberg, Mike. *Lost in Michigan: History and Travel Stories from an Endless Road Trip*. Saginaw, MI: Etaoin Publishing, 2017.
Usitalo, Kath. *100 Things to Do on Mackinac Island before You Die*. St. Louis, MO: Reedy Press, 2018.

MINNESOTA

Atkins, Annette. *Creating Minnesota: A History from the Inside Out*. St. Paul: Minnesota Historical Society Press, 2008.
Shuler, Jack. *The Thirteenth Turn: A History of the Noose*. New York: Public Affairs Books, 2014.

MISSISSIPPI

Busbee, Westley, Jr. *Mississippi: A History*. Malden, MA: Wiley-Blackwell, 2015.
Salinger, Sharon V. *Taverns and Drinking in Early America*. Baltimore, MD: Johns Hopkins University Press, 2004.

MISSOURI

Christensen, Lawrence, Brad Lookingbill, and William E. Parrish. *Missouri: The Heart of the Nation*. 4th ed. Hoboken, NJ: Wiley-Blackwell, 2019.
Offutt, Jason. *Haunted Missouri: A Ghostly Guide to the Show-Me-State's Most Spirited Spots*. Kirksville, MO: Truman State University Press, 2007.
Spencer, Thomas M., ed. *The Other Missouri History: Populists, Prostitutes, and Regular Folk*. Columbia: University of Missouri, 2005.

MONTANA

Spritzer, Don. *Roadside History of Montana.* Missoula, MT: Mountain Press, 1999.

Stevens, Karen. *More Haunted Montana: Haunted Places You Can Visit—IF YOU DARE!* Helena, MT: Riverbend Publishing, 2010.

NEBRASKA

Boye, Alan. *A Guide to the Ghosts of Lincoln.* Lincoln: University of Nebraska Press, 2013.

Luebke, Frederick. *Nebraska: An Illustrated History.* 2nd ed. Lincoln, NE: Bison Books, 2005.

NEVADA

Bowers, Michael W. *The Sagebrush State: Nevada's History, Government, and Politics.* Reno: University of Nevada Press, 2015.

Cavanaugh, Liz, and Michelle Broussard Honick. *Ghosts, Gangsters, and Gamblers of Las Vegas.* Atglen, PA: Schiffer Publishing, 2009.

NEW HAMPSHIRE

D'Agostino, Thomas. *Haunted New Hampshire.* Atglen, PA: Schiffer Publishing, 2007.

Thompson, M. W. *The Rise of the Castle.* New York: Cambridge University Press, 1991.

Whitney, D. Quincy. *Hidden History of New Hampshire.* Charleston, SC: The History Press, 2008.

NEW JERSEY

Archbold, Rick, and Ken Marschall. *Hindenburg: An Illustrated History.* New York: Grand Central Publishing, 1994.

Dick, Harold G., and Douglas H. Robinson. *The Golden Age of the Great Passenger Airships: Graf Zeppelin and Hindenburg.* Washington, D.C.: Smithsonian Books, 1992.

Zwillenberg, Elias. *New Jersey Haunts.* Atglen, PA: Schiffer Publishing, 2010.

NEW MEXICO

de Aragón, Ray John. *Enchanted Legends and Lore of New Mexico: Witches, Ghosts & Spirits.* Charleston, SC: The History Press, 2012.

Stanko, Stephen, and Wayne Gillespie. *Living in Prison: A History of the Correctional System with an Insider's View.* Santa Barbara, CA: Greenwood, 2004.

NEW YORK

LaMonica, Lisa. *Haunted Catskills.* Charleston, SC: The History Press, 2013.
Reitano, Joanne. *New York State: Peoples, Places, and Priorities: A Concise History with Sources.* New York: Routledge, 2015.
Revai, Cheri. *Haunted New York City: Ghosts and Strange Phenomena of the Big Apple.* Mechanicsburg, PA: Stackpole Books, 2008.
Shorto, Russell. *The Island at the Center of the World: The Epic Story of Dutch Manhattan and the Forgotten Colony That Shaped America.* New York: Vintage, 2005.

NORTH CAROLINA

Little, Benerson. *The Golden Age of Piracy: The Truth Behind Pirate Myths.* New York: Skyhorse, 2016.
Ready, Milton. *The Tar Heel State: A History of North Carolina.* Columbia: University of South Carolina Press, 2005.
Wilson, Patty A. *Haunted North Carolina: Ghosts and Strange Phenomena of the Tar Heel State.* Mechanicsburg, PA: Stackpole Books, 2009.

NORTH DAKOTA

Aasen, Larry. *North Dakota.* Chicago, IL: Arcadia Publishing, 2000.
Kisacky, Jeanne. *Rise of the Modern Hospital: An Architectural History of Health and Healing, 1870–1940.* Pittsburgh: University of Pittsburgh Press, 2017.

OHIO

Cayton, Andrew. *Ohio: The History of a People.* Columbus: Ohio State University Press, 2002.
Kachuba, John. *Ghosthunting Ohio.* Cincinnati, OH: Clerisy Press, 2004.
Katz, Michael B. *In the Shadow of the Poorhouse: A Social History of Welfare in America.* New York: Basic Books, 1996.

OKLAHOMA

Blanton, De Anne, and Lauren Cook. *They Fought Like Demons: Women Soldiers in the Civil War.* New York: Vintage, 2003.
Bouziden, Deborah. *Oklahoma Off the Beaten Path: A Guide to Unique Places.* Lanham, MD: Rowman & Littlefield, 2015.

Grann, David. *Killers of the Flower Moon: The Osage Murders and the Birth of the FBI.* Reprint ed. New York: Vintage, 2018.

Ricksecker, Mike. *Ghosts and Legends of Oklahoma.* Atglen, PA: Schiffer Publishing, 2011.

OREGON

Chandler, JD (sic). *Hidden History of Portland, Oregon.* Charleston, SC: The History Press, 2013.

Hayes, Derek. *Historical Atlas of Washington and Oregon.* Oakland: University of California Press, 2011.

PENNSYLVANIA

Miller, Randall M., and William Pencak, eds. *Pennsylvania: A History of the Commonwealth.* University Park: Penn State University Press, 2002.

Nesbitt, Mark, and Patty A. Wilson. *Haunted Pennsylvania: Ghosts and Strange Phenomena of the Keystone State.* Mechanicsburg, PA: Stackpole Books, 2006.

RHODE ISLAND

D'Agostino, Thomas. *Haunted Rhode Island.* Atglen, PA: Schiffer Publishing, 2005.

Lamphier, Peg A. *Kate Chase and William Sprague: Politics and Gender in a Civil War Marriage.* Lincoln: University of Nebraska Press, 2003.

SOUTH CAROLINA

Edgar, Walter B. *South Carolina: A History.* Columbia: University of South Carolina Press, 1999.

Schlosser, S. E., and Paul Hoffman. *Spooky South Carolina: Tales of Hauntings, Strange Happenings, and Other Local Lore.* Guilford, CT: Globe Pequot Press, 2011.

SOUTH DAKOTA

Hoover, Herbert T., and Edward P. Hogan. *A New South Dakota History.* Sioux Falls, SD: The Center for Western Studies, 2009.

Hunhoff, Bernie. *South Dakota Curiosities: Quirky Characters, Roadside Oddities & Other Offbeat Stuff.* Guilford, CT: Globe Pequot Press, 2010.

TENNESSEE

Buxton, Geordie. *Haunted Plantations: Ghosts of Slavery and Legends of the Cotton Kingdoms.* Charleston, SC: Arcadia Publishing, 2007.

Finch, Jackie Sheckler. *Tennessee off the Beaten Path: A Guide to Unique Places.* Guilford, CT: Globe Pequot Press, 2013.

TEXAS

Calvert, Robert, Arnoldo De Leon, and Gregg Cantrell. *The History of Texas.* 5th ed. Malden, MA: Wiley-Blackwell, 2014.

Williams, Scott, and Donna Ingham. *Texas: Famous Phantoms, Sinister Sites, and Lingering Legends.* Guilford, CT: Lone Star Books, an imprint of Globe Pequot, 2017.

UTAH

Cogley, Christopher, and Rich Briggs. *Utah's Greatest Wonders: A Photographic Journey of the Five National Parks.* Springville, UT: Plain Sight Publishing, 2017.

Weeks, Andy. *Haunted Utah: Ghosts and Strange Phenomena of the Beehive State.* Mechanicsburg, PA: Stackpole Books, 2012.

VERMONT

Bushnell, Mark. *Hidden History of Vermont.* Charleston, SC: The History Press, 2017.

Thelin, John R. *A History of American Higher Education.* Baltimore, MD: Johns Hopkins University Press, 2004.

VIRGINIA

Heinemann, Ronald L., John G. Kolp, Anthony S. Parent Jr., and William G. Shade. *Old Dominion, New Commonwealth: A History of Virginia, 1607–2007.* Charlottesville: University of Virginia Press, 2008.

Rhea, Gordon C. *Cold Harbor: Grant and Lee, May 26–June 3, 1864.* Baton Rouge: Louisiana State University Press, 2002.

Taylor, L. B. *Haunted Virginia: Ghosts and Strange Phenomena of the Old Dominion.* Mechanicsburg, PA: Stackpole Books, 2009.

WASHINGTON

LeWarne, Charles Pierce. *Washington State.* 3rd ed. Seattle: University of Washington Press, 2003.

Porter, Roy. *Madness: A Brief History.* New York: Oxford University Press, 2003.

Stansfield, Charles, and Alan Wycheck. *Haunted Washington: Ghosts and Strange Phenomena of the Evergreen State.* Mechanicsburg, PA: Stackpole Books, 2011.

WEST VIRGINIA

Lawless, Seph. *Abandoned: Hauntingly Beautiful Deserted Theme Parks.* New York: Skyhorse, 2017.

Williams, John Alexander. *West Virginia: A History.* Morgantown: West Virginia University Press, 2003.

WISCONSIN

Axelrod, Alan. *The Gilded Age: 1876–1912: Overture to the American Century.* New York: Sterling, 2017.

Bell, Devon. *Haunted Summerwind: A Ghostly History of a Wisconsin Mansion.* Charleston, SC: The History Press, 2016.

Huhti, Thomas. *Wisconsin.* 7th ed. Berkeley, CA: Moon, 2017.

WYOMING

Moffitt, Linda. *Haunted Wyoming.* Atglen, PA: Schiffer Publishing, 2011.

Reeves, Richard. *Infamy: The Shocking Story of the Japanese American Internment in World War II.* New York: Henry Holt, 2015.

Index

Page numbers in **bold** indicate location of main entries.

African Americans
   in Georgia, 69
   in Illinois, 85
   in Kansas, 103
   in Louisiana, 115, 116
   in Maine, 125
   in Minnesota, 148
   in Ohio, 222
   in South Carolina, 249
   in Tennessee, 262, 263
   in Texas, 270
   in Virginia, 286
Airships, 189–190
Alabama, **1–6**
   Boyington Oak, 3–4
   Dr. John Drish House, 4
   Eliza Battle (steamboat), 4
   Gaineswood, 4–5
   Kenworthy Hall, 5
   Sloss Furnaces, 2–3
   Sweetwater Mansion, 5–6
Alamo (Texas mission), 269
Alaska, **7–12**
   Badarka Road, 9–10
   Begich Tower, 10
   Fairbanks Memorial Hospital, 10–11
   Historic Anchorage Hotel, 11
   Hotel Captain Cook Inlet Tower Hotel, 11
   Motherlode Lodge, 11–12
   Red Onion Saloon, 7–9
   Wendy Williamson Auditorium, 12
American Dream (concept), 25, 202
Amusement parks, 298–300
Arizona, **13–18**
   Bird Cage Theatre, 15–16
   Copper Queen Hotel, 16–17
   Hotel San Carlos, 17
   Jerome Grand Hotel, 17
   Oliver House, 17–18
   Thornton Road Domes, 18
   Vulture Mine, 13–15
Arkansas, **19–24**
   Allen House, 21–22
   Basin Park Hotel, 22
   Crescent Hotel, 20–21
   Gurdon Light, 22–23
   Judge Parker Court House, 23
   King Opera House, 23
   Monte Ne Ruins, 24
   Old Malco Theatre, 23–24
   Peel Mansion, 24

Bankhead, Tallulah, 133
Battlefields, 286–288
Begich, Nick, 10
Belasco, David, 201
Bernstein, Leonard, 137
Blackbeard (Edward Teach), 185–186, 209–210, 252, 253
Blade, Maxwell, 23
Blair Witch Project (movie), 263
Boggs, Hale, 10
Bonanza (television series), 169
Bonnet, Stede, 253–254
Borden, Lizzie, 135
Bourbon, 109–111
Brady, Matthew, 56
Breweries, 158–160
Bridges, 92–93
Broadway (New York Theater District), 201, 241, 264
Brothels, 7–9
Brown, John, 300

Brown, Margaret Tobin (Molly), 34
Burr, Aaron, 204, 241, 242

Calamity Jane (Martha Jane Cannary), 256, 257
California, **25–32**
   Alcatraz, 28
   Bodie (town), 29
   Cecil Hotel, 29
   Donner Memorial State Park, 28
   Greystone Mansion, 29–30
   Hollywood, 26
   Hotel del Coronado, 30
   Los Coches Adobe, 30
   Queen Mary (ocean liner), 30–31
   Whaley House, 31
   Winchester Mystery House, 31–32
Canals, 129–130
Cannary, Martha Jane (Calamity Jane), 256, 257
Carnegie, Andrew, 104
Cassidy, Butch, 313, 314
Castles, 183–184
Caves, 80–81
Cemeteries, 66–68
Centralia, Pennsylvania (town), 238–240
Chicago, Illinois, 29, 81, 85–87, 88, 89, 95, 97, 220, 298, 303
Civil War
   in Alabama, 5, 6
   in Arizona, 15
   in California, 25
   in Colorado, 33
   in Delaware, 47, 50
   in District of Columbia, 55
   in Georgia, 66, 68, 69, 70
   in Indiana, 92
   in Iowa, 100
   in Kansas, 103
   in Louisiana, 117, 119
   in Maine, 125
   in Maryland, 129, 131
   in Massachusetts, 137
   in Mississippi, 154, 156
   in Missouri, 158, 161, 162, 163
   in Montana, 165, 169
   in Nebraska, 172
   in Nevada, 178
   in New Mexico, 197
   in North Carolina, 209, 211, 213
   in North Dakota, 217, 219
   in Oklahoma, 225, 226–227, 229
   in Pennsylvania, 241, 242
   in Rhode Island, 244, 245
   in South Carolina, 250, 252
   in Tennessee, 262, 264
   in Texas, 267, 271
   in Vermont, 280, 282
   in Virginia, 286–287, 288, 289
   in West Virginia, 297, 298, 300, 301
   in Wisconsin, 303, 305
   in Wyoming, 309
Cody, William "Buffalo Bill," 312–313
Cold Harbor (Civil War battle), 286–288
Colleges and universities, 280–281
Colorado, **33–39**
   Cheesman Park, 36
   Hotel Colorado, 36–37
   Mattie's House of Mirrors, 37
   Melting Pot (restaurant), 37
   Molly Brown House, 34
   Riverdale Road, 37–38
   Silver Cliff Cemetery, 38
   St. Elmo Ghost Town, 38
   Stanley Park Hotel, 35–36
   Third Bridge, 38–39
Connecticut, **40–46**
   American Shakespeare Festival Theatre, 42–43
   Bara-Hack, 43
   Dudleytown, 43–44
   Hannah Cranna's Grave, 44
   New Haven Green, 44–45
   Remington Arms, 40–42
   Winsted Wildman, 45
Corey, Giles, 136
Crucible, The (play), 136
Custer, Elizabeth, 165, 217
Custer, George Armstrong, 165–166, 217, 256

Deadly jobs, 1–3
Deadwood, South Dakota (town), 256–257
Deadwood (television series), 257
Delaware, **47–52**
   Addy Sea, 49
   Christiana Fire Company Station, 50
   Deer Park Inn, 48–49
   Fort Delaware, 50
   Headless Horseman, 50–51
   Rockwood Mansion, 51
Distilleries, 109–111
District of Columbia, **53–59**
   Capitol Building, 56
   Ford's Theatre, 54–56

Index

Halcyon House, 57
Hay-Adams Hotel, 57–58
Octagon House, 58
Old Stone House, 58
Smithsonian, 56
Walsh Mansion, 58–59
White House, 59
Yellow House, 57
Donner Party, 26–28

Earp, Wyatt, 16, 103, 256
Edison, Thomas, 189
Environmental disasters, 238–240
Eureka Springs, Arkansas (town), 20–21, 22
Exorcist, The (movie), 107, 160

Factories, 40–42
Flamingo Hotel, 177
Florida, **60–65**
Apollo 1 Launch Complex, 62–63
Castillo de San Marcos, 63
Coral Gables Biltmore Hotel, 63–64
Cuban Club, 64
Don CeSar Hotel, 64–65
Key West Cemetery, 65
St. Augustine Lighthouse, 61–62
Vinoy Renaissance Hotel, 65
Ford, John, 274
Forests and woods, 86–87
Franklin, Benjamin, 133, 153, 193, 215, 237
Franklin, William, 193

Georgia, **66–71**
Bonaventure Cemetery, 67–68
Hay House, 68–69
Laurel Grove Cemetery, 69
Madison Square, 69–70
Marshall House, 70
Pirates' House, 70
Roswell, Georgia (town), 70–71
Sorrel-Weed House, 71
Gettysburg (movie), 241
Gettysburg, Pennsylvania (Civil War battle), 241–242
Gone with the Wind (movie), 66
Grand Hotel (Mackinac Island, Michigan), 141–142, 143
Grant, Ulysses S., 86, 282, 286, 288, 294

Hamilton (play), 241
Hamilton, Alexander, 240–241, 242

Hangings, 147–148
Hawaii, **72–78**
Hickam Air Force Base, 75
Highway 1 (Oahu), 75–76
Hilton Hawaiian Village, 76
Honolulu Airport, 76
Iao Theater, 76–77
Iolani Palace, 73
Molokai, 73–75
Nu'uanuPali Highway, 77
Pearl Harbor Naval Station, 77–78
Health spas, 19–21
Hickok, James Butler "Wild Bill," 256, 257
Hillerman, Tony, 195
Hindenburg (airship), 189–190
Hollywood, California, 17, 26
"Hoosier," 91
Hospitals, 215–216
Hot Springs, Arkansas (town), 19, 23
Hotels, 34–36

Idaho, **79–84**
Bates Motel, 81
Brig at Farragut State Park, 81–82
Canyon Hill Cemetery, 82
Old Idaho State Penitentiary, 82–83
Owyhee Plaza Hotel, 83–84
Shoshone Ice Caves, 80–81
Illinois, **85–90**
Bachelor's Grove Cemetery, 87
Congress Plaza Hotel, 87–89
Hotel Baker, 89
Robinson Woods, 86–87
Showmen's Rest, 89–90
Immigration, 201–202
Indiana, **91–96**
Carolina Street Demon House, 93
Culbertson Mansion, 93–94
Edna Collings Bridge, 92–93
Elkhart Civic Theatre, 94
French Lick Springs Hotel, 94–95
James Allison Mansion, 95
Roads Hotel, 95
Stepp Cemetery, 95–96
Whispers Estate, 96
Inns, 47–49
Iowa, **97–102**
Black Angel of Fairview Cemetery, 99
Black Angel of Oakland Cemetery, 99
Edinburgh Manor, 99–100
Malvern Manor, 100

Iowa (*cont.*)
   Mason House Inn, 100–101
   Roseman Covered Bridge, 101
   Squirrel Cage Jail, 98–99
   Villisca Ax Murder House, 101–102
Islands, 140–142

Jails, 98–99
James, Jesse, 97, 114, 161, 258
Japanese Americans, 310–311

Kalaupapa (Molokai), 73–75
Kamehameha, King of Hawaii, 72, 77
Kansas, **103–108**
   Brown Grand Theatre, 105
   Brown Mansion, 105–106
   Fort Leavenworth, 106–107
   Hutchinson Public Library, 104–105
   Stull Cemetery, 107–108
   Wilbur's Grocery, 108
Kennedy, Jacqueline, 54
Kentucky, **109–114**
   Bobby Mackey's Music World, 111–112
   Buffalo Trace Distillery, 110–111
   Camp Taylor, 112–113
   Cave Hill Cemetery, 112
   Kentucky State Penitentiary, 113
   Liberty Hall, 113–114
   Old Talbott Tavern, 114
King, Stephen
   as Maineresident, 122, 124
   and Mount Hope Cemetery, 126
   and Ohio State Reformatory, 223
   and Stanley Hotel, 35, 207

Las Vegas, Nevada, 176–178
Lee, Robert E., 286, 300
Lemp family, 159–160
Lemp Mansion, 159–160
L'Enfant, Pierre, 53, 56
Lennon, John, 203
Leprosy (Hansen's disease), 73–75
Lewis, Meriwether, 48, 164, 173
Lewis, Sinclair, 150
Lewis and Clark Expedition
   and Idaho, 79
   and Montana, 164
   and Nebraska, 173
   and North Dakota, 214
   and Oregon, 231
   and Washington, 292
Libraries, 104–105

Lighthouses, 61–62
Liliuokalani, Queen of Hawaii, 73
Lincoln, Abraham
   assassination of, 54–56, 148
   and Civil War, 244
   and Emancipation Proclamation, 262
   as Illinois resident, 86
   and Lincoln Memorial, 99
   and Morrill Act, 280
   and Mudd House, 131
   naming Arizona, 13
   and transcontinental telegraph, 274
   and White House, 59
Lincoln, Mary Todd, 56, 282, 293
Little Bighorn, 165–166, 217
Longfellow, Henry Wadsworth, 156
Los Alamos National Laboratory, 195
"Lost Colony" (Roanoke Island, North Carolina), 208
"Lost Dutchman" mine, 13–14
Louisiana, **115–121**
   Arnaud's Restaurant, 118
   Calcasieu Parish Courthouse, 118
   Dauphine Orleans Hotel, 118–119
   LaLaurie Mansion, 119
   Loyd Hall Plantation, 119
   Magnolia Plantation, 119–120
   Marie Laveau Gravesite, 116–118
   Myrtles Plantation, 120
   Oak Alley Plantation, 120
   Old State Capitol, 120
Louisiana Purchase
   enacting of, 118
   and Iowa, 97
   and Kansas, 103
   and Louisiana, 115, 116
   and Minnesota, 146
   and Missouri, 158
   and Montana, 164
   and North Dakota, 214
   and Oklahoma, 225
   and South Dakota, 255
Lovecraft, H. P., 247

Madison, Dolley, 54, 58, 190
Madonna (singer), 236
Main Street (book), 150
Maine, **122–127**
   Biddeford's City Theater, 124
   Carriage House Inn, 124
   Kennebec Arsenal, 125
   Lake George Regional Park West, 125

Index

Maine State Prison, 125–126
Mount Hope Cemetery, 126
Museums of Old York, 126–127
Strand Cinema, 127
U.S. Route 2A, 123–124
Manhattan Island (alleged sale to Dutch), 200
Marx, Harpo, 282–283
Maryland, **128–133**
    Baltimore County Almhouse, 130–131
    Chesapeake & Ohio (C&O) Canal, 129–130
    Dr. Samuel Mudd House Museum, 131
    Edgar Allan Poe House Museum, 131–132
    Glenn Dale Hospital, 132
    Lord Baltimore Hotel, 132–133
    Maryland State House, 133
    St. Paul's Cemetery, 133
Mason-Dixon Line, 47, 51, 129
Massachusetts, **134–139**
    Highwood Ghost, 137
    Hoosac Tunnel, 137–138
    Houghton Mansion, 138
    Salem Witch Hunts, 135–137
    Spider Gates Cemetery, 138
    Taunton State Hospital, 138–139
    USS *Salem* (ship), 139
    "Witch House," 136–137
Mental Hospitals, 292–294
Michigan, **140–145**
    Bruce Mansion, 142–143
    Detroit Masonic Temple, 143
    Felt Mansion, 143
    "Hippie Tree," 145
    Landmark Inn, 143–144
    Mackinac Island, 141–142
    River Raisin National Battlefield Park, 144
    Traverse City State Hospital, 144–145
Midnight in the Garden of Good and Evil (movie), 67, 68, 70
Miller, Arthur, 136
Mines and mining, 13–15
Minnesota, **146–151**
    First Avenue and 7th St. Entry, 149
    Fitzgerald Theater, 148–149
    Forepaugh's Restaurant, 149–150
    Gibbs Farmhouse, 150
    Minneapolis City Hall, 147–148
    Palmer House Hotel, 150
    Wabasha Street Caves, 151
Mississippi, **152–157**
    Chapel of the Cross Cemetery, 154–155
    Grand Opera House, 155
    King's Tavern, 153–154
    Longfellow House, 155–156
    McRaven House, 156
    Stuckey's Bridge, 156–157
    Waverly Mansion, 157
Missouri, **158–163**
    Exorcist House, 160
    Governor's Mansion, 160–161
    Jefferson Barracks, 161
    Jesse James Farm, 161
    Lemp Mansion, 159–160
    Ravenswood Farm, 161–162
    Thespian Hall, 162–163
Molokai (Hawaiian island), 73–75
Monroe, Marilyn, 17, 26
Montana, **164–169**
    Chico Hot Springs Lodge, 166–167
    Grand Union Hotel, 167
    Little Bighorn Battlefield National Monument, 165–166
    Many Glacier Hotel, 167
    Montana Territorial Prison, 167–168
    Philipsburg Opera House, 168
    Pollard Hotel, 168
    St. Charles Hall, 168
    Virginia City, 168–169
Monument Valley (Utah), 274
Moore, Annie, 202
Morrill Land Grant Colleges Act, 280, 281
Morrison, Herbert, 189
Mudd, Dr. Samuel, 131
Murder, 244–245
Murder She Wrote (television series), 30, 122
Museums, 171–172

Natchez Trace, 48, 152, 156
Native Americans
    in Arizona, 13
    in California, 25, 28
    in Colorado, 37, 38
    in Connecticut, 38
    in Delaware, 48
    in Florida, 60, 63
    in Georgia, 66
    in Idaho, 79, 80
    in Illinois, 85, 86–87
    in Indiana, 91
    in Iowa, 97

Native Americans (*cont.*)
  in Kansas, 103
  in Kentucky, 109
  in Louisiana, 115, 116
  in Maine, 122, 123
  in Maryland, 127
  in Massachusetts, 134, 137
  in Michigan, 140, 141, 144
  in Mississippi, 152, 155, 156
  in Montana, 164–166
  in Nebraska, 170
  in Nevada, 176, 177, 179
  in New Hampshire, 182
  in New Jersey, 188
  in New Mexico, 194–195
  in New York, 200, 206
  in North Carolina, 208
  in North Dakota, 214
  in Ohio, 219
  in Oklahoma, 225, 226, 228, 229–230
  in Oregon, 231
  in Pennsylvania, 237
  in South Carolina, 249, 252
  in South Dakota, 255
  in Tennessee, 261
  in Texas, 267, 268, 270
  in Utah, 273
  in Virginia, 285, 288
  in Washington, 291, 294
  in West Virginia, 297
  in Wisconsin, 303, 306
  in Wyoming, 309
Nebraska, **170–175**
  Alliance Theater, 172
  Antelope Park, 172
  Bailey House, 172–173
  Ball Cemetery, 173
  Blackbird Hill, 173
  Centennial Hall, 174–175
  Museum of Shadows, 171–172
  Platte County Historical Society and Museum, 175
Nevada, **176–181**
  Hoover Dam, 178–179
  Las Vegas, 177–178
  Mackay Mansion, 179
  Mizpah Hotel, 179–180
  Rhyolite, 180
  Westgate Hotel, 180–181
  Yellow Jacket Mine, 181
New Hampshire, **182–187**
  Amos Blake House Museum, 184–185
  Chase House, 185
  Isles of Shoals, 185–186
  Kimball Castle, 183–184
  Mount Washington Hotel, 186
  New Hampshire State Hospital, 186–187
  Ocean-Born Mary House, 187
New Jersey, **188–193**
  Burlington County Prison, 190–191
  Devil's Tower, 191
  Emlen Physick Estate, 191–192
  Grenville Hotel, 192
  Hotel Macomber, 192–193
  Inn of Cape May, 192
  Lakehurst Naval Air Station, 189–190
  Proprietary House, 193
New Mexico, **194–199**
  Cloudcroft Lodge Resort and Spa, 198–199
  Dawson Cemetery, 196
  Dona Ana County Courthouse and Jail, 196
  Double Eagle Restaurant, 197
  La Fonda de Santa Fe, 197
  La Posada de Santa Fe, 197–198
  Luna Mansion, 199
  Penitentiary of New Mexico, 195–196
New York, **200–207**
  Amityville Horror House, 205
  Broadway, 201
  Dakota Apartments, 202–203
  Ellis Island, 202
  Hyde Hall, 205
  Iron Island Museum, 205–206
  Merchant's House Museum, 203–204
  Morris Jumel Mansion, 204
  Sagamore Hotel, 206–207
  Washington Square Park, 204–205
North Carolina, **208–213**
  Attmore-Oliver House, 211
  Biltmore Estate, 211
  Carolina Inn, 211–212
  Carolina Thea, 212–213
  Executive Mansion, 213
  Teach's Hole, Ocracoke, 209–210
North Dakota, **214–218**
  Children's Museum at Yunker Farm, 216–217
  Custer House, 217
  Harvey Public Library, 218
  Medora Fudge and Ice Cream Depot, 218
  St. Joseph's Hospital, 216

Index

Ohio, **219–224**
    Ceely Rose House, 222
    Cincinnati Music Hall, 220–222
    House of Wills, 222
    Lorain Palace Theater, 223
    Ohio State Reformatory, 223
    Stivers School for the Arts, 223–224
Oklahoma, **225–230**
    Cain's Ballroom, 227–228
    Cherokee Strip Museum, 228–229
    Constantine Theater, 229
    Fort Gibson National Cemetery, 226–227
    Fort Washita Historic Site, 229
    Gilcrease Museum, 229–230
Oregon, **231–236**
    Crystal Ballroom, 233
    Hollywood Theatre, 233–234
    Hot Lake Hotel, 234
    Kell's Irish Restaurant & Pub, 234
    Multnomah County Poor Farm (McMenamin's Edgefield), 234–235
    Old Town Pizza, 235
    Pittock Mansion, 236
    Shanghai Tunnels, 231–233
    White Eagle Saloon, 236
OSHA (Occupational Safety and Health Administration), 3

Penn, William, 237
Pennsylvania, **237–242**
    Centralia, 238–240
    Eastern State Penitentiary, 240
    First Bank of the United States, 240–241
    Fort Mifflin, 241
    Gettysburg, 241–242
    Logan Inn, 242
Pet Sematary (movie), 126
Pirates and piracy, 70, 185–186, 187, 209–211, 253, 254, 268
Plantations
    Bonaventure, 67
    Carnton, 264
    and Chinese laborers, 73
    as economic system, 262–263
    Edgewood, 288
    Ferry Plantation House, 288–289
    Gaineswood, 4
    Kenworthy Hall, 5
    Loyd Hall, 119
    Magnolia, 119–120

    Myrtles, 120
    and North Carolina, 208
    Oak Alley, 120
    and slavery, 129, 152
    and South Carolina, 250
    and Tennessee, 262
    and West Virginia, 297
    Wheatlands, 262
Poe, Edgar Allan
    and Deer Park Inn, 48–49, 51
    and Edgar Allan Poe House Museum, 131–132
    and Maryland, 129
    and Providence Athenaeum, 247
    and tuberculosis, 251
Popham Colony, 122
Potter's Fields, 220–222
Prairie Home Companion (radio program), 149
Presidio system (Spanish forts), 262–263
Presley, Elvis, 181, 261
Prisons, 195–196
Prostitution, 7–9
Providence Plantations (Rhode Island colony), 243
Psycho (movie), 81

Railroads, 274–275
Relocation centers, 310–311
Remington Arms, 40–41
Rhode Island, **243–248**
    Breakers Mansion, 245–246
    Chestnut Hill Cemetery, 246–247
    Providence Athenaeum, 247
    Slater Mill, 248
    Sprague Mansion, 244–245
River Raisin Massacre (War of 1812 battle), 144
Roads and highways, 123–124
Rosemary's Baby (movie), 203

Salem Witch Trials, 134–137
Shanghaiing, 231–233
Shawshank Redemption, The (movie), 223
Shining, The (movie), 35–36, 207
Siegel, Benjamin, 177–178
Smithsonian Institution, 56, 73, 171
Somewhere in Time (movie), 142
South Carolina, **249–254**
    Dock Street Theatre, 251–252
    Folly Beach, 252
    Greenville Tuberculosis Hospital, 251

South Carolina (*cont.*)
   Pawleys Island, 252
   White Point Gardens, 253–254
South Dakota, **255–260**
   Deadwood (town), 256–257
   Devil's Gulch, 258
   Easton's Castle, 258
   Homestake Opera House, 258–259
   Hotel Alex Johnson, 259
   Old Minnehaha Courthouse Museum, 259
   Orpheum Theatre, 259–260
Sprague, Kate Chase, 245
Sprague family, 244–245
Stanley Hotel, 35–36, 207
Summer Homes, 303–305
Swearengen, Al, 257

Tanglewood, Massachusetts (music festival), 137
Taverns, 153–154
Teach, Edward. *See* Blackbeard
Tennessee, **261–266**
   Bell Witch, 263
   Carnton Plantation, 264
   Orpheum Theatre, 264–265
   Pegram Family Cemetery, 265–266
   Rotherwood Mansion, 266
   Wheatlands Plantation, 262–263
Texas, **267–272**
   Devil's Backbone, 270
   Hotel Galvez, 270–271
   Jefferson Hotel, 271
   Littlefield House, 271–272
   Presidio La Bahia, 269–270
Theaters
   Alliance Theater, 172
   American Shakespeare Festival, 42–43
   Biddeford's, 124
   Bird Cage, 16
   Broadway (New York Theater District), 201
   Brown Grand, 105
   Capitol (Salt Lake City), 276
   Carolina Theatre, 212
   Constantine, 229
   Dock Street, 251–252
   Elkhart Civic Theatre, 94
   Fitzgerald, 148–149
   Ford's, 54–56
   Grand Hotel, 142
   Grand Opera House (Meridian, Mississippi), 155
   Grand Opera House (Oshkosh, Wisconsin), 306
   Grauman's Chinese, 26
   Hollywood Theatre (Portland, Oregon), 233
   Iao Theater, 76–77
   King Opera House, 23
   Lorain Palace, 223
   Mount Baker, 294–295
   Old Malco, 23–24
   Orpheum (Memphis, Tennessee), 264–265
   Orpheum (Sioux Falls, South Dakota), 259–260
   Philipsburg Opera House, 168
   Strand Cinema, 127
   Thespian Hall, 162–163
   Wendy Williams Auditorium, 12
Titanic (ocean liner), 34
Tombstone, Arizona (town), 15, 16
Tombstone Epitaph (newspaper), 18
Tuberculosis, 250–251
   and Colorado, 34
   Glenn Dale Hospital, 132
   Greenville Tuberculosis Hospital, 251
   and Mercy Brown, 246–247
   and Roads Hotel, 95
   and Vermont Police Academy, 283–284

Universities and colleges, 280–281
University of Alaska, 12
University of Vermont, 281
Unsafe workplaces, 1–3
USS *Arizona*, 79
Utah, **273–278**
   Ben Lomond Hotel, 275–276
   Capitol Theatre, 276
   Devereaux Mansion, 276–277
   McCune Mansion, 277
   Mountain Meadows Massacre, 277–278
   Rio Grande Depot, 275

Valentino, Rudolf, 26
Vanderbilt, Alice Gwynne, 245–246
Vanderbilt, George, 211
Vermont, **279–284**
   Brattleboro Retreat, 281–282
   Equinox Golf Resort and Spa, 282
   Lake Bomoseen, 282–283

Marble Mansion Inn, 283
University of Vermont, 281
Vermont Police Academy, 283–284
Virginia, **285–290**
  Boxwood Inn B&B, 288
  Cold Harbor Battlefield Park, 286–288
  Edgewood Plantation, 288
  Ferry Plantation House, 288–289
  Fort Magruder Hotel, 289
  Staunton Train Depot, 289–290
Voodoo, 116–118

Wagon trains, 25–28
Washington, **291–296**
  Fort Vancouver National Historic Site, 294
  Mount Baker Theatre, 294–295
  Northern State Mental Hospital, 293–294
  Oxford Saloon, 295
  Starvation Heights Sanitarium, 295–296
West Virginia, **297–302**
  Droop Mountain Battlefield, 300
  Harpers Ferry (town), 300–301
  Lake Shawnee Amusement Park, 299
  Lewisburg (town), 301
  Trans-Allegheny Lunatic Asylum, 301–302
Whiskey Rebellion, 110
Williams, John, 137
Wisconsin, **303–308**
  Dartford Cemetery, 305–306
  Grand Opera House, 306
  Maribel Caves Hotel, 306–307

Pfister Hotel, 307–308
  Summerwind, 304–305
Witch hunts, 134–137
Wizard of Oz (movie), 103
Women soldiers, 226–227
Wonderful Wizard of Oz (book), 258
World War II
  and Bates Motel, 81
  and Brig at Farragut State Park, 81
  and Carriage House Inn, 124
  and growth of air travel, 177
  Hickam Air Force Base, 75
  and *Hindenburg*, 181
  Hotel Colorado as naval hospital, 36
  internment of Japanese Americans, 310–311
  Manhattan Project at Los Alamos, 195
  Pearl Harbor, 75, 77–78
  Queen Mary as troopship, 31
  and rail travel, 275
  and Vulture Mine, 15
  and Wabasha Street Caves, 151
  and workplace safety, 3
Wounded Knee Massacre, 255
Wyoming, **309–314**
  Fort Laramie Historical Site, 311–312
  Heart Mountain Interpretive Center, 311
  Historic Plains Hotel, 312
  Irma Hotel, 312–313
  Occidental Hotel, 313–314
  Wyoming Territorial Prison, 314

Young, Brigham, 273, 274

About the Author

Nancy Hendricks, PhD, is an award-winning author whose book *Senator Hattie Caraway: An Arkansas Legacy* was named by *Cosmopolitan* magazine as one of the "Twenty Political Books Every Woman Should Read."

Her previous books include *America's First Ladies: A Historical Encyclopedia and Primary Document Collection of the Remarkable Women of the White House*; *Popular Fads and Crazes through American History*; and *Daily Life in 1950s America*, all for ABC-CLIO, as well as *Notable Women of Arkansas: From Hattie to Hillary—100 Names to Know.*

Her writing can also be seen on *Smithsonian.com* as well as in ABC-CLIO books such as *Historic Sites and Landmarks That Shaped America*; *Disasters and Tragic Events: An Encyclopedia of Catastrophes in American History*; *Political Groups, Parties, and Organizations That Shaped America*; *Technical Innovation in American History*; and *Women in American History*. In addition, she is a major contributing author for the *Encyclopedia of Arkansas*.

As a playwright, professional productions of her works include *Miz Caraway and the Kingfish, Second to None*, and *Boy Hero: The Story of David O. Dodd.*

Hendricks is a founding member of the proposed National Women's History Museum in Washington, D.C. She is the recipient of a Pryor Award for Arkansas Women's History, the Arkansas Governor's Arts Award, National Society Daughters of the American Revolution Women in American History Award, and the White House Millennium Award.

www.ingramcontent.com/pod-product-compliance
Lightning Source LLC
Chambersburg PA
CBHW081144230426
43664CB00018B/2792